Hudson Valley
Faces & Places

Hudson Valley

Faces & Places

Patricia Edwards Clyne

THE OVERLOOK PRESS
Woodstock & New York

First published in the United States in 2005 by
The Overlook Press, Peter Mayer Publishers, Inc.
Woodstock & New York

WOODSTOCK:
One Overlook Drive
Woodstock, NY 12498
www.overlookpress.com
[for individual orders, bulk and special sales, contact our Woodstock office]

NEW YORK:
141 Wooster Street
New York, NY 10012

∞ The paper used in this book meets the requirements for paper
permanence as described in the ANSI Z39.48-1992 standard.

Cataloging-in-Publication Data is available from the Library of Congress

Book design and type formatting by Bernard Schleifer
Manufactured in the United States of America
ISBN 1-58567-662-4
1 3 5 7 9 8 6 4 2

For Augie

Contents

V. MAKING THEIR MARK

VI. CORNUCOPIA

VII. WARFARE

VIII. PLACES NONPAREIL

Preface

WHERE DOES THE HUDSON VALLEY BEGIN AND END? Ask six different people and you're apt to get a half-dozen different answers ranging anywhere from the river's start at Lake Tear of the Clouds in the Adirondack Mountains to the Atlantic Ocean, where the Hudson's channel extends out many miles. For the purposes of this book, however, I chose such simple parameters as the eleven New York counties bordering the river at its southern end: Rockland, Orange, Ulster, Greene, Albany and Saratoga counties on the west, with Westchester, Putnam, Dutchess, Columbia and Rensselaer on the east. That, frankly, is the Hudson Valley I know best, though New York County (Manhattan) is frequently featured, not so much because I was born there, but because it's so often tied in with its more northerly neighbors, as evident in chapters like "The Curse of the Cornwall Quaker." As for "The Legend of Charlotte Temple," set almost entirely in Manhattan, I plead guilty to simply loving the story and wanting to share it with others, while relying on its slender link to Albany.

Most ties are much stronger, since the region has been the setting for so much of our country's history—be it the defining early days of one president (James Garfield) or the heroic last battle waged by another (Ulysses S. Grant). So, too, with industry: iron, cement, leather, steam, and even radio all left indelible marks on the valley, as did its writers, artists and musicians, only some of whose colorful stories are collected here.

As so many writers before me, I have ever been ensorceled by the beauty of this incomparable place I am so happy to call home, and I have included chapters on some of my favorite venues—from waterfalls and castles to parks and even cemeteries, always with an eye to locating such sites so that others may enjoy them too.

This leads me to comment on the "regionality" of the book. True it is that every chapter is unique to the Hudson Valley, yet each one is also universal insofar as the themes encompass basic human experience—from love, loss and betrayal to bravery, beauty and accomplishment, with a haunt or two thrown in for good measure. Indeed, the murder of Richard Jennings could easily have occurred elsewhere, just as the kind of courage exhibited by Enoch Crosby is not exclusive to our region. Nor do we have a patent on perversity such as shown by the infamous Matthias the Prophet, or—conversely—the deep spirituality of Graymoor's founders. What we do have is an amazing amalgam of faces and places—one that perhaps reflects William Blake's famous line about seeing "a world in a grain of sand."

—PATRICIA EDWARDS CLYNE

Aiséirí, 2005

I. Enterprise Zone

1. Hemlocks, Hides, and Chutzpah—The Tanning of Zadock Pratt

IN TODAY'S CONSERVATION-CONSCIOUS CLIMATE, THE CATSKILL MOUNTAIN tanlords of earlier centuries—those leather-making moguls who felled whole forests for the tannin-rich tree bark necessary to their trade—are pretty much considered environmental pariahs. That is, with one exception. A Greene County man named Zadock Pratt seems to have escaped such condemnation, despite the fact that in the early 1800s he operated what has been called "the largest tannery of the time."

How that came about is the fabric from which legends are formed, and few men are more fabled than this tragedy-touched humanist whose business acuity was offset by a streak of eccentricity.

Zadock Pratt's story starts in the Rensselaer County community of Stephentown, where he was born on October 30, 1790. Named after his father, a Revolutionary War veteran whose health had been permanently impaired by incarceration on a British prison ship, Zadock was already shouldering some of the workload when his family moved west to the Schoharie County village of Middleburgh in 1797. A few years later they relocated to Greene County, where the elder Pratt established a small tannery at Jewett, and Zadock began learning how to make leather. There was little time for formal education, although Zadock's mother did manage to teach him how to read by using the Bible—the source of many of the proverbs he liked to quote in later life.

By the age of 19, having invented some tannery pump improvements, Zadock obviously was destined for a career in leather. Equally obvious was his penchant for feats of physical endurance; he regularly swam in chill mountain streams until winter froze them over, and he reportedly once hiked 40 miles in a single day without a sip of water, let alone any food.

Such strength was to serve him well in the coming years of nearly non-stop labor. After completing an apprenticeship with a saddlemaker named Luther Hays in the neighboring town of Durham, 21-year-old Zadock went to work for his father. Within a year he had managed to save enough of his $10 monthly wage to open a store, where he slept under the counter as an added economy.

This business had to be put on hold when the intensely patriotic Zadock enlisted in the Army during the War of 1812 and was sent downstate to Brooklyn Heights. As a compnay steward dealing with the commissary, he fought the corruption then so prevalent in the military, and became known for his own fairness and never-failing honesty—traits that may have helped him seal a private sale to the Navy of 100,000 ash-wood oars he shipped to New York City from the Catskills. Money made from that venture, plus the profitable sale of his Greene County store stock prior to the postwar recession he had predicted would occur, allowed the savvy 25-year-old to go into business with two of his brothers when he returned home in 1815.

Having partners gave Zadock time to turn his attention to matters of the heart, and in 1817 he married a Connecticut belle called Beda Dickerman. But the good fortune that attended Zadock's business ventures deserted him in matrimony. A mere seven months after the wedding, his bride died from tuberculosis—the same disease that was to claim Beda's younger sister Esther, who became Zadock's second wife in 1821.

Less than three years later, Esther also was dead and the grieving Zadock plunged himself into work: the family business, as well as holding local government posts and serving with the state militia. He even funded a re-enactment of the 1796 Battle of Lodi, when Napoleon defeated the Austrians in Italy's Lombardy region. The stage for this mock battle was the Greene County town of Windham, with Zadock supplying everything from band instruments and gunpowder to souvenir sashes for the officers. It wasn't the only such simulation either; Zadock continued to enjoy war games, and it is said that over the years more than one farmer was handsomely compensated for a bombarded barn.

"Tanner, Master of Arts, Member of Congress, Farmer and Banker" was the way Zadock Pratt described himself. But that tells only part of the story of this eccentric visionary who overcame family tragedy to lead an extraordinary life.

The summer of 1842 found Zadock scouting potential tannery sites, for he had decided to dissolve the partnership with his brothers and strike out on his own. Searching through surrounding counties, he almost purchased a tract in Ulster's Pine Hill, but opted instead for the small settlement of Schohariekill in the northwestern corner of Greene. There at the junction of the Batavia Kill and Schoharie Creek, his $14,000 savings were sufficient to buy land and build a tannery. But first the diplomatic Zadock was careful to assure residents—made wary by "pirate" tanners in the past—that he intended "to live *with* them, not *on* them."

Zadock kept his promise, planning not only the tannery but a whole community complete with 100 houses for his workers and a broad main street bordered by 1,000 trees. Knowing the economic dangers of a single-industry town, he also encouraged other businesses, including an iron foundry, hat factory and woolen mills, in addition to establishing a newspaper. No wonder then that in 1833 the village was named Prattsville.

Eventually Zadock founded the Prattsville Bank, issuing bank notes bearing his own portrait—bills that reportedly were highly regarded on Wall Street because of Zadock's reputation as a businessman. Wall Streeters might well have fainted, however, had they known that Zadock didn't always demand collateral for bank loans, oftentimes relying solely on his intuition and what he saw in an applicant's eyes or hands. Apparently this was a dependable yardstick too, since those unsecured loans always were repaid. As for Zadock's tannery, it was completed in June 1825, measuring 170 feet long by 43 feet wide. This was soon enlarged to an "immense wooden structure 530 feet in length . . . and two and a half stories high," containing "300 tanning vats," as described in Patricia E. Millen's book, *Bare Trees.*

Manufacturing leather was hard smelly work, but Zadock was always in the thick of things, rising at 5 a.m. so he could join his men for 6 o'clock breakfast. His house (now the Pratt Museum on the village's Main Street) was only a short distance away, and supposedly even the slightest disruption of machinery during the tannery's night shift would awaken Zadock. His response was equally quick whenever a business opportunity presented itself, as in the winter of 1847 when the Mexican War caused the price of leather to skyrocket. Zadock promptly loaded a sleigh with leather and drove his team of four gray horses all the way down the frozen Hudson River to the New York City market.

He dreamed of matching the reputation England then enjoyed for producing the finest sole leather—a dream realized by the 1840s and reinforced by medals won at the 1851 World's Fair in London—but Zadock did not allow his tannery to become an obsession. In fact, one day in 1839 when he was in

Washington, D.C., serving his first term as a U.S. Congressman, word came that he was needed at home because a flood had destroyed part of the tannery. Zadock didn't feel it would be right to desert his congressional duties for personal concerns, and advised tannery workers simply to "do the best you can."

The nation's capital was never quite the same after Zadock's two congressional terms (1837-39 and 1843-45). It is claimed he never missed a roll call, and he proposed a number of far-sighted projects, among them a transcontinental railroad to the Pacific. The establishment of the Bureau of Statistics is also credited to Zadock, as is the almost unbelievable feat of reducing the cost of postage (from 25¢ to 5¢) in 1838. He was not averse to a bit of political blackmail either: when in 1845 his plea for much-needed renovations of the White House fell on deaf ears, he warned his colleagues in Congress that if they didn't pass a bill appropriating the money, he would "proceed to have the work done, pay every dollar of the expense out of [his] own pocket, and *publish it to the world.*" The bill passed posthaste.

It is interesting to speculate what Zadock might have accomplished had he continued in politics and been elected governor of New York. For some reason, though, he refused the nomination when chosen by the Democratic Party at their 1848 convention in Syracuse. Perhaps he simply wished to spend more time with his family.

In 1829 Zadock had married Abigail Watson, a tanner's daughter from Rensselaerville in Albany County. This third union seemed a happy one, with a son George born in 1831, followed by a daughter Julia. But death seemed to dog Zadock's loved ones. Abigail passed away on February 5, 1834 and an infant daughter succumbed soon after. Zadock waited a short time, then married Abigail's sister Mary, possibly just to have someone to raise his children.

As teenagers, Zadock's children, George and Julia, attended school in Poughkeepsie, with George showing unusual aptitude as a linguist. He chose to follow in his father's footsteps though, serving in Congress, the state militia, the Prattsville Bank, and of course the tannery business. (Although Zadock closed his Prattsville tannery in 1846 because all the hemlock trees had been felled within a 10-mile radius, he was involved in other leather-making concerns, including Ulster County's Samsonville Tannery, in which he gave George half-interest.)

A Pratt dynasty was not to be, however. George was wounded during the Civil War's Second Battle of Manassas (Bull Run) and passed away in Albany on September 11, 1862. His son, George Jr., was to die in childhood. These losses deeply affected Zdock, but he was not one to descend into bitterness, and went on with what remained of his life, even marrying for the fifth time at the age of 79. The bride, Susie Grimm, was all of 28.

In keeping with his colorful life, there is a curious incident associated with Zadock's death 18 months later, in 1871. Local tradition tells of his nearly completed coffin—fashioned from hemlock, of course—being washed out of the carpenter's shop by a flood, with the rushing water carrying it to Zadock's back door, where it smashed into pieces. Some might see this as a sign of Zadock's love for his home, or maybe his wish not to be buried in the village's Pratt-Benham Cemetery, since his original plan had been to be entombed in a crypt excavated in the rocky prominence overlooking the village. Unfortunately, the gray sandstone there proved too dense, water constantly dripped through the cracks, and the half-finished crypt was abandoned—one of the more remarkable of the large carvings Zadock commissioned for what might be termed a miniature Mount Rushmore.

Now a public park with National Historic Landmark status, Pratt's Rock's large carvings range from a bas-relief horse and a hemlock to busts of Zadock and his son, along with other biographical symbols, and stone seats for trekkers following the cliffside trail bordering Route 23 just east of the village. The carving resulted from a chance meeting between Zadock and an unemployed stonecutter, who was given the task when he appealed for help. Zadock wasn't one for handouts, but he'd find work for anyone requesting it. One of the few exceptions was a lad who had been cheated out of his wages in New York City and was hiking back home to Otsego County when Zadock met him along the road. Zadock wasn't carrying any money with him, nor pen and paper, so he scratched out a check on a piece of bluestone he picked up from the roadside, and instructed the lad to take it to the Prattsville Bank. The teller, familiar with Zadock's sometimes offbeat behavior, readily cashed the rock.

Incidents like that—perhaps more than any business prowess—have kept Zadock's memory fresh. Indeed, people still talk about the Fourth of July when

A chance encounter with an unemployed stonemason prompted Zadock Pratt to decorate a Greene County cliff with a bevy of biographical bas-reliefs. Shown here is a scroll recalling Pratt's role in establishing the U.S. Bureau of Statistics, plus the traditional arm-and-hammer symbol of labor.

he jokingly donned a heavy fur coat, hitched his horse to a sleigh, and drove over to the Hudson-shore city of Catskill for the festivities. Also how in 1847, as they passed through Prattsville, the prisoners recently pardoned for their part in the Anti-Rent War were greeted by a brass band arranged for by Zadock, who also provided them with a banquet and transportation home. And there is a late-in-life anecdote about the silver-haired Zadock's dignified entry into a Jewett church one Sunday that prompted a youngster to ask his mother, "Is that God?"

All of this still does not fully account for why Zadock is remembered with affection and respect while other tanlords are not. The rest of the reason has to do with hemlocks. Unlike other tanlords who stripped off the bark and left the trees to rot, Zadock utilized the lumber for village betterment: a plank road, a covered bridge, and housing. In additon, he sincerely believed that land stirpped of hemlock trees made the very best pasture for dairy cattle, and proceeded to prove his point by operating a farm on 365 deforested acres that produced "record yields of butter and milk." By 1884, 99 farms could be counted in the township, so there has been little faultfinding with that remarkable tanlord-turned-dairyman, Zadock Pratt.

2. Emperors of the Airwaves

MOST OF YONKERS HAD ALREADY RETIRED FOR THE NIGHT BUT A single light still shone in the tower room atop the stone mansion at 1032 Warburton Avenue. Alone amid the maze of electrical equipment tht filled the room, 21-year-old Edwin Howard Armstrong listened intently to the staccato sounds emanating from a small box on the workbench before him. Then snatching up the box, Armstrong raced downstairs to wake up his sister Edith by dancing around her bedroom and shouting, "I've done it! I've done it!"

What the young inventor accomplished in his tower laboratory that September night in 1912 would revolutionize the infant radio industry—an industry destined to dramatically alter American society, with much of its stranger-than-fiction story rooted right here in the Hudson Valley.

Just as no single individual can be credited with the discovery of radio, it was a trio of men who made it successful: the litigious Lee de Forest, self-styled "father of radio," who patented the seminal audion tube, yet couldn't explain how it worked; communications czar David Sarnoff, the one-time impoverished Russian immigrant who never let friendship stand in the way of business; and most of all Edwin Howard Armstrong, the daredevil inventive genius of Yonkers, whose life was inextricably entwined with the other two.

Armstrong's penchant for sometimes reckless physical feats may well have been a reaction to a childhood bout with chorea that invalided him for two years, and in 1902 prompted his parents, John and Emily, to move from the Chelsea section of Manhattan to what they felt was the healthier air of Westchester County. Their choice was a turreted house on the Yonkers heights overlooking the Hudson, where the ailing 12-year-old Edwin was forced to confine his fascination for anything mechanical to book-reading and model-building.

It was not time wasted, however, for when the blue-eyed Armstrong finally recuperated and began attending Public School 6 on Ashburton Avenue, he became a hero among neighborhood children because of his ability to fix broken toys. Then later, when he was not playing a fever-pitch game of tennis at the Hudson River Country Club, or satisfying his lifelong urge to scale high places like the Palisades, he might be found standing by the highway, toolbox in hand, waiting for some car to break down—as they frequently did in those early days—so he could fix it.

But repairing what others had built would never satisfy Armstrong, who in 1904 had been given a copy of *The Boy's Book of Inventions*, containing a chapter on Guglielmo Marconi's wireless telegraphy. And by the time he entered Yonkers High School the following year, Armstrong knew without a doubt that he wanted to be an inventor. What's more, as he was to record in later years, "The decision favored wireless."

Aided by his parents, who not only bought some of the needed equipment but allowed him to set up shop in the highest point of the house where transmission would be best, Armstrong was soon exchanging messages with other wireless buffs in the vicinity. Among them was Tom Styles, who lived just down the hill from Armstrong's house, and Carman "Randy" Runyon, Jr., whose home on North Broadway was well within range of Armstrong's experimental broadcasts. As Tom Lewis records in his excellent study, *Empire of the Air*, when Runyon finally met Armstrong in person, he was overwhelmed by his new friend's exacting description of a transformer he had designed. But smiles were in order when the ever-honest Armstrong concluded, "The only trouble with [the transformer], it's too big to get out of the house." Runyon and he were to remain friends for life.

Another local radio enthusiast, William "Bill" Russell, joined Armstrong in fabricating and flying large antenna kites, but in 1910 these were supplanted by a 125-foot antenna mast. Armstrong's sister Edith pitched in with the construction of this wooden pole in the south yard of their home, sending up tools by rope to the fearless-of-heights inventor as he precariously swung from a bosun's chair high above Warburton Avenue. Supposedly one of the neighbors, worried that Armstrong might fall from his perch, phoned his mother one day to say how nervous it made her to watch. "Don't look then," advised Emily Armstrong, whose serene confidence in her son never seemed to falter.

The noted author and inventor Charles Underhill lived nearby at the Pincrest estate, and welcomed after-school visits from Armstrong, who peppered him with questions. By patiently answering whatever the boy wanted to know and by providing him with books, Underhill did much to advance Armstrong's knowledge of electromagnetism. But it was a chance remark that may have had the greatest impact. One day when

Armstrong confessed concern over an electrical connection he had made that worked better than the directions given in a book, Underhill told him not to worry over what some book said; that he was "an original thinker."

This kind of encouragement was complemented by Underhill's contributions of needed equipment, including an audion tube—the first Armstrong had ever seen, and something that would bring him both triumph and trouble. Patented by Lee de Forest in 1906, the audion looked like a lightbulb but was able to detect radio waves and regulate their flow. The only problem was a weakness in reception, which Armstrong set about remedying around the time he enrolled at Columbia University in 1909.

Unwilling to give up his home laboratory, Armstrong commuted by motorcycle—a high school graduation gift from his parents—between Columbia's Morningside Heights campus and Yonkers. His route took him past the Riverlure mansion that Lee de Forest was then building in the Bronx at Spuyten Duyvil, providing Armstrong with a daily reminder of his determination to improve on the audion tube. Success came during Armstrong's junior year at Columbia, when he invented the regeneration circuit that fed radio waves back through the audion tube, thereby increasing its strength and eliminating the need for earphones. Radio could now be heard through a speaker, and true broadcasting began.

No one could have been prouder of Armstrong than his electrical theory professor at Columbia, Michael Pupin. A Serbian immigrant who had literally pulled himself up by his bootstraps to become a distinguished teacher and inventor, Pupin had earlier lived in Yonkers at 7 Highland Place, but apparently never met Armstrong until the 6-foot, sandy-haired junior took his course. It is interesting to note that Pupin once said, "If I can inspire one student to do research that will lead to one important scientific discovery, I will consider that more worthy of mention than any money I amass." Certainly Armstrong fit the bill.

Sixteen months after awakening his sister Edith with shouts of "I've done it!" Armstrong was demonstrating his regenerative circuit to the Marconi Company's chief inspector—an equally young and far-seeing man named David Sarnoff. The friendship forged that frigid January night in 1914 would endure for more than three decades, during which Armstrong was to become embroiled in the longest patent suit in history, and still manage to invent the superheterodyne circuit that is the basis for every present-day tuner and channel selector in both radio and television sets.

This second of Armstrong's greatest inventions was made while he served in the Army Signal Corps during World War I, and it greatly enhanced the marketing potential of the "radio music box" that David Sarnoff had proposed in 1916 as one day sitting in every American parlor. Nor was Sarnoff wrong. By 1924, one-third of all the money being spent for furniture in the country went for radios. As for the mid-Hudson region, its earliest commercial broadcasting station is believed to have been built in 1933 by Peter Goelet at his family's Glenmere Lake mansion in the Orange County township of Chester. But that's getting ahead of our story.

Prior to his enlistment in the Army, Armstrong had been teaching at his alma mater, Columbia University, where he had made use of its extensive laboratory facilities. So when he left the service in September 1919, after contracting anthrax in France, he rejoined the Columbia faculty as soon as he recovered his health, and set about improving his superheterodyne circuit. By now his premature balding—accelerated by the anthrax infection—had left his head nearly hairless, and a residual neck and shoulder twitch—from his childhood bout with chorea—annoyed him. But Armstrong was otherwise hale and hearty—and still ensorceled by heights.

That was something David Sarnoff discovered in May 1923, when Armstrong decided to perch astride the globe surmounting the Radio Corporation of America's 115-foot tower atop the 21-story Aeolian Hall on Manhattan's 42 Street. It wasn't the first time Armstrong had scaled the RCA tower either, and Sarnoff—now vice president and general manager of the corporation—was furious at the inventor who had recently sold his new superregeneration circuit to RCA for an amazing $200,000 in cash and 60,000 shares of stock. Yet other than prohibiting RCA employees from allowing Armstrong access to the tower, there was little Sarnoff could do to curb his friend's antics, and the two resumed their amicable relationship . . . at least for the time being.

Armstrong was to profit from this relationship in another way as well. For it was in Sarnoff's office that he met the RCA chief's lovely auburn-haired secretary, Marion MacInnis. Armstrong had never been a ladies' man, and quite likely had never even dated anyone, including any of the various girls his sister Edith had purposely brought home with her when she was attending Vassar College in Poughkeepsie. Yet Armstong was immediately smitten by Marion, pursued her with a persistence heretofore reserved for his work, and on December 1, 1923 they were married.

Meanwhile, Armstrong remained locked in a bitter court battle with Lee de Forest that had started in 1914 over rights to the regenerative circuit. Suit followed countersuit for 20 years until 1934, when the U.S. Supreme Court outraged the scientific community by making a final ruling in de Forest's favor. Armstrong's shock at the injustice of the decision was compounded by the lack of support shown by his old friend David Sarnoff, now president of RCA—a corporation that stood to profit from Armstrong's loss. Still the relationship between the two men remained outwardly cordial, and Armstrong continued setting up equipment in the RCA facility atop the Empire State Building for testing his latest discovery.

In the past Sarnoff had often expressed the wish that someone would invent a "little black box" to eliminate radio static. Armstrong now claimed to have the problem solved by something he called frequency modulation (FM). However, to market Armstrong's method would mean scrapping existing radios for more expensive models, and Sarnoff wasn't about to commit such commercial suicide in the middle of the Depression. Besides that, Sarnoff was more interested in developing television, and in July 1935 Armstrong was tersely told to remove his equipment from the Empire State Building.

Deeply hurt but undaunted, Armstrong proceeded to make the first public broadcast of an FM program from Yonkers, where his childhood chum, Carman "Randy" Runyon, operated an amateur station at his North Broadway home. The next step was to build some FM receivers and erect a 400-foot antenna on the Palisades at Alpine, New Jersey. FM was then on its way, but so was trouble.

When Sarnoff finally made an offer, Armstrong flatly refused, and the powerful president of RCA went for the jugular. Succeeding years of litigation ate away Armstrong's fortune, along with his physical and emotional health, and finally his marriage failed. On the night of January 31, 1954, the distraught inventor carefully donned overcoat, gloves and scarf. Then he removed the air-conditioner from a window in his 13th floor apartment at Manhattan's River House, and stepped out into space. It was the 40th anniversary of his demonstration of the regeneration circuit to Sarnoff—a date the two men had always marked by messages to each other in friendlier times.

*   *   *

Marion MacInnis Armstrong was to carry on her husband's crusade in the courts, first winning a $1 million settlement from RCA that covered the cost of succeeding lawsuits against other companies that had impinged on Armstrong's patents. Finally in 1967—thirteen years after Armstrong's death—the litigation ended. He had won.

The Warburton Avenue house in Yonkers was destroyed by fire in 1982, but from the site it's easy to see Armstrong's tall FM tower across the Hudson —still dominating the Palisades, and still operational.

3. An Illuminating Tale

WHEN ARTIST-PHOTOGRAPHER DON HERRON DECIDED TO BUY A 19th century house in Newburgh's historic East End neighborhood, he knew the Orange County property possessed a notable pedigree, but only later did he learn how literally electrifying was the legend, right down to a modern-day mystery.

Unobtrusive on the outside, though not without charm, Herron's three-storey, high-stooped structure fronting on First Street is one of five attached townhouses designed by one of Newburgh's leading architects, Thornton M. Niven—a cachet that could have contributed to the quintet being called Quality Row. Certainly the prominent citizens who lived there added an air of elegance too, yet a tradition perists that "Quality Row" was simply a sarcasm stemming from a local tiff over some shade trees the original residents planted.

Central to that controversy was the Rev. John Brown, pastor of St. George's Episcopal Church on Grand Street. In 1828, Brown purchased part of the land once owned by the Rev. Joshua Kockerthal, leader of the Palatine Germans who had come to Newburgh in 1709. Brown originally used this historic parcel for a garden in which "he had all manner of fruit trees," then in 1836 he built the first house—No. 114—in Quality Row.

Four other clapboard buildings soon followed—one east of Brown's, the other three on the west side—with No. 116 right in the middle and boasting perhaps the best construction, thanks to its lumber-dealer owner James Graham Clinton. As the son of Revolutionary War General James Clinton, the nephew of Governor George Clinton, and the younger half-brother of Erie Canal builder DeWitt Clinton, the lumberman also had access to the family homestead in the Little Britain section of nearby New Windsor. (A monument can be seen on the west side of Bull Road, just off State Route 207.)

Hence, the unusually wide panels on some of the main floor's interior doors almost surely came from the huge walnut trees occurring in a rare stand of virgin timber on the Clinton farm.

James G. Clinton enjoyed his richly appointed home for only a few years. Elected to the U.S. Congress in 1841, he sold No. 116 to Newburgh lawyer David W. Bate. Nor did Bate live there long. Upon becoming a county judge in 1847, he found a buyer in Dr. Nathaniel Deyo, and for several generations thereafter the house remained in that family.

During those decades, a doctor's shingle usually swung outside, for John Van Zandt Deyo followed in the footsteps of his father Nathaniel, setting up offices at No. 116's brick-fronted, above-ground basement, where the dining room and kitchen initially had been located. Both Deyos also taught medicine, which could account for a macabre discovery made many years later. But first came the electrifying event mentioned earlier.

Two years after John Deyo began practicing medicine in 1877, scientists meeting at Saratoga Springs watched as a young inventor demonstrated an "electro-chemical telephone." While this device was not destined to be his most memorable invention, the "brilliant results" Thomas Alva Edison achieved on that August day in 1897 may have influenced a pair of Newburgh textile manufacturers to take a chance on his later and greater development of incandescent lighting while it was still in its infancy.

Edison's main focus for this new industry was on building central generating stations to serve large numbers of customers. And in 1881 he set up shop in New York City, planning his first district lighting system for an area of Lower Manhattan around Pearl Street. But Edison didn't shy away from individual customers either, with the result that Newburgh already was hosting two so-called "isolated stations"—installed in the mills of the aforementioned textile manufacturers, James Harrison and James Taylor—when Manhattan's Pearl Street Station went on line in September 1882.

A centralized system was still the most practical answer to large-scale lighting, however, and the successful Pearl Street Station was soon being toured by a contingent of city fathers from Newburgh. Aided by Edison's agent, Charles T. Hughes, they then set about raising capital for a Newburgh plant—not so easy a task, Hughes wrote to Edison in August 1883, saying he "never saw such hard scratching to raise a little money as it is here where plenty of people have lots of it." Hughes, it should be added, was also working the other side of the river, trying to promote an Edison plant in Poughkeepsie. But while he found the "very nice" Newburghers to be somewhat "old fashioned and cautious" when it came to electric lighting, he felt the other city's folk were "the slowest and most skeptical on earth."

The Edison Electric Illuminating Company of Newburgh eventually overstrode the stumbling blocks, and on March 31, 1884 its brick generating station at Montgomery and Third streets began operation—the second such Edison plant in New York State, and one that is still in use today. (A plaque on the building and a curbside historical marker describe the site.) As for recipients of the service, on Easter Sunday evening, April 13, 1884, the First (now Calvary) Presbyterian Church on South Street dramatically came aglow with the new 10-candle-power lighting. Reportedly it was the first fane in the state to be fitted with Edison incandescent bulbs.

While there is ample evidence of Edison's visit to Newburgh on April 24, when he inspected the new generating station, only local tradition tells of his earlier trips to supervise construction. Supposedly during some of those visits he stayed with the Deyo family on First Street, and installed part of the wiring needed to convert No. 116 from gas illumination to electricity.

But would an eminent inventor be apt to take on so menial a task? Actually Edison liked nothing better than rolling up his sleeves to work alongside his men, even helping to dig trenches and lay cable during the development of his Lower Manhattan lighting district. On opening day, it was Edison who connected the lamps in the offices of one of his backers, J.P. Morgan. Then later at Newburgh, another staunch supporter was banker Moses C. Belknap, who just happened to be married to the sister of Dr. John Deyo. So the story of the inventor as electrician at No. 116 seems plausible, especially when present owner Don Herron points out the antique knob-and-tube wiring, or turns on the main-floor foyer's overhead lantern with its genuine Edison bulb.

Electricity wasn't the only reason Edison visited the Hudson Valley. Neil Baldwin records in his biography, *Edison: Inventing the Century*, that the "most consuming obsession in Thomas Edison's career" was the profitable processing of iron ore. The Hudson Valley of course abounds in iron, as does the surrounding region, but the post-Civil War availability of richer and cheaper ore from the West caused many of the mines to close down. Edison figured that by utilizing the magnetic properties of the metal, he could extract enough iron from eastern ore to make it marketable. As early as 1880 he had patented a magnetic ore separator and installed his machines at such sites as the Sunk mines, east of Dennytown Road in what is now Clarence Fahnestock State Park in Putnam County. And to transport ore, Edison once owned the narrow-gauge railway that ran from the Croft and Todd mines down to a blast furnace on the south side of Annsville Creek in the Westchester County town of Cortlandt.

Edison also bought 194 acres near the present-day Cornell Mine Trail atop Rockland County's Bald Mountain, where some old trenches attest to his mining activities. But the 1892 opening of the vast Mesabi Range in Minnesota spelled the end of Edison's "most consuming passion," and in 1928 the Bald Mountain property became part of Harriman State Park. (A word of caution: old mines can be dangerous and are best investigated from the outside only.)

Much more might be said of Thomas Edison's ties to the Hudson Valley, including his friendship with Ulster County naturalist John Burroughs, or the former boy-telegrapher's presence in the Orange County village of Harriman when in November 1911 Edison was present at the dedication of a monument to the first railroad telegraph message, sent between Harriman and Goshen in January 1851. (The plaque is missing, but the boulder base of the monument can be seen by the old railroad depot on Grove Street.) However, it's time to head back to Newburgh's 116 First Street, and the controversy occasioned by the contents of the old cedar box discovered there during December 1981.

By that time the Deyos no longer owned the house and the Crosbie family had just moved in. It was teenage Lorne Crosbie who was exploring the attic crawl space when he spotted the narrow, 3-foot-long box on a ledge. Thinking it might be an old musket case, he eagerly pried open the lid, only to find what appeared to be just some oily old newspapers. Then the boy's disappointment turned to total shock: wrapped in the paper was a human arm!

Strongly smelling of what Lorne Crosbie's mother Dorothy later described as cloves, the arm was well preserved, with veins still containing vestiges of blood, and it obviously had been amputated many years before by someone knowledgeable in anatomy. Police investigators called in by the Crosbies also determined that it was a right upper limb from someone approximately sixty years old, that phenol had been used as a preservative, and some dissection had taken place, with the skin drawn down to the fingers. But to whom did the limb belong? How did it get into the attic crawl space? And most of all, had there been foul play?

Decades later the mystery remains unsolved, though it definitely dates to the tenure of the Deyos. An inscription on the lid of the box suggests it was either sent from or to John Van Zandt Deyo, and the arm was wrapped in May 1876 editions of the *Newburgh Weekly Journal*—a time when Dr. Nathaniel Deyo was still practicing and his son John was about ready to enter the profession. This led to speculation that the limb was used by them for anatomy lessons, but there is no proof of this, or of any of the darker rumors that circulated—rumors which escalated when the box also yielded a separately wrapped, left-hand pinky pierced by a piece of linen cord, much like a rabbit's foot charm.

Another interesting sidenote to the story concerns the Crosbies, who fully expected their find to be returned to them after the investigation. The authorities thought othewise, citing statutes dealing with dead bodies, and it was only after the Crosbies consulted a lawyer that they were given back the box—empty.

The arm? It eventually wound up at the Biology Department of Orange County Community College in Middletown, where it was used for awhile as a teaching tool, but at last report it has been relegated to a laboratory refrigerator, still wrapped in its1876 newspaper. In regard to the long-missing pinky, it is all but forgotten.

That suits No. 116's owner just fine, for Don Herron would prefer his home to be known more for its beauty than the bizarre. Since buying it in June 1994, the Texas-born Herron has worked hard at restoring the townhouse, plus adding his own touches such as painted trompe l'oeil drapes in the master bedroom and murals in both dining room and parlor. At the same time he is quick to point out the house was in amazingly good condition considering its age, with the double-hung, 6-over-6 windows on the main floor retaining most of their original "wavy-glass" panes. Some of the hearths even have "heatilators," made up of a wood- or coal-burning chamber covered by cast iron for heat radiation (the 19th century answer to inefficient fireplaces).

Despite the mid-year purchase of No. 116, and the fact that he maintains a studio in Manhattan, where he works as a multi-dimensional artist-photographer, the tall soft-spoken Herron managed to have his home ready for Newburgh's annual Christmas Candlelight House Tour in December 1994—the first time a Quality Row residence had been included. And as of this writing (2003), the house continues to be a frequently featured stop on the tour, providing the public with an unbeatable opportunity to enjoy a literally embellished legend.

*   *   *

The Christmas Candlelight House Tour is sponsored by the Historical Society of Newburgh Bay and the Highlands, headquartered in the Crawford Mansion on Montgomery Street, and open to the public.

4. From Sharecropper Shack to Hudson Valley Villa—
The Odyssey of Sarah Breedlove Walker

PUZZLEMENT . . .

GASPS OF ASTONISHMENT . . .

EXCLAMATIONS OF "IMPOSSIBLE!"

THAT WAS HOW *The New-York Times* DESCRIBED REACTIONS OF IRVINGTON residents in 1917 when a newcomer named Walker built a palatial home in their exclusive Westchester County community. For not only was Walker a self-made near-millionaire and a woman, but she was also black. The lady, however, had a knack for beating seemingly insurmountable odds. With an alleged assist from famed tenor Enrico Caruso, the shock waves eventually died down in Irvington, and any residual amazement was mainly over Madam C.J. Walker's remarkable rise from poverty.

What has to be one of America's most inspiring rags-to-riches stories began on a Louisiana plantation a couple of days before Christmas 1867, when former slaves, Minerva and Owen Breedlove, welcomed the first child in their family to be born free. They called their baby girl Sarah, and somehow imbued her with the strength to survive their harsh existence as sharecroppers whose only shelter was a dirt-floor shack. The parents didn't survive, though. Minerva died during an outbreak of cholera that ravaged the lower Mississippi River region in 1873, and Owen passed away in 1875, leaving 8-year-old Sarah in the care of her older married sister Louvenia.

Penniless in a period lacking child labor laws and with few social services, the sisters endured the dawn-to-dusk drudgery of field work, accompanied by Louvenia's husband Jesse Powell. But when racial violence worsened in Louisiana, and cotton crops faltered at the same time a deadly epidemic of yellow fever swept the land, Sarah and the Powells moved across the river to Vicksburg, Mississippi. Yet any hope of a better life in Vicksburg was canceled out by the cruelty Sarah suffered at the hands of her hot-tempered brother-in-law.

Partly to escape that abuse, at the age of 14, Sarah eloped with a man named Moses McWilliams, and for a time it seemed that happiness might be hers—especially after the birth of her only child, a daughter she named Lelia, on June 6, 1885. Then three years later, Moses died; one report holds that he was murdered by a lynch mob, but that has never been confirmed.

The more northerly city of St. Louis, Missouri, offered better employment opportunities, if not safety, so Sarah soon moved upriver with Lelia. Though unable to read or write, Sarah was determined to educate her daughter, and she labored long hours as a laundress and cook in order to save enough money to eventually send Lelia to Knoxville College in Tennessee.

It was while bending over the washboard one day, her back aching, that Sarah began worrying about what would happen when she grew older and

Born into a family of ex-slaves, Madam C.J. Walker overcame poverty, abuse and illiteracy to become one of the country's first self-made million-airesses, as well as a force for civil rights.
PHOTO COURTESY A'LELIA BUNDLES/
WALKER COLLECTION

was no longer able to do such strenuous work. Strangely enough, another physical problem was to provide the answer. Sarah found herself going bald. Aware of how much her appearance meant to her livelihood as well as to her self-esteem, Sarah searched for a preparation that promised to remedy hair loss. There were several such tonics too, for baldness was not uncommon among women like Sarah, who had experienced long years of inadequate diet, poor hygiene and stress, plus the scalp-tugging, wrap-and-twist method then popular for styling African-American hair.

Having experienced some regrowth with a substance devised by St. Louis businesswoman Annie Malone Pope-Turnbo, when Sarah moved to Denver, Colorado, in 1905, she went as a sales representative for Pope-Turnbo's "Wonderful Hair Grower." Sarah felt, however, that a more effective product was possible, and within a year she had come up with her own hair-growing formula which she said had been revealed to her in a dream.

She also had married newspaperman Charles Joseph Walker on January

4, 1906, and began calling herself Madam C.J. Walker, since the title added a certain cachet to the line of hair products she was creating. As for selling them, she first when door to door in Denver, her now full head of shining hair a perfect testimonial. Then when local ladies proved receptive, she began a mail-order business and tirelessly solicited retail stores to stock her preparations, in addition to recruiting hundreds of women as commissioned agents able to earn two or three times the average wage.

Within four years, Madam—as she was now known—permanently headquartered her fast-growing company in Indianapolis, Indiana, with a complex containing a training school for the agents she called "hair culturists," a beauty salon, and a large factory turning out such products as Madam C.J. Walker's Wonderful Hair Grower, her Vegetable Shampoo, and a hair dressing called Glossine.

Not everyone applauded Madam's progress. Her development of a wide-toothed "hot" comb fueled a debate over whether black women should straighten their hair. Disagreements as to company growth also contributed to Madam divorcing her husband. She even had to battle the legendary black leader, Booker T. Washington, for recognition as a businesswoman.

The latter incident occurred in January 1912, when 45-year-old Madam sought to address the National Negro Business League's Chicago convention. But she was repeatedly turned down by the league's founder, Booker T. Washington, who apparently didn't think too much of female entrepreneurs. Finally on the last day of the convention, Madam stood up in the audience and demanded, "Surely you are not going to shut the door in my face!" And she proceeded to tell convention-goers how she "built my own factory on my own ground." So impressive was her presentation that in succeeding years she was invited back as a featured speaker at the convention.

By now a self-possessed, fashionably dressed figure, Madam did not regard making money as an end in itself; more important was what could be done with it, particularly education. As soon as she was financially able, she addressed her own illiteracy by hiring personal tutors, reportedly learning to write so well that for awhile the bank refused to honor checks bearing her beautiful signature. Reading, meanwhile, became her avocation, with literature and American history her favorite subjects.

Education for others of her race was equally important to her. Madam annually contributed thousands of dollars to schools, in addition to making large donations to orphanages, retirement homes, and the YMCA. She could also be counted on for other causes, and was instrumental in saving the Washington, D.C., home of abolitionist Frederick Douglass.

At a 1924 convention, agents of her hair-care products gathered on the rear terraces of Madam C.J. Walker's Irvington-on-Hudson mansion, Villa Lewaro, now a National Historic Landmark.

Plans for building a brand-new home of her own didn't develop until 1916, when Madam moved to Manhattan, where her daughter Lelia was running the New York branch of the business at 108-110 West 136 Street, in a Harlem townhouse that had been converted to a combination residence and beauty school. With her company now numbering 20,000 agents in the United States, Central America and the Caribbean, Madam could well afford a country estate too, and she set about finding a suitable piece of property— something easier said than done. Madam reportedly first set her sights on the Flushing area of Queens County, but "met with such resistance that she had to abandon her plans," and look elsewhere. Next came Irvington, where the $60,000 purchase price for a 4.5-acre parcel on North Broadway purportedly was inflated by brokers in an effort to keep her out. Madam paid anyway.

Ground was broken early in 1917 for the graceful Italian Renaissance villa that was designed for Madam by Vertner Woodson Tandy, the first African-American architect registered in New York State. Another noteworthy friend, Enrico Caruso, supposedly interceded on Madam's behalf when controversy arose during construction. It was also the famed tenor who dubbed the building Villa Lewaro, using the first two letters from each name of Madam's daughter, *Le*lia *Wa*lker *Ro*binson. (For awhile she was married to a man named John Robinson.)

Deemed a "wonder house" by *The New-York Times*, the 34-room residence with its 2-storey columned portico became such a landmark that Hudson River steamboats making the night run to Albany were known to train their lights on the Irvington shore so passengers could glimpse Villa Lewaro's cream-colored exterior. But the marble-staircased interior was even more striking—from the grand entry foyer and solarium to a massive drawing room where Isadora Duncan may have danced. For Madam intended the 3-storey house to serve as an inspiration to others of her race, as well as a gathering place for prominent people of the day, and she furnished it accordingly—right down to a gold-plated piano and matching phonograph in the music room.

That Madam still found satisfaction in simple things amid all that splendor is evident in a letter she wrote on August 14, 1918, two months after moving into her new home. Calling herself a "farmerette," she tells of being in the garden every morning at six o'clock, "pulling weeds," and also "putting up fruit and vegetables by the wholesale." On the other hand, she welcomed modern conveniences, equipping the villa's master bedroom with a "needle shower" much like today's Jacuzzis, and keeping a quartet of cars. The larger automobiles were operated by her chauffeur, but Madam defied convention by doing her own driving of a smaller, electric model.

She became more politically challenging too, particularly after race riots in the summer of 1917 resulted in the lynching and burning of blacks. On July 28, Madam fearlessly joined 10,000 others in the Negro Silent Protest Parade down Manhattan's Fifth Avenue, the only sounds being that of muffled drums and marching feet. Shortly afterward, she went to Washington, D.C., with a party of black leaders, hoping to convince President Woodrow Wilson to support a federal law against lynching. The President was "too busy" to meet with them, but that didn't discourage Madam. At a convention of her agents in Philadelphia later that summer, she made a stirring speech about not allowing patriotic loyalty to prevent speaking out against wrong. "We should protest," she urged, "until the American sense of justice is so aroused that such affairs as the [race riots] . . . be forever impossible." The convention-goers concurred, promptly sending off a telegram to Pesident Wilson.

At Madam's behest, the following year's convention telegraphed Washington about fair treatment of black soldiers. While supporting her country's involvement in World War I by raising thousands of dollars during bond drives, Madam was fiercely opposed to racial discrimination in the armed forces. She had no qualms about publicly stating her position either, and hosted a conference at Villa Lewaro to duscuss the problem.

Friends and family expressed concern about how this might affect her business, and even more so that the added stress was exacerbating the hypertension from which she suffered. Madam didn't seem to have a slow speed, though, not even during the first and only Christmas she spent at Villa Lewaro, when she also celebrated her fifty-first birthday.

A houseguest named Hallie Queen left reminiscences of a hostess who retired early on December 24, but awakened at midnight to wish everyone a merry Christmas . . . of Madam "waiting for us before a glowing fireplace" for gift-giving on Christmas morning . . . of her humble prayer preceding breakfast . . . and of an eclectic group of guests that numbered, in part, a minister, a mathematician, a politican, a sculptor, and "a sailor from a recently torpedoed vessel." Then after carols in the music room and dinner in the "beautiful state dining room with its . . . rich indirect lighting," everyone motored down to Manhattan to attend a basketball game. Madam, it seems, was an avid fan, and even got to throw out the ball that night.

Four months later, while on a business trip to St. Louis, Madam became gravely ill and was brought back to Irvington in a private railroad car. Typical of her practicality, she used the time to update her will. Kidney failure brought about by hypertension caused her death on May 25, 1919, and after a funeral service at Villa Lewaro she was buried in the Butternut section of Woodlawn Cemetery in the Bronx.

Madam's daughter, who had amended her name to A'Lelia, took over as president of the Walker Company, while acting as a patroness of the arts. Poet Langston Hughes called A'Lelia the "joy goddess" of the Harlem Renaissance, and in addition to having a 1921 movie "The Secret Sorrow" filmed at Villa Lewaro, she is said to have kept the mansion "roaring" with her parties throughout the 1920s.

All that ended with the onset of the Great Depression. When Villa Lewaro proved too expensive to maintain, its magnificent furnishings were auctioned off in 1930, most of them selling for a fraction of their worth. Fortunately one of the most unusual pieces—a $25,000 player organ whose outlets in various parts of the house allowed A'Lelia Walker to literally pipe guests awake in the morning—was built into the music room wall and could not be moved.

A'Lelia Walker died at age 46 in 1931, and the following year Villa Lewaro was purchased as a rest home for members of the Companions of the Forest. It was still being used for that purpose in 1976 when listed on the National Register of Historic Places—a designation that meant nothing to a developer in the 1980s, who wanted to destroy it and build condominiums in its stead. It was saved, believe it or not, by two trees. For Irvington has an ordinance protecting arboreal treasures, and the property boasts a more than 250-year-old Chinese ginko, plus an American beechnut that's been around for more than three centuries.

A subsequent owner of Villa Lewaro mounted a restoration effort that was later taken over by Helena and Harold E. Doley. An investment banker then of middle age, Doley had dreamed of owning the house ever since he first saw it when he was in his twenties. The dream came true in 1993, and despite the problems involved in redecorating an old house—not to mention strangers sometimes knocking on the door, thinking the private house was a museum to be toured!—Doley remained delighted with his acquisition.

Concerned that Madam Walker would be accorded a proper place in the history of our country, Doley also joined Madam Walker's great-great-grand-daughter, author A'Lelia Perry Bundles, in campaigning for a commemorative stamp to honor the woman the *Guiness Book of World Records* called America's first self-made millionairess. (Madam's actual net worth was only about $600,000 when she died, but that adds up to over $6 million in today's economy.) Happily their effort was rewarded in 1998, when the U.S. Postal Service issued a 32-cent stamp featuring a handsome portrait of the entrepreneur. Madam surely would have loved it!

Villa Lewaro remains a private residence, but its graceful facade can easily be seen near the southwest corner of Fargo Lane and North Broadway (Route 9) in Irvington. In addition, strollers along the Old Croton Aqueduct Trail, a block to the west, are treated to views of the terraced back portion of the mansion.

5. Set in Cement

THE SUMMER SUNLIGHT SENT DOZENS OF RAINBOWS DANCING IN THE spray from the mighty cascade that gave the Ulster County hamlet of High Falls its name, while the foliage along the banks of the Rondout Creek had never been brighter. But beauty was not in the eye of James S. McEntee on that day in 1825.

As an assistant engineer on the then abuilding Delaware & Hudson Canal, McEntee viewed the falls as an obstacle to be circumvented via a series of locks, and the Rondout in terms of an aqueduct to carry boats across another innavigable part of the creek. All were projects requiring cement that would set under water—so-called hydraulic cement which was available from only one site in the whole state, a place far out in western New York. And that was why McEntee turned his back on the summer beauty to concentrate on the chunks of burned limestone being pounded into powder at the local blacksmith's shop.

What happened next was probably the closest thing to a miracle that McEntee ever witnessed. When water was poured over it, the powder slowly began to harden. It was natural hydraulic cement, and it had been mined right in the neighborhood. What's more, as it later turned out, there seemed to be an endless supply in the hills bordering the Rondout all the way from High Falls to Kingston.

The discovery of a cheaper, more convenient source of cement may not sound as exciting as a gold strike, but the boom times it triggered could easily compete with any Old West tale. For cementing the D&H Canal was only the start of an industry that would literally recontour the landscape, and in the process contribute one of the more colorful chapters in the canon of Hudson Valley history.

Within a few months of the lime-burning experiment at High Falls, a man named John Littlejohn contracted to supply the canal builders with locally produced cement, and by the Spring of 1826 he was quarrying rock for a kiln he'd constructed just west of Bruceville Road. From there, the burned limestone was taken for crushing to the nearby mill of Simon (or

Simeon) DePuy, whose handsome stone tavern later became the landmark Depuy Canal House restaurant along Route 213.

Littlejohn did well with his new business. Yet for some reason, as soon as he had fulfilled his contract with the canal company, he closed up shop. The infant cement industry was thus left to languish—but not for long. A few miles farther along the Rondout, Judge Lucas Elmendorf (for whom Lucas Turnpike is named) was soon running a cement operation utilizing a mill owned by Jacob Lowe Snyder. Supposedly it was on Snyder's land that the original sample of natural cement had been found, but the locality came to be called Lawrenceville for still another industry pioneer, Watson E. Lawrence, who was in business there as early as 1827.

Cement-making was then a primitive process, dependent on the vagaries of weather, water-powered mills, and wood-burning "pot" kilns that barely produced 25 barrels of cement during the best of weeks. Lawrence replaced those inefficient ovens with his own design of "draw" kilns fired by coal. The fuel was brought up the D&H Canal, which had opened in 1828 and ran right past Lawrenceville. Canal boats also freighted out the finished product at a most reasonable rate: 3½¢ per mile per ton of cement in 1831.

Another boost was provided by Lawrence's partner in the Rosendale Cement Company. A former federal employee, John P. Austin managed to

elicit government endorsement of their product, which not only was used in the Brooklyn Navy Yard drydock, but for Westchester County's Croton Aqueduct, completed in 1842. This undoubtedly helped other cement manufacturers too. For the town of Rosendale was formed in 1844, and the natural cement produced within its borders generally was referred to geographically—as it still is today—despite the brand names of individual companies. Government projects specifying Rosendale cement did not necessarily reflect unfair favoritism either. The

The manufacture of cement required limestone to be "cooked" in large stone kilns. Many of these sturdy structures still stand, including ones along Binnewater Lane, north of the village of Rosendale.

product was quite simply superior, far exceeding strength requirements, and so durable that it once took a pair of wrecking companies nearly a year to demolish a warehouse made of Rosendale cement

As the product's popularity grew, cement works began springing up in adjacent towns, and attracting an army of immigrant workers. But the greatest concentration of companies remained in Rosendale: at Binnewater, Creek Locks and Hickory Bush, clear down the alphabet to Tillson and Whiteport, the latter named for cement-maker Hugh White. Mention might also be made of LeFever Falls, where D&H Canal lock #6 became known as the Rock Lock due to the limestone diggings nearby.

Nowhere was the industry's growth more evident than in the village of Rosendale, which for awhile was transformed into a rip-roaring hub of hard-working, harder-drinking miners, cement-burners, "canawlers," and—after 1872—Wallkill Valley Railroad men. It was a setting conducive to tall tales, including one about an Irish cement worker who singlehandedly bested a gang bent on beating him up. Supposedly Jack Dillon faced his foes on the narrow bridge then spanning the Rondout at Rosendale, and since there was only room for two abreast to come at him, the burly "bogtrotter" flailed away with both fists until he'd floored the whole bunch!

The Irish are also credited with the huge support pillars in limestone mines being called "leggos." For it is said they frequently voiced their fear that if one of the pillars "let go," all the others would follow and the whole ceiling fall. In actuality, those colossal columns—carved out as the limestone was mined around them—were probably even stronger than needed, some of them measuring 50 feet in circumference, and as solid today as they were more than a century ago. That doesn't mean there weren't disasters. Unknown numbers of men were maimed or killed in all kinds of accidents. Take the time a teamster named Bergen died at the horse-powered tramway in Maple Hill. A broken piece of harness was what caused a loaded cable car to plunge out of control as it left the quarry there.

Of much greater extent was the disaster that took place at Joppenberg Mountain, where the New York & Rosendale Cement Company excavated limestone on several levels. (Joppenberg is the mountain on the northern side of the railroad trestle crossing the Rondout at Rosendale.) Four separate cave-ins occurred during the morning of December 19, 1899, sending boulders and buildings sliding down the mountain to block both the roadway and the D&H Canal. Meanwhile, the trestle was rocked by a boiler explosion and the tracks twisted like pretzels. Yet amazingly the more than 100 men working on the mountain escaped unscathed.

Of the many landmarks to Rosendale's once-flourishing cement industry, the most unusual has to be Pumba, a large rhinoceros sculpture-cum-kiln. The work of artist Judy Sigunick, Pumba stands on the grounds of the village's Recreation Center on Route 32.

At the time of the Joppenberg landslide, Rosendale cement was still in demand, having been used in such prestigious projects as the wings of the U.S. Capitol (1859), the Brooklyn Bridge towers (1883), and the Statue of Liberty pedestal (1886). Closer to home in Westchester County, Rosendale cement was chosen for Horace Greeley's Chappaqua farm barn (1865), which was later remodeled into the Aldridge Road residence called Rehoboth. On Abruyn Street in the Ulster County city of Kingston, the lovely old Ponckhockie Church (1870) can be found, built by the Newark Lime & Cement Company for its workers, while just across the road is another cement structure, the Union Free School (1871). And the following year saw concrete being used for a Westchester County version of a Rhineland castle—the Squire House near the junction of Maple Place and North Highland Avenue (state route 9) in Ossining.

As for Rosendale itself, the village library on Route 213 is constructed of limestone chunks set in natural cement mortar—an eye-catching landmark that started out as a church in 1876. Nor should the more modern "Pumba" be missed in the riverside park at the junction of Routes 32 and 213. A huge cement rhinocerous that is both a sculpture and a kiln, "Pumba" commemorates Rosendale's history as "the center of the cement industry."

By the late 1870s interest in natural cement was beginning to crumble due to competition from portland cement, which was first produced in the

United States in 1875. Natural cement was far more durable, but the port-land kind—processed from limestone, shale and gypsum—set faster and was therefore more economical. And in 1920 there was only one cement plant still operating in Rosendale, whose population had plummeted from over 6,000 in 1900 to less than 2,000. However, the owner of that remaining company, Andrew J. Snyder II, the great-grandson of the previously mentioned Jacob Lowe Snyder, had faith in the future of natural cement—especially since studies were showing that portland cement disintegrated over a period of time. What was needed was a product combining the durability of natural cement with the rapid hardening of portland, and before long a blend called masonry cement was on the market.

Snyder's masonry cement—used in building Dutchess County's Green Haven Prison (1939) and more than 500 New York Thruway bridges—was so successful that in the 1950s his Rosendale plant couldn't keep up with the demand, despite operating around the clock. It all ended less than a decade later though, when chemists came up with a cheap substitute for natural cement. Snyder had also planned on producing portland cement at a state-of-the-art plant he built in 1961. However, a host of problems beset the aging entrepreneur and in 1970 he closed down the last of Rosendale's cement works.

It was the end of an era, but not of the region's entire cement industry, which continued at places like Cementon in Greene County. Meanwhile, the echoing emptiness of Ulster County's vast limestone mines—some of them stretching for more than a mile underground—encouraged new uses, if not legends. As early as the 1930s, some of the abandoned mines were being called caves and touted as tourist attractions. And what could be more enticing than stories of bank loot left in one of the mines, or that bootleggers piped their booze from subterranean stills to waiting boats on the Rondout? There was even a rumor that you could use connecting mines and caves to trek underground all the way from Rosendale to Kingston.

Better documented is the fact that in 1935 Andrew Snyder II leased his unused Beach Mine off Binnewater Road to a family of mushroom growers. The damp, dark mine, with its near-constant coolness of around 55 degrees F., was ideal for the tasty fungus, and reportedly over 5 tons of mushrooms per day were harvested during the peak years of underground farming which ended in 1960.

Another such man-made cave served as a cooler for locally grown corn awaiting shipment to market, while the mine entrance atop Joppenberg Mountain was the setting for some scenes in the 1965 movie, *The Agony and the Ecstasy*. In more recent times, a mine along Route 213 became the water source for a company that fills swimming pools, and one of the caverns in back of the nearby Williams Lake Hotel has hosted a weirdly echoing concert featuring a didjerido, a wind instrument of the Australian aborigines. Nor is that the only site for social gatherings. The Widow Jane Mine on the old Snyder Estate has hosted a variety of events, from spelunker training to Halloween parties.

Perhaps even more intriguing—and of a more permanent nature—is the underground information-storage company called IMAR (Iron Mountain at Rosendale), which moved into the aforementioned Beach Mine back in the 1970s. Behind the 20-ton steel door that now blocks off the entrance lies a subterranean village complete with streets, mini-motel, and small houses for the safekeeping of vital records. The motel is a holdover from Cold War days when some of IMAR's corporate customers wanted employee accommodations in case of emergency—something that gave rise to stories that the mine would be used as a fall-out shelter for the local populace, or that a special suite had been set up for the President of the United States in the event of nuclear attack.

Security concerns of course preclude public access to IMAR, but so much else remains of Rosendale's 30-square-mile cement district—280 acres of which have been listed on the National Register of Historic Places since 1992—that even a driving tour along area roads offers stunning views of sturdy stone kilns and the sun-dappled maws of pillared mines. Better yet, add a visit to the old Snyder Estate on the north side of Route 213 between High Falls and Rosendale. It's easy to find it too. Just look for the Brooklyn Bridge! No kidding. The cement magnate was so proud of his product being used in the towers of that mighty span, he gated his driveway with a replica of the bridge.

Nor did Snyder distance himself from his business. His home—now called Century House—is a few minutes' stroll from the kilns that cooked the limestone coming from the nearby, cemetery-topped Widow Jane Mine. All of these, along with a barn museum, D&H Canal slip, carriage house exhibits and other features, make the Snyder Estate a fascinating microcosm of the once-flourishing world of cement. And for a fitting finale, visitors might like to stop by the grave of A.J. Snyder II in Rosendale's Rural Plains Cemetery on Elting Road. It is said that a lifetime spent battling seepage in his mines made Snyder insist on several pre-interment tests to make certain his crypt was watertight!

6. Steamin' Down the River

"TALK ABOUT STEAM TRANSPORTATION IN THE REGION, AND MOST people think of railroads; speak of saling the river, and it's wind-driven ships that generally come to mind." So notes artist William Gordon Muller who—along with other dedicated Hudson Valley maritime historians— has worked long and hard at changing that perception to include the majestic paddlewheel steamers that plied the river for over a century and a half.

"No era was more romantic or dramatic," Miller maintains, recalling how, as a six-year-old, he got his first glimpse of a sidewheel steamer when his mother took him picnicking in Manhattan on an Inwood Park hill overlooking the Hudson. The steamboat was the multi-decked *Hendrick Hudson*, built at Newburgh in 1906 but still magnificent when Muller saw her in 1942. And as this floating palace went by—dazzling white in the summer sun, flags flapping, passengers waving, orchestra playing, and froth cascading from fast-beating paddles—the young boy watching her fell utterly and forever in love. Thereafter, he returned to the hill on a daily basis, often with sketchbook in hand, and whenever offered the choice of an outing, he invariably opted for a river trip. Though his favorite excursions were to places like Westchester County's Indian Point Park in Buchanan, and he loved the more extended Hudson cruises his family took when on their way to visit relatives in upstate New York, he was equally content with shorter rides on some of the steam ferries that were still in operation.

Eventually Muller's interest encompassed all aspects of steam-powered watercraft, from tugboats to ocean liners, but the Hudson held a special place in his heart, and at the age of 16 he secured a summer job as a purser on one of the Day Line's steamers. Two summers later, when he was offered the post of quartermaster on the *Alexander Hamilton*, Muller "jumped at this opportunity to join the pilothouse staff," for it meant he would learn how to navigate the river and perhaps someday realize his dream of becoming a steamboat captain. Unfortunately, passenger travel on the Hudson was even then declining, and in time Muller was forced to discard his dream for a more secure job with an advertising agency. What he learned during the long hours he spent in the pilothouse of the *Alexander Hamilton* never left him, however, and when friends finally convinced him to strike out on his own as a marine artist, Muller was soon lauded not only for his exceptional talent and a style reminiscent of the Hudson River School of painting, but how he combined them with a thoroughgoing knowledge of his subject that compellingly recreated the colorful history of steamboating.

A highpoint of that history occurred in mid-August 1807, when people gathered along the Hudson's shore witnessed "the devil going up the river on a sawmill." At least that was how one startled resident of Rhinecliff in Dutchess County described the spark-spitting, smoke-belching phenomenon then making its 5-mile-an-hour way from New York City to Albany, defying both wind and tide. To others, it looked more like a "boat driven by a teakettle" or a "backwoods sawmill mounted on a scow and set afire," and some derided it as "Fulton's folly." But that didn't bother Chancellor Robert R. Livingston of Columbia County, who proudly stood on deck beside the vessel's designer, 42-year-old, painter-turned-inventor Robert Fulton.

More than a decade before this historic voyage, Livingston had recognized the potential for steam navigation on the Hudson, and he sponsored the work of an English inventor named Nesbit, who set up shop at a dock on North Bay, below Tivoli in Dutchess County. Where Nesbit failed, Fulton followed, living in a cottage by the bay while he experimented with various designs for what is remembered today as the *Clermont*—the "first successful steamboat."

That quotation, along with the vessel's name, comes with a caveat, since the *Clermont's* success perhaps was due as much to the steamship monopoly enjoyed by Fulton and Livingston as to its design. As for the name *Clermont*, that was an after-the-fact appellation pinned on her by Cadwallader D. Colden in his 1817 biography of Robert Fulton, and referred only to the vessel's hailing port in Columbia County (home of her co-owner, Chancellor Livingston). For some reason the name stuck, despite the fact—pointed out by Donald C. Ringwald in his history of the *Hudson River Day Line*—that throughout the vessel's seven-year career, she was known as the *North River Steam Boat*. (North River, of course, was what the Hudson used to be called.)

Although the 20-year monopoly the state legislature granted to Fulton and Livingston initially retarded the growth of river steamboating and kept rates high, the new mode of transportation proved immensely popular among those who could afford it. Indeed, it became a mark of distinction to travel in this manner, as was apparent in 1818, when the remains of Revolutionary War hero Richard Montgomery were removed from Canada (where he had fallen at the 1775 Battle of Quebec) to be reinterred in New York City, and the steamship *Richmond* was chosen for the Hudson segment of the journey. Upon reaching Annandale in Dutchess County, the Richmond stopped opposite Montgomery Place, where the general's widow waited on the portico overlooking the water. Then after the onboard military band played Handel's "Dead March" and a gun salute sounded, the *Richmond* slowly proceeded downriver.

Drama of a different sort was meanwhile being played out by rival interests seeking to break the stranglehold imposed on them by the Fulton-Livingston monopoly. The climax came in 1824, when the case of Gibbons vs. Ogden was brought before the U.S. Supreme Court, with none other than the fiery Daniel Webster arguing that "the people of New York have a right to be protected against the monopoly." Chief Justice John Marshall was in complete agreement, and his ruling regarding such state laws being "repugnant to the Constitution" opened wide the floodgates for steamboat development.

Further encouragement, especially for steam freighting, came the following year (1825), when the opening of the Erie Canal was celebrated with a "Wedding of the Waters." This grand bit of hoopla began at Cohoes in Albany County, the eastern terminus of the canal. There the steamer *Chancellor Livingston* met the lead boat of a celebrity-laden flotilla, and towed it down the Hudson, amid the booming of a route-long network of shoreline cannons. Then in the Lower Bay a cask of Erie water was poured overboard to symbolize the joining of the Atlantic Ocean to the Great Lake at the western end of the canal.

Equally favorable for the burgeoning steam freight business was the completion of the Delaware and Hudson Canal in 1828, linking the coal fields of northern Pennsylvania with the Hudson, and causing the Ulster County port of Rondout to boom. So did practically every other riverside community from Troy and Poughkeepsie to Peekskill and Nyack, with many of them eventually establishing their own steamboat routes, such as the Saugerties Evening Line and the Catskill & Albany Line. But they were mere midgets in comparison to early giants like the Hudson River Steamboat Association (made up of several shipowners), and the People's Line, presided over by Putnam County-born Daniel Drew.

Boatyards also flourished, with Orange County's New Windsor claiming the first steam freighter to be constructed on the Hudson—the aptly named *Experiment* of 1828. Three years earlier, the first safety barge appeared on the river in answer to a growing public fear of steamboat boilers exploding. Attached to a towing steamboat by a hawser, sometimes with a swivel gangplank to facilitate boarding, these barges provided the utmost in safety but proved too slow-moving to turn much of a profit in the increasingly competitive river trade. So they soon were taken out of service, even though the concern they had addressed was certainly well founded.

As more and more steamboats appeared on the river, competition for passengers grew ever more fierce. Price wars raged so that at times the $7 fare (originally set by Fulton's *North River Steam* Boat) for passage from New york City to Albany dropped to 50¢ or less. Dockside hawkers would tout one boat over another, often making outlandish claims to lure customers. Even scheduled stops might be ignored if a captain was trying to make time, or else passengers would be picked up or landed "on the fly." That dangerous practice depended on the steamer's momentum to wash a tethered rowboat toward the dock, where passengers had scant seconds to jump out or in. Then the small craft was hurriedly hauled back.

Speed seemed to be what sold the most tickets, and in their lust to claim the fastest craft, captains engaged in ofttimes tragic races. One of the worst of these disasters occurred on a snowy night in April 1845, when the *Swallow*—trying to outrun the *Rochester* and the *Express*—rammed into an islet called Noah's Brig (now Swallow Rocks) just off Athens in Greene County. Fifteen lives were lost as the *Swallow* broke apart and sank, but that did not halt the insane racing on the river. It took an even greater tragedy to do that.

As described in the chapter about Andrew Jackson Downing, when the *Henry Clay* caught fire during a race with the *Armenia* on July 28, 1852, scores of passengers were killed—a senseless loss of life that finally spurred Congress into enacting a strict law governing the inspection and safe operation of steamboats. From then on, seamboat men centered mainly on providing their passengers with the most comfortable and dependable means of travel available—a concentration given added compulsion by the mid-1840s advent of railroads offering swifter service. But not even the private cars of millionaire railroad magnates could match the commodiousness of the passenger steamships, which provided inspiration for many artists of the Hudson River School: Poughkeepsie's Jim M. Evans, Wappinger's Clinton W. Clapp, and Newburgh-born Samuel Ward Stanton, to name only three.

Grand saloons, two decks in height, featured carved mahogany furniture, deep carpeting, crystal chandeliers, and fine murals, with just as much decoration devoted to the multi-windowed dining rooms noted for their excellent cuisine. Promenade decks ran the length of the steamers, every inch of which was freshly painted, varnished or polished. For passengers desiring additional diversions there were concerts, dances, writing rooms, free souvenir guidebooks, plus tours of the pilothouse or engine room, and the *Hendrick Hudson* even sported plate-glass panels on the inner side of the paddlewheel housing for viewing the churning water.

Whereas earlier vessels had been used for either daytime or night runs, the newer models were designed for a specific service, with the second deck of night boats devoted to staterooms offering sleeping accommodations. Two of the best remembered of these night-runners were the *Saratoga*, which the Citizen's Line operated between New York City and the Rensselaer County city of Troy, and the Catskill Evening Line's *Kaaterskill* that only went as far north as Coxsackie in Greene County. Main stops for both were at Hudson in Columbia County, and Catskill in Greene.

Construction of those floating palaces continued through the first three decades of the 20th century, when the *DeWitt Clinton, Robert Fulton,* and *Peter Stuyvesant* were built, all of them with room for thousands of passengers per trip. The *Washington Irving* was considered the grandest, both in terms of passenger capacity (6,000) and decor, the latter inspired by Spain's Alhambra castle, which the ship's namesake had written about. And it might have been even grander, had the artist Samuel Ward Stanton lived to complete his commission for decorating the *Washington Irving*. Unfortunately, Stanton—famous not only for his paintings, but as editor of the *Nautical Gazette* and author of the classic *American Steam Vessels*—went abroad to make preliminary sketches of the Alhambra, and decided to return home on a brand-new steam liner. He and all his sketches were lost when the *Titanic* sank on April 15, 1912.

Despite the grandeur of the 20th century floating palaces, best loved of all the passenger steamboats was the older and smaller *Mary Powell*, built in 1861

Perhaps the best-loved steamship of all those that once plied the Hudson, the Mary Powell *glides past Storm King Mountain in this painting by William Gordon Muller.* PHOTO COURTESY OF THE ARTIST

for Absalom Anderson of Rondout. Deservedly called "the queen of the Hudson," this slim and swift vessel was part of the river scene for more than half a century, never experiencing a major accident nor the loss of a single passenger's life, and so prompt that people on shore were said to set their clocks by her passing. (The *Mary Powell's* wheel and other memorabilia are on display at Loughran House—part of the Senate House State Historic Site on Fair Street in Kingston, Ulster County. The steamship's bell can be found nearby at the Hudson River Maritime Center.)

Steam transportation on the Hudson managed to weather two world wars and the Great Depression, but its end was near, owing to changing lifestyles and technology. By 1949, regular steamboat service between Albany and New York City had ceased. The many riverside amusement parks that once enticed excursionists were fast fading too: Ulster's Kingston Point facility was auctioned off that year, and Indian Point Park was soon to become a nuclear power plant. In 1971, the last of the old-time floating palaces, the *Alexander Hamilton,* made her final run to Poughkeepsie, eventually winding up at the South Street Seaport in Manhattan, where steamboat buffs tried to preserve her by forming the Alexander Hamilton Society. They succeeded in placing the steamer on the National Register of Historic Places, but suffered defeat when the *Alexander Hamilton* was capsized by a storm in 1977.

One of the society's founders was William Muller, whose disappointment in not saving the steamship on which he had served made him all the more determined to keep alive a period of Hudson River history that seemed in danger of being lost. As an advisor to the National Maritime Historical Society, in 1978, he issued a plea in that organization's journal *Sea History* for "a vitally needed Hudson River maritime center at a mid-Hudson port." Rallying behind him were such men as Donald Ringwald of Kingston, who had also worked on Hudson steamers; Roger W. Mabie, former Esopus Town Supervisor and steamboat crewman; long-time river pilot and captain William O. Benson; and well-known writer Arthur G. Adams, all of whom played a leading role in establishing the Hudson River Maritime Center museum on the Rondout Creek waterfront at Kingston in 1980.

During the years since its inception, the center has become an important repository of maritime memorabilia, with one of its most impressive outdoor exhibits the 1898 steam tug *Mathilda*. Muller, too, continued to rack up credits in preserving the past. In 1985, he designed the *Andrew Fletcher* and the *DeWitt Clinton,* two replicas of turn-of-the-century steamers which for awhile were used as cruise boats at the aforementioned South

Street Seaport. And in 1990 he completed large paintings of four of the Hudson's most famous steamboats for the refurbished *Dayliner*, which was renamed the *New Yorker*, and operated as a charter dinner boat—reportedly the largest inland waterway vessel in the United States—until it was turned into a floating casino.

Less obvious were some of Muller's other commitments, a case in point being his participation in a 1989 project undertaken by the White Plains Historical Society to honor James Bard, a painter of the Hudson River School, who concentrated almost exclusively on steamboat subjects. Though Bard's works now sell for $125,000, he rarely received more than $25 per painting, and when he died in 1897 he was buried in the pauper's section of the White Plains Rural Cemetery on Route 22. Nine decades later, when Bard's overgrown grave was rediscovered, community leaders and other concerned citizens banded together to erect the marble monument that now graces the last resting place of this early recorder of the river's steamboats. With dedicated history buffs like those, interest in the Hudson River's bygone era of shipping should never run out of steam.

II. Arts and Crafts

7. Fanfare

I N THIS AUTOMATED AND AIR-CONDITIONED AGE, YOU MIGHT THINK THAT such cooling tools as hand-held fans have become archaic, if not altogether forgotten. Yet quite the contrary is true, a case in point having occurred at the modern-day summer races in Saratoga Springs. There, in her family's grandstand box abutting the racetrack's finish line, the undisputed queen of Saratoga society—Marylou Whitney—was rarely seen without a fan in hand on hot afternoons. And she usually had several other fold-up fans tucked away in her purse for people (men included) wanting to borrow one. "After all," she once pointed out, "nothing quite takes the place of a fan when you're outdoors."

For that matter, indoors too—as in the days before the Casino in Saratoga Springs' Congress Park was air-conditioned. To insure that their guests stayed comfortable at the annual summer ball they hosted at the Casino, Mrs. Whitney and her husband, Cornelius Vanderbilt "Sonny" Whitney, would hand out fans to everyone. Fans, however, were much more than mere breeze-makers for Mrs. Whitney, who was known to send fans in lieu of birthday cards, marking across the leaf—the broad band connecting the fan's upper sticks— "I am a fan of . . ." for the recipient. But even more memorable is the "Gone With the Wind" party she once gave, when each guest received a fan printed with a picture of Clark Gable. Nor was she alone in this interest, as was evident in 1993 when Tiffany's auctioned off dozens of celebrity-designed fans to benefit the New York Philharmonic orchestra.

While all this helped to keep fans in the public eye and thereby preserve their popularity, it is only one facet in the fascinating story of an art form almost as old as man—an art form particularly well appreciated in the Hudson Valley, where mystery adds fillip to a magnificent fan collection not brought to light until the 1990s.

Fans likely date back to some cave-dweller's discovery that by waving a large leaf he could either cool himself off or coax his campfire. But by the time ancient Egyptians were employing palm fronds and ostrich feathers for fans, the idea had grown to include the whisking away of flies and the winnowing of grain. In fact, our word "fan" comes from the latin *vannus*, an instrument for separating chaff from grain. As for the fly-whisks, this type of fan occurred in most cultures, with the early Christian church's *flabella*—originally intended for keeping insects out of the Eucharistic wine—evolving into ceremonial works of art.

The Orient, of course, is most closely associated with fans, having the longest continuous record of their use (starting in China around 2700 B.C.), and a culture in which a distinct fan etiquette developed. Even more important were the innovations that come out of the Far East. The Chinese, for example, are thought to have initiated painted decorations on fans, while Japanese legend credits a 7th century man with inventing the folding fan after observing a bat in flight. These folding fans were an immediate success when introduced into Europe during the early 1500s by Portuguese sailors returning from the Orient. Whether bejeweled or a less-expensive brisè, it wasn't long until fans were considered as much a part of a person's dress as was a pair of shoes. And that goes for men as well as women. Non-folding—called fixed, or rigid—fans remained in fashion too, with the variety of materials for both types rivaled only by the different styles and myriad uses that eventually came about.

The most intriguing use was for silent communication, whereby a lady could convey whole sentences through a mere flick of her fan. An apology, for instance, could be offered by drawing the fan across the eyes, but when pulled through the hand it registered revulsion. And a desire for friendship was indicated by dropping the fan—a ploy that the fashion-conscious writer Oscar Wilde called upon to foreshadow the happy ending of his 1892 play *Lady Windemere's Fan.*

A study of fans in regional collections reveals that Hudson Valley dwellers relied chiefly on overseas imports for this kind of finery, but that does not mean fan-making was unknown in the New World. Native people fashioned feathered fans from whatever birds were available, with North American Indians attaching special significance to the eagle. Indeed, it was thought by some groups that being fanned by an eagle wing during battle would resuscitate a warrior. On a more peaceful note, the Shaker society which in 1776 had its American start at Niskayuna, northwest of Albany, helped to support itself through the sale of turkey feather fans they called "wings." These fans were also fabricated at such society enclaves as Mount Lebanon on present-day Route 22 in Columbia Conty, and the nearby Shaker Museum in Old Chatham has a fine example. (At the time of this writing—2003—the museum was scheduled to be moved to Mount Lebanon.) Braided palm leaf fans were fashioned too, a few of which have been preserved by the Shaker Heritage Society on Albany Shaker Road in the town of Colonie.

Not far from there, three other collections reflect much more of the amazing variety of fans that enhanced the region's artscape while echoing its social history—only a mere sampling of which can be given here. (Please note that not all of the fans described are on permanent display. For current information contact individual sites.) As might be expected in a summer spa area where the wealthy were wont to water in Victorian times, the Historical Society of Saratoga Springs in Congress Park owns some remarkable pieces—from a hatchet-shaped Egyptian fan and a miniature model known as an "imperceptible," to an 1805 Scottish souvenir and a 1927 Art Deco advertisement for a Parisian store. There are "personality pieces" too, including a fan that purportedly belonged to the renowned soprano Lillian Russell, plus an 1830 brisé carving from a local tree complete with biblical quotations written on the fan-sticks and signed by a "Louise Cowen." Brisé, by the way, simply means short. A few miles to the south, on Charlton Street in Ballston Spa, the Saratoga County History Center—Brookside—boasts a "flirtation fan" with a tiny oval mirror for some 19th century lovely curious to see what was going on behind her. And for local interest, there is a painted fan brought back from Cuba by an area resident named Ellen Betts, who served as a Red Cross nurse during the Spanish-American War of 1898.

Some of the oldest fans in the region are housed at the Albany Institute of History and Art on Washington Avenue in the state capital. For example, a pair of matching "hand screens" dates back to 17th century China, and a paper-plus-ivory piece is traced to Margarita Ten Broeck, whose husband Dirck was mayor of Albany from 1746 to 1748. No date, however, has been assigned to an unusual water buffalo hide-and-horn fan from Java, or a set of undecorated parchment folds reputedly meant to hold poetry written by dinner guests in China. But another fan with blank folds—this one for autographs—is unquestionably from 1895, since that is the date written in by two of the signers.

There is a tale told of an Albany brewery that in the decade prior to Prohibition attempted to appease the wives of topers by handing out inexpensive fans decorated with the company's sudsy logo. Whether it worked is not known, though printed advertising fans have long been part of the scene, including some at the aforementioned Albany Institute. Political campaign and commemorative fans deserve mention as well, with a presidential portrait fan to be found in the Franklin Delano Museum on Route 9 in Dutchess County's Hyde Park. And just down the river in Newburgh, Washington's Headquarters State Historic Site on Liberty Street has a one-of-a-kind commemoration of the place rendered on a wooden fan by a local 19th century painter, William Roe, Jr.

Large collections from several generations of a single family are relatively rare, which is why the hundred or so fans at Locust Grove— the Samuel F.B. Morse Historic Site on South Street (Route 9) in Poughkeepsie—are considered such a treasure. Having belonged to members of the wealthy Young family, the fans recall all kinds of occasions, one especially happy event being the May 1883 marriage of Martha Innis to William Hopkins Young. For this the bride had borrowed the stunning white satin wedding fan that her mothr, Ann Bevier Hasbrouck Innis, had carried in 1855.

Death was not ignored by fan-makers either, and at the Madam Brett Homestead on Van Nydeck Avenue in Beacon, visitors can see one of the mourning fans that were once common. Also on display there, it might be added, is an interesting "fireplace fan" dating back to the days when women held up such shields to protect their wax-based makeup from melting in the heat of the flames!

According to Tom DeLeo, a fan expert from Cortlandt Manor in Westchester County, the popularity of fans plummeted in the 1920s. This has been attributed to the newfound freedom of flappers to drink and smoke in public, and with hands thus occupied, they had no way of holding a fan. But certainly the advent of air-conditioning and cooler less-corseted clothes had a great deal to do with it. Whatever the case, there was a concurrent decline in fan-collecting. The hobby never entirely died out though, thanks to appreciative people like the late Orange County writer, Alice Curtis Desmond of Balmville. A pair of fine pierced-ivory fans she had carefully preserved in shadowbox frames now graces the Crawford House headquarters of the Historical Society of Newburgh Bay and the Highlands on Montgomery Street in Newburgh. Then there were some serendipitous finds, such as two of the fans displayed at the Vanderbilt Mansion Visitors Center on Route 9 in Hyde Park. One—a magnificent black "cockade" fan with metallic silver stars and crescent moon—was found in the estate's pavilion, while a smaller gold-on-black Oriental fan was recovered from the back seat of the family Packard shortly after Louise Vanderbilt's death in 1926.

But the greatest treasure was unearthed in the 1990s when author Mary E. Rhoads began updating her *Fan Directory*. This guide for collectors was first published in 1983, a year after the not-for-profit Fan Association of North America (FANA) was founded in answer to a resurging interest in decorative fans. And by 1992 it was apparent that a second editon was needed. Upon learning that the Hammond Museum on Deveau Road in the Westchester County community of North Salem had an uncatalogued collection stored in their basement, the author called upon fellow FANA member Tom DeLeo to check it out since he lived not far from the museum. DeLeo then wrote to Hammond Director Geralyn Huba, and in February 1993 the two of them—along with Assisant Director Abigail Free—began sorting through the dozens of dusty shoeboxes and suitcases that had remained undisturbed for three decades. The rest is history—more than 700 exquisite pieces of hsitory, to be exact, all tinged with a mystery that may never be solved. For no one knows why a New York City woman named Lavinia Mockridge decided to give her valuable fan collection to the Hammond in the early 1960s, or why the museum's founder Natalie Hays Hammond never did anything with it. Both ladies are now dead and no explanatory documents have been recovered, so it's anybody's guess. What isn't guesswork is the quality and exceptionally broad spectrum of the collection. An 18th century Japanese warrior's fan with heavy iron guards for weapons . . . a Battenberg lace peacock appliqued on painted silk by its 19th century French artist . . . a sumptuous silk and point D'Alencon lace masterpiece whose gold coronet and chain help to place it in the Russian imperial court of the early 20th century . . . a trick fan that appears to fall apart when opened . . . ethnic items from the Pacific . . . a gentleman's fan in the shape of a cigar . . . red Bakelite and black rubber pieces likely used to introduce the industrial possibilities of those materials . . . even a feathered confection that belonged to the famed innovator of the fan dance, Sally Rand. And that's only some of this collection whose value goes far beyond mere monetary amounts.

Truly, those hand-held fans, along with others in various Valley museums—whether locally fabricated or acquired from afar by some regional resident—add a distinctly decorative dollop to our heritage. In a word: fantabulous!

8. Wherefore Edith Wharton

THE LITTLE GIRL'S BROWN EYES GREW WIDER AND MORE APPREHENSIVE the closer the horse-drawn carriage came to the castle-like house on the heights overlooking the Hudson at Rhinecliff in Dutchess County. The arched windows with their beetling red-brick brows seemed to stare back at her, and it was only at the urging of her mother that the child slid off the carriage seat to start their summer stay with the stone-faced spinster standing on the front steps.

The girl did not know it then, but this ornate mansion—built in 1853 by her old-maid aunt, Elizabeth Schermerhorn Jones—supposedly spurred neighboring nabobs to embellish their own estates, and thus the expression "keeping up with the Joneses" had been born. Yet even if the child had known, it would not have swayed her from "hating everything at Rhinecliff," nor would it have stayed the terror she suffered in an upstairs bedroom one night when she was sure "there was a wolf under my bed"—an experience she would later draw upon in her role as one of the most popular American authors of the early 20th century. It was a popularity well-deserved, since the writer was Edith Wharton, the first woman awarded a Pulitzer Prize for fiction, and someone as adept at supernatural chillers as with the social commentary seen in her classic *The Age of Innocence*. And throughout both writing genres run the ofttimes intriguing threads that inexorably tie Wharton to the Hudson Valley.

There are ancestral strands as well, including some spun as far back as the 1690s when Wharton's Huguenot great-great-grandfather "came from the French Palatinate to participate in the founding of New Rochelle" in Westchester County. But as the auburn-haired author went on to say in her autobiography, *A Backward Glance*, her favorite forebear was the freedom-loving Ebenezer Stevens, whose artillery aided in the American victory at Saratoga during the Revolutionary War. It was not just his army exploits that won Wharton's heart, however. It was also the way Stevens later dubbed his Long Island estate Mount Buonaparte in honor of the new French republic's military hero, then abruptluy dropped the second noun when Napoleon declared himself emperor in 1804. In fact, when Wharton eventually built her own mansion in the Berkshires of western Massachusetts, she called it The Mount in memory of her great-grandfather's home.

When Washington Irving referred to the Hudson a being bordered by the "stately towers of the Joneses, the Schermerhorns and the Rhinelanders," he might well have been describing the wealthy Manhattan family into which Edith Newbold Jones was born on January 24, 1862. More than a decade separated her birth from that of her two older brothers, so this daughter of George Frederic Jones and the former Lucretia Stevens Rhinelander was pretty much raised as an only child, with private tutors and an Irish nurse nicknamed "Doyley."

It may have been through Doyley's Gaelic folktales that the future writer first encountered the supernatural, but it was an uncle who awakened her appreciation of the natural world by taking young Edith for a walk in the Westchester County marshes of Mamaroneck one spring day when "the earth was starred with pink trailing arbutus." After that woodland ramble, she was aware of a "secret sensitiveness to the landscape"—a communion with nature which was to provide comfort and inspiration throughout her life.

Probably because it occurred so early in her childhood, Wharton did not record a date for the Mamaroneck adventure, nor do we know exactly when she first visited the Dutchess County house of "intolerable ugliness" that she refers to as Rhinecliff. Both events, however, had to have taken place before 1866, when the four-year-old girl and her family left America for a lengthy stay in Europe. And the author's ability to vividly recall those milestones nearly 70 years later, when she penned her autobiography, indicates much more than her self-professed photographic memory. For two of Wharton's abiding interests in adulthood turned out to be gardening and architectural design.

Actually the home of Wharton's Aunt Elizabeth was not all that awful-looking, nor was it really Rhinecliff. The latter is the name of the riverside community in the town of Rhinebeck, while the man-

Childhood visits to her aunt's gloomy Gothic mansion in Rhinecliff surely influenced some of Edith Wharton's later essays into the supernatural.

sion is known as Wyndcliffe. In addition, when it ws later owned by beer baron Andrew Fink, the turreted brick bastion—in time a sadly gutted shell off Mill Road—was informally called Fink's Castle. (Local tradition also attests that, lest any player get parched, the suds king ran an underground, gravity-fed beer tap from the basement to his tennis courts by the Hudson shore a half-mile away!)

No matter what its name or who owned it, Wharton's childhood opinion of her aunt's house never changed, even upon "rediscovering it some years later." That is another event she does not date, but it could easily have occurred during the early 1900s when she lived just across the New York border in the Massachusetts town of Lenox. By that time, Wharton had shocked the upper-crust society to which she belonged by becoming a wage-earning writer. (Proper ladies didn't do such things in those days.) She also had made the mistake of marrying Edward "Teddy" Wharton, an amiable if psychologically ailing gentleman of no particular profession, who was 13 years her senior and did not share her intellectual pursuits.

One thing the Whartons did share was a love of the four-storey, white-stucco villa they built—mainly with Edith's money—in the Berkshires. The architect Edith chose was Francis Hoppin, whose similarly designed Blithewood (presently part of Bard College n Dutchess County) was completed around the same time that construction commenced on The Mount in 1901. (Located on Plunkett Street in Lenox, The Mount is now open to the public during the warmer months.)

The following year was a banner one for Wharton. Not only did she and Teddy move into their new home, but her first nvoel, *The Valley of Decision*, was published. What's more, she began a friendship with fellow writer Henry James that turned the tide of her writing. For it was the Manhattan-born expatriate—a score of years older than Edith, and already famous for such books as *The Bostonians*—who wrote to Wharton praising her European-based novel, then added that she should now "Do New York!"

Wharton took Henry James' advice and was working on *The House of Mirth*—set in New York City and the Hudson Valley—when he came to visit her at The Mount during the summer of 1904. Both of them delighted in driving around the countryside in Wharton's new automobile, but because she didn't record much about their destinations it is uncertain if they ventured any farther west than the Shaker community at New Lebanon in Columbia County. James might have insisted on seeing Linwood, the one-time home of his uncle Augustus, which had deeply impressed him when he visited there as a lad. If so, then this could have been the time Wharton

Now part of Bard College, Blithewood as seen here bears similarities to Edith Wharton's Berkshire mansion, the latter built a year later and both buildings designed by architect Francis Hoppin.

rediscovered Wyndcliffe, since that "sour specimen of Hudson River Gothic" stands just up the road from Linwood. (The Linwood estate, which James described in his 1913 memoir, *A Small Boy and Others*, later became a retreat run by the Sisters of St. Ursula.)

It has been said that another nearby estate, Staatsburgh State Historic Site (formerly Mills Mansion), was the model for Bellomont in *The House of Mirth*. Readers—as well as viewers of the same-named, 1981 TV movie, starring Geraldine Chaplin—will recall that the heroine Lily Bart's train ride north past "Garrisons" (Putnam County) would have brought her into Dutchess County. But while the Mills Mansion may have some features similar to the fictional Bellomont, it was a way of life rather than a specific building that Wharton was bent on describing—a life of materialistic excess that she deplored. And when it came to excess, the mansion's real-life mistress, Ruth Livingston Mills, was an expert. Reportedly she gave one party so lavish that the dining room's long banquet table was heaped with sand into which precious gems had been buried. Guests were then supplied with tiny shovels to unearth the treasures!

In her autobiography, Wharton went to great lengths in denying "the exasperating accusation of putting flesh-and-blood prople" into her books. Yet as Eleanor Dwight points out in a well-researched study of *Edith Wharton—an Extraordinary Life*, "all her life, people would read her fiction and discover themselves or their friends in it." For example, there is *The Age of Innocence*, Wharton's Pulitzer Prize-winning novel of 1920, which several times has been made into a motion picture: a 1924 black-and-white silent version; a 1934 black-and-white talkie starring Irene Dunne; and the 1993 technicolor rendition that has been deemed one of director Martin Scorsese's best works. Starring Daniel Day-Lewis, Michelle Pfeiffer and Winona Ryder, the latter version was shot mainly in the Rensselaer County city of Troy, whose downtown brownstones provided a perfect backdrop for Wharton's Victorian-era drama; so, too, the Burden Iron Works office building at the foot of Polk Street, where some interior scenes were filmed. And farther south on Route 9H in Kinderhook, the Luykas Van Alen House—a 1737 National Historic Landmark maintained by the Columbia County Historical Society—was called the Patroon's House in the movie, its interior serving as a trysting place for the ill-fated lovers, Newland Archer and Countess Olenska.

As for others of the novel's cast, the characer of Mrs. Welland is almost surely modeled on Wharton's own mother; Julius Beaufort on the Manhatan millionaire August Belmont; and there is even speculation about M. Rivière resembling the English tutor rumored to have been Wharton's real father. (Nothing was ever proven—or disproven—about her possible illegitimacy.)

Wharton herself can be glimpsed in the two main characters she created for *Hudson River Bracketed* (1929) and its sequel *The Gods Arrive* (1932). Although neither work is as well known as her 1911 novella *Ethan Frome* (which became a 1993 movie starring Liam Neeson), both of these later books are much more personal, and of particular interest to Valley residents. Briefly stated, the saga concerns a young writer named Vance Weston, who finds inspiration in an old Hudson Valley house, and in a married woman not his wife. Wharton's familiarity with the frustrations authors face—along with her own unfulfilling marriage and subsequent infidelity that preceded a 1913 divorce, the loss of her beloved home in the Berkshires, and her eventual expatriation to Europe—add a realistic tang to the tale.

So do local stories that pinpoint certain Hudson Valley settings as being those Wharton was writing about. One tradition holds that Wharton had the aforementioned Wyndcliffe in mind when she described the romantic retreat called The Willows. The only trouble is that the two houses are not much alike—a mistake that the architectural-minded author would never have made. Nor is it likely that Wharton would have chosen a house she hated as the model for a charming cottage where creativity and caring flourished.

Wyndcliffe seems better suited to Wharton's superb ghost story, "The Lady's Maid's Bell," which is set in a "big and gloomy" house "on the

Hudson." As for the fictional Willows, that place looks more like the present-day house-museum called Wilderstein, a brown wooden villa with a corner tower that can be seen a short distance north of Wyndcliffe off Morton Road. But that is only speculation, as are comparisons of other places in Wharton's novel to sites in and around Rhinecliff, including Mt. Rutsen (now part of Ferncliff Forest—accessible from Mt. Rutsen Road) being the site of Thunder Rock.

Such stories citing local sources may have been spurred in part by a conversation that takes place early in *Hudson River Bracketed*, when a character reads a passage from Newburgh architect Andrew Jackson Downing's book on *Landscape Gardening*. Of course, the book and its author are real—see the chapter on "God's Own Gardener"—but the reference to Downing choosing the Willows "as one of the most perfect examples of Hudson River Bracketed" is pure poetic license on Wharton's part. That some readers may have taken it as the truth is understandable though, in view of the fact that Downing did indeed divide the architectural styles he discussed into six main categories, one of which was Hudson River Bracketed—something Wharton notes in the frontmatter of her novel. The name, by the way, refers to decorative brackets placed beneath the eaves of regional villas.

Interestingly enough, Wharton's two books about the writer Van Weston —in some ways a summing up of her own experiences, without the strictures imposed by autobiography—were the last novels she completed before her death in 1937. For awhile thereafter, her fame seemed destined to die as well, but after decades of decline Wharton was rediscovered and became one of the hottest properties around, be it on the movie screen, via video, or the printed word—her own prose plus at least three biographies—and in 1996 she was elected to the National Women's Hall of Fame.

Bravo, Edith. It couldn't have happened to a finer writer!

9. The Modest Colossus of American Music

THE FIFTEEN-YEAR-OLD LAD SAT IDLY FINGERING THE KEYS OF AN OLD piano at the Fairmont Hotel in the Greene County community of Tannersville. It was an activity far easier than the berry-picking he had done earlier this summer of 1916, when he and some other students from Brooklyn's Boys High School had headed up the Hudson to Ulster County, substituting for wartime draftees on a Marlborough farm. However, he was still wrestling with a difficult decision about the future.

In his middle-class merchant family, music was a mainstay—but only as an avocation, not a profession—and the teenager had recently realized he wanted to spend his life as a musician. Fortunately, help with his quandary came from a slightly older scholar also staying at the hotel, who became his friend, listened appreciatively to his amateur piano compositions, then later supported his decision to study music abroad. And while many momentous milestones were to occur in the long productive career of the "Dean of American Composers," Aaron Copland, the Tannersville incident remains a landmark, as well as an introduction to the late musician's lesser known but lifelong links to the region.

Copland returned to Marlborough for the berry-picking season of 1917, but when his graduation from high school the following June gave him greater freedom in job choices, he found steady work as a piano player while taking music lessons with a private teacher. The summers of 1919 and 1920 were spent performing in such Catskill Mountain resorts as Schoharie Manor near Greene County's Elka Park—appearances that allowed him to save enough money to realize his dream of studying music in Europe. This was the move that his Tannersville friend prodded Copland to make, and in 1921 the budding composer arrived in France for what he later described as "the decisive musical experience of my life."

Returning to the United States in 1924, Copland had already completed his first large work, the music for a ballet called *Grohg*, and was commissioned by no less a personage than his teacher, the renowned Nadia Boulanger, to produce an *Organ Symphony* for her upcoming American tour. Yet neither this

nor the recognition he was beginning to receive from other parts of
the music world served to inflate
his ego. For Copland's greatest gifts,
aside from his musical genius, were
his modest and even-tempered
goodwill, abetted by a sometimes
astounding ability to laugh at himself
with a wonderfully wide grin that lit
up his blue-gray eyes. Copland
apparently was incapable of professional jealousy too, preferring to help
his fellow composers whenever he
could, and in the meantime promote
American music. The latter was
accomplished in myriad ways,
among them his 1927 debut as a
lecturer at Manhattan's New School
for Social Research, which eventually
led to his first book, *What to Listen
For in Music.*

*Aaron Copland is remembered not only for his musical
talent, his modesty, and his concern for upcoming
artists, but also for his even-tempered goodwill, as
revealed in his wide grin.*

In January 1930, Copland abandoned his Manhattan apartment for a
quiet home on Hook Road in the Westchester County town of Bedford.
There he began work on his first major piano composition, *Piano
Variations*—a 17-page score he completed that summer when he went to the
artists' retreat of Yaddo in Saratoga Springs as a composer-in-residence. It
was the first of several seasons he spent at Yaddo, usually ensconced in a picturesque stone tower studio that once served as an icehouse. And it was while
strolling the grounds of the lovely old estate that Copland came up with the
idea for the music festivals held there, starting in 1932—festivals for show-
casing new music that supposedly were the first such events of the kind in
the United States.

Although creative artists were especially hard hit by the deepening
Depression, Copland's characteristic simplicity of lifestyle helped him through
those troubled times as he explored additional avenues of music. These
ranged from a major orchestral work titled *Statements* (1935), and a short
opera for children called *The Second Hurricane* (1936), to the ballet *Billy the
Kid* (1938), and his first film credit, *The City*, which was a documentary
shown at the 1939 World's Fair in New York's Flushing Meadow.

The summer of 1939 found Copland renting a house at Woodstock in Ulster County, where he worked on his *Piano Sonata* and a segment concerning the folk hero *John Henry* for CBS Radio's School of the Air series. Never one for all work and no play, he still found time at Woodstock for tennis with friends—and a good thing too, since Hollywood came calling that autumn, allowing Copland a mere six weeks to complete a full musical score for the movie *Of Mice and Men.* Copland never did get hooked on Hollywood, though his musical scores for such films as *Our Town* and *The Red Pony* are said to have set new standards, and in 1950 he won an Oscar for *The Heiress.* Aside from foreign travel, he stayed mainly in the East, devoting more than 20 summers to the Berkshire Music Center in Massachusetts and the associated Tanglewood festivals, beginning in 1940. As is obvious from its title, the East also flavors Copland's most famous work, *Appalachian Spring,* for which he won the Pulitzer Prize in 1945. The ballet's "Simple Gifts" melody, now a familiar standby in most schools, was borrowed from a hymn that seems to reflect Copland's own approach to life—a hymn from the Shaker sect that had its American start here in the Hudson Valley.

A year after winning the Pulitzer Prize, Copland happened to visit some friends in the Snedens Landing section of Palisades. Ensorceled by this southeastern corner of Rockland County, with its enclave of creative people and relatively easy access to Manhattan, he rented a centuries-old dwelling known as the Ding Dong House—a nickname derived from the ferry bell that once graced its arched gate. Comprised of three uniquely stepped sections set amid old-fashioned gardens and a lawn leading down to the Hudson, the spacious house was just the place Copland needed to compose his widely acclaimed Emily Dickinson song cycle. The work started out as a single Dickinson poem set to music, but grew to a dozen songs as Copland read more and more by and about her. Indeed, he later recorded in his autobiography how friends visiting him during this period kidded him about always having an Emily Dickinson book in his hands.

A story that does not appear in his autobiography but survives as a local tradition concerns the neighborhood garbage collector, Bob Hauser, who was also an accomplished musician. According to Palisades historian Alice Haagensen, Hauser was picking up garbage at the Ding Dong House one day when he heard Copland "playing a passage over and over and stopping abruptly in the same place," as if stuck for inspiration. Thereupon Hauser is said to have joined the composer at the piano, and completed the piece for him. Still another local legend tells of the time Copland was hosting a party that got a tad wild and someone pushed actor Laurence Olivier over the edge of an embankment. Or was it the aristocratic Olivier who did the shoving? Versions vary except for the happy outcome that no one got badly hurt.

Copland had hoped to purchase Ding Dong House when his three-year lease expired. The owners wouldn't sell, however, and it was to be several years until he found another property that suited him. Meanwhile, he added to his accomplishments by being the first American composer named Norton Professor of Poetics at Harvard University, where he lectured during the academic year of 1951-52. His well-attended talks were subsequently turned into a book, *Music and Imagination*, though Copland in his typical self-effacing style initially had been worried that his "words might not be eloquent enough."

Having enjoyed the Hudson view from his Snedens Landing home, it is not surprising that when Copland finally purchased a house in 1952, it offered a similar prospect, only this time it was on the Westchester County side of the river in the Crotonville section of Ossining. Originally a barn belonging to the historic Shady Lane Farm, the structure had been remodeled into a lovely residence boasting a two-storey-high room that took up most of the interior. On one end of this huge room stood a Baldwin piano at which Copland completed his only full-length opera, *The Tender Land*, with the multi-talented Erik Johns as librettist. The piano itself was noteworthy in that Copland generally used Steinways. Upon his move to Ossining, however, the Baldwin company offered to supply him with a piano so long as they could periodically replace it, then sell the used instrument as a genuine "Copland piano." It was an offer no composer could refuse.

One invitation that Copland would gladly have turned down came on May 22, 1953, when he received a telegram from Senator Joseph McCarthy directing him to appear before the Senate Permanent Subcommittee on Investigations. The hearing into his alleged communist affiliations took only two hours and Copland acquitted himself well, but the mere fact that he had been called to testify was to reverberate in many nasty ways, including anonymous letters, canceled performances, and passport problems. Even his patriotic *Lincoln Portrait* (1942) was once presented on national television without any credit given to its composer. Copland tried to treat the hearing humorously, sometimes mimicking the way committee counsel Roy Cohn pronounced "communist" with a bovine moo. But the toll in time and money was exceeded only by the terrible emotional drain—something recalled decades later in 1980 when Copland was celebrating his eightieth birthday and a glowing tribute to him was read into the *Congressional Record*, saluting "this country's greatest living composer . . ." and "his tireless efforts on behalf of American music." Learning of this, Copland quipped, "Has anyone told Roy Cohn?"

At that time Copland was living in the Westchester County town of Cortlandt, where in 1960 he had purchased a secluded home called Rock Hill. Though well loved, his converted barn in Ossining had proven unsuitable due to the lack of separation between studio and living room. Plus that, the neighborhood was beginning to be built up, and Copland ever fretted about his music disturbing others. It therefore seemed as if Rock Hill's unknown architect had designed the understated wood-sided house with Copland in mind, since a spacious studio featuring floor-to-ceiling windows occupied one end, and the living room was at the other end. Set on two-and-a-half hilly but well-landscaped acres overlooking the Hudson, the house was reached via a winding driveway through the woods that assured privacy as well as a measure of soundproofing.

This was a period in his life when Copland could easily have afforded lavish surroundings. Yet he retained his simple ways, working at a desk someone had made for him from slabs of wood set atop sawhorses, and sleeping in a bare-bones bed covered by a plain chenille spread. As for the hallway's mirrored niche that held his Oscar, that might have seemed a touch of vanity, except for the fact that the niche was already there when Copland moved in. He merely and matter-of-factly made good use of the space.

Copland contentedly lived at Rock Hill for the last 30 years of his life, composing such pieces as the lovely piano solo *Down a Country Lane* (1962), *Connotations* for the opening of Philharmonic Hall in Manhattan's Lincoln Center (1962), *Inscape* for the New York Philharmonic Orchestra's 125th anniversary (1967), and *Duo for Flute and Piano* (1971). His inspiration began to fade though, so instead of composing, Copland concentrated more on conducting, having made his debut as a conductor with the New York Philharmonic in 1958. Encomiums were accumulating too: dozens of honorary doctorates, plus the 1964 Medal of Freedom—the highest civil honor conferred by the President for service in peacetime—to name only some.

At an age when most men would have long since retired, Copland continued to concertize, as well as to travel extensively, and to co-author with Vivian Perlis a two-volume autobiography. Nor did he neglect his fellow musicians, whether professional or local school groups, who made a mecca of Rock Hill. In addition, Copland actively supported area efforts like the Paramount Center for the Arts in Peekskill. He was 82 when he gave his last concert, and did not slow down until he realized his memory was failing. As

Set off from the road on a wooded lot, Rock Hill was Aaron Copland's home for the last 30 years of his life, affording the composer both privacy and soundproofing.

his long-time friend, Erik Johns, recalled, the doctor Copland consulted told the composer there was nothing that could be done about his memory; to just "Forget it"! Typical of Copland, he didn't find the phrase cruel or offensive, but often repeated the anecdote with great mirth.

Following his death on December 2, 1990, Copland's ashes were taken to Tanglewood in the Berkshires, but Rock Hill is considered by many to be the most tangible monument to the man who contributed so much to American music. Yet it is a monument that almost wasn't. For his will set up a trust called the Aaron Copland Fund for Music, which was to use his assets for assisting young American composers. And what better way to raise revenue than by selling Rock Hill? Fortunately local music lovers rallied to save the house. Initially led by Peekskill impressario Edward Mashberg, the group formed the non-profit Copland Heritage Association in 1993, hoping to convince the town of Cortlandt to obtain a long-term lease on Rock Hill so that it could be turned into a "living memorial." Not only did Cortlandt Supervisor Linda Puglisi and the Town Board endorse the idea, but the Copland trust was enthusiastic too, putting aside the possibility of a $400,000 house sale for a token rental of $1 a year, and in 1994 a lease was signed.

Transforming the dream into a reality wasn't easy, since Rock Hill required substantial repair, as well as additional furnishing and an operating budget. But eventually Copland House—its present-day name—became operational, and since 1998 it has been hosting a variety of activities, not the least of which is awarding short-term residencies to deserving composers. Because of the peace and privacy essential to such a program, the house—added to the New York State Register of Historic Places in 2002, when it also became the property of Copland House, Inc.—is not generally open to the public except for a couple of community-welcome days during the year. Meanwhile, its presence is very much felt through a touring ensemble of musicians, along with other events.

At one time there was talk of lobbying to have a National Aaron Copland Day declared, but it was felt that emphasis might best be placed on year-round recognition of the composer's goals, rather than a single day. In fact, it was Copland's friend, Erik Johns, who once pointed out that the modest composer probably would have insisted any such national holiday should be called simply American Music Day.

10. *Mining the Valley's Iron Art*

S TRETCHING FROM THE RAMAPO MOUNTAINS ON THE SOUTHWEST TO the Taconics on the northeast, the Hudson Valley's vast iron heart provided the region with its first major industry—an industry evident in the many old mines and furnaces that still dot the landscape, as well as some of the finest ornamental ironwork to be found anywhere. And there is no better way of fully appreciating that decorative art form than by first seeing how it all started.

Folks able to rack up a few miles on a hiking trail should not miss the concentration of iron mines in Harriman State Park in Orange and Rockland counties. Among those mines easily found are the Hasenclever complex visible from the Red Cross Trail south of Tiorati Brook Road; Dunn Mine on the east side of the Nawahunta Fire Road; Boston Mine on Island Pond Road; Pine Swamp and Hogencamp mines off the Dunning Trail west of Lake Skannatati; plus two extensive excavations along the old Surebridge Mine Road, one called the Greenwood and, a short distance south, the Surebridge. Keep an eye out, too, for the remains of small villages that once surrounded some of these places; no matter what the season, it's impossible not to be aware of the harsh life miners endured in these isolated communities.

It goes without saying that such mines should be viewed from the outside only, which is why many of those in other parks are off-limits to the public, including some in Rockland County's Sterling Forest and Clarence Fahnestock in Putnam County. But in the latter park it's still possible to view from Route 301 a huge horizontal tunnel—gated at either end—that reveals how miners followed an ore vein as it dipped down into the earth. And in Sterling Forest, stone steps and crumbling walls recall the mining community that once flourished along Old Forge Road, near its junction with West Lake Road. (The large ruin with a still-standing fireplace was the miners' meeting hall.) Nearby a massive charcoal furnace—enclosed by a worse-for-wear wooden portico—stands at the corner, while farther down West Lake Road can be seen various ore-handling buildings, including a crusher and hoist-house that served the mine running *beneath* Sterling Lake. The park's shore-side visitors center was opened on Old Forge Road in 2003, and is a boon to anyone interested in the iron industry. In addition, a distinctive double-arched furnace, located on the Orange Turnpike just north of Southfields, is now part of the park, but the fencing and construction done to stabilize the structure—while necessary—are detractious.

For those who don't care for woods-walking, the Clove Furnace Historic Site farther north on Route 17 in the Orange County hamlet of Arden offers a unique view of 19th century ironmaking—from a restored, four-chambered hot-blast furnace to a small museum housed in one of its original buildings—all within steps of the parking lot. Easy walking is likewise offered at Fort Montgomery State Historic Site, on Route 9W north of the Bear Mountain Bridge. Although focusing on a Revolutionary War battle that took place there, the site also contains a fenced-off iron mine along one of its paths.

On the other side of the river, in Columbia County, the Copake Falls section of Taconic State Park contains the furnace and a few other remains of what was once the bustling Copake Iron Works—now part of the maintenance area, and only a short drive from the park entrance on Route 344. Nearby, too, is the Roeliff Jansen Historical Society, housed in a former Methodist church, featuring a fund of local lore—iron and otherwise. Farther south, one of the loveliest of former ironmaking sites can be found in the Dutchess County town of Union Vale, where the 500-acre Tymor Forest on Bruzgul Road offers a scenic trail skirting a furnace pond that takes strollers past such remains as a smelting furnace, rock crusher, quarry, dynamite shed, and slag heap. Part of this complex, but not in the park, is the anthracite-powered Beekman Furnace stack on Furnace Road. It is on private property, but may be viewed from the road, as can the wonderfully preserved Wassaic charcoal kilns—which provided fuel for area ironworks—on Furnace Bank/Deep Hollow Road in the nearby town of Amenia.

While in no way comprising a complete map of early iron enterprise in the Valley, the aforementioned sites should serve as a prelude to the ornamental side of the industry—a side that did not truly come of age until the 19th century, even though some decorative pieces were produced before then. Abetted by improved technology, decorative ironwork fit in with a love of the elaborate which had its heyday during the 1837-1901 reign of England's Queen Victoria. The earliest and most widespread use of ornamental iron was for fencing, especially in riverside cities like Troy and Newburgh, where the high stoops and recessed areaways of row houses required protective railings, as did the balconies and porches of other buildings. It was also in these indus-

Top: *distinctive because of its high double arches, the Southfield iron furnace operated until 1887, and is now preserved in Sterling Forest State Park.*

Bottom: *Northeastern Dutchess County hosts many mementoes of the early-day iron industry, including these well-preserved charcoal kilns in Wassaic.*

trial centers that master blacksmiths were found who could hammer the heated metal into works of art. Because of its purity and pliability, wrought iron was particularly suited to the marvelous melange of scrolls, arrows, arches, acanthus leaves and other motifs used in these early 19th century fences, though cast-iron pieces were sometimes incorporated.

As the penchant for iron enclosures grew to include larger areas such as parks and cemeteries, foundry-made cast iron began taking over, largely because it was cheaper than the hand-wrought kind, and the reusable molds for molten metal produced more uniform pieces. Competition became keen among cast-iron manufacturers, who in their zeal to have the most popular fence patterns, were not averse to copying a competitor's design. Yet despite this practice, manufacturers infrequently sought patent protection, one of the few exceptions being John T. Davy of Troy, who in 1851 became the first American to obtain a design patent for what he called an Elizabethan pattern. Later patents usually covered construction rather than pattern, one example being the fence around the Mohawk Street YMCA in Cohoes, Albany County. As for Davy's Elizabethan design, check out 705 Third Avenue in the Rensselaer County community of Lansingburgh.

Around the time that Davy secured his patent, there was also a trend for

fencing off family plots in cemeteries, and it is in such protected places that some of the best specimens of this kind of ornamental ironwork are found today, especially the cemetery on Troy's Oakwood Avenue. There are some oddities too: somehow a magnificent cemetery-plot gate and fence wound up in front of the old Sally Tack Tavern (now a private residence) on Route 209 in the Ulster County hamlet of Stone Ridge, while part of the fence that once graced the New York City Hall now borders the Bloomingburg burial ground on Route 17M in Orange County. Those transplants serve as reminders of how

Troy's Oakwood Cemetery is noted for its outstanding ornamental ironwork used mainly in fences like that enclosing the tomb of Civil War General George H. Thomas.

changing times have taken a toll on our cast-iron legacy. Too often in the past, when tastes veered away from iron fences, they were simply dismantled. Still others were sacrificed to wartime scrap drives, as happened to the fence surrounding Orange County's Hambletonian Monument in the village of Chester—a site that later sported a unique replacement made possible by local citizens.

Such community caring is also the clue to the more preferred preservation of original ornamental ironwork, which in this region ranges far beyond the aforementioned fencing to encompass everything from lawn furniture and fireplace backs to prefabricated building facades. A leader in the latter development was Catskill-born James Bogardus, who in 1848 manufactured the 5-storey facade for New York City's first building with an all-iron front. In an era when fire often destroyed whole neighborhoods, the protection afforded by iron added to the popularity of the new facades, which could be cast much quicker than stone could be cut, and were much lighter too. Those were some of the advantages that convinced the commander of Albany County's Watervliet Arsenal to choose cast iron for a gun carriage storehouse that was constructed there in 1859—currently considered the "only all-iron building in America still used for its original purpose," and one that can be viewed during public tours of the arsenal on Broadway.

That some exterior segments of the Watervliet storehouse resemble stone is not surprising, since iron was often made to look that way. The facade of the Ezra Waterbury House on Warren Street in the Columbia County city of Hudson is a good example of this, and is thought to be the only iron-fronted building in the Northeast that was constructed exclusively as a residence. Other notable facades include the cast-iron storefronts found on Main and Partition streets in the Ulster County village of Saugerties.

Another interesting innovation can be seen on Troy's Third Street, which boasts some "brownstone" stoop posts that are really iron, whereas the pillared portico of Newburgh's former library on Grand Street shouldn't be missed. And getting back to fencing, the Grove Street headquarters of the Historical Society of Sleepy Hollow and Tarrytown boasts a handsome black-painted iron enclosure, as does the Purdy Homestead at Purdy Station in the Westchester County town of North Salem.

While cast iron remained in fashion, all up and down the river foundries flourished, their spark-spitting smokestacks crimsoning the night skies—a sight perhaps reprehensible in our present pollution-conscious time, but one that inspired 19th century artists and authors alike. Of the many industrial scenes painted by Hudson River School artists, Jasper Francis Cropsey's 1879 *Foundry* may be the most dramatic, matched only by Harry Fenn's inferno-like *Poughkeepsie, and Its Foundries at Night*, which was used as the frontispiece for William Cullen Bryant's second volume of *Picturesque America* (1872-1874). Bryant, by the way, regarded such scenes as "strangely beautiful," adding that the Hudson's foundries "light the river like weird beacons . . . the sound of their great furnaces . . . the panting of giants."

The West Point Foundry at Cold Spring was probably the most widely depicted, though, with John Ferguson Weir's famous painting of the furnace room now owned by the nearby Putnam County Historical Society on Chestnut Street. The largest foundry in the country at mid-century— with its property now protected as Foundry Cove Historic Preserve, accessible from Chestnut Street—it was most famous for munitions and machinery. In fact, the space projectile Jules Verne wrote about in his 1865 novella, *From the Earth to the Moon,* supposedly was a product of the West Point Foundry. More factually, the foundry also produced cast-iron building components, as well as lawn furniture for Washington Irving's Sunnyside estate in Sleepy Hollow.

The Valley's vast array of cast-iron lawn and garden items is a study in itself, and many of the great estates that are now open to the ublic—notably Montgomery Place in Dutchess County's Annandale—have large collections. But even from-the-road viewing of private gardens can be rewarding, as in the case of one old house on Newburgh's Montgomery Street, where a life-size cast-iron dog guards the grounds.

Outdoor lighting fixtures are still another study; the lampposts in front of Albany's Fort Orange Club on Washington Avenue being some of the finest, as are fountains like the tall, star-topped sipping station at Congress Park in Saratoga Springs. The latter city, it should be added, is a veritable museum of ornamental ironwork, including the Saratoga Race Course, where equine railings and treillage recall the superb craftsmanship of the McKinney family's Albany Architectural Iron Works. Although the company remained in business long after other foundries began closing down in the 1880s, it eventually had to abandon its castings and wrought-iron products in favor of steel, the metal which now dominates the market.

Today only a few foundries still operate in the Hudson Valley, and blacksmiths who can fabricate fine wrought iron are equally rare, so it is all the more important to preserve the ornamental ironwork which has survived. And that must also include practical pieces now used for decorative purposes, a case in point being the massive chain that once spanned the Hudson to prevent the British from coming up the river during the Revolutionary War. Links from the chain now rest on Trophy Point at the United States Military Academy—a respectful note to both our military and industrial history.

11. Legacy of an Itinerant Limner

MIRACLES DO OCCUR. AT LEAST THAT SEEMS TO BE THE CASE WITH Ammi Phillips, the regional folk painter whose rescue from obscurity has depended not only on some decidedly artful detective work, but at times on sheer serendipity. Consider, for example, the portrait of Harriet Campbell (Mrs. Marinus Fairchild) that in 1992 was donated to the Sterling and Francine Clark Art Institute, just across the New York/Massachusetts border in Williamstown. Painted around 1815 when the subject was a young girl in the Washington County town of Greenwich, the portrait was later brought to the Berkshires by Harriet's daughter Sarah, who resided in North Adams, Massachusetts, until her death in 1937.

The unsigned canvas by then had lost its frame and was in such parlous condition that it would have been thrown out had it not been for a friend named Carre Eldridge. She retrieved it from the trash heap simply out of respect, and stored it in her attic. There it remained for many years until Mrs. Eldridge's son Oliver happened to recognize a painting in Harvard University's Fogg Art Museum as being "wonderfully similar." Closer inspection revealed that the two full-length portraits were indeed related, both having come from the brush of "the best, most prolific, and the most inventive American country painter of the 19th century"—an accolade given Ammi Phillips by the late art historian Mary Childs Black of Germantown, Dutchess County, who helped bring about his current recognition.

How is it possible that a painter producing more that 500 commissioned portraits over a 50-year period could remain relatively unknown until recent times? To arrive at an answer, it is best to begin in Colebrook, Connecticut, where Ammi Phillips was born on April 24, 1788, the middle son in what became a family of seven children. ("Ammi," b the way, is not a French derivation as some people have supposed; rather it is an Old Testament name pronounced "Am-eye.") Little else is recorded of his early years, but since it is known that several portraitists (or "limners") plied their trade in western Connecticut during that period, it is safe to say the boy was exposed to, if not influenced by, their work, and may even have received some lessons.

During a lifetime spent as an itinerant painter, Ammi Phillips embraced different styles, one of the finest evident in his portrait of a "Young Man From Gaylordsville," done around 1823.

PHOTO COURTESY OF PAUL SARDELLIA

Sometime after 1810 (when census records show he was still living with his parents), Phillips struck out on his own as an itinerant limner, heading north from Colebrook to the Berkshires, where in 1811 he completed his earliest known commissions. These portraits, though primitive and out of proportion, nevertheless sold, and Phillips was soon sufficiently solvent to afford a wife—Laura Brockway of the Rensselaer County community of Schodack, whom he married in the neighboring town of Nassau on March 8, 1813. By now Philllips was a more accomplished painter, having developed an almost dreamlike style featuring soft pastels such as those found in the Harriet Campbell painting and its near-twin, also a girl named Harriet (Leavens). The latter lived in Lansingburgh (now part of Troy), where Phillips and his wife soon settled, likely because of the transportation benefits and centrality of the Hudson-shore city. For Phillips' commissions were beginning to come from across the river as well as along New York's eastern border—from Albany and Catskill to Chatham, and as far north as Bennington, Vermont.

The practice in those days was for a painter to work in the home of his patron, often executing several portraits of family members while living there or at a nearby inn if his own house was too distant. Nor were these itinerant limners averse to doing side jobs like sign-painting, though we know of only two instances when Phillips supplemented his income in such a manner. One was a banner he purportedly painted in Dutchess County for the 1844 presidential campaign of James K. Polk, and the other a signboard done two decades earlier for the Vail Tavern in the Orange County city of Goshen. That sign—showing an eagle on either side—became so well known that when the establishment changed hands, the new owner named it the Eagle Hotel. The campaign banner also brought its image-bearer success in that Polk won the election, but neither it nor the sign can be seen today. The hotel was destroyed by fire in 1841, while the banner remains unlocated.

Phillips was probably too busy for much moonlighting, especially during the decades of the 1820s when he did the most extensive traveling of his career. Economics dictated this, for his family grew to include five children, and a portrait garnered him at most $10. (One of the few original sales slips that survive shows that on September 29, 1824 Phillips was paid $20 for painting an Orange County couple, Hannah and Alexander Thompson of Crawford.) In contrast, a 1986 sale of a Phillips portrait brought in $181,000, and later his *Little Girl in Red* reportedly sold for just under $1 million.

There's a big difference between $1 million and $10, but the more modest amount was still a fairly handsome stipend in Phillips' day, and his popularity tended to disjoint the nose of at least one more formally trained painter. In a letter of September 9, 1825, Kingston-born John Vanderlyn grudgingly allowed that "moving about through the country as Phillips . . . does must be an agreeable way of passing ones [*sic*] time." This may have been true for the young limner trying to make a name for himself, but as Phillips approached middle age, he began to cut down on the time he was away from home, particularly after the death of his wife on February 2, 1830. The family was then living in Rhinebeck, where Laura Phillips was laid to rest in the graveyard of the Dutch Reformed Church on South Street.

Needing a caregiver for his underage children, if not necessarily a companion, Phillips defied convention by remarrying a mere five months later. The July 15 ceremony took place in the Dutchess hamlet of Bangall, for the bride—22-year-old Jane Ann Caulkins—came from the neighboring town of Northeast. Despite the difference in their ages—Phillips was then 42—the union apparently was a happy one, which may account in part for the artist altering his style to one which Mary Black called "infinitely more languid and more highly stylized . . . with a new gracefulness in the poses of the women." This is readily seen in the largest of Phillips' known paintings, a 58-by-44-inch canvas done at Saugerties in 1838, which depicts Mrs. Stephen Ostander and her son Titus—one of the few double portraits the artist did.

As for Phillips' most unusual commission, that had to be the quartet of portraits which an Amenia lady, Sarah Totten Sutherland, ordered to give to her four daughters in 1840—each painting of Mrs. Sutherland identical except for slight differences in the right corner of her lace collar. Mention of those quadruple portraits brings to mind an associated tale which holds that at home Phillips would make up a stock of canvases with bodies to which he need only paint in the heads of clients when working in their houses! Admittedly Phillips did employ certain shortcuts, such as standard poses, to expedite his portraits, but the headless body story seems only good for a laugh.

Amusing, too, is an anecdote concerning Phillips' 1840 painting of Nelson De La Vergne, which was described in Isaac Huntting's' 1897 *History of Little Nine Partners* as looking "more natural that Nels[on] does himself." Yet there is more than just entertainment value here, for the anecdote hints at the realism Phillips used to compete with the emerging technique of photography. The development of daguerreotypes in the late 1830s doomed the careers of many itinerant limners, but not Phillips, who continued painting until 1850. The census for that year lists him as a portraitist living with his wife and children in Jane Ann's home town of Northeast, and on June 14, 1850 a cousin is recorded as getting married in their house. From then on, though, we know practically nothing of Phillips' whereabouts or his work for nearly a decade.

The mysterious period ends with the 1860 census, which shows Phillips, his wife, and one grown daughter living in the Berkshires at Curtisville (now Interlaken). Then in his seventies, Phillips nevertheless managed to turn out nearly two dozen more portraits before he died on July 11, 1865. For almost a century after he was buried in Dutchess County's Amenia Island Cemetery on East Main Street, the region's most prolific folk painter remained largely unrecognized. Part of this was attributable to Phillips himself, who signed less than a dozen of his portraits, made inscriptions on only a few more, and changed his style several times during a half-century of painting. Some families, of course, had records pertaining to ancestral portraits, but the great bulk of Phillips' work went unidentified or assigned to others.

Whereas no one person can be said to have rediscovered Ammi Phillips, a great deal of credit goes to Barbara and Lawrence Holdridge. Their 1958 purchase of a signed portrait—that of Putnam County's George C. Sunderland, done in 1840—led them on a quest that eventually linked Phillips to several other limners. All of them turned out to be Ammi, as the Holdridges demonstrated in the early 1960s. Since then, other portraits have been identified, including the one of Harriet Campbell that now graces the Clark Institute collection; indeed, it was the Holdridges who authenticated it for Oliver Eldridge. And today examples of the limner's work can be found in fine museums across the country—from the National Gallery in Washington, D.C., and New York's Whitney, to Fort Worth's Amon Carter collection, and the Henry Ford Museum in Dearborn, Michigan. But some of the best remain right here in the Hudson Valley: among them a half-dozen portraits of the Hasbrouck family at Ulster County's Locust Lawn on Route 32 in Gardiner, and seven at the Senate House on Kingston's Fair Street.

Of the latter septet, four are notable not so much because the subjects were related—Phillips often painted several members of the same family—but because these portraits of the DeWitt/Sleight clan were only brought to light by someone cleaning out a Clinton Street barn in 1909. Still another portrait—that of innkeeper Hannah Masten Radcliff—is possibly the only one of the group that Phillips actually painted in Kingston, despite the fact that the seven people depicted all had ties to the city. In addition, these seven portraits showcase some of the techniques emblematic of the artist: for instance, the direct and penetrating gaze of the subject; attention to fabric, especially the detailed lace of the ladies' headgear; and the use of book titles to denote vocation, as in *Horne on the Psalms* being held by the Reverend Thomas DeWitt.

Other places in the region with Ammi Phillips paintings are the Albany Institute of History and Art on Washington Avenue; Greene County's Bronck House on Route 9W in Coxsackie; Putnam County's Boscobel Restoration on Route 9D in Garrison; and the Ulster County Historical Society on Route 209 in Stone Ridge. But don't go looking for a likeness of Ammi. Ironically, despite the large legacy he left us, there is no portrait of the itinerant limner.

12. Satanstoe Revisited

WHENEVER JAMES FENIMORE COOPER IS MENTIONED, IT'S ONLY natural to think of Cooperstown, the central New York community his father founded, and where the author lived for much of his life. Or else Cooper's name evokes upstate scenes like the ones he depicted in such novels as *The Deerslayer* and *The Last of the Mohicans.* Yet equally salient, if not as well known, are his Hudson Valley connections—especially the relatively short but seminal time he spent in Westchester County.

An even briefer time was spent in Burlington, New Jersey, where Cooper was born on September 15, 1789, the twelfth child of a successful land speculator who was then planning a village along the shore of Otsego Lake. Cooper had just celebrated his first birthday when his father William decided to move the family there—a decision opposed by his mother Elizabeth. She reportedly refused to budge from her chair on the day of departure, and had to be carried out to the waiting wagon.

That recalcitrant streak seems to have been passed down to Cooper, who could be quite testy later in life, though he also possessed great charm and readily made friends. The latter trait was evident as early as 1800 when Cooper was sent to board at a small parish school run by a Reverend Ellison in Albany. There he met William Jay, youngest son of Chief Justice John Jay, and the two became close friends, eventually attending Yale College together. Jay was to graduate; Cooper did not. Youthful high spirits, coupled with a disinterest in study and a dislike of New Englanders, culminated in a couple of pranks during his junior year—a donkey placed in a professor's chair, plus some gunpowder set off in a schoolroom. Cooper was thereupon expelled from Yale, despite one teacher's description of him being "a fine sparkling beautiful boy of alluring person & interesting manners."

Deciding that his son might fare better in the navy, William Cooper—now a judge and an influential politician—shipped James off as a common sailor, there being no naval academies in those days. The young man did well on his trans-Atlantic voyage before the mast, and on January 1, 1808 was commissioned a midshipman, serving aboard such vessels as the *Vesuvius* and

Not far from the present-day Mamaroneck Free Library where this Warren Chase Meritt painting can be seen, James Fenimore Cooper was married in the home of his bride's father on New Year's Day, 1811. (Photo courtesy of the Mamaroneck Free Library)

Wasp until 1810, when he was granted a year's furlough. Cooper never did return to the navy. Upon meeting the lovely Susan Augusta De Lancey of Mamaroneck in Westchester County, he promptly proposed, and the couple was married on New Year's Day, 1811, at the home of the bride's father, former Loyalist John Peter De Lancey. Shortly thereafter, Cooper resigned his commission, mainly to please his 18-year-old bride, but also because the death of his father had left him with extensive upstate holdings to oversee. Judge Cooper, it might be noted, had died in December 1809, after being hit from behind by an opponent when leaving a political meeting in Albany.

The newlyweds divided their time between Cooperstown and Mamaroneck, with the thought of eventually settling on a farm by Lake Otsego. But fate intervened in the form of a treasured family nurse—or so tradition tells—who during one of their stays at Cooperstown decided to quit her job and marry some local sinner. Supposedly Susan Cooper was so upset by this event she convinced her husband that only a protracted stay with her parents would help. Cooper obliged, and in 1817 they moved in with Susan's family at Heathcote Hall, whose hilltop location at Mamaroneck's present-day Cortland Avenue afforded fine views of Long Island Sound near De Lancey's Neck, the southernmost extension of which was called Satan's Toe (now known as Edgewater Point). It was probably while residing at the De Lancey home that Cooper was treated to tales about the site: how ancient Indians had driven the devil from Westchester County, forcing Satan to flee across some rocks to Long Island, and how his fiery toe had burned into the last section of shoreline it touched—hence, Satan's Toe. But it would be several more decades before Cooper utilized the legend in making his own indelible mark on American literature.

Had it not been for a casual comment, Cooper might never have embarked on a writing career. This conversational catalyst occurred in 1819, after Cooper had built a home he called Angevine on some Scarsdale property owned by the De Lanceys along Mamaroneck Road. One night as Cooper was reading aloud to his ailing wife, he suddenly set aside the insipid novel, saying, "I could write you a better book myself." Amused at her husband's comment, Susan challenged him to pick up his pen, with the result that *Precaution* appeared the following November—a dismal imitation of Jane Austen's *Persuasion* that Cooper had the good sense to publish anonymously.

Fortunately the failure of his first novel didn't deter Cooper. Encouraged by his friend William Jay as well as Susan, he soon embarked on another book, this time showing better judgment by following the cardinal rule of good writing: know your subject. The setting Cooper chose was the Hudson Valley during the Revolution, augmenting his own considerable knowledge by interviewing local residents who had lived through those trying times. He also made trips to the Katonah home of William Jay's father, John, and it was the elderly statesman who provided Cooper with the protagonist of his new book, *The Spy*. (See the chapter about Enoch Crosby, "Shoemaker-Spy of the Revolution.")

An immediate success when it appeared in 1821, *The Spy* was followed by *The Pioneers*, the first of Cooper's five Leatherstocking tales featuring the quintessential woodsman Natty Bumppo. By this time (1823), Cooper had moved his family to New York City, where they lived for only a few years until the author decided that Europe offered more. Actually he might have done better had he remained at home, for his seven-year stay abroad served to negatively alter his perception of America. Yet it was also a period when he produced the classic *Last of the Mohicans*, as well as such maritime tales as *The Red Rover* and *The Water-Witch*, the latter two drawing upon Hudson Valley legends of Captain Kidd, as did some of his subsequent books. (In all, Cooper authored over thirty novels, plus travel books.)

Upon his return to New York in 1833, Cooper soon demonstrated his disenchantment with the country he had once championed. Declining a dinner in his honor, he petulantly declared that there were "no longer any Americans of the old breed," and for the next five years he concentrated mainly on works dealing either with Europe or his disillusionment.

It was in the Katonah home of Chief Justice John Jay that James Fenimore Cooper heard about the Revolutionary War spy who was to become the hero of Cooper's next book.

American readers reacted as might be expected: his books remained largely unbought, while the press panned him to the point of libel. Cooper retaliated by bringing suit, and while he often won his cases, the price he paid was public neglect—a neglect sadly accorded *Satanstoe*, which is now considered by some scholars to be one of the finest American historical novels ever written. Cooper's disgruntlement, it should be pointed out, did not extend to his family. He and Susan were said to have a serenely happy marriage marred only by the death of two of their seven children.

After *Satanstoe* appeared in 1845, Cooper told a friend, "You see what anti-rentism is about? It is the great American question of the day." Indeed it was, and Cooper—having replaced his earlier democratic ideals with a faith in the power wealth wielded—sided with Hudson Valley landowners like the Livingstons and Van Rensselaers in their dispute with tenant farmers. (See the chapters on "Winging It" and "Echoes of Big Thunder.") This stand did little to endear Cooper to an already alienated public, and for awhile *Satanstoe* was virtually ignored. Its creator, however, had planned it to be the first of a trilogy collectively called the Littlepage Manuscripts, so he forged ahead with the companion volumes, *The Chainbearers* (1845) and *The Redskins* (1846).

Together those volumes constitute the closest thing to an autobiography that Cooper would compose. (Perhaps because of his poor public image, he even made a deathbed demand that no biography be written about him—a request respected by his author daughter Susan, who also burned many of his papers after he died at Cooperstown on September 14, 1851, a day short of his sixty-second birthday.) For in following three generations of his fictional family—from *Satanstoe*'s optimistic, America-loving Corny Littlepage, to Corny's great-grandson, who in *The Redskins* finds the country "diminutive and mean" after living in Europe—Cooper touches upon many of his own experiences, meanwhile revealing how his philosophy changed to favor aristo-cratic landowners. The entire trilogy, therefore, is must reading for anyone interested in the anti-rent movement or Cooper in toto. But only in *Satanstoe* is the author at his best, presenting a vivid portrait of the Hudson Valley during the mid-1700s, particularly Albany and the De Lancey lands in Westchester County. And for those who may have thought Cooper dull, it should be noted that few modern-day chillers can compete with his chapters describing a race against death, when the ice on the Hudson breaks up as par-tygoers are crossing from Kinderhook to Albany.

In calling this important novel *Satanstoe*, and using that setting as the Littlepage family seat throughout his trilogy, Cooper paid a lasting homage to the happy period he spent in Westchester, where his writing talent first flowered. It is a tribute that has been well reciprocated by county residents over the years, as seen in such place-names as Mamaroneck's Leatherstocking nature trail, Cooper Avenue, and Fenimore Road. Where the latter meets Boston Post Road, the old De Lancey mansion—moved from its Heathcote Hill site—later served as a restaurant, while a local theatre group was called the Fenimore Players, and the high school cafeteria was decorated with murals depicting scenes from his novels. The cafeteria is not generally open to the public, but a painting of Cooper's marriage ceremony can be seen at the Mamaroneck Free Library on Library Lane.

As for Cooper's life in Scarsdale, his Angevine home—referred to by his neighbors as Cooper's Folly, due to its odd architecture and poor workman-ship—was demolished long ago. There are other landmarks, though, includ-ing the Harvey Birch Room at the Wayside Cottage (maintained by the Junior League of Central Westchester, and open to the public by appoint-ment). And just a short distance north along the Post Road (Route 22), the Cooper Memorial stands near the corner of Olmstead Avenue.

Considering all this, it is safe to say that outside of Cooperstown there is nowhere the author is better remembered than in Westchester County—a memory that goes beyond his cantankerous and caustic public persona to take into account the peaceful and loving life he shared for forty years with the devoted lady he discovered in Mamaroneck.

13. The Sweet Magic of Sugar Loaf

SUGAR LOAF IS NOT AN UNCOMMON NAME, ESPECIALLY IN THE NORTHEAST, where more than one bald-topped mountain resembles the conical loaves of sugar once used in colonial kitchens. But of all the many Sugar Loafs, only the one in Orange County has a manifold magic that lures and endures.

Ask a hiker what this magic is and he will probably say it is to trek along the trails of the legend-laden mountain which gave its name to the hamlet lying at its base.

Ask a craft collector, and the answer is certain to concern Sugar Loaf's dozens of distinctive shops, run by artisans who are as dedicated to their work as they are to preserving the heritage of this centuries-old hamlet.

The history buff will reply that Sugr Loaf is a living textbook, with each house a chapter and every lane offering some footnote of local lore. Likewise, the photographer and painter find enchantment in the vistas which change with each corner turned and at every bend in the serpentine road.

As for the lover of Americana, the magic is in the story of this tiny community—a community that flourished, faltered and nearly died, only to recover and return to what it was in the early 1700s when it began. Prior to that time, even though Orange County had been established in 1683, the land was inhabited mainly by Leni Lenape Indians, with Sugar Loaf their sacred mountain. Visible for miles around, this 1200-foot cone of rock was both beacon and burial ground for those long-ago indigenous people, as well as for other native Americans passing along the adjacent Wawayanda Path. A well-defined

A crafts village since the early 1700s, Sugar Loaf continues to entice visitors with its singular shops and scenic setting, along with entrancing tales.

route even in pre-colonial times, the Wawayanda Path connected two important Indian ceremonial sites: one near Philadelphia, and the other just north of Newburgh.

The awe with which the Indians regarded Sugar Loaf Mountain has been carried over to this day, for its boulder-strewn flanks harbor many a mystery, including the origin of a strange series of rock cairns that some researchers think may have been left there by prehistoric travelers other than Indians. A more conservative view is that these heaps of rock are merely the result of field-clearing efforts on the part of farmers who settled there sometime after 1703, when European land speculators purchased more than 190,000 acres from local chieftains.

Although tract housing may seem to be a modern real-estate concept, the idea was in operation in this area during the early half of the 18th century, when a couple named Mary and Samuel Clowes began buying parcels of land. They envisioned a cluster of stores built on the scenic knoll at the western base of Sugar Loaf Mountain, which would serve as a commercial center for the farmers then settling the surrounding countryside. With this goal in mind, the land was subdivided and sold—and the hamlet of Sugar Loaf was born.

By the time the Revolutionary War broke out in 1776, Sugar Loaf was a thriving community, its main road (the old Indian path) having been widened and renamed the Kings Highway—a name that was retained even after America won its independence from Great Britain. This route was vital to the development of Sugar Loaf as a center for craftsmen and merchants, as well as for the farmers who shipped their wheat, butter and eggs to New York City, 60 miles to the southeast. The road also brought in commerce, as wagonloads of coal from Pennsylvania, en route to New England, rumbled through Sugar Loaf. Weavers, tanners and tailors soon joined the blacksmiths, sawyers, coopers, millers and distillers who made Sugar Loaf their home. So, too, came the makers of soap, carpets, wagons, candles and cheese. And even though Sugar Loaf never grew beyond its bounds as a hamlet, it prospered for nearly two centuries until 1919, when passage of the Volstead Act presaged economic decline.

Prohibition meant that local distillers no longer bought produce from the apple orchards which were a mainstay of Sugar Loaf's economic structure. Trade at stores and taverns fell off sharply, and all business was affected. Another major area of industry—dairy farming—also declined due to competition from upstate milk producers, and by the time the Great Depression of the 1930s cast its dark shadows over the land, Sugar Loaf was in serious trouble. Some of the hamlet's businesses did weather the Depression, and there was even a slight resurgence during the 1940s when a group of organic farmers moved into the area, but economic problems continued to plague Sugar Loaf. Within another decade, its commercial vitality was so depleted that Sugar Loaf's death seemed imminent.

Destiny deemed otherwise.

While no single factor was solely responsible for Sugar Loaf's rejuvenation in the 1960s, its great natural beauty certainly was a major contributor. People seeking scenic serenity found Sugar Loaf to be an affordable haven, with vistas that fanned the creative flame in anyone artistically inclined, be he poet or painter, potter or photographer. Another factor was the craft revival that swept the country during the decade of the '60s. New craft communities sprang up, while older ones flourished from fresh infusions of talent and trade. In this heady atmosphere of appreciation for hand-wrought items, it was only natural for Sugar Loaf's beginnings to be recalled, and for its collection of ancient buildings to be recognized as an ideal showcase for artists and craftsmen.

Two of the earliest artisans to install themselves on Sugar Loaf's main street were the nationally famous woodcarver/painter Jarvis Boone and barnsider Walter Kannon. (A barnsider—Kannon's own coinage—is a recycler of old barns.) Their restoration efforts and energetic espousal of Sugar Loaf's virtues encouraged other craftsmen to move there, and before long dozens of shops had opened for business. Then in 1993 the hamlet became home to a handsome theater for the performing arts. Called the Lycian Centre, it was the brainchild of Richard Logothetis, a local stage lighting expert. Commercialism, however, is not the hallmark of Sugar Loaf, for most of the craftsmen consider the hamlet their home, and they are as concerned as older residents in retaining the comfortable atmosphere and community spirit of rural America. That they have accomplished this can perhaps best be shown by taking a brief tour of Sugar Loaf.

Most visitors reach Sugar Loaf by driving south on Kings Highway (County Route 13) from NY Route 17—a two-mile stretch that caterpillars past handsome homes and paddocks filled with horses. The equine industry came early to Sugar Loaf, for one of its first settlers was Hugh Dobbin— how's that for an appropriate name?—who pastured and traded horses on the southeastern slope of the mountain. It is said that Dobbin's wife Elizabeth gave Sugar Loaf its name. There is also a tradition that in her later years Elizabeth was accused of witchcraft. But those are just tales handed down from the past, and the only sure thing is that Hugh Dobbin introduced what was to become an important segment of the Sugar Loaf scene: the horse farm.

One of the most dramatic views of Sugar Loaf Mountain comes as drivers top a rise in the road and leave behind a row of ancient maple trees that border Kings Highway on either side. No sign is needed to explain that the rocky prominence is Sugar Loaf. Its bald summit distinguishes it from all others in the vicinity, and it is easy to understand why the Indians considered it sacred. Meanwhile, some of the man-made features along the road deserve attention too, including a sturdy but graceful Greek Revival house originally called Bairdlea (now Fury Brook Farm), built in 1856 by a farming family whose roots in this area were planted almost a century before that. There is also an old wood-walled well alongside the road that is the reason for a rustic lane leading east to Mine Hill being called Wellsweep Lane. Overshadowed by Sugar Loaf Mountain, which rises just behind it, Mine Hill was once thought to contain a rich deposit of iron ore. Today only the gaping maws of several abandoned pits remain as mute reminders of 18th and 19th century prospecting ventures that never proved profitable.

Just before crossing the railroad tracks into the main part of Sugar Loaf, there is another example of the inhabitants' dedication to making over instead of tearing down. The brick building on the left was erected as a school in 1839, and later served as a firehouse. A few hundred feet farther along, the Sugar Loaf Post Office occupies a building that used to be part of a poultry farm and hatchery. It is worth a visit inside, if only because this is one of the tiniest post offices to be seen, and its old-fashioned air also serves as a kind of time machine to ready newcomers for the ambience of Sugar Loaf proper. Then as the railroad tracks are crossed a glance to the left reveals an old caboose and depot that recall the days when trains still ran through Sugar Loaf, with the station now rehabbed into a restaurant.

The greatest concentration of craftsmen lies farther up the hill along Kings Highway, but before proceeding there, a right-hand turn into Woods Road is recommended. For down this road is an old house dating back to the Revolution, when it was owned by a British sympathizer who died during the war. It is said that his widow and four small children were callously evicted from the house when the property was confiscated by the Americans, and what happened to the hapless five is not known. The house was then purchased by Nathaniel Knapp and after him by Minard Sutton, both of whom operated creameries during the days when Sugar Loaf was famous for its dairy products. And in more recent times, the building became the home of different businesses.

Backtracking down Woods Road to Kings Highway, a small but delightful sculpture garden welcomes strollers to sit for a spell before continuing to the crest of the hill. There, just after the turnoff to Pines Hill Road, two white buildings face each other, the smallest of which is also the oldest: a two-storey white structure with full-length upstairs porch that was the hamlet's first tavern—a time when Sugar Loaf applejack was known far and wide. As for the other white-pillared building across the street, that is the United Methodist Church, with an interesting old burial ground along one side and in the back. Serving as both the religious and community center of Sugar Loaf, this handsome Greek Revival fane—built around 1853—and its more recent Fellowship Hall, host many of Sugar Loaf's social events, whereas the whole hamlet is the setting for the longstanding and popular Arts and Crafts Fair held each Columbus Day weekend.

Among the famed artists associated with Sugar Loaf is the late Swiss-born surrealist Kurt Seligmann, whose 55-acre farm on White Oak Drive is now being preserved by the Orange County Citizens Foundation, with public tours of the art-filled house and barn occasionally held. Art and antiques also adorn the Barnsider restaurant, down the road from the Methodist Church. Beneath this road, it is interesting to note, runs a tunnel connecting the church with two old houses. Tradition holds that in antebellum days the church served as a "station" on the Underground Railroad, and the tunnel was used as a refuge for escaped slaves making their way north.

Formerly a general store, the Barnsider is an impressive renovation effort by the aforementioned Walter Kannon. Authentic wide-plank floors and weathered beams contribute to the homey atmosphere of this eatery which boasts a picture window in the upstairs dining room affording an unforgettable view of Sugar Loaf Mountain. But beware of being mesmerized by the mountain—something that can easily happen as people relax in this comfortable setting. For those who tarry too long may miss seeing the rest of Sugar Loaf's shops, each of which is like a mini-museum, and some of which have areas where visitors can watch the resident artist or craftsman at work. Nor should one's rambles be restricted to Kings Highway, since interesting sights await the explorer of side streets such as Romer's Alley and Mill Lane. Still another street that should be explored is the one leading to Scott's Meadow, where rows of one-time chicken coops have been converted into shops. At the foot of this sloping lane flows the Otterkill Creek, where the ghost of Hugh Dobbin's son supposedly has appeared periodically since his drowning more than two centuries ago. Yet there is nothing spooky about this placid place, which used to be the launching point for hikes up Sugar Loaf Mountain.

That trail was obliterated when in the early 1990s a side road skirting the hamlet was constructed, and hikers nowadays access the mountain from a field on the east side of the Sugar Loaf Bypass (County Road 13A).

It takes less than an hour for fit hikers to reach the summit of the mountain, and although the trail may be steep, there are plenty of places to rest, and the view from the top is spectacular. In fact, some people maintain that it is only from the sun-baked summit of Sugar Loaf that the enchantment of both mountain and hamlet can be fully savored. Whatever the answer, the magic is undeniably there—a magic that transports you back to the rurality which is the taproot of American society, and makes you glad to be there.

III. LADIES' DAY

14. The Day Harriet Tubman Raided Troy

When the day dawned clear and crisp on April 27, 1860, it was to be expected that the Rensselaer County city of Troy's sidewalks would soon be filled with folk. But it was not the near-perfect weather that brought forth the thousand-strong throng which by early afternoon had collected at the northeast corner of State and First streets, where U.S. Commissioner Miles Beach had offices on the second floor of the Mutual Building. The cause was a young black man named Charles Nalle, who had just been brought in as a fugitive slave from a Virginia plantation.

Although few in the crowd were personally acquainted with Nalle, his arrest meant the first time the provisions of a decade-old Fugitive Slave Law were to be carried out in Troy. And with the country poised on the brink of civil war, feelings were running high—especially so in a city serving as a stop on the Underground Railroad that freighted escaped slaves to safety.

How Charles Nalle came to be captured piqued the curiosity of the crowd, for the tall, light-complexioned coachman had been in Troy for only a few weeks, having moved there from the town of Sand Lake about a dozen miles away. Rumors circulated that the fugitive had been betrayed by Horatio Averill, an attorney the illiterate Nalle had trusted to write letters for him to relatives in the South. Once Nalle's whereabouts became known to the Virginia farmer who owned him, an agent had been sent north to bring the escapee back under the terms of the federal Fugitive Slave Law, which was in force even though slavery had been abolished in New York State.

About 11 o'clock that Friday morning, Nalle's employer had sent him to buy some bread.

It was at the bakery that Nalle was arrested by a U.S. deputy marshal, then manacled and brought before Commissioner Beach. The proceedings to send Nalle south were speedy, but so was the way word spread throughout Troy.

A sea of people was soon surging around the Mutual Building. Not everyone favored the fugitive and scattered fights broke out. Freeing Nalle seemed the overriding sentiment though, particularly after his landlord shouted above the din that the spectators would soon see an enslaved man "come forth . . . to be taken to the depot, to go to Virginia by the first train. . . ." But first they were to witness Nalle's frantic attempt to escape such a future by scrambling out a second-story window, only to be jerked back by his captors.

Adding to the drama was the arrival of attorney Martin Townsend, who volunteered as Nalle's lawyer. Townsend then sped off to the chambers of Supreme Court Judge Gould, several blocks away on Congress Street, where he was granted a writ of habeas corpus. This meant Nalle must be taken over to Judge Gould—something easier said than done, considering the crowd.

Among that mass of people was a small black woman, whose seemingly advanced age and decrepit condition caused others to make way for her to hobble up the steps to Commissioner Beach's hastily convened court. There she waited until deputies started downstairs with Nalle. Then discarding her geriatric guise, she sprang to the window, shouting, "Here they come!"

Her compatriots below were ready when Nalle reached the street, with the small black woman struggling to wrench him from the grip of his guards. "Take him!" she urged the crowd. "Drag him to the river! Drown him! But don't let them send him back!"

Neither cudgels nor billy clubs could break her hold on Nalle, and the pair was swept along by a tsunami of battling bodies that crested with an all-out fistfight in front of the Congress Street office of Judge Gould. The outnumbered lawmen were losing the contest, but they managed to hold on to Nalle until the human wave pushed them west to Dock Street, where a skiff was waiting to ferry the freed fugitive across the Hudson River.

While the badly battered Nalle was being rowed over to the Albany County community of West Troy (now Watervliet), his champion—the small black woman—exhorted all supporters to follow in the regular ferry, for she anticipated more trouble. The *Troy Whig* later reported that there was a "rush for the steam ferry-boat, which carried over about 400 persons and left as many more—a few of the latter being soused in their efforts to get on the boat." Those that made it across the river found Nalle already arrested and locked in Justice Stewart's second-floor office near the ferry landing. It seems that a West Troy constable named Becker just happened to spot the still-manacled Nalle on the street, and figured that anyone in handcuffs belonged behind bars.

By the time the ferryboat passengers discovered Nalle's whereabouts, Constable Becker had been joined by two other officers, who quickly barricaded the door. Fists pounded on the portal, followed by stones, and the policemen began firing above the heads of the mob. This caused a brief retreat as one besieger cried, "They've got pistols!"

"Who cares?" shouted another. "They can only kill a dozen of us—come on!"

Hundreds surged forward once again, with a huge black man at the forefront. Instead of pummeling the door, he managed to wrench it open, only to be struck down by a hatchet wielded by one of the officers inside. Ironically, it was the felled man's body blocking the door that prevented the policemen from closing it, and rescuers were able to reach in for Nalle. Amid whizzing bullets, the fugitive was rushed to the nearby Witbeck livery stable. There, the small black woman, now bloodied and shoeless, her clothes in shreds, directed wagon-driver Hank York to head west for Schenectady—and a safe house along that route of the Underground Railroad.

Charles Nalle was never apprehended, nor was the woman who one newspaper termed the "Moll Pitcher of the occasion," and the Troy raid remained a prime topic for days afterward. During that time some interesting sidelights surfaced: questions concerning the legality of the documents dealing with Nalle's detention, suggestions that certain officials might have purposely absented themselves from the city during the fray, and even a dramatic disclaimer by Horatio Averill about betraying the fugitive. Yet the identity of the small black woman was not revealed.

In a May 2 story captioned simply "A Character," the *Troy Whig* described her abolitionist activities in detail, saying she was "well known in this city," but that "*no one appears to be acquainted with her name*"! That last bit of editorial fudge was probably meant to protect her, since the article concludes favorably, "If Mrs. Stowe wants a heroine for some future 'Uncle Tom's Cabin,' we suggest this singular female."

However, Harriet Tubman—for that was the name of Nalle's rescuer—had no need of the fiction writer's pen. In fact, at the time of the Troy raid, when she was about 40 years of age, Tubman already had experienced the equivalent of several tragedy-touched lifetimes of adventure, and

Called the Moses of her people, Harriet Tubman fearlessly led hundreds of fugitive slaves through the Hudson Valley to freedom.

she still had more to go, making her one of America's truly great heroines.

Like Charles Nalle, Harriet Tubman was born a slave, and she experienced all the cruelties of the plantation system, including a severe head injury caused around 1833 when an overseer threw a 2-pound iron weight at another field hand, striking Tubman instead. Then about 13 years old, Tubman recovered after several months in bed, but for the rest of her life she suffered brutal headaches as well as bouts of apparent narcolepsy.

Her tendency to suddenly fall into a sound sleep, no matter where or when, could be both funny and frightening, as occurred one day when some friends found the illiterate Tubman in a park snoozing away beneath a poster offering a $40,000 reward for her arrest! At the time that happened, Tubman had gained fame as a fearless "conductor" on the Underground Railroad. She herself had escaped captivity in 1849, but she kept returning to her native Maryland for family members and anyone else who wished to risk the journey north. She was amazingly successful too, and in the decade preceding the Civil War she made an estimated 19 trips to guide perhaps as many as 300 escaped slaves to freedom—little wonder, then, that she came to be called the Moses of her people.

As flexible and intuitive as she was intelligent, Tubman was a strategist extraordinaire. She always tried to start a northern flight on a Saturday night, since owners were not apt to discover—or advertise—their slaves missing until Monday. Pursuers might literally be put off-track by her taking a *southbound* train, and she made certain that any agent nailing up wanted posters was shadowed by someone who quickly tore them down. Communicating with potential escapees could be a problem too—one that Tubman solved in part by sending messages through pertinent verses in spirituals she sang as she passed a plantation, usually disguised as a harmless old crone. Whether or not a verse was repeated meant something too.

Standing barely five feet tall, but physically powerful from early years working as a woodcutter, Tubman had an equally strong will that she enforced with a gun carried on all trips north. "Move or die!" she was known to tell any fugitive afraid to continue, but usually she was followed without question, even one time when she felt it necessary to hide her "passengers" under a mound of manure with only straws for breathing.

Her means of transportation might be anything from shanks' mare to a railroad car or a hired wagon like the one with which she rescued her elderly parents in 1857. And since the Underground Railroad track she took almost invariably brought her to the Manhattan end of the Hudson River—which she followed north to Albany or Troy—boats were also an option. This route was a favorite because Hudson-shore communities offered a wide selection of safe houses at which she could stop, and she was able to count on the support of such "stationmasters" as Moses Pierce in Westchester County's Pleasantville, or Edward Hesdra of Nyack in Rockland County. But due to the necessary secrecy surrounding the Underground Railroad at that time, there is no way of knowing all the places she stayed with her "passengers." Likely sites, however, include the Peter Roe house on the Cornwall/New Windsor border in Orange County, Poughkeepsie's AME Zion Church in Dutchess, the Terpenning home at Esopus in Ulster, and a tunnel leading from the Hudson River to Columbia County's Clermont estate.

Tubman eventually extended her activities to encompass the whole abolitionist movement, and she had been on her way to a large anti-slavery rally in Boston when she happened to stop off in Troy to visit friends that fateful April Friday in 1860. It was those friends who hid her after Nalle's escape, nursing her wounds until she could continue her journey.

When the Civil War broke out in 1862, Tubman headed for South Carolina, serving as a nurse to soldiers while also aiding newly freed slaves, and even doing some spying along with scouting behind Confederate lines. Yet when she sought compensation for her services after the war, she was refused. Tubman wasn't so much seeking the money for herself; she wanted to provide for her parents, as well as orphans and other helpless people at the home which Orange County-born Secretary of War William H. Seward had helped her to buy in the central New York city of Auburn.

Congress did not approve a pension for her until 1897, and then only a piddling $20 a month, but that didn't stop her from establishing the Harriet Tubman Home for Aged and Indigent Colored People. Nor did modest means keep her from continuously campaigning for temperance, women's suffrage, and educational opportunities.

Finally physical infirmity forced the nonagenarian to enter her own facility, where she died two years later on March 10, 1913. She was accorded full military honors at her funeral and further recognition came the following year, when Booker T. Wahington addressed a memorial service that saw a portrait plaque placed on the Cayuga County Courthouse in Auburn. There was also a World War II liberty ship christened the *Harriet Tubman*. For many, however, the most meaningful accolade came on February 1, 1978, when the U.S. Postal Service brought out a stamp commemorating the "Moses of her people"—the first stamp in the Black Heritage U.S.A. series, and issued on the opening day of Black History Month.

15. Minding Her Manners

THE TUXEDO PARK AUDIENCE WAS SMALL IN NUMBER BUT THEIR applause echoed through the posh clubhouse of the gated comunity that Pierre Lorillard IV recently had constructed in the Ramapo Mountains of southeastern Orange County. Responding to the recognition, the young performer took her bows on the ballroom stage as Lorillard turned to the girl's father, Bruce Price. "You must stop her," Lorillard said brusquely. Then seeing the other man's puzzlement, he explained, "She's too good."

This time Price nodded his understanding, and not just because he was Lorillard's chief architect for Tuxedo Park. Although amateur theatricals such as the one they had just witnessed were acceptable in their upper-class society of the late 1880s, it was scandalous for anyone to become a professional entertainer, no matter how talented she might be. Therefore, by parental decree, teenage Emily Price's first appearance on the Tuxedo stage was also her last. She would not become a formally trained architect either, despite displaying an early aptitutde for house design—an "absolutely true sense of scale" was how her father put it when she had accompanied him to construction sites. Destiny, it seems, had other grander plans for Bruce and Josephine Price's only child. As much a rule-breaker as she was a standard-setter in adulthood, their daughter met adversity with action and carved out a career that made her name synonymous with social etiquette. But it is by her married name that the world best knows her—Emily Post.

Born in Baltimore in October 1873, Emily was five years old when her parents moved to New York, where they acquired a home near Manhattan's Washington Square. Winters were spent there, then in the spring they would transfer to one of the four cottages Bruce Price built for himself among the numerous other structures he designed at Tuxedo Park. The later's winding roads and wooded hills easily became Emily's favorite, and in a 1961 biography Edwin Post Jr. recalled how his mother's "old affection for Tuxedo bloomed again each year with the daffodils. No other place called her so urgently."

Certainly during the decades she lived there, Emily amassed many a Tuxedo memory, ranging from the momentous to the amusing. A local tra-

dition, for instance, says that once when
Pierre Lorillard invited some sportsmen
friends for a day of deer hunting, young
Emily's pet doe—replete with pink ribbon
around its neck—unexpectedly trotted out
to greet them. The laugh was on Lorillard,
who apparently didn't hold it against his
architect's daughter. In fact, years later, when
her engagement was announced, attended
by talk of where the newlyweds might reside,
Lorillard reportedly declared, "Tuxedo Park
should not, must not, lose Emily!"

Bruce Price obviously felt the same way
too, for he assured Lorillard that he was
deeding over one of his cottages to Emily as
a wedding present—a gift that proved a
godsend in the trying times ahead. The
marriage took place at Tuxedo on June 1,
1892, little more than a year after Emily
had made her debut and met the handsome investor, Edwin Main Post, who
became her husband. They were a most
attractive couple too, for the blue-eyed
Emily had grown into a tall   willowy

*Possessing a flawless complexion framed by
light-brown hair, teen-aged Emily Price (later
Post) was photographed around the time of
her debut into New York society. (Copyright
Emily Post Institute)*

woman with a wasp waist and a "dazzling white" complexion framed by light-
brown hair—someone so graceful and poised that a social commentator of
the day, Ward McAllister, deemed her one of only three young women in
New York society who could properly cross a ballroom floor alone. But aside
from superficial similarities, Emily and Edwin had very little in common.

Their union endured for more than a decade, however, and for awhile
seemed fairly happy as their family grew to include Edwin Jr., born in 1893,
followed two years later by another son, Bruce. As much as she enjoyed
motherhood, Emily craved other employment, so in 1902 she welcomed the
challenge when someone suggested that the letters she'd written to her father
during a European vacation might be made into a book. Only instead of a
travelogue, she turned the correspondence into a novel, *The Flight of the
Moth*. The project was completed at her Tuxedo cottage, which had been
winterized so that the Posts could live there year-round, and the boys were
able to attend the Tuxedo Park School under Headmaster Leon Bonnet.

Their happiness was shadowed, though, when Emily's beloved father died a few months before *The Flight of the Moth* appeared in the summer of 1903.

There was also a growing gulf between Emily and Edwin, whose mother didn't approve of ladies earning money as writers and prophetically compared her daughter-in-law to contemporary novelist Edith Wharton—*a divorceé.* But for the present, the marriage continued to appear outwardly solid, and the widowed Josephine Price moved into Emily's house after turning over the largest of the family's Tuxedo cottages to her daughter. The cellar of that lovely hillside home was the setting for some of the family's most hilarious moments, when Edwin—senior, not junior—decided to raise diamondback turtles for the terrapin dinners he relished. It all seemed simple enough: plop the creatures into a cellar pen and pick them at your leisure. The only problem was that the sharp-beaked reptiles didn't stay put, and their reaction to roundup efforts elicited many a howl of laughter—or pain.

Pain of a different sort struck the family in 1905, the same year Emily's second novel, *Purple and Fine Linen*, was published as a magazine serial. That summer, the editor of a weekly New York scandal sheet called *Town Topics* attempted to blackmail Edwin Post over his affair with a showgirl. Deciding to go public instead of pay, Edwin assisted the authorities in trapping the blackmailer's go-between, but in the process he lost Emily.

Awarded a divorce and custody of the two boys, Emily found herself in financial straits. Edwin's business investments had not been going well, and she had little more than her Tuxedo property and what she earned as a writer. Calling herself Mrs. Price Post—a coinage that might be considered her initial step in setting social standards—Emily concentrated on composing magazine articles as she cut down on everyday expenses. She could have strolled down Easy Street by marrying any one of several wealthy suitors, but she savored her newfound independence and chose to make her own way. Meanwhile she lived at Tuxedo even during the severest of seasons, such as the winter of 1908-09, when an editor who had come to discuss changes in her new novel literally disappeared in a 9-foot snowdrift after leaving the cottage. Luckily Emily was looking out the window, rescued the poor fellow, and *The Title Market* appeared later that year.

Long before this Emily had been advised to write about the things she knew best, so her stories—some of which were later expanded into novels like *The Eagle's Feather* (1910)—frequently concerned society figures and the contrast of American and European cultures. Sticking to one thing can be tiring though. Sometimes she contributed jokes to magazines, first testing them out on her mother. If Josephine didn't laugh or disapproved, Emily figured the joke was marketable!

Eventually landing a magazine contract for a series of travel articles, Emily set out with her son Edwin and a female companion on a cross-country drive to California in the spring of 1915—a pre-motel period when the highway system was still in its infancy and ladies just didn't go on such motor jaunts. Yet the trip was a rousing success, and so was her resulting book, *By Motor to the Golden Gate* (1916).

With her sons now grown, and having inherited her late mother's estate, Emily no longer had to work as hard as she did. But she was by nature a productive person, with "idleness" not in her vocabulary. (Stories that speak of her abed until afternoon sometimes neglect to mention that she routinely woke up at 5:30 a.m., and worked in bed on manuscripts and such until lunchtime.) Nevertheless, she expressed no interest when in 1921 an editor approached her about doing a book on etiquette. Not only did Emily consider the subject "stupid and stuffy," but she

The hillside cottage that her father designed in Orange County's Tuxedo Park remained Emily Post's home for many years.

had become involved in another type of work she thoroughly enjoyed—that of making project models for architects, as well as modernizing and redecorating houses. Still, the editor persisted to the point of sending her a sample of the kind of manners books then on the market. That did it. Incensed by what she read, Emily agreed to produce a "small book" on etiquette, since "the whole subject can be reduced to a few simple rules."

The simplicity, she soon discovered, lay only in her timeless definition of etiquette: "A code of behavior that is based on consideration, kindness, and unselfishness." Setting down specific rules was a much more complex matter. Holing up in her Tuxedo home, Emily tackled the project with typical thoroughness, relying not just on her own knowledge, but researching publications and consulting with friends. Piles of notes accumulated under individual subject cards tacked up in her workroom, and for many months she reportedly rarely left the house during the week except to have tea at the Tuxedo Clubhouse. Sundays remained a time for her family.

When it was published in July 1922, Emily's "small book" had grown into a 627-page volume that soon topped the best-seller lists for non-fiction, and went through eight printings within a year. Its original title, *Etiquette in Society, in Business, in Politics and at Home*, was subsequently simplified to *Etiquette, the Blue Book of Social Usage* (with appropriately colored cover), and Emily revised it periodically over the next four decades. But one thing never changed: her wit, wisdom and concern for all society, not just the upper crust. Emily might be a blue blood, but never a bluenose, and she couldn't resist having some fun with naming the book's characters: Mrs. Toplofty, Mr. Stockan Bonds, Edith Worldly, and a Southern couple called Davis Jefferson are only some. As for Mrs. Three-in-One, introduced in the 1927 edition of *Etiquette*, that was Emily's sympathetic response to the many women who wrote asking how to manage households single-handedly.

Emily had thought she pretty much covered all the bases with the 1922 book, but letters from readers kept pouring in, and she felt obliged to answer each one, either by personal note or by sending a pamphlet she'd prepared on the subject. The only advice she would not give was on matters of the heart. Responses might also be made via a radio program she began hosting in 1929 and continued for eight years. It was an opportunity she initially turned down because she thought her voice "too thin." Finally convinced to audition, she proved such a sensation that when President Franklin Delano Roosevelt began broadcasting his Fireside Chats, he said the finest compliment paid him was "You're as good as Emily Post."

To illustrate just how much her judgment was relied on, a story is told of the day Emily stopped in at Tiffany's to find out the proper wording for a certain kind of invitation. Not recognizing her, the head of the stationery department said he'd look up the information, and promptly produced a copy of her *Etiquette!*

A direct and simple way of dealing with matters had a lot to do with why Emily commanded such a large following, which eventually included readers of her daily column, "Social Problems," appearing in more than 150 newspapers across the country. Common sense and unflappable self-assurance figured in too, along with her capacity for adjusting to a changing world. Take the time some fellow dining with her accidentally skidded his chop across the table and asked in utter embarrassment what he should do. "I would pick it up and start all over again," came her calm answer. Then when the tables were turned on another occasion and it was Emily who spilled some cranberries, she cheerfully reminded chiders that she was "a human being, not a robot."

As for dunking—as in doughnuts—she initially maintained that it was "but one step above eating with one's knife." But when a mini-Civil War began festering over whether to dunk or crumble Southern corn pone in pot liquor, she diplomatically suggested that "when in Rome, do as the Romans do." And speaking of diplomacy, it was Emily who worked out a protocol code for the U.S. State Department, which had no fixed rules prior to that. On the other hand, she could stir up controversy when it suited her, such as the time she publicly opined that British Queen Mary wore her skirts too long. More important, in the 1930s, Emily took a strong stand *against* Prohibition, even though she was a teetotaler. Yet that might not have shocked some readers half as much as when she stated that "No rule of etiquette is of less importance than which fork to use." Queries continued, however, and when she got 15 letters on the subject in a single day, she'd had it. "Oh, use any one," was her exasperated reply.

By that time, Emily had left Tuxedo for the convenience of a New York City apartment, which she remodeled, using many touches from her Orange County home. She also bought a building on Martha's Vineyard, where she spent many of her remaining summers, employing her decorative talents and continuing to give full rein to her love of color: yellow closet interiors, Chinese-red bedroom walls, and even a blue typewriter she personally painted. More books were produced too, including one on *Motor Manners* and a cookbook compiled with the help of her son Edwin, who also assisted her in setting up the Emily Post Institute to perpetuate her work.

As much as she loved living in Manhattn and on Martha's Vineyard, Tuxedo meant "home" as well. Therefore, when Emily died at her apartment on September 25, 1960, she was brought back to Orange County and laid to rest in the churchyard of St. Mary's-in-Tuxedo. And it goes without saying that her tombstone is the epitome of good taste.

16. The Curse of the Cornwall Quaker

A LIGHT SNOWFALL HAD FROSTED LOWER MANHATTAN, BUT BY THE time Gulielma Sands left her cousin's Greenwich Street house on the frigid evening of December 22, 1799, stars had appeared in the sky and the thoroughfare was thronged with horse-drawn sleighs as well as pedestrians. One of those passersby later testified to seeing the beautiful pale-skinned girl with the pitch-black hair. Then in the press of people, 22-year-old Gulielma simply disappeared.

Eleven days elapsed before Gulielma's battered body was fished from a well in nearby Lispenard Meadows. But after that, events moved swiftly, with a suspect arrested the very same day in a case that was to become one of the most celebrated in the annals of New York crime—a case as remarkable for its strange aftermath as for its sensational murder trial and the famous figures involved.

The victim herself had neither wealth nor renown—far from it. The product of what was politely referred to as an "irregular union," Gulielma had been born in the Orange County town of Cornwall, where her unwed mother Mary Sands was part of a prominent Quaker family. So was Catherine Sands Ring, Gulielma's older cousin, who had married millwright Elias Ring in 1790 and subsequently moved to Manhattan. Aware that the frail Gulielma was ill-suited to farm life, and perhaps hoping the girl might escape the bane of her illegitimate birth by living elsewhere, Catherine traveled to Cornwall in September 1796 and brought her cousin back to New York City. Elma—as Gulielma was familiarly known—could attend a local school for young ladies while residing at the Rings' three-story boarding house.

All went well until July 1799, when Catherine rented a room to a young bachelor named Levi Weeks. The close attachment he soon formed with Elma might have been kept in check by Catherine, had she been around. However, a yellow fever epidemic struck the city that summer, and in September the auburn-haired Quaker matron took her children upriver to the safety of Cornwall, leaving the Greenwich Street house in the care of her husband Elias. Interestingly enough, the illness-prone Elma stayed behind too. The reason why was obvious to Catherine as soon as she returned home at the end of October. The affair between Elma and Levi had escalated to the point of impropriety, but when her cousin confessed that she and the boarder were secretly betrothed, Catherine breathed easier. While Levi was only starting out as a carpenter/builder, his future was secure in the employ of his wealthy older brother Ezra Weeks, and a girl of Elma's standing could scarce have expected such a match. The only disturbing note was Levi's insistence on a private wedding unbeknownst to either family. . . .

Elma had also confided to her cousin that the nuptials were slated for the night of December 22, so when Catherine heard the front door close around 8 o'clock that evening, she assumed the two elopers were on their way. Then two hours later, Levi returned by himself, denying any knowledge of Elma's whereabouts, let alone the role of bridegroom.

Midnight passed, then the morrow, and still no sign of Elma. Meanwhile, Levi never wavered in his story, not even on Christmas Eve when some teenage boys found a woman's muff floating on the surface of the Manhattan Well—less than a mile from the Rings' boarding house—and neighbors recalled hearing cries for help on the night Elma disappeared. The logical next step was to probe the well with nail-studded poles, but probably because of the holidays this was not done until the day after new year's.

As soon as Elma's corpse was recovered from the well on the afternoon of January 2, Levi Weeks was arrested, and a coroner's inquest scheduled for the next day. The finding of "murder by some person or persons as yet unknown" quickly resulted in Levi's indictment, with his trial set for March 31, 1800 at the City Hall located on the corner of Broad and Wall streets. During the intervening time, there was a steady festering of public feeling against Levi, fostered in part by the distribution of anonymous handbills hinting of his guilt, in addition to rumors of a ghostly girl writhing around the Manhattan Well. The defendant therefore could not have been surprised by the shouts of "Hang him!" coming from the crowd on the opening day of the trial. Nor was Levi unprepared, having in his corner three of the sharpest legal minds in Manhattan: Aaron Burr, Alexander Hamilton, and Henry Brockholst Livingston.

How could a young carpenter afford such top-shelf counsel? He couldn't. But Levi's older brother Ezra certainly could and did. As for Burr and Hamilton working together, in the years prior to their infamous duel, the two lawyers were frequently seen in the same courtroom, one of the most memorable cases being the 1785 Cheesecock Patent trial held in the Orange County village of Chester. Other officers of the court had even stronger regional ties. Albany-born John Lansing, Chief Justice of the state supreme court, presided over the Weeks trial, while the third member of the defense team was part of the powerful upriver family founded by Robert Livingston. And in the prosecution's chair sat Assistant Attorney General Cadwallader Colden, grandson of the same-named Orange County physician/historian.

Although Colden couldn't produce anyone who actually saw the crime committed, his parade of several dozen witnesses was effective in detailing for the all-male jury how and why Levi might have murdered Elma—right down to the health of Ezra Weeks' horse, which the prosecution contended pulled the sleigh that brought the victim to the Manhattan Well. And considering his careful attention to calling character witnesses for Elma—especially the beyond-reproach Quaker Catherine Sands Ring—Colden obviously anticipated what line the defense would take to clear their client.

Nor did Aaron Burr waste any time before dishonoring the dead. Using the defense's opening address to depict Elma as a loose-moraled liar, Burr went on to paint Levi lily white, and lest the jury rely on "presumptive evidence," he reminded them of several similar cases involving the wrongful conviction of innocent young men.

While the defense could prove that Levi had visited his brother Ezra's house on the evening in question,there were no witnesses for a 15-minute period when the accused said he was walking home. This the defense attempted to dismiss as unimportant, maintaining that Elma had taken her own life! But the condition of the corpse—shoeless, her gown ripped open, strangulation marks on her throat and other abrasions—indicated that Elma had put up quite a struggle, as described by two different doctors the prosecution had called, including Burr and Hamilton's own personal physician David Hosack.

One way to take the focus off Levi was to show that others had enjoyed the dead girl's favors, and the defense had no qualms about questioning Elias Ring's relationshiip with Elma during the time his wife Catherine had been in Cornwall. However, the most melodramatic moment of finger-pointing occurred when a lighted candle was held up to the face of Richard Croucher, a former lodger at the Ring house who was among the courtroom spectators. One version of the story has Burr illuminating Croucher's less than handsome countenance with a pair of candelabra and shouting, "Behold the murderer," while another account credits Hamilton with the candle trick. Whatever the case, it had the desired effect of diverting the jury's attention away from the defendant.

Judge Lansing may also have influenced the outcome of the case by running his court nearly non-stop. The trial continued from 10 a.m. on March 31 to 3 a.m. on April 3, with only one adjournment to allow the jurors some sleep. And in his charge to those jurors, Lansing bluntly stated, "the proof was insufficient to warrant a verdict against" the accused. No wonder then that the weary jury took all of five minutes to decide that Levi Weeks was *not guilty*!

A cannonade couldn't have created a greater impact. Angered over what was considered an unfair verdict, the public was further aroused by newspaper accounts favorable to Levi, and the word "bribery" was soon being bandied about—especially when brother Ezra attempted to change the conclusion of a published trial report by offering a cash incentive to the transcriber. Failing that, Ezra then tried to buy up every one of the 1500 copies printed. The trial, it might be added, was reputedly the first criminal case since the Revolution to be reported verbatim.

There were some interesting connections too. John McComb, the crucial defense witness who corroborated Levi's presence at Ezra's house on the night Elma died, went on to design The Grange, Alexander Hamilton's estate (now a National Memorial open to the public at 287 Convent Avenue in upper Manhattan), which was completed two years after the trial. The builder was Ezra Weeks, who also supplied the wooden pipes for the Manhattan Company's water system, which included the well in which Elma was found. And it was Aaron Burr who owned the Manhattan Company, having set it up in order to start a bank—what later became the Chase-Manhattan—but that's another story.

As innocuous as these connections may have been, Catherine Sands Ring certainly suspected something nefarious. For at the close of the trial she is said to have accosted Alexander Hamilton, saying in a most un-Quakerlike manner, "If thee is permitted to die a natural death, I shall be brought to believe in the injustice of God!"

Why she would single out Hamilton is a mystery, but four years later he was mortally wounded in the duel with Aaron Burr, and died at a house on Jane Street, a short distance north of the Manhattan Well. Catherine's curse, as some people called it, also seemingly reached past Hamilton to touch others involved in Levi's acquittal. Three months after the trial, the subject of the candle trick, Richard Croucher, was convicted of raping a girl at the Rings' boarding house and eventually he was executed for yet another crime. As for Aaron Burr, he survived until his eightieth year, though tragedy dogged his steps following the 1804 duel. And strangest of all was the fate of Judge Lansing. Visiting New York City on December 12, 1829, he left his hotel to post a letter aboard an Albany-bound boat and never returned—a mystery that to this day remains unsolved.

Five years prior to Lansing's disappearance, Elias Ring had died of yellow fever in Mobile, Alabama, where he was building some flour mills, and Catherine moved back to Cornwall. There she transformed her childhood home into a summer boarding house which gained fame as Rose Cottage, but is now preserved as the Sands-Ring Homestead on Main Street (open by appointment). Catherine never forgot the murdered girl, and in her declining years would "sit, the centre of an admiring throng, and tell . . . the sad history of Cousin Elma." That quotation comes from *Guilty or Not Guilty. The True Story of the Manhattan Well*, published in 1870 by Catherine's granddaughter, Keturah Connah. Though highly romanticized, the book cites incidents that only someone close to the case might know, including the claim that many years after the murder, two separate confessions by accomplices proved Levi Weeks had indeed killed Elma. If he did, nothing more could have been done about it in the courts, even if Levi were found. But he had disappeared after threatening crowds hounded him from New York shortly after the trial.

Sad to say, Elma once more would up missing too. She had been interred in the Quaker section of the Houston Street Burial Ground on January 6, 1800, but when the property was sold in 1874 and the graves moved elsewhere, hers was not among those recorded as being transferred. A clue to this mystery may have been provided by Catherine's granddaughter Keturah, who wrote that the grave had been obliterated by the "march of improvement"— probably when Houston Street was widened around 1840. The former graveyard, by the way, is now the site of the Liz Christy Bowery-Houston Community Garden on the northeast corner of Bowery and Houston streets.

The lack of a last resting place didn't stop Elma's story from being of interest to succeeding generations. Theodore S. Fay's once widely poopular 1835 novel, *Norman Leslie*, drew upon the murder, and periodically the press would publish a rehash, as occurred in 1869, when a man living near the intersection of Spring and Greene streets was digging in his garden and supposedly unearthed the old well. Halloween usually prompted a retelling of the murder too, for Elma's ghost—along with those of Burr and Hamilton—purportedly appeared from time to time. In fact, in the 1950s, a sanitation worker who had parked his truck in an alley near the well reported a woman's figure had risen out of the ground, and in December 1974 an artist living in an adjacent loft building looked out her window to perceive a female wraith amid phantom water pipes. But the best tale has to be the one where another neighboring loft dweller swore that an apparition of Elma emanated from his water bed!

The well itself is located in the basement storage room of a Spring Street building now housing the Manhattan Bistro—a restaurant whose employees have experienced any number of weird occurrences—from exploding ashtrays and faucets that turn themselves on, to wine bottles flying off the bar shelves, a spectral figure seen reflected in the shiny stainless-steel splash guard of a kitchen stove, and lights that suddenly go out for no apparent reason.

One of the restaurant managers, Tommy King, remains unperturbed despite several years of dealing with what he believes to be the ghost of Gulielma Sands. However, he freely admits his first encounter with the spectre was nothing less than nervewracking. It seems that one night as King was entering the room where the tall brick well is located, just before he turned on the lights, he heard a woman's sad voice repeating, "I'm sorry." Startled, since he knew no one else could have gotten into the locked room, King still managed to say, "It's okay. I'm not here to hurt you," and the voice became silent.

At other times the presence has demonstrated a proclivity for practical jokes. King relates that one evening when he was seated in the well room talking with another employee, the chair went flying out from under him just as if someone had jerked on one of the legs—but no one was there beside the two of them, and the door was locked. Three other employees were with King another day when they brought some boxes down to the storage cage that lines one side of the well room. After they unlocked the cage and carried in the boxes, they turned to leave, only to discover the cage door closed behind them and the padlock secured—yet the room outside the cage was empty, the outer door locked. They had to shout for someone in the restaurant upstairs to come down and let them out—after which none of the three employes would ever again enter the well room.

King's latest experience occurred in 2003, when he was alone in the restaurant after closing time and went into the basement to put away some things. Suddenly he heard footsteps overhead, like a woman in high-heeled boots clicking across the first-floor dining room above. Although positive he had thoroughly

The Manhattan Well where the body of Gulielma Sands was found is now located in the basement of a Spring Street restaurant.

checked the place, King ran upstairs shouting, "Who's there?" But of course there was no answer. The footsteps had stopped too. All the doors were locked. The security sensors had not gone off, nor had the burglar alarm.

Some people maintain that such phenomena occur when an untimely death causes a spirit to restlessly roam the scenes of its demise. And the murder of Gulielma Sands has never been solved. Despite his acquittal, Levi Weeks remains the prime suspect, but other suggestions have ranged from Richard Croucher and Ezra Weeks to Elias Ring. And one biographer of Alexander Hamilton even accused Catherine Sands Ring! None of those allegations was proven beyond a doubt, and with the passage of nearly two centuries it began to look as if little more might be learned—that is, until the late 1980s when Estelle Fox Kleiger was compiling her in-depth study of *The Trial of Levi Weeks*, and surprising news of the long-gone subject surfaced. It seems that far from being a pariah, Levi Weeks wound up in Natchez, Mississippi, where his New York notoriety hadn't followed him. For awhile he prospered as an architect, then in 1819—at the age of 43—he died "from a debilitating illness."

Could it have been the curse of the Cornwall Quaker, Catherine Sands Ring?

17. Winging It

THE POWERFUL HORSE RESPONDED TO THE PRODDING OF ITS RIDER'S booted heels and extended its stride to a full gallop down the King's Road. It was late summer in Dutchess County, with stands of sumac already displaying their clusters of dark-red fruit against still-green leaves that complemented the blue sheen of the Hudson River occasionally glimpsed through the foliage on the right. But for the lone rider, her Quaker-gray dress whipping behind her, such beauty signaled only that the year was soon to die—as would her beloved husband William if she didn't succeed in her journey south to New York City.

Mehitabel Wing Prendergast tried not to think of the dangers she would be facing on the 80-mile ride from Poughkeepsie to the tip of Manhattan Island. Nor did she dwell on the three children she had left behind in the care of her family, especially little Jedediah who had been born last May, a couple of months after her 28th birthday. Instead, Mehitabel watched the road ahead while her mind's eye focused on the past and memories of the charming Kilkenny Irishman who had come courting her in 1754.

Initially, Elizabeth and Jedediah Wing had not thought much of a match between their comely 16-year-old daughter and a non-Quaker 11 years her senior. But William Prendergast persisted and Mehitabel soon left her parents' Quaker Hill home for the nearby farm her bridegroom had rented where today's Dutcher Golf Course is located in the town of Pawling.

The land was arable, but the terms of the lease were atrocious, and when trouble began brewing between other tenant farmers and large landowners like the Beekmans, Prendergast took up the cause that came to be called the anti-rent rebellion. In keeping with her pacifist Quaker upbringing, Mehitabel counseled her husband to try conciliation. This William did, even journeying down to the Yonkers manor house of Frederick Philipse (now a state historic site open to the public). But such manorial lords cared little for those less fortunate: eviction of tenants, incarceration, or corporeal punishment continued to be meted out for any real or imagined arrears.

On November 21, 1765, a contingent of tenant farmers marched

through Fredericksburgh (present-day Patterson in Putnam County) to a
tavern where they prevailed upon Prendergast to be their leader. He had a
talent for it too, drilling his growing band of dissidents into a military unit,
while he exhorted them to "Pay your honest debts as honest men should—
but not a shilling for rent!"

Over the next several months the anti-rent protest spread throughout
the Hudson Valley at such an alarming rate that on April 2, 1766
Governor Henry Moore issued a proclamation against it. Prendergast's
answer was to waylay the messenger bringing the news to Dutchess
County. The rebel leader also extended his operations to Westchester
County, where two tenant farmers had been arrested and sent to Fort
George at the foot of Manhattan. Prendergast decided to rescue the pair,
gathering sympathizers as he marched south, along with a conundrum
concerning names. It seems that tenant farmers on some of the large downriver estates were calling themselves Sons of Liberty—a title already appropriated by landlords like John Van Cortlandt, whose home was threatened
by arson if he did not acknowledge the rioting tenants' name claim.
Fortunately little came of this other than an amusing observation by
British Captain John Montrésor (see Chapter 19) that "the Sons of Liberty
[are] great opposers of the Rioters as they are of the opinion no one is enti-
tled to Riot but themselves."

Meanwhile, Prendergast received warning that Fort George was extremely
well guarded and hence he had little chance of rescuing the farmers incarcerated
there. This prompted him to turn back at Kingsbridge, deftly deflecting any hint
of defeat by restoring evicted Westchester County tenants to their farms, and
declaring that "officials who persisted in serving warrants or in spying on tenants should be dragged and ridden on rails."

Prendergast was not long in carrying out his threat. The target was
Samuel Peters, a local magistrate known for readily sentencing rentless farmers to jail. However, after being ducked in cold water, dragged through the
springtime mud, flailed with a whip, and then ridden around on a rail, Peters
reportedly was only too glad to swear on a Bible that he would not testify
against his tormentors.

He didn't have to.

On May 6, 1776, Governor Moore issued another proclamation, placing the militia on standby and offering a reward of £100 for Prendergast.
This brought forth at least one bounty hunter, as well as an unexpected bit
of burlesque when a New York City alderman named Brevington welcomed
the company of a genial stranger as both traveled north along the road to

Dutchess County. The other horseman was such a good listener that Brevington wound up boasting of his plot to capture Prendergast and reap the reward. Wishing Brevington luck, the smiling stranger turned off at the next crossroad, and only later did the alderman learn that his pleasant companion was also his prey.

On a more serious note, Prendergast mobilized a mob that stormed the Poughkeepsie jail on June 10, freeing John Way , a Dutchess County tenant farmer. Ten days later, the 28th Regiment of Grenadiers was dispatched from Albany with orders to apprehend the rebel leader. Marching toward Quaker Hill, the soldiers were crossing a bridge on June 28 when firing broke out and several of their number fell wounded. Shot in the knee, a grenadier named George Henry was taken to a hospital in Manhattan, where his leg was amputated on July 27 and he died five days later. The coroner called it "willful murder by persons unknown," but the outcome of Prendergast's subsequent trial indicates the blame was placed on him.

It is not known whether Prendergast was even present during the skirmish on the bridge. Nor is it certain how he came into custody of the authorities. Some say he was captured along with 60 or so fellow rebels. Other accounts credit Mehitabel with convincing her husband that enough blood had been shed, and if he surrendered with a promise to cease his antirent activities, surely he would be pardoned.

If, indeed, Mehitabel caused him to cede, just imagine her consternation when Prendergast was promptly indicted for *high treason* and placed in chains aboard a sloop bound for New York City. The authorities, it seems, feared another storming of the Poughkeepsie jail if they held Prendergast there—especially since all the other rebels had been charged with much less serious crimes—so he was incarcerated elsewhere until his trial on August 6, 1766.

This time Mehitabel was not so trusting. After packing a saddle bag for a contingency plan, she arrived in the Poughkeepsie courtroom on August 6, determined to defend her husband since no lawyer seemed so inclined. "Solicitously attentive to every particular," one reporter wrote, "she never failed to make every remark that might put" Prendergast's "conduct in the most favorable point of view." He was no traitor, she argued, but someone simply seeking justice.

Needless to say, Mehitabel's unexpected and effective advocacy did not set well with the prosecuting attorney, who demanded that she "be removed from the court, lest she too much influence the jury." Judge David Horsmanden didn't agree, and when the prosecutor insisted the attractive Mehitabel's "very looks" could have an impact, Horsmanden wryly remarked that "For the same reason" the prosecutor "might as well move the prisoner himself be covered with a veil."

Despite Horsmanden's efforts and Mehitabel's eloquence, the verdict was a foregone conclusion, since the jury was composed of landowners unsympathetic to the plight of tenant farmers. "Guilty!" was their announcement after a trial lasting 24 non-stop hours. The judge, however, refused to accept the verdict. Aware of the terrible punishment he would have to impose for high treason, he sent the jury back to reconsider the case. It wasn't any use, though. They soon returned to repeat their guilty verdict, forcing Horsmanden to sentence the defendant to death by hanging.

Mehitabel delayed only long enough to hear Horsmanden set the execution date for September 26—weeks away, but of immediate concern in that some of her husband's friends were already murmuring about marching on the jail to free him. Nor were matters made any less tense by Sheriff James Livingston's promise of a handsome stipend plus anonymity for anyone who would assist with the execution. There really was no time to waste, and Mehitabel was thankful she had anticipated the verdict and come prepared to race down to New York City, where she planned to appeal directly to Governor Moore for a stay of execution. (It should be noted here that some reports give Albany as Moore's location and Mehitabel's goal, but Fort George in Manhattan is the site most frequently associated with her ride.)

Exact details of Mehitabel's long journey may be missing from the historical record, but there is no question of her securing an immediate audience with Governor Moore. Although the gallant Quaker must have been physically spent, her persuasive powers were intact; so much so that Governor Moore is said to have been moved to tears by her plea and assured Mehitabel that "Your husband shall not suffer." Thereupon he stayed the execution until word could be received regarding a royal pardon—an appeal to the British king that Mehitabel also composed.

Yet her mission was far from finished. Mehitabel still had to get back to Poughkeepsie with Prendergast's reprieve before the volatile situation there turned violent. Somehow she climbed back into the saddle, spurring her horse for home. Her round-trip journey of 160 miles reportedly took three days and a trio of horses to complete—a mission given even greater weight by the fact that Mehitabel succeeded in reaching Poughkeepsie before any mob action made matters worse.

On December 11, 1766, King George III granted Prendergast a pardon. He and Mehitabel were then free to continue farming their Pawling property while they tended their growing family—eventually numbering 13 children.

But the problems of tenant farmers had not been solved (see Chapter 43), and the Prendergasts grew increasingly dissatisfied with their prospects, particularly after the Revolutionary War. Prendergast, you see, had sided with the king rather than with the patriots, so in 1784, he abandoned the Pawling farm and moved his family to Pittstown in Rensselaer County. They remained there until 1805, when the lure of better land to the west impelled yet another move. Although Mehitabel was then 67 and her husband 78, their sense of adventure was in no way diminished, and they set off with some of their children—and their children's children—first trying Tennessee, then settling in western New York's Chautauqua County, where one of their sons founded the city of Jamestown.

Atop a gentle knoll on their Chautauqua farm, not far from the creek that bears their name, William and Mehitabel Prendergast were buried—he in 1811; she the following year, almost on the 46th anniversary of her courageous ride. Yet there is no hint on either tombstone of their place in history. For that one must visit the cemetery on Quaker Hill Road in Pawling, where a bronze plaque commemorates Mehitabel. As for the husband she saved, a historic marker recalling the 1766 skirmish stands at the junction of Mooney Hill Road and Route 292 in Patterson.

It is well that we remember them.

18. A Soul that Burned for Freedom

THE MULATTO NURSEMAID SIGHED AS SHE ENTERED HER ROOM IN THE mansion's third-floor servants' quarters. The bed seemed to beckon her bone-tired body, but she bypassed it for a seat at the table, where a pile of writing paper awaited her pen.

A frown creased the forehead of the handsome heavyset woman. A few years earlier, in 1853, when her employer—the well-known writer Nathaniel Parker Willis—had moved his family to the Orange County town of Cornwall, the nursemaid had envisioned a quiet country retreat in keeping with "Idlewild," the name Willis had given his new home. Instead, the 18-room Hudson River Gothic house frequently oveflowed with visitors, increasing her workload already made heavier by Willis' deteriorating health and the addition of two more children to the family. But domestic duties were not the only hindrances to the autobiography she was determined to complete. As an ex-slave and former fugitive, hers was a shocking story involving nearly seven years' confinement in an attic crawlspace—a narrative in which she dare not name her current employers, or even let them know she was writing it. Troubling, too, was her experience with the sexual subjugation of female slaves. Should she—could she—tackle such a taboo subject in antebellum America?

It wasn't until 1858 that Harriet Ann Jacobs finally finished her autobiography and several more years elapsed before she got it published, using the pseudonym of Linda Brent, and changing the name of every person in her otherwise non-fiction narrative. Nor does it take too many pages for readers of the book to understand why Jacobs chose this approach to her no-holds-barred account of the brutality of slavery. Actually she herself did not suffer greatly during the first decade of her life at Edenton, North Carolina, where she was born into bondage in the autumn of 1813.

In fact, when her mother died in 1819, Jacobs became part of her owner's household, where she was treated kindly, and not only taught domestic skills like sewing, but also how to read and spell.

All that changed with the death of her mistress. The then 12-year-old

Jacobs was willed to the infant daughter of an Edenton doctor named James Norcom, whose wife would spit into a kettle rather than see her slaves enjoy any leftovers from the dining room. The doctor was no nicer, and Jacobs soon witnessed countless cruelties—from an attempt to cheat her grandmother out of her freedom, to a slave hung from ceiling joists and beaten half to death, as well as a young black woman abruptly sold to a slave trader when she gave birth to a fair-skinned baby possibly sired by Norcom.

Jacobs had barely turned 15 when the doctor began casting a lecherous eye in her direction, but she was already in love with a free black man who wished to marry her. There was no way Norcom would consent to that, and in time the lover went away, leaving Jacobs to deal with what she termed the doctor's "persecutions" of her, in addition to the vindictiveness of his now suspicious wife. Then when Norcom began building a cottage in which he planned to install her as his concubine, the panic-stricken Jacobs accepted the attentions of a sympathetic white lawyer named Samuel Sawyer and soon was pregnant with his child. She apparently had hopes this might cool Norcom's ardor enough for him to sell her to Sawyer, who could then free her, along with their baby boy Joseph.

Alas, the teenaged mother misgauged the much older Norcom. He would gladly have kept her at his home had it not been for his wife, who thought he had fathered Jacobs' baby and threatened to kill Jacobs if the girl set foot in the house. Jacobs therefore was allowed to stay with her grandmother, a former slave with her own home in Edenton. It was there in 1833 that Jacobs' second child by Sawyer was born—a girl she called Louisa. The infuriated Norcom grew more and more abusive, in one instance throwing Jacobs down a flight of stairs, and another time cutting off all her hair, yet he still lusted for her. Refusing all offers from potential buyers, Norcom vainly kept trying both bribes and threats to gain her sexual submission.

Finally, in 1835, Norcom sent Jacobs to work on a nearby plantation, where she soon learned he was going to bring her children to be "broke in." That did it. Figuring he wouldn't subject the youngsters to such hardship if she was not there to witness it, Jacobs ran away in June. Family and friends—even a slave holder's wife—helped to hide her, and she was variously shuttled from one lady's bedroom closet to a cubbyhole beneath another's kitchen floorboards, and then to a snake-infested swamp. Meanwhile, Norcom plastered the region with wanted posters in which he offered a reward for the return of his "light mulatto, 21 years of age, about 5 feet 4 inches high" who "spoke easily and fluently, and has an agreeable carriage and address."

With all escape routes being watched, there seemed little chance of

Jacobs reaching safety in the North, so she secreted herself in the small garret above a storage shed attached to her grandmother's house. Freezing in winter and stifling in summer, this "dismal hole" measured a mere 9 feet by 7 feet, with the highest point of its sloping roof only 3 feet. Yet Jacobs managed to survive there for nearly seven years—from August 1835 until June 1842—aided by family members who risked their own freedom to supply her with necessities hauled up through a secret trapdoor. Only rarely did she risk a brief respite in the storeroom below, and in later years she would be plagued by bouts of rheumatism likely stemming from this period, but there were also some positive aspects to her confinement. Besides teaching herself to write, Jacobs devoured every book that came her way, thereby furthering her education when she wasn't supporting herself by sewing items that family members sold for her. She also devised a system whereby she mailed letters to Northern friends who would then send the missives back to Edenton as if posted by Jacobs from a free state—a ploy that worked so well that Norcom more than once went searching for her in some Northern city.

Jacobs even managed to see her two children, albeit from afar. Their father finally had purchased them through an agent, and placed them in the care of Jacobs' grandmother. Therefore, whenever Joseph and Louisa were in the street below, Jacobs could watch them via a peephole she had carved in the outside wall of her garret. It was heartbreaking to be so near and yet so distant, but she dared not risk everyone's safety by revealing her hideaway to children so young. Eventually Jacobs did enjoy a brief meeting with her son and daughter in the storeroom, but it would take until 1843 for the three of them to be reunited. In the year preceding that happy event, it had become obvious that Jacobs could not remain much longer in the garret. It was falling apart and so was her health. So "at a price that would pay for a voyage to England," a friend bought passage for her aboard a Philadelphia-bound vessel, and during the ten-day trip Jacobs brought life to her nearly crippled legs by "constant exercise . . . and frequent rubbing with salt water."

Abolitionists in Philadelphia helped Jacobs reach New York City, where she soon secured a job tending the baby daughter of Mary Stace Willis, wife of writer Nathaniel Parker Willis. A deep bond developed between the two women, especially after Jacobs accompanied the family on a Hudson River cruise to Albany aboard the steamship *Knickerbocker*. For when Jacobs was refused service in the dining saloon because of her color, Mrs. Willis promptly gave the nursemaid her own cup of tea, and called for another.

At that time, Mary Willis did not know her nursemaid was a fugitive slave, but she may have suspected something when they continued their trip

Harriet Jacobs was employed as a nursemaid at Idlewild—the Cornwall home of writer Nathaniel Parker Willis—when she penned her now classic autobiography, Incidents in the Life of a Slave Girl.

to Saratoga Springs, and she saw how nervous Jacobs became "in the midst of a swarm of Southerners" also staying at the United States Hotel. Jacobs' fears were well founded. Upon the family's return to New York City, she learned her presence there had been reported to Norcom and that slave catchers were probably already on their way to apprehend her. The news forced Jacobs to confide in Mary Willis, who promised all the help she could give and promptly sought legal advice from the Kinderhook-born Superior Court Judge Aaron Vanderpoel and another lawyer. Both men felt it best for Jacobs to flee farther north, which she did, settling in Boston with her two children.

Their stay there ended with the childbed death of Mary Willis in March 1845. The bereaved husband decided that his 3-year-old daughter Imogen would benefit from a trip to see her late mother's parents in England, and he prevailed upon Jacobs to come along as nursemaid. Jacobs didn't particularly care for Nathaniel Parker Willis, who she considered to be pro-slavery, but she felt beholden to his dead wife. Plus that, the salary was better than what she could make as a seamstress, and she wanted her own children to have a comfortable life.

Jacobs came home from Europe in 1846 to find out that her North Carolina owner was still searching for her in New York. She therefore went again to Boston, spending a couple of years there before moving to western New York and the anti-slavery community in Rochester, not far from where her daughter was then attending school. Manhattan offered better economic opportunities though. So in September 1850, despite passage of the Fugitive Slave Law that made her position even more precarious, Jacobs returned to New York City, where she helped a local group keeping track of slave-hunting activities. Meanwhile, paid employment was provided by Nathaniel Parker Willis, whose new wife had recently given birth and needed a nursemaid.

Cornelia Grinnell Willis proved as close an ally as her predecessor. More than once when Jacobs was in danger of being apprehended as a fugitive slave, the second Mrs. Willis arranged for her flight to a safer place. But best of all, following the death of Dr. Norcom, Mrs. Willis managed to buy her nursemaid's freedom. The year ws 1852, and although Jacobs was now at liberty to go wherever she chose, she remained with the Willis family, who had decided to move to Orange County. Two years earlier, when they had summered at the Sutherland boardinghouse in Cornwall, Nathaniel Parker Willis had become so enchanted with the Hudson Highlands he purchased 50 acres near what is now Idlewild Avenue. But it was not until a doctor warned the ailing writer he must abandon the city for a healthier climate that the Willises had architect Calvert Vaux design a many-gabled mansion on the edge of a scenic Cornwall glen.

Jacobs already had plans for telling her life story when she moved with the Willises into their new home in July 1853. Originally she'd had an abolitionist friend approach Harriet Beecher Stowe with the idea that the author of *Uncle Tom's Cabin* might do the writing. But Stowe rubbed her the wrong way, and Jacobs decided to tackle it herself, after warning the aforementioned abolitionist friend not to "expect much" because she could only offer "truth but not talent." God, she went on to say, had not provided her with the latter gift, though He had given her "a soul that burned for freedom." That was more than sufficient, since she actually did possess great narrative power, plus the courage to reveal the full horror of slavery, including graphic details as to why it was "more terrible for women." Jacobs did not, however, use real names, and for more than one reason kept her project secret from the Willises during the five years of late-night writing sessions on Idlewild's upper floor. But upon the book's publication, the Willises easily recognized themselves as the pseudonymous Bruce family, and must have found it interesting that Jacobs gave her children's father the same surname as Cornwall's prominent Sands family. In addition, Dr. Norcom was dubbed Flint—no doubt for its descriptive image, but Jacobs may also have heard Nathaniel Parker Willis mention a same-named nemesis from his Boston childhood.

There must have been days Jacobs despaired of ever seeing her book in print. Upon completion of the mansucript, she went to England in May 1858, hoping to arrange publication, but was turned down. The following year a Boston publisher accepted the manuscript on the condition that the noted abolitionist author Lydia Maria Child would contribute a preface. Child agreed and even edited the manuscript—only to have the company go bankrupt before publication. Then in 1860, when still another publisher that had contracted for the book went belly-up, Jacobs decided to print it herself.

Incidents in the Life of a Slave Girl finally appeared in 1861, just before the outbreak of the Civil War. And although Jacobs was accorded a modicum of celebrity, she—along with the rest of the country—was soon caught up in the conflict. Heading south, Jacobs at first focused her efforts on the plight of the "contraband"—homeless slaves within Union Army lines—but wound up active in all kinds of relief work, from distributing supplies to organizing orphanages both during and after the war.

As busy as she was, Jacobs did not forget those who had befriended her. Late in 1866, when Nathaniel Parker Willis was in the final stages of a neural disorder, Jacobs helped Cornelia Willis tend the hallucinating man until his death at Idlewild on January 20, 1867. The bond between the Willis and Jacobs families did not end there either. Three decades after Nathaniel Parker Willis was interred at Mount Auburn Cemetery in Cambridge, Massachusetts, Harriet Jacobs was laid to rest in a nearby plot. And when her daughter Louisa was buried beside Jacobs in 1917, it was Willis' daughter Edith who erected the headstone.

By that time, *Incidents in the Life of a Slave Girl* had been pretty much forgotten. And of those who did read the book, some insisted that its editor, Lydia Maria Child, must have been its author—not Jacobs. The controversy might still be going on were it not for a Pace University professor named Jean Fagan Yellin, who devoted decades to documenting Jacobs' life and work—including the discovery of a cache of letters that proves beyond a shadow of a doubt that Jacobs authored *Incidents*. A resident of Goldens Bridge in Westchester County, Prof. Yellin produced a fully annotated edition of *Incidents* (Harvard University Press, 1987) in which she identified the pseudonymous characters. And then she went to work on a biography of Jacobs, as well as a collection of her papers—the latter work purportedly the first scholarly edition of the papers of a black woman.

At long last that unsung heroine of the Hudson Valley—Harriet Jacobs—was getting her song!

19. The Legend of Charlotte Temple

PEOPLE STILL VISIT THE INCONSPICUOUS GRAVE IN THE NORTHEAST section of New York City's historic Trinity Churchyard.

They come, despite the fact that the original nameplate has been replaced by a hastily carved pseudonym.

They come, even though the body no longer lies beneath the weathered brownstone marker.

In earlier days, this grave was a favorite trysting spot for lovers, who would bypass the nearby monuments of such historic figures as Alexander Hamilton and Robert Fulton, to gaze at the simple headstone of a lonely girl few people knew but many remembered. So it was with two famous writers. One would tell the girl's story to the world. The other would use parts of it in one of the best known short stories ever written in the English language. And so it is today that, from time to time, fresh roses still appear on this unpolished brownstone slab. For while Hamilton and Fulton may impress the mind, it is the tragic story of Charlotte Temple that stirs the heart.

Her name was really Charlotte Stanley, and in 1774 she was still attending school in England when she fell in love with Lieutenant John Montrésor. Since the handsome, 38-year-old British officer neglected to tell Charlotte he was already married, he had little trouble in persuading her to elope with him to America, where he was then stationed as an army engineer.

It was not long after their arrival in New York City that the teen-aged Charlotte discovered Montrésor's perfidy. But by then it was too late—she was pregnant.

Home was three thousand miles away, yet even if it were only three miles, Charlotte felt she could not return to shame her clergyman father. There remained only one choice: to reside in the house Montrésor had rented for her at what is now the corner of Pell Street and the Bowery, near Chatham Square. Meanwhile, Charlotte's seducer returned to his home and family on Montrésor's (now Randall's) Island located a few miles to the north.

As the months passed, Montrésor's visits to the small rented house became less frequent; finally they ceased altogether. According to Charlotte's

Although her grave is now empty, people still pay their respects to Charlotte Temple in Manhattan's Trinity Churchyard. (Photo courtesy of Stephen Paul DeVillo)

biographer, a fellow officer had conspired to convince Montrésor that the girl had been unfaithful to him. In a way, Montrésor welcomed the news, since his ardor for Charlotte already had cooled, and this untrue story provided an excuse for him to stop seeing her. But although he abandoned Charlotte, Montrésor did not intend to abandon his financial responsibility, and he gave his "friend" money to bring to the house near Chatham Square.

Seeing this as an excellent way of furthering his plan to obtain Montrésor's mistress for himself, the unscrupulous officer secretly pocketed the money, leaving Charlotte destitute. The plot did not work, however. Instead of turning to this man for aid and comfort, Charlotte withdrew into herself, then became ill—and soon enough the officer lost interest in her as well.

There were no more visits to the small house near Chatham Square—neither by Montrésor nor by his fellow officer. Then late in December 1775, the penniless Charlotte, her pregnancy near term, was evicted. For days, the solitary and seriously ill girl walked the winter streets of New York City. Eventually she was given refuge by a poor servant's family, and it was in their hovel at what is now 24 Bowery that Charlotte gave birth to a daughter. It was also there that Charlotte's father found her, having followed her trail all the way from England.

Charlotte Stanley did not survive the added burden of childbirth. And before he went back to England with his newborn grandchild, the Reverend

Stanley buried his daughter Charlotte in Trinity Churchyard on lower Broadway.

The following year saw the acceleration of the Revolutionary War, during which time Charlotte's grave remained unvisited except by the now remorseful Montrésor. With his return to England in 1778, Charlotte's tragic story might well have been forgotten, were it not for Montrésor's cousin, the novelist Susanna Rowson.

In an era when over-ripe sentimentality, a touch of scandal and tedious sermonizing were the key ingredients of popular fiction, Mrs. Rowson immediately saw the commercial possibilities in the tale she heard first from a woman who had known Charlotte during her ill-fated New York stay. Then when whispered allusions by family members substantiated the story, Mrs. Rowson went to work, changing little except the name of the characters, and even those only slightly. Charlotte Stanley became "Charlotte Temple" and Montrésor was altered to "Montraville."

To her credit, Mrs. Rowson was apparently sincere in her desire, which was stated in the preface of her novel, *Charlotte Temple*, to "be of service to some who are so unfortunate as to have neither friends to advise, or understanding to direct them, through the various and unexpcted evils that attend a young and unprotected women in her first entrance into life." Financial necessity having thrust her into the male-dominated society of her day, Mrs. Rowson could well express the outrage she felt over Charlotte and similar unfortunate girls she had heard about. Thus, she ended her story on a haunting note of retribution—a note that would be taken up and enlarged five decades later by the master story-teller Edgar Allan Poe. Before that occurred, however, Mrs. Rowson's book would become an all-time best-seller, enjoying over 200 separate editions. In fact, from the time it was published in 1791, until Harriet Beecher Stowe's *Uncle Tom's Cabin* appeared in 1851, *Charlotte, A Tale of Truth* (its original title) was probably the most widely read novel in America.

Since Mrs. Rowson steadfastly maintained that the story was true, with only "a slight veil of fiction" thrown over the whole, it was not long until the real name of the heroine became known. Thereupon, sympathetic readers began the pilgrimages to Trinity Churchyard that continue to this day.

In 1800, one of those who made their way to Charlotte's grave was a wealthy young Englishwoman who stood there for many minutes, her lovely face paled by sadness. Charlotte's daughter Lucy—the hapless infant born in a New York City hovel in 1775—had come to take her mother home. Arrangements were soon made, and Charlotte's quarter-century-old casket was disinterred for shipment to England. Then Lucy did a strange thing.

Before she left the land of her birth, she had a new and larger, dolmen-like monument erected over the now empty grave: a brownstone slab supported by four pillars, with a rectangular plaque inscribed to "Charlotte Stanley" and bearing the family coat of arms.

In time, the supporting pillars became unstable and the brownstone slab was laid flush on the ground. Then during the rebuilding of Trinity Church in the early 1840s someone made off with the plaque. Public reaction to this act of vandalism can best be gauged by an incident which had occurred a decade earlier. When, in 1835, the city proposed extending Pine Street through part of Trinity Churchyard, Philip Hone (one-time mayor of New York) objected to the plan because of Charlotte Temple. "She was treated shamefully while she lived," Hone had explained. "And I am firmly opposed to any injury to her grave now that she is dead." The plan was scuttled.

Another man later recalled, "When I was a boy," during the 1830s and '40s, "the story of Charlotte Temple was familiar in the household of every New Yorker. The first tears I ever saw in the eyes of a grown person were shed for her."

Well aware of the depth of public sentiment, William H. Crommelin, foreman of Trinity's stone-cutting crew, ordered the name be chiseled into the headstone to replace the plaque that had been stolen. That "Charlotte Temple" was inscribed rather than "Charlotte Stanley" is not unusual, for it was by the former name that people knew her best. Nor is it unusual that her story so impressed Edgar Allan Poe that traces of it can be found in his classic tale, "The Cask of Amontillado," published in November 1846, not long after the nameplate incident.

Poe, then living in New York City, had surely read the most popular novel of his day, and perhaps had visited Charlotte's grave in Trinity Churchyard. Likely, too, he had learned the details of the tragedy at closer hand, for he was friendly with the family of painter Samuel Osgood, who was related to Susanna Rowson. Poe may also have heard about Montrésor long before he learned of Charlotte Temple. For Poe had been a cadet at West Point from June 1830 to February 1831, and it is likely that the well-known army engineer and mapmaker of the preceding century had been mentioned in connection with Poe's studies at the military academy.

Picking up the retributive note on which Mrs. Rowson had ended her book, Poe set about crafting a story of supreme vengeance, in which the narrator bears the name of Charlotte's seducer. Deceptively simple, "The Cask of Amontillado" is a chilling step-by-step account of how one Montresor (Poe dropped the accent over the "e") entices his one-time friend Fortunato into a

wine cellar, where he proceeds to wall him up alive. Poe does not have
Montresor reveal his reason for revenge. However, in Mrs. Rowson's novel,
motive enough can be found. In it, she relates how Montrésor's friend had lied
about Charlotte's fidelity, then did not deliver the money to her, and was thereby indirectly responsible for the girl's death.

Mrs. Rowson records that, following Charlotte's burial, Montrésor
learned for the first time what his friend had done. Finding the officer
drunk, Montrésor then killed him in a sword fight. "The Cask of
Amontillado" parallels this, except that the genius that was Poe's could never
be satisfied with such a pat ending. Therefore, Poe had his Montresor bury
the other man alive. What more poetic justice could there be for someone
who had caused a young girl to be buried before her time?

But Poe was not finished with his tale. Murder must not go unpunished,
and retribution—as Mrs. Rowson wrote—"treads upon the heels of vice, and
. . . tho not always apparent, yet even in the midst of splendor and prosperity,
conscience stings the guilty and 'puts rankles in the vessels of their peace.'"

So it was that Poe added his master stroke of retribution—one that is
"not always apparent" to readers—at the very end of "The Cask of
Amontillado." In a deathbed confession fifty years after walling up
Fortunato, the narrator Montresor utters these final three words: "*In pace
requiescat!*" Though the dead Fortunato has rested in peace, the still-living
Montresor has not. Nor had the real-life Montrésor.

The son of a famous British military engineer, John Montrésor followed
in his father's footsteps and already had a long and distinguished career both
as a combat soldier and engineer—including the demolition of old government buildings at Albany and the construction of new ones in 1765, and sur-
veying the New York-New Jersey border in 1769—when he met Charlotte
Stanley during a brief trip to England in 1774. A year later, in December
1775, having been promoted to the rank of captain, Montrésor was named
Chief Engineer of America by King George III, and it seemed that nothing
would halt his ascendancy.

Then Charlotte Stanley died in a lonely servant's hovel.

Mrs. Rowson says that "to the end of his life [Montrésor] was subject to
fits of melancholy, and while he remained at New York frequently retired to
the church yard, where he would weep over the grave, and regret the untimely fate of the lovely Charlotte Temple." But remorse and melancholy were to
be the least of the afflictions visited upon the real-life Montrésor.

The first hint came shortly after the colonists declared their independence, when in September 1776 Montrésor was given the dangerous task of

entering the American camp to inform them that the British had executed Nathan Hale as a spy. Reportedly what made the assignment even more odious was that Montrésor had given Nathan Hale his word as a gentleman to deliver some personal papers the condemned spy had entrusted to him—papers which were of no military value, yet were still confiscated by Montrésor's superior, and never brought to Hale's grieving family.

A little more than a year later, on January 1, 1777, all the buildings on Montrésor's island estate were burned to the ground, and not long after that, he incurred the displeasure of British General Sir Henry Clinton. Thus forced to return to England, Montrésor left behind in a New York graveyard not only the girl who had been his mistress, but three of his sons who had died in childhood. In a diary written during that time, Montrésor recorded he was "very ill," with "a fistula coming on *peu-á-peu.* . . . My wounds breaking out," among them a "restless ball" suffered during an ambush in 1755, which remained in his body even though there had been many "incisions cut to remove it." In addition, he had "a dreadful hydrocele—in short, my existence rather doubtful should my complaints increase for want of proper assistance."

Ill health continued to plague Montrésor, as did his bitterness over not being promoted to the rank of colonel. By the same token, his caustic comments as to why the British lost the war made him less than welcome in some circles. Added to all this was financial difficulty. His wife's family had been "reduced from opulence to poverty," his own Amrican holdings had literally gone up in smoke, and he complained in his journal of being "tormented by a court of inquisition at the Creditors' Office."

Despite his reduced wealth, Montrésor was able to purchase an estate in Kent, England, where he retired, following a not always pleasant tour of the Continent during 1785-86. But fate was not finished with him. Once again, flames destroyed his estate, as well as the nearby home of one of his sons. Nor did Montrésor's problems with debt diminish, and in 1799 he was incarcerated in Maidstone prison. There he died at the age of 62, having known no peace from the retribution that "treads upon the heels of vice."

Charlotte (Stanley) Temple had been avenged.

IV. Marchers to a Different Drum

20. *The Poughkeepsie Seer*

LIGHTNING LEAPFROGGING ACROSS THE ORANGE COUNTY SKY BRIEFLY augured relief from the midsummer heat that was making the birthing process even more burdensome for the 33-year-old woman on the sweat-soaked bed. Then the rumbling thunder followed the flashes east toward the Ramapo Mountains and Mrs. Davis was left to swelter, her moans drowned out by the drunken dialogue of her husband Samuel celebrating the impending birth of their sixth child.

They had both hoped for another son to help balance their daughter-dominant family, yet when this came to pass later on that sultry August day in 1826, Mrs. Davis displayed little delight. Poverty and the primitiveness of their Blooming Grove home contributed to this depression, as did the alcoholism of her cobbler husband. But mainly it was due to the baby being born with a caul—a veil-like membrane swathing its head. Although subscribing to the widely held superstition that fame and fortune came to such children, Mrs. Davis was nevertheless apprehensive about her frail baby's future, and worried that "He's born to see trouble, or—somethin' else—I don't know what." So perhaps to enhance his chances, she went along with the suggestion of an inebriated neighbor, Thomas Maffet, that the boy be named after the Battle of New Orleans hero and current presidential hopeful.

Andrew Jackson Davis did indeed grow up to achieve celebrity status, and for a while was even better known than the like-named contemporaries with whom he is often confused: regional architect Alexander Jackson Davis, and Newburgh's noted landscape designer Andrew Jackson Downing. Any similarity between the three men ends there, though. For the charismatic and still controversial cordwainer's son was a leading current in the tidal wave of spiritualism that washed across the western world during the mid-19th century.

Known as the "Poughkeepsie Seer," Andrew Jackson Davis quite literally mesmerized audiences during the heyday of spiritualism.

PHOTO CREDIT DOVER PUBLICATIONS

Rooted in the age-old belief that the dead survive as spirits and can communicate with the living, the movement attracted millions—England's Queen Victoria, John Ruskin, William Butler Yeats, and Arthur Conan Doyle, to name only some of the more famous adherents—and it eventually encompassed any associated occult practice. But spiritualism's initial momentum was mainly generated by the 18th century work of Swedish author Emanuel Swedenborg, a former scientist turned seer, and the Austrian physician Franz Anton Mesmer, for whom the precursor of modern hypnotism—mesmerism—is named.

It is doubtful that Andrew Jackson Davis ever heard of either man during his boyhood, since he rarely went to school—five months total attendance, according to his own accounting—and both parents were barely literate. On the other hand, he was early introduced to the occult by his deeply superstitious mother, who possessed an uncanny ability to foretell the future. She "saw," for instance, Andrew's near drowning in a stream, and on another occasion dreamed of the exact spot in the road where he was later injured by an ox cart.

By the time those events occurred, the family had relocated across the Hudson to Dutchess County, first to the John Myers farm, then that of Bart Cropsey, both in Staatsburg, and later to a series of tenant houses in and around the town of Hyde Park. Their transience was directly related to Samuel Davis' intemperance. Despite skills as a shoemaker and weaver, abetted by stints as a farm laborer, he rarely made enough money to cover both his tavern tab and the rent. Then tragedy struck.

The sudden death of Andrew's older sister, Julia Ann, though foreseen by Mrs. Davis, so shocked and saddened Samuel that he abandoned his dissolute habits. Determined to take better care of his family, he moved them to the village of Hyde Park in the spring of 1837, and got a job at John Hinchman's shoe factory. Andrew, nearly 11, tried working too, but his chronic ill health, clumsiness and lack of education soon got him discharged from Belden Delamater's plaster mill. He couldn't even make it as a porter in the home of Hyde Park lawyer W.W. Woodworth, and wound up hoeing corn at the nearby David Hosack farm (the latter now part of Vanderbilt Mansion National Historic Site on Route 9).

It was there that the pubescent boy—already somnambulistic—began experiencing aural phenomena: "sweet, low and plaintive music," along with a voice that suggested travel to Poughkeepsie. Why Poughkeepsie? The voice didn't say. But when Samuel Davis decided to move there in the autumn of 1839, 13-year-old Andrew felt right at home. In fact, for the rest of his life he referred to Poughkeepsie as his "native village," and in some ways it certainly was.

For a brief period, Andrew attended the Lancaster School on Church Street, where the educational philosoophy of English Quaker Joseph Lancaster was followed, and the students literally taught themselves. But then his mother became ill and Andrew was needed as a wage-earner. He was still receiving messages from his mysterious voice, and one day when he heard it say something about "a little leaven," he immediately set out for Matthew Vassar's brewery (near the present-day Cunneen-Hacket Cultural Center on Vassar Street). There he purchased a pail of yeast, convinced for the nonce that he was destined to be a door-to-door leavening salesman!

Other messages were accompanied by visions, as on the February day in 1841 when Andrew returned home to find the family's crude rented house turned into a heavenly palace at the moment of Mrs. Davis' death. Though something only he could see, the vision of a better abode for his beloved mother enabled the teenager to accept what might otherwise have been unendurable, and in the meantime helped prepare him for even more mysterious experiences.

In the autumn of 1843, an itinerant lecturer named J. Stanley Grimes appeared on the Poughkeepsie stage, using members of the audience to demonstrate mesmerism. Andrew Jackson Davis was among the volunteers, but for some reason he did not fall into the hypnotic trance that Grimes easily induced in others. Even so, the 17-year-old was fascinated, and when Poughkeepsie tailor William Levingston later asked if he might try his hand at mesmerizing him, Davis readily agreed. Trance induction, it should be noted, became quite the rage in Poughkeepsie following Grimes' appearance, with "almost everybody . . . mesmerizing each other," as Slater Brown pointed out in his 1970 study, *The Heyday of Spiritualism*.

Levingston succeeded in mesmerizing Davis with the very first attempt on December 1, 1843, and in ways he had not anticipated. For even when blindfolded, Davis reportedly could read from the newspaper, or "see" the time on someone's watch. His greatest gift, however, was the ability to clairvoyantly diagnose illness, and he and Levingston were soon holding clinics where only the well-to-do were charged a fee. There is no way of knowing how accurate Davis may have been. Certainly some of his prescribed remedies were medieval to say the least—for example, to treat deafness, oil boiled from the hind legs of 32 weasels—but the majority of his patients hailed him as a healer.

All this might have turned the young man's head had it not been for a combination sleepwalk and allegorical dream that took him across the ice-bound Hudson one night early in 1844. Based on the description given in his 1857 autobiography, *The Magic Staff,* Davis wound up on Illinois Mountain in the Ulster County town of Lloyd, then trekked back over the frozen river to Poughkeepsie, where he woke up in the Rural Cemetery on South Avenue. Along the way he encountered several spirits, including that of Emanuel Swedenborg and second-century Greek physician Galen. Both lectured Davis on being "an appropriate vessel for the influx and perception of truth and wisdom." Then Galen presented him with a magic staff containing all the medical information he would need.

Skeptics guffawed at such alleged goings-on and called Davis a humbug, yet were at a loss to explain how an uneducated lad could suddenly display a doctor's knowledge. One disbeliever who decided to find out was the Reverend Gibson Smith of the Mill Street Universalist Church. Upon challenging Davis, the clergyman was invited to attend a mesmeric session, with the result he not only became a true believer but influenced the next step in the young seer's career. This involved Smith posing philosophical questions to the mesmerized Davis, then writing down his responses—a practice that soon convinced Davis his were divinely inspired revelations of universal import, and therefore deserved wider circulation. Leaving Smith and Levingston behind, he headed for New York City.

While residing at 24 Vesey Street in lower Manhattan, Davis delivered no less than 157 "trance lectures" between November 28, 1845 and January 25, 1847, and in the process became one of Manhattan's most talked about personalities. For witnesses to these mesmeric sessions told astounding stories of Davis correctly quoting ancient Hebrew texts, and learnedly discoursing on all sorts of subjects, from archeology and geology to mythology.

Contributing to the air of credulity was the Poughkeepsie Seer's serene comportment, along with his appearance. No longer the gawky rustic, Davis had grown into a handsome young man—sensuous of mouth and serious of gaze—whose high forehead was framed by dark hair that reached down to a full beard. (He wore a beard throughout his adult life, believing that razors—along with alcohol and tobacco—were the bane of mankind.) As for his calm demeanor, whenever Davis felt in need of support or inspiration, he'd hop aboard a steamboat and head up the Hudson for Poughkeepsie. There he was welcome to stay with friends like the Samuel Laphams on Washington Street— only a short walk to the foot of Main Street, where he could take the ferry across the river to Illinois Mountain, and communion with his guiding spirit Galen.

Davis' attainment of his majority in August 1847 was made even more memorable by the appearance of his lectures in book form: *Principles of Nature, Her Divine Revelations, and a Voice to Mankind.* Despite this ponderous title, the book was an immediate success, reportedly selling 900 copies the first week. Eventually it went through more than a dozen editions, and became the bible of modern spiritualism, since it was the Poughkeepsie Seer who defined the movement and gave it much of its terminology.

By that time Davis had won international recognition through his books (ultimately totaling 26), lecture tours, and articles, if not from the various reform organizations he worked with, or the Progressive Children's Lyceum he founded in New York City. To his way of thinking, social reform went hand in hand with spiritualism as a means of attaining universal harmony, yet the combination made controversy his constant companion. A scandal at the start of his first marriage hadn't hurt either, and while famed bridge engineer John A. Roebling called Davis "one of the great men of all time," clergyman and orator Henry Ward Beecher considered him an "impudent pretender."

Davis, however, was never shown to be a "table-rapper" engaged in the kind of fraudulent parlor tricks that have so often been associated with spiritualism. In fact, on the thirtieth anniversary of the movement in 1878, he had no qualms about denouncing "magical spiritualism." He also encouraged practicing spiritualists to earn legitimate degrees, and in 1880 the 54-year-old Davis took his own advice. Three years after enrolling in New York City's United States Medical College, Davis was awarded a degree in medicine, as well as a doctorate in anthropology—triumphs that were tempered by the dissolution of his second marriage and a growing disenchantment with pseudo spiritualists invading the movement. Deciding to distance himself, he moved to Boston, where he produced a few more books, while devoting the rest of his life to the practice of traditional medicine.

Andrew Jackson Davis died in 1910, but the controversy concerning him continues to this day, particularly the question of how, as an unschooled country boy, he could have demonstrated such a depth of knowledge. Psychic? Swindler? Or simply an avid newspaper reader with a photographic memory? Mayhap the answer lies somewhere on Illinois Mountain.

SOME SPIRITED ASIDES

Although Andrew Jackson Davis has been credited with founding spiritualism, the movement officially began in the western New York community of Hydesville in Wayne County, where on March 31, 1848 mysterious sounds were heard in the home of John Fox. His daughters were to become the most notorious of all "table-rappers."

The Fox sisters' first appearance in the Hudson Valley was almost their last. While giving seances at Albany's Van Vechten Hall during February 1850, a clergyman named Staats accused them of "blaspheming against the holy scriptures." A special seance convinced the authorities to the contrary, and the sisters continued their triumphant tour to Troy and then on to New York City.

Horace Greeley's Turtle Bay farm in Manhattan was the scene of numerous seances, some of which were held by the Fox sisters. The famed singer Jenny Lind was present at one of the sittings and accused Greeley of initiating the sounds that were heard, but the newspaperman contended the rappings were real.

Poughkeepsie remained a center for spiritualism long after Andrew Jackson Davis departed. In 1852, a group of "spiritual believers" held their first meeting in the home of William Levingston, Davis' initial mesmerizer, while a former employer, Main Street shoemaker Levi M. Arnold, wrote a series of "sermons" that were published in both pamphlet and book form.

By 1853 there were an estimated 40,000 spiritualists in New York State, including Court of Appeals Judge John Worth Edmonds, who was forced to retire when his beliefs became known.

Senator Nathaniel P. Tallmadge was another Poughkeepsie man who embraced spiritualism. He served as president for the Society For the Diffusion of Spiritual Knowledge when it was founded in New York City, and his four daughters all became well-known mediums.

21. A Maverick Among Us: Charles Bouck White

THE MILD MAY MORNING WAS SO SERENE BEES COULD BE HEARD buzzing amid the apple blossoms that had transformed the orchard-clad slopes of Marlborough Mountain into a fragrant white bouquet. It was the kind of scene that lured tourists to this southeastern section of Ulster County, and even though it was early for the 1921 summer season, Leonia Swifle paused in her housekeeping to glance hopefully out the window of the McElrath farm and boardinghouse. What she saw, however, was not some would-be boarders motoring up the mountin. Instead, a lone young woman with a large suitcase was stumbling down the rutted road that curved past the farm—a stranger whose distress was apparent as she turned into the front gate.

By the time the housekeeper reached the porch, the sobbing stranger had collapsed in a chair. Several minutes then elapsed before she recovered enough to blurt out a bizarre story barely understood by the housekeeper, since the young woman spoke mostly in French, with only bits of broken English. It was enough, though, for the authorities to be notified that the 19-year-old wife of Charles Bouck White apparently had been abused by her much older husband. It was also sufficient to set off a self-appointed posse of masked men who made a late-night call at the alleged wife-beater's home farther up the road from the McElrath farm. Tying a burlap bag over White's head, they drove him nearly 20 miles southwest to a wooded area near Snake Hill in the Orange County town of New Windsor. There he was partially tarred and feathered, beaten with switches, then released to wander for miles through the darkened countryside until he finally found a sympathetic farmer at the town of Newburgh's Orange Lake.

No stranger to notoriety, Charles Bouck White had made more than one headline in New York City prior to his 1918 purchase of a primitive farmhouse high atop Marlborough Mountain. So as soon as they got wind of his latest troubles, newspaper reporters from all over the metropolitan area con-

Author, artisan and social activist, Charles Bouck White adopted the simple robe of a penitent and adhered to an austere lifestyle even after his pottery became popular.

verged on Marborough; even one from the usually staid *New-York Times.*

Being in the center ring of a media circus certainly had not seemed likely when White was born into a well-to-do family in the Schoharie County village of Middleburgh on October 10, 1874. After graduating magna cum laude from Harvard University, he briefly worked as a newspaper reporter before entering Union Theological Seminary, and he was ordained a minister in 1904. White's ministry—first in western New York, then in Brooklyn—remained unremarkable until "verging off," as he once said, "sensibly and perpetually into social work," with a stint from 1908 to 1913 as Head Resident of New York City's Trinity Neighborhood House. It was during this time (1910) that White penned *The Book of Daniel Drew*, a still highly readable "autobiography" based on papers found in the Carmel (Putnam County) home of the self-made, 19th century financier responsible for the term "watered stock." (The book, by the way, supposedly was one of the sources for a 1937 movie, "The Toast of the Town.")

Although subtitled a "Glimpse of the Fisk-Gould-Tweed Regime From the Inside," the Drew book didn't draw nearly as much enemy fire as did the 1911 *Call of the Carpenter*, in which White depicted Jesus as a social agitator. Nor were the inhabitants of White's hometown especially happy with his use of real names and local events in his 1913 novel, *The Mixing,*. However, acts other than authorship were what landed White in jail.

A deepening disenchantment with both church and government led to White's espousal of Socialism as well as the union movement, and in 1914 he was briefly incarcerated for going to the aid of some female strikers in a Brooklyn factory when they were threatened by goons. A longer prison term—six months of hard labor on Blackwells (now Roosevelt) Island—came after a scuffle resulting from his challenge to debate the immorality of being rich with the pastor of Calvary Baptist Church on Manhattan's Fifth Avenue, where members of the Rockefeller family worshipped. But it had been White's attempt to bed the homeless on the cushioned pews of an upper-crust church that caused him to be ousted from the religious establishment. Not to worry: White simply formed his own Church of Social Revolution, welcoming all radicals as he adopted the simple robe of a penitent.

White's new garb was a way of showing his sadness over the suffering he had observed during a European stint as a war correspondent in the summer of 1915. His anti-war sentiment was even more apparent the following spring, when he and his followers publicly burned the flags of ten different nations, including that of the United States. Arrested and brought to trial, White insisted the burning was done solely to melt the banners into a single "flag of Internationalism." The jury didn't buy that and neither did the judge. Pronouncing a sentence of 30 days, the judge reportedly remarked he wished it could have been 30 years.

When the United States entered World War I in 1917, White did an attitudinal about-face, patriotically crisscrossing the country in an attempt to get other radicals to back the war effort. In addition, he maintained that government reform eventually could be realized through peaceful political process instead of violent revolution—a position that got him kicked out of the Socialist Party. That didn't seem to cause him any anguish, for White was already involved in other projects, not the least of which was moving to Ulster County. Before doing so, however, he launched one last crusade in New York City: a 1919 petition to the Board of Aldermen to secede from the Union rather than submit to Prohibition. (White was no toper, but he well knew a "wet" republic would reap more revenue than a "dry" municipality. Plus that, he was an admirer of old Italian city-states, believing that smaller units worked better than unwieldy governments.)

Needless to say, the secession petition didn't pass, and White left Manhattan for Marlborough. There he concentrated on improving the 20 acres he owned on the east slope of the mountain, with an eye to creating a refuge for radical thinkers. Socialist William Sanger, for instance, purchased a small parcel from White and built a cabin where his wife—birth control advocate Margaret Sanger—allegedly escaped when things got too troublesome for her in New York City.

Only a crumbling fireplace remains of Sanger's cabin, but White's buildings (now privately owned) still stand soldidly at the end of the road: the old farmhouse he remodeled by adding a porch, plus a fireplace with concrete pennants featuring some of his sayings; a tidy residence made from stones he hauled up the mountain in his Model-T Ford; and a pump house he constructed with an exterior plaque proclaiming: "For A United States Constitutional Convention That Shall Restore Local Self-Determination 1921."

White was still working on that pump house when he took time off for a trip to France, having developed an interest in peasant pottery. Paris worked its magic. Within three months of meeting a young Frenchwoman named Andree Emilie Simone, the 46-year-old White married her on April 21, 1921, and they soon set sail for America.

Each was to tell a different version of almost immediate marital discord, with newspapers adding their own embroidery. But one thing is clear: neither spouse got the partner expected. When the bride realized her husband intended for her to share his rustic life—existing mainly on bread and eggs while learning to become a radical, and bearing only "brain-children" (the books she would help him write)—Andree literally took French leave. As for her accusation of assault, it is interesting to note that Andree dropped the charge a day after making it. Nor did White leave any impression of violence on one of the people who knew him then. Frank Nicklin, who lived on Marlborough Mountain all his life, was only a boy when his father sold some of his land to White, but even after 75 years Nicklin warmly recalled the kindly neighbor he "never heard tell a lie," and one who "always kept his word."

Charles Bouck White did not contest his wife's suit for a marriage annulment that was granted on grounds of fraud by Poughkeepsie Judge Joseph Marschauser in July 1921. The tall, attractive woman then left the area, having received many publicity-generated offers ranging from marriage to movie roles. White left too, first settling for a short time in Vermont, then spending five years in Malden, Massachusetts, where he studied pottery-making. This interest took him back to Paris and to the French Riviera as he perfected a new ceramic process of glazing that did not require firing—something he called "protest pottery" in that it was created without the "insolence of machinery" and therefore was "lifting its voice against an age that is going mad for gadgets." Collectors nowadays know it better as Bouckware.

In 1933, White returned to the Hudson Valley, renting a Chestnut Street studio in Albany until he found another mountain retreat—this time the site of an old lime kiln set on five fissured acres high on the Helderberg escarpment overlooking the state capital. The selling price was $300, for the remote property offered little other than a far-reaching view and fractured limestone that could be used as building material. But that was all White needed. After subsisting in a cave-like crevice during that first winter of 1933-34, springtime found him erecting a tall wooden teepee that served in part as the signature on some of the pottery he later produced.

Other buildings followed, eventually forming a unique stone complex White variously called his "triumph of incompetency" or "island of sanity," and more formally "Federalberg"—the latter a reference to his belief in a society of cities instead of nations, and his hope that the complex might become "a beacon for the return to municipal civilization." But for most people it was simply the Helderberg Castle.

Whereas his earlier buildings at Marlborough had been of rough but regular design, White now allowed the shape of the stone to dictate dimensions, and it is said that no two windows at Federalberg were alike. The effect was not as disharmonious as might be supposed, due in part to White's unerring eye for finding unusual stones, such as an anthropomorphic pillar that guarded the outside stairway of his studio.

Called Middlemight, due to its central location among the complex's several other buildings, the two-story studio sported a couple of cone-topped towers, along with Gothic archways, a large stone cistern, and even a sunken garden. Nearer the road stood a stolid round tower, while on the other end of the property, at the edge of the cliff, White erected another large, martello-type structure he dubbed the Tower of Hiawatha. This was in deference to his professed Mohawk lineage, as well as the close proximity of the Vale of Tawasentha (now a Town of Guilderland park on Altamont Road),

Utiliziang limestone from is acreage high on the Helderberg escarpment west of Albany, Charles Bouck White built a castle-like complex featuring this workshop he called Middlemight.

immortalized—albeit geographically misplaced—in Henry Wadsworth Long-fellow's poem, *Hiawatha*.

The spectacular view from the tower's parapet was enhanced by a compass White installed so that visitors could readily identify landmarks. It is doubtful, though, that any of his neighbors were thrilled with the public-address system he also placed there in order to share his love of symphonic music with those in the valley below, and the structure became known as the Singing Tower. By that time White had been joined at Federalberg by two Swedish brothers, Sigurd and Karl Bergstrom, who helped with both the buildings and Bouckware. And although life at Federalberg was never easy—the bathtub drain, for example, was strategically set over a crack in the rock, and a pair of pliers took care of aching teeth—it did get better as Bouckware gained in popularity.

Stores began stocking White's pottery, while an occasional student came to learn his process of "cold glazing," and Bouckware was exhibited at the 1939 World's Fair in Flushing Meadow. White even got commissions, and not just for his pots, plates, and vases that were made mainly with colored shards set in clay. One family renovating an old Rensselaerville farmhouse in the late 1930s had blue Bouckware tiles made for all their fireplaces.

Without question, one of the selling points of the pottery was its creator. White liked nothing better than to sit outside on a summer day, his sun-bronzed skin almost masking the "City of God" tattoo on his chest, and philosophize with visitors in a melodious voice that prompted one little girl to call him Bob White instead of Bouck White. The wealth of knowledge coming from this shabbily dressed man could be compelling too, as in the case of some doctors who went hiking in the Helderbergs one afternoon and wound up being treated to a well-grounded talk on pneumococcus typing.

Having given up ever finding a wife to share his primitive existence, White fully intended to live out his remaining days at the Helderberg complex, but World War II interfered. Gas rationing stemmed the flow of visitors, while an ugly rumor circulated that White was a spy utilizing carrier pigeons to send secrets to Nazi Germany. All this and a cerebral hemorrhage convinced him to abandon Federalberg, and in 1943 the 69-year-old White entered the Home for Aged Men in the Albany suburb of Menands.

From time to time reporters came to call, for White could always be counted on as "good copy," be it reminiscences about his early years, or relating how a chance discovery of a cross chiseled into a boulder near his Helderberg "castle" contributed to the Bouckware logo—a cross within a square, a rectangle, or a double triangle (teepee). He had thoughts about the future too, and he made newspaper headlines with his 1947 proposal for developing the Hudson River's mud flats between Watervliet and Kingston into a "little Venice."

Such dreams did not materialize, nor did those of Federalberg's new owner, Gabriel Cordovez, who envisioned an artist's colony there. Shortly after his purchase of the property in 1944, Middlemight burned, and little else was attempted except for the 1946 addition of a nonsectarian shrine dedicated to Gold Star mothers. Vandalism became a problem, and the site was sold several more times until its acquisition in the 1990s by a professional couple dedicated to preserving it as a private enclave.

But in a way it will ever be the domain of Charles Bouck White, whose ashes were placed in the rock fissures of Federalberg following his death at age 76 on January 7, 1951. Certainly his spirit is symbolized in the hand-laid stones of the remaining buildings—possibly more impressive than some of his pottery that has not weathered the years too well. Still Bouckware has its own charm—as apparent in specimens preserved in such places as the New Scotland Historical Society near Federalberg, and the Albany Institute of History and Art on Washington Street—if only as the mark of one of the Valley's most original mavericks.

22. The Saugerties Bard

HE USUALLY COULD BE HEARD BEFORE HE WAS SEEN ENTERING SOME Hudson Valley village during the decades preceding the Civil War. Cooking pots clanging and harness bells jingling, his rickety, flag-bedecked wagon would come rolling down the road, a bevy of barking dogs running alongside. And rising above this din was the sound of a well-played violin—sometimes a flute or fife—presenting one of the popular tunes of the day. The words, however, were those of the wayfarer, who began to sing as soon as his halted wagon was surrounded by a sufficient audience of towns-folk. The subject of the lyric, like the melody, was always something with which they were familiar: maybe a sensational murder.

> An awful tale I will relate
> Of lads that met a cruel fate,
of a recent disaster . . .

> Farewell to the *Reindeer* that in glory and pride
> Did once on the Hudson most beautifully glide,
or a patriotic theme . . .

> A terror to all nations, if perchance they be foes
> Is the American flag, wherever she goes,

with the simple rhyming verses belying the balladeer's educational back-ground. Nor did his dress give any hint of an earlier, easier life. Garbed all in gray with hoary hair and beard blending in with his shabby suit, the man peo-ple called the Saugerties Bard would finish his song and travel on, barely eking out an existence by selling broadsides of his verses for perhaps a penny apiece.

Things hadn't always been like that. Born Henry S. Backus in northern Greene County during 1801, the Saugerties Bard came from a notable mil-itary family. His father, Colonel Electus Backus, was a talented musician, and before his death from wounds received in the 1813 Battle of Sackets Harbor in western New York, he had instilled in young Henry a love of mar-tial themes. That love did not extend to soldiering, though. Whereas his younger brother Electus Jr. entered West Point in 1820 and eventually achieved the same Army rank as their father, Henry restricted his military activities to giving lessons in the bugle, fife and drum.

Proving to be an able instructor, Backus decided to devote his life to teaching school, first in Greene County, then in the Ulster village of Saugerties. It was there that he met and married Ann Elizabeth Legg, and the 1830 Census shows their family included a daughter between the ages of 5 and 10. What the Census did not reveal was the death of another daughter, Sara Ann, who had succumbed shortly after her first birthday— a sorrow that may have begun the process by which Backus' mind "received a peculiar bias." That was the polite way a 19th century newspaperman named Van Der Sluys described what happened to Backus after his beloved wife also died. Saugerties historian Pauline Hommell gave the year as 1845 in her book *Teacup Tales*, and went on to tell of a ghostly presence seen at the same window where Mrs. Backus used to sit awaiting her husband's return from school.

The death of his loved ones had depleted Backus of any desire to teach. For awhile he sought solace in a bottle, then "became rabid" with religion, finally winding up in the lunatic asylum run by Dr. Samuel White in the Columbia County city of Hudson. (The building is now the Hudson Area Library at 400 State Street.) Responding to the asylum's gentle regime— unusual for its day—Backus was subsequently released and returned to Ulster County, apparently only "partially cured." At least that was the assessment of Nathaniel Booth when Backus walked into his store in Kingston on February 11, 1851. The visit awakened decades-old memories of the time Booth had been the Bard's student, and later that day the storekeeper included a lengthy discussion of Backus in the detailed diary he kept.

Booth harbored little love for Backus, who had "often warmed my back to quicken my wits." The diarist also recalled his old schoolmaster's "rattan-ruler" as well as "a certain Lignum Vitae inkstand cork that often found my head in its way." (For those unfamiliar with the tree, lignum vitae is a hard, solid, heavy wood.) Add to that a later affront, when the disapproving Backus had barged into a social gathering and "jerked" his daughter away from a dancing partner who just happened to be Nathaniel Booth, and it's easy to understand why the tone of the diary entry might be a tad disparaging.

While conceding that Backus had once been an "excellent teacher" who also held an advanced degree in the Masonic order, Booth couldn't help poking fun at the advertising jingles that the "Poet Lauriate" [*sic*] was turning out for local merchants, including one that went:

> I John Thomas
> Make no promise
> Like Pie crust to be broken.

Probably penned on a need-to-eat basis, these brief "commercials" have been largely forgotten and fortunately so, since even at his best Backus had a limited talent for versification. Yet his songs possessed a certain charm, especially when played and sung by their sweet-voiced creator—a quality recorded by the aforementioned *Kingston Weekly Leader* columnist Van Der Sluys in 1897. Even after many decades, the journalist remembered a summer evening, presumably in 1852, when he heard a bird's call followed almost immediately by an improptu song from the Saugerties Bard, who happened to be passing by:

> In rural strains, with right good will,
> Loud sings the lovely whip-poor-will. . . .

Much less mellifluous was the chance encounter several years later in 1855 when a defrocked Baptist preacher named Joseph R. Johnson was walking along a Saugerties road. Having just been acquitted—though still suspected—of drowning his wife and child in Esopus Creek, Johnson gladly accepted a lift in a wagon whose driver obviously did not recognize him. Pleasantries were exchanged and when Johnson learned the driver was a wandering minstrel, he asked to hear one of his songs. The Saugerties Bard promptly complied with the composition currently most popular:

> The Baptist priest went sailing
> On the Esopus' rippling tide,
> But soon returned a wailing;
> Drowned were his child and bride. . . .

Before the startled Backus could begin the second verse, his passenger had shot over the side of the wagon and scurried out of sight!

Around the time this happened, Backus extended his travels to the Mohawk Valley as well as to other towns along the Hudson, and it is said that sometimes he even went as far north as Canada. But home was Saugerties, where he was welcome to work on his verses in the back room of the store owned by a sympathetic friend, John Swart. It may well have been there that Backus compiled his *Ulster County Almanac for 1855*, which included a wide selection of his songs covering regional events—from the 1850 Albany County case of "Dunbar, the Murderer," to the 1852 "Burning of the *Henry Clay*" steamship in the Hudson, along with the 1853 arrival of "John Mitchell, Irish Patriot in Exile," and the 1854 "Powder Mill Explosion at Saugerties."

The exact number of songs Bckus wrote is uncertain, but it is believed that one of his most productive periods followed the publication of his almanac, when he spent a few years in and around Manhattan. His reason for going there also is not known, though it might have had something to do with the fact that from 1855 to 1857 his brother Electus was serving as the Army's Superintendent of General Recruiting Services at Fort Columbus on Governor's Island in Upper New York Bay. Whatever the case, Backus helped to preserve in song some of the city's more sensational murder cases, plus such mayhem as the police riots of 1857, and the cotemporaneous "Dead Rabbits' Fight With the Bowery Boys" gang of the notorious Manhattan neighborhood known as Five Points.

That the Saugerties Bard was not cut out for city life had been evident in "My Heart's in Old 'Sopus Wherever I Go"—a poignant 1855 ballad supposedly sung by a homesick sailor and surely composed by Backus to please listeners in the town of Esopus, south of Kingston, but a song that seems to be something of a personal testament too:

> I sigh and I vow if e'er I get home
> No more from my dear native cottage I'll roam;
> The harp shall resound, and the music shall flow;
> For my heart's in Old 'Sopus wherever I go.

Writing about the upriver city of Hudson's reaction to the completion of Cyrus Field's transatlantic cable in August 1858—a song called "The Queen's Telegraph Message and President Buchanan's Reply"—may have prompted Backus to return to more familiar scenes. For apparently his only other surely dated New York City pieces concern a murder that occurred there on October 26, 1858.

Long years as an itinerant troubadour had taken their toll. Backus' health was failing and there were fewer friends to greet him as he drove his wagon from one Hudson Valley village to another. Finally on the morning of May 14, 1861, Katsbaan hotelkeeper James H. Gaddis found the emaciated Backus unconscious and nearly frozen in a shed near where present-day Malden Turnpike meets Route 32 just north of Saugerties village. After reviving the poor fellow, Gaddis brought Backus to the village. There the Saugerties Bard was charged with vagrancy and, though obviously very ill, he was transported a dozen bumpy miles to the Kingston jail, at that time located in the basement of the county courthouse on Wall Street. A doctor was called who prescribed some potions; these were discarded by another physician who also left medicine but never returned to check on the patient in the locked cell.

For several days Backus is said to have thrashed about on his cot, unattended and suffering. Then on the morning of May 20, Van Der Sluys wrote, "he turned his face to the wall and breathed his last."

With no family or friends claiming the body, Kingston officials notified Saugerties to come get their Bard, and according to Pauline Hommell he was buried there in a pauper's grave without ceremony—not even a song. Nor is the exact location remembered. Quite possibly Backus lies near the grave of his beloved daughter Sara Ann in the Mountain View Cemetery on Main Street, but nobody seems to know for sure.

For awhile after his death it appeared that the Saugerties Bard might be forgotten. But broadside publishers continued to include his songs in their books, folklorists gathered stories about him, and today the New York State Library at Albany has a collection of his compositions. Nor has he been ignored by modern-day folk musicians, whose repertoires often contain a Backus verse or two. Perhaps the greatest tribute, however, came from SUNY-New Paltz professor Harry R. Stoneback. A songwriter and folk music performer as well as a teacher and poet, Stoneback helped to keep memory's flame burning with his own ballad, "The Death of the Saugerties Bard," which ends:

> All up and down the Hudson Valley
> And New York City too
> You can hear him a-singing if you listen hard
> Henry Backus—here's to you.

23. *Obstinate Becky*

"You could lock me up until the Resurrection day . . . I never will tell!"

ALL EYES IN THE PACKED NEW YORK CITY COURTROOM FOCUSED ON
the diminutive figure in the witness box. Drab in mourning dress,
but with eyes as dark and flashing as the jet eardrops she wore, 62-
year-old Rebecca Jones nodded as if to punctuate her declaration that even
lifetime incarceration could not change her repeated refusal to testify in this
1884 trial concerning her late employer's last will and testament. Nor did
this lady from Saratoga County's Ballston Spa seem in the least upset when
Surrogate Judge Rollins found her in contempt of court and remanded her
to the Ludlow Street Jail in lower Manhattan. With a laugh, Rebecca Jones
thanked the Surrogate as she shook his hand, demanding, "Why didn't you
do it the first day [of the trial]? You would have saved me from being bothered and fretted to death by the lawyers and the rest of them."

Thereupon the uncooperative witness, amid an admiring crowd of spectators, set off with a deputy sheriff for the prison. It was there that someone
said to her, "You certainly are an exception to the rule that women cannot
keep a secret"—a remark picked up by reporters who filled the city's newspapers with sympathetic stories about "Silent" or "Obstinate Becky" for the
better part of a year.

Back in Ballston Spa, people who had known Becky since 1841, when
her family moved there for Schoharie County, probably weren't surprised at
her obdurate stance at the trial. After all, it was the bold Becky who had literally kidnapped her brother Joseph from a Virginia hospital during the
Civil War. It seems the young soldier had survived several battles unscathed,
only to be struck down by dysentery. Aware of the deplorable conditions in
Army hospitals, Becky headed south, determined to bring her critically ill
brother home. But when she reached him, she was told Joseph could not be
moved without a formal discharge. Her solution, as related in her own
words: "I . . . armed myself with four men and a gun in my hand . . . picked
up the cot and . . . put my brother on the [train] . . . for N.Y. State."

Rebecca Jones was said to have a "Heart of Gold" by the artist who painted her portrait while she was jailed for being "Obstinate Becky."
REPRODUCED BY PERMISSION OF THE
SARATOGA COUNTY HISTORY CENTER

The home she brought him to was on West High Street in Ballston Spa—a house Becky purchased for her family after years of saving practically every penny from her meager salary as a domestic for wealthy families in nearby Saratoga Springs. In fact, when she began her 40-year service with the Gordon Hamersley family, Becky possessed but a single dress, which she carefully washed and ironed each night so she would be "nice & tidy" the next day.

New York City dwellers who only summered in Saratoga when they weren't vacationing abroad, the Hamersleys became like a second family to Becky, especially after Mrs. Gordon Hamersley died and Becky was put in charge of running the household. Becky's candor and common sense also caused both Gordon Hamersley and his son Lewis to seek her advice; so much so that after accompanying them to the Rensselaer County city of Troy around 1880, Becky was consulted as to whether a young woman they met there might make a suitable bride for Lewis. Apparently Becky approved the match, as did the elder Hamersley, and the couple married. But family friction soon developed. In Becky's opinion, Gordon Hamersley then "worried himself to death," followed to the grave not long afterward by his son, the bridegroom Lewis. And it was Lewis' will, bequeathing $7 million to his lovely blonde widow, that was being contested by other family members in the court battle of 1884.

Before the trial took place, Becky returned to Ballston Spa, where she was approached by agents of the contestants to appear as a witness; reportedly they offered her $50,000 if she would answer just four questions. Though the money would have kept the never-married Becky comfortably fixed for the rest of her life, she flatly refused. She also evaded an official subpoena, and eventually two New York City detectives were sent to bring her back.

Having found refuge in the home of a Saratoga friend named Mrs. Davis, Becky was astonished when the out-of-town detectives approached the house—allowing her scant time to hide in the granary—just as if they had been told where to look. Indeed they had, and Becky never got over the hurtful fact that it was her nephew—someone she had financed through Eastman College in Poughkeepsie—who had turned her in.

What Becky did get over, albeit in a purely physical way, were the steps of the railway coach taking her to New York City. Figuring that their prisoner was secure so long as the train was moving, the two detectives went into the smoking car for a few puffs. That was all Becky needed. Somewhere between Ballston Spa and Mechanicville, she leaped off the train, missing the coach steps, and miraculously landing unhurt in a mud-filled ditch. Then the past-60 lady, who "wouldn't weigh 100 pounds dripping wet," trudged over berm and brook to reach Ballston—only to be recaptured.

This time the detectives made ceertain Becky reached Manhattan in time for her April 30 appearance. But that didn't mean they could get her to testify. No one could. Claiming the Hamersleys had told her to "keep still" about family matters, and that she must respect the dead, Becky turned a deaf ear to lawyers, friends and even the trial judge, who finally had to find her in contempt of court.

"I am ready for my bread and water!" Becky melodramatically declared on the day she was incarcerated in the Ludlow Street Jail. She soon discovered, however, that conditions were "not near so dismal as . . . was pictured," including the bill of fare. Her first breakfast there, according to one newspaper report, consisted of "Raspberries and cream, one loaf of home-made bread, five hot rolls, three hard-boiled eggs, two cups of Java coffee, large sirloin steak and a glass of country milk." No wonder she likened her appetite to that of a "Sullivan County ten-year-old wolf"!

As for Becky's cell, it was actually a comfortably furnished chamber measuring 15 by 10 feet, with a "bright carpet on the floor," plus bed, bureau, rocking chair, and even a "merry little clock" on the mantel. Flowers from sympathetic admirers had turned the place "into a grotto of roses," with a large Maltese cat to keep Becky company when she wasn't entertaining visitors, attending religious services, exercising in the jail yard, answering the many letters that came to her from all over the country, or reading the newspapers supplied to her every day. She even enjoyed a mild flirtation with one of her jailers.

Becky's every movement was grist for the media mill, which duly ground out such inconsequential items as the former housekeeper's "horror" over the jail kitchen's improperly stored teacups that "should always be dovetailed and not stand up like soldiers." What most reporters were hoping, of course, was that during an interview Becky might let slip some of her secrets—or that they would

be able to break the story when she finally tired of being in jail and agreed to testify in the stalemated court case. But Becky wasn't about to do either.

The summer of 1884 gave way to autumn and then winter arrived with
little change at the Ludlow Street Jail, other than that its most famous prisoner had her portrait painted—two portraits, in fact, both funded by
reporters, who presented one to Becky in a frame with a plaque proclaiming
her "Heart of Gold."

Finally, as spring approached, the principals in the Hamersley will case
reached an out-of-court settlement, and Becky was released from prison on
March 28, 1885. Returning to Ballston Spa and the West High Street house
she called her "Cosy Castle," Becky maintained her silence, amid public
curiosity further piqued by monthly checks that began arriving for her,
reportedly sent by one of the Hamersleys. Whether those checks were the
result of a pre-arranged plan or an after-the-fact thank-you is anybody's
guess, since Becky clammed up about this too. The only thing certain is that
the payments continued until her death on March 19, 1905.

Those last two decades of her life saw the once-lovely Becky growing ever
more eccentric. Attending funerals became her favorite pastime. It didn't matter to her if the deceased was a stranger; Becky would show up carrying a
peeled onion in her handkerchief so she could shed some tears. Her dress
deteriorated too: her stockings often didn't match, and she would shift her left
shoe to her right foot and vice versa, supposedly to ensure even wear. Nor was
she temperate of mood, becoming a "great one to swear," as her grand-
nephew Christian Burnham later recalled, and on one occasion she tossed
dynamite into her furnace just because she was upset about something.

Yet Becky's sense of duty never diminished. She purchased burial plots for
family members and made sure each grave had a headstone—including her own.
And it is in the village cemetery on Ballston Avenue that Becky finally spoke up
in a self-composed epitaph expressing her sentiments, if not her secrets . . .

> Ah, me. As we fall by the wayside
> And lie sleeping the long dreamless sleep
> How soon we're forgotten by others
> How long will our dearest friends weep?
> But I care not how soon they forget me
> Or if no wreath is laid on my brow
> If they gather the roses of kindness
>   And keep away now.
> OBSTINATE BECKY

24. Death on Zion Hill

A CHILL NOVEMBER WIND WAS NOT ENOUGH TO DETER THE CURIOUS from converging on Bedford village for the start of the Westchester County Court's 1834 fall session. Nor was the crowd disappointed in the flamboyant figure about to be tried for murder.

Standing "taller than most," with steel-gray eyes nearly matching a flowing beard and long hair "the color of ashes," the man called Matthias the Prophet stared back at the spectators, his sinewy form enfolded in a purple cloak. Then with a stately grace, the 46-year-old defendant removed his outer garment to reveal green pants belted by a crimson sash, snowy lace ruffles at his wrists, and a claret-colored frock coat with a line of large silver stars paralleling each lapel—an outfit as sensational as the stories of sexual improprieties leading up to the alleged murder.

Trial-goers expecting to listen to the lurid details were in for a letdown though. The presiding judge became ill, forcing a postponement of the trial until the following April, when it would be transferred to White Plains. In the interim, Matthias was to be held in the White Plains jail, while his guilt or innocence remained public question #1. It was a question of particular interest to residents of the Hudson-shore village of Sing Sing, near where Matthias and his followers had been staying off and on for over a year in the two-storey farmhouse of Benjamin and Ann Folger. The Folgers themselves were relative newcomers to the area, having purchased the 29-acre estate known as Heartt Place in April 1832. But the couple had been quickly assimilated into the community, with Benjamin buying up real estate and both becoming active with the local Baptist church—that is, until the advent of Matthias the Prophet.

Matthias was not his real name, nor did he preach any recognized religion. However, some of his precepts surely stemmed from the strict Presbyterianism practiced in Coila, a Washington County enclave of mostly immigrant Scots about 10 miles east of Hudson, where he had been born Robert Matthews in 1788. Orphaned before his eighth birthday, Matthews grew up a nervous sickly soul who reportedly possessed clairvoyant powers and conversed with spirits. On a more mundane level, he managed to master carpentry, which is mainly how he supported his wife and children as he moved from one place to another, finally settling in Albany around 1826.

This was when Matthews' lifelong preoccupation with religion took a manic turn. Believing his mission was to convert the whole city, he marched through Albany carrying a white banner proclaiming "Rally Round the Standard of Truth." The truth, it turned out, was Matthews' personal spin on Old Testament doomsday prophecies, along with his perceived role as a modern-day messiah. Most folks thought him more crackbrained than convincing. Hence, when Matthews proclaimed the impending destruction of Albany and fled the city with three of his small sons in tow—against the wishes of their mother—the authorities arrested him for lunacy and he spent a fortnight in the city's almshouse. More arrests followed, persuading him to prophesy farther afield.

Adopting the name of Matthias—the disciple chosen by the 11 other apostles to take the place of Judas Iscariot—and sporting a huge spade of a beard, in 1831 he left his family to fend for itself while he wandered for a year in western New York and Pennsylvania. May 1832 found Matthias in Manhattan, where he showed up at the Fourth Street home of Elijah Pierson, asking to speak to the well-known and wealthy religious reformer. The housekeeper answering the door later recalled she "instantly thought he was Jesus"—a resemblance that also impacted on Elijah Pierson. Within a week Pierson had turned over his pulpit to the bearded newcomer whose "stare projected power and danger."

Pierson also pretty much turned over his pocketbook, as he and another wealthy follower supplied whatever the prophet desired. There was a lot Matthias desired too: sumptuous meals served with specially engraved silver, an extensive wardrobe of finely tailored clothes, along with a carriage drawn by matched horses to drive him down Broadway or to the Battery as he exhorted onlookers. For props the prophet might display a huge chain and key to lock up the devil on the doomsday Matthias predicted for 1851. Only those converted to his "kingdom" would survive in a golden city built by him somewhere in western New York—a New Jerusalem whose land would be measured with the carpenter's rule he carried.

It was in Elijah Pierson's house that Matthias was introduced to one of his host's business associates, Benjamin Folger. Brought up in the city of Hudson, Folger was a well-educated hardware merchant not easily influenced by others. Nor was his wife Ann. However, within ten months, when Matthias showed up one August day at their Sing Sing home with obvious intentions of staying, both Folgers had been won over by the prophet's preaching and welcomed him with open arms. As he had done with Pierson, Matthias soon took over the Folger household. He renamed the place Zion Hill (or Mount Zion) and moved in his few followers, including Pierson's former housekeeper, Isabella Van Wagenen—an ex-slave from Ulster County more familiar to modern-day readers as Sojourner Truth, the name she adopted in later years. Van Wagenen, it should be noted, never took part in the sexual misadventuring at Zion Hill that soon started with co-ed nude bathing and escalated to the coupling of Ann Folger and Matthias—all with due religious reasoning, of course.

As might be expected, Benjamin Folger was not too happy about losing his wife's favors, but with Matthias' blessings he was soon bedding none other than the prophet's 18-year-old daughter, who during January 1834 had left her new husband behind in Albany to travel down to Westchester County and visit her father at Sing Sing. When his bride didn't return to Albany, Charles Laisdell headed for Zion Hill. The young Mrs. Laisdell, however, was reluctant to part with her newfound lover Folger, so the bridegroom obtained a writ of habeas corpus which he presented to Sing Sing magistrates holding court at Crosby's Tavern on February 17, 1834. The proceedings were brief. The magistrates simply ordered the girl to return to her rightful spouse. But the case was sufficient to cause a public uproar.

Wherever he went in Sing Sing, Matthias encountered catcalling crowds as well as threats of tar and feathering. Interestingly, none of this anger seemed directed at Benjamin Folger, though he was visited by two prominent villagers politely pleading that he send his "houseguests" away. Just as politely Folger refused, and a month later he sold Zion Hill to Elijah Pierson for $7,700. Pierson then leased the property to Matthias for $1 a year.

Despite the fact that he had acquired a Matthias-sanctioned bedmate, Benjamin Folger had deepening doubts about the prophet's so-called kingdom. Still yearning for his own wife Ann, he began plotting to take her away from Zion Hill, even if it meant battling Matthias. And when Folger shared these plans with villagers during a drinking spree in a Sing Sing tavern on June 1, 1834, they promised to help him.

On the other hand, Ann Folger had no intention of being separated from Matthias. Utilizing her considerable charms, she convinced her husband to call off his scheme. But Folger's friends in the village were not so easily swayed, and soon enough a man named Taylor came up with a strategy for getting rid of the hirsute holyman of Zion Hill. Actually, when Taylor approached Zion Hill in the guise of a policeman on June 3, he was simply trying to win a bet with tavern buddies that he could procure the prophet's beard as a trophy. Showing Matthias a fraudulent arrest warrant, Taylor suggested the prophet cut off his beard before being taken to the village, lest an angry mob do it for him. Matthias submitted to Taylor's razor, but when they reached Sing Sing, the so-called warrant was declared "defective," and the prophet was released. He then headed posthaste for Manhattan, where he remained until the following month when he felt it was safe to return to Sing Sing.

Elijah Pierson was among the few followers joining Matthias for supper at Zion Hill on July 28, 1834. Dessert was a big bowl of fresh blackberries that Matthias and Pierson had picked earlier in the day. Of the four people dining, only Pierson ate any substantial amount; Matthias none at all.

When Pierson became violently sick to his stomach and collapsed the following afternoon, little heed was paid other than to put him to bed, since he was known to suffer from seizures. Even when his condition worsened, no doctor was called, no medicine administered, for members of Matthias' kingdom believed sickness could be cured solely through prayer. And on August 6, Elijah Pierson breathed his last.

A coroner's jury did not order an autopsy, having decided that Pierson died of natural causes. But dark rumors persisted and the coroner finally ordered the body exhumed for further examination on August 18. Four doctors felt there was evidence of poisoning, and sent Pierson's stomach to the noted New York botanist John Torrey for confirmation.

Matthias' kingdom was crumbling too—something for which he blamed Ann Folger. Arguments raged on Zion Hill, and one morning the two Folgers were sickened by some coffee served them by the prophet's staunch supporter, Isabella Van Wagenen. This may have been what decided Ann Folger to return to her husband. Whatever did it, Benjamin Folger took steps to solidify their reconciliation by offering Matthias $630 to buy land and move his kingdom farther west.

As soon as Matthias departed with the money on September 19, 1834, Folger went to the New York City police, accusing the prophet of defrauding him. Two policemen then apprehended Matthias in Albany, where he had stopped off to see his legal wife. He was brought to Manhattan aboard the steamboat *Champion* and formally charged with embezzlement..

Thanks to the efforts of Isabella Van Wagenen and Matthias' longsuffering wife Margaret, the prophet was represented at the November trial by two of Manhattan's finest lawyers, Henry Western and N. Nye Hall. They were the ones who advised Van Wagenen to sue Benjamin Folger for slander when—possibly in an attempt to discredit her as a defense witness—he began circulating stories that she had tried to poison him and his wife with arsenic-laced coffee at Zion Hill. Van Wagenen did sue and eventually was awarded $125 in damages.

Faced with such a top-notch legal team and knowing his case lacked sufficient evidence, District Attorney Hoffman motioned to end the prosecution. The judge agreed, having no problem dismissing the charges since he knew the Westchester County authorities were waiting to arrest Matthias for the murder of Elijah Pierson.

When his much delayed murder trial took place in White Plains the following April, Matthias made the most of his moment in the media spotlight, protesting the secrecy of the grand jury system, and instructing all farmers to forget about plowing because the spring thaw would not occur until he was set free. He also warned that if he were found guilty, an earthquake would destroy White Plains, leaving "not an inhabitant . . . to tell the tale."

The question has been raised as to whether those "prophecies" swayed the jury. Admittedly it was a superstitious era and there were stories of Matthias having once cursed a man who soon afterward died a horrible death. But truth be told, District Attorney William Nelson's case just didn't stand up to the onslaught of defense lawyer Henry Western, who had obtained an affidavit from Dr. John Torrey stating that Elijah Pierson's stomach had shown no signs of poisoning. As for the earlier autopsy, Western easily demonstrted that it had been mishandled.

On the fourth day of the trial, Judge Charles H. Ruggles instructed the jury to find Matthias not guilty. This they did, without even retiring to the jury room. But Matthias was not yet off the hook. District Attorney Nelson immediately asked for the arraignment and trial of Matthias for beating up his daughter, the aforementioned Mrs. Laisdell, when she had visited Zion Hill!

This trial was short, with both sides trying to avoid full disclosure of the sexual goings-on at Zion Hill that would surely sour the jury. In the end, what it boiled down to was not so much whether Matthias had beaten his daughter, but whether in doing so he had appropriated Charles Laisdell's "rights of a husband over the body of his wife." The jury thought he had, and Judge Ruggles sentenced Matthias to three months in the county jail, plus 30 days for contempt of court.

By the time Matthias was released from jail in the summer of 1835, his kingdom was finished, its followers scattered. Even the wife who had stuck by him through so many tribulations no longer wanted him around. The Folgers still lived at Zion Hill, but that name would be only a memory after the house was sold in 1836 to the Reverend William Creighton. He called it Beechwood, and began the first of many alterations that eventually turned it into a showpiece bordering the Albany Post Road. Somewhere along the line a story surfaced about Matthias' ghost haunting the property. Supposedly he had murdered "five beautiful young virgins," then buried them in the basement, after which he himself was immured alive in a wall oven where his bones were discovered in the early 1900s. A fitting finale perhaps, but the truth is a tad more mysterious.

Although there was some talk of Matthias drowning shortly after his release from jail, it is surely known that he showed up at the Mormon settlement at Kirtland, Ohio, on November 5, 1835, seeking an audience with Joseph Smith. The Mormon leader wanted nothing to do with a man he considered "the devil in bodily shape," and sent Matthias on his way—a wandering that reportedly wound up in Little Rock, Arkansas, in 1839. But the people there didn't want him either. The last that was heard of him, the prophet-turned-pariah was preaching to Indians in the Iowa Territory during 1841. Who knows, the Indians may have tired of his teaching too. . . .

25. Plan 9 from Poughkeepsie

UNLIKE SOME OF THE YOUNGSTERS HORSING AROUND IN THE DARKENED Poughkeepsie movie theater, seven-year-old Ed Wood Jr. sat ensorcelled by the tall, black-caped figure staring back at him from the screen. Then the actor's heavily accented voice intoned, "Dra . . . cu . . . la." And even though motion pictures were no longer a novelty in that year of 1931, Bela Lugosi's portrayal of the vampire had an impact few of the film's viewers would forget—certainly not the captivated boy, who went on to make his own brand of Hollywood history.

There was little in the boy's background to suggest such a future. Born on Poughkeepsie's Franklin Street on Ocober 10, 1924, and named for his factory-worker father Edward Davis Wood, "Junior"—as relatives called him—is said to have inherited a story-telling talent from his mother, Lillian Phillips Wood. But other than that, his mania for movie-making seems to stem mainly from the Saturday matinees he started attending in the 1930s.

What a marvelous make-believe world that was, with feature-length films accompanied by serials whose cliff-hanger endings ensured a youngster's return the following week. The Flash Gordon series starring Buster Crabbe was a '30s hit, while the '40s saw cowboy Buck Jones in the popular "Rough Riders." Both were lifetime favorites of Ed Wood, whose mother once said that whenever he wasn't in school or at work, he was at the movies.

Actually Wood's boyhood was not quite so circumscribed. While he never went out for sports, he did join the Boy Scouts, played drums in a local band, was with a singing group that appeared on Major Bowes' Amateur Hour on radio, was an avid reader, and enjoyed family outings to the Ulster County hamlet of Kripplebush, where the old Wood homestead stood across from the fire hall.

The dark-haired, blue-eyed boy with the cleft chin also had a host of friends while attending Columbus Elementary on Perry Street, and later Poughkeepsie High School on North Hamilton Street. For as his cousin Tom McDonald recalled, "He was a very happy person. Even as a kid he was always smiling, and you were glad to have him around." But films took up

The family homestead in the Ulster County hamlet of Kripplebush was where Ed Wood spent many childhood vacations. (Photo reproduced by permission of Ruth Donnelly)

more and more of Wood's attention, especially after he got his first movie camera—a 16mm Kodak with which he "shot" his cops-and-robbers playmates—and later worked as an usher at both the Stratford Theater, at Cannon and Liberty streets, and the Bardavon, on Market Street. So fascinated was he by motion pictures that he would cull through the trash bins in back of the theaters for promotion photos thrown out after a film's run, and he wound up with an impressive collection. But it was a real-life image that proved to be the most memorable: the night when cowboy star Ken Maynard was appearing in person and his horse fell through the stage as Wood watched from the wings. Fortunately no great harm was done to man or beast, and years later in Hollywood Maynard and Wood would laugh over how their friendship started on a splintered Poughkeepsie stage.

Wood by then was heartthrob handsome, and might have headed for Hollywood much earlier than he did, had it not been for the Japanese attack on Pearl Harbor. Within six months of that infamous December day in 1941, 17-year-old Wood and two of his buddies, George Kesseck and Frank Wirsch, enlisted in the Marines. Wood was sent to the Pacific, where he survived such blood baths as the Tarawa invasion, but suffered from tropical disease and battle wounds. Despite this, he not only managed to complete his enlistment, he even wrote a play about the Marines. He called it *Casual Company*, and it was staged at the Poughkeepsie High School shortly before his discharge in 1946.

The following year found Wood finally in Hollywood, after taking some classes in acting and creative writing, then traveling for awhile with a carnival. Reportedly he worked in the carnival's freak-show, portraying the half-man/half-woman, or the geek—the later role so demeaning that usually only down-and-out winos would accept it. Both parts proved strangely prophetic, for the two most damaging quirks in Wood's personality turned out to be his fondness for booze and a fetish for female clothing.

Neither trait caused him much trouble to start, and he embarked on a life at times so bizarre that the award-winning 1994 movie, *Ed Wood*, was given a comedic spin. Based on Rudolph Grey's 1992 biography,

Photographed around 1950 when he was an aspiring Hollywood actor, producer and director, Poughkeepsie-born Ed Wood evolved into one of moviedom's cult figures. (Photo reproduced by permission of Ruth Donnelly)

Nightmare of Ecstasy, the film deals mainly with Wood's first decade in Hollywood —an optimistic time when he gave up steady work as a production coordinator at Universal Studios, and supplemented acting stints with producing his own movies on a shoestring. Limited funds frequently led hm to outlandish situations, including a late-night raid on Republic Studios to "borrow" a huge fake octopus, and then there was the contract with a clergyman who invested in a Wood movie only on conditon that the whole cast be baptized in a swimming pool. (They were.)

Wood also had a knack for improvising props, be it a cardboard coffin "varnished" with water, or automobile hubcaps sliding down piano wire to simulate flying saucers. The latter were seen in the 1956 sci-fi film *Plan 9 From Outer Space*, which has been called the worst movie ever made, and earned Wood the title of Hollywood's least-talented director. *Plan 9 From Outer Space* also marked Bela Lugosi's last movie appearance. Wood, it seems, had never forgotten his 1931 encounter with the veteran vampire on a Poughkeepsie movie screen, and when he finally met Lugosi in person during 1953, a firm—if somewhat wacky—friendship was forged. In addition to writing scripts for the aging, drug-addicted actor whose career was on the decline, Wood kept watch over Lugosi to the point that he supposedly went along on the older man's honeymoon. Lugosi was flattered by the attention, and reciprocated by giving Wood the best performances his debilitated body could muster, even when it meant wrestling a pseudo octopus in an ice-cold swamp (*Bride of the Monster*, 1955). And ironically enough, when Lugosi died in 1956, it was while reading a script Wood had written for him called *Final Curtain*.

A few years earlier, Lugosi had appeared in *Glen or Glenda*, a movie Wood wrote and directed which has been deemed autobiographical because it deals with transvestism. While it's true that Wood sometimes donned female clothing, and had a particular fondness for angora sweaters, how much was true transvestism and how much was pure—pardon the pun—put-on is not so easily assessed. Take the time Wood told his wife Kathy that his transvestism was the result of his mother dressing him as a girl during early childhood. None of Wood's many baby pictures in family albums show any sign of such cross-dressing, nor do relatives recall it occurring. As for his love of angora, Wood's cousin Ruth Donnelly of Stone Ridge in Ulster County treasured a blue sweater he sent her, though she had no idea whether it was something he wore.

Wood rarely returned to the Hudson Valley after moving to Hollywood, but he did keep in touch with his family, usually through late-night phone calls that hinted of his deepening dependence on alcohol. Letters were something else. Surviving samples show a chatty and upbeat style, or in the case of a 1963 condolence note concerning the death of his beloved Grandmother Phillips, a wealth of warm memories of Poughkeepsie—walking with his grandmother from the Hedding Methodist Church on Clover Street to her home on Allen Street, filming her in her flower garden with his first movie camera, how she nursed him when he caught his foot in the spokes of a bicycle wheel, and in later years how he took her to see *Sonny Boy* and *The Shepherd of the Hills* in the old Stratford Theater.

Wood was close to his parents too, and Rudolph Grey's biography includes a description of how he proudly watched his father help President Franklin Delano Roosevelt lay the cornerstone for the Poughkeepsie Post Office in 1937. (A World War I veteran, the elder Wood was by then working for the post office.)

When it came to his cousins, Ruth Donnelly was the dearest to Wood, having been born only five days before him. Her scrapbooks are full of clippings, playbills and other memorabilia he mailed to her starting in 1949. There are paperback books too, for Wood eventually began writing pulp fiction to supplement an income rarely enriched by his movies. Most of his books were of the kind then known as tit-lit, but he wasn't overtly ashamed of them and only sometimes used a pseudonym for the dozens he turned out between 1963 and 1978. When he did use a pen name, it was often a play on words such as "Akfdov Telmig" (read it backwards). This sense of humor was an essential part of his nature, and Ruth Donnelly recounted how he could do a hilarious take-off on Adolph Hitler, complete with a man's black comb as a mustache. He didn't use words as weapons, though—something inexperienced actors particularly appreciated when the congenial Wood directed their performances with a calming choice of words.

Wood's talent for turning a phrase was coupled with an almost unbeliev-able writing speed. It is said he once wrote a complete screenplay in a single day of non-stop typing, and that he took even less time with one of his nov-els. True or false, the fact remains that he was a prolific writer, churning out short stories, TV scripts, political speeches for one-time Los Angeles mayor Sam Yorty and nightclub reviews, in addition to his books and movies. Not all of them were of the "brand X" variety either, and it can only be wondered what he might have accomplished had he slowed down to more carefully craft his creations; most of all, had he set aside the bottle.

Clearly he could do neither. On December 10, 1978, exactly one month after his fifty-fourth birthday, Ed Wood died of a heart attack. Rarely sober, he had been evicted from his run-down apartment a few days earlier. The media paid little heed to his passing, and only a handful of mourners showed up at the memorial service. His cremated remains were then committed to the open sea.

For a long time afterward, whenever the name of Ed Wood was men-tioned by other than friends or family members, it was usually with derision for his work, his lifestyle, or both. Gradually, however, as a new generation was introduced to his movies through film festivals, TV and video tapes, he gained a following. Then came Rudolph Grey's biography and the movie, *Ed Wood*. Starring Johnny Depp in the title role, the film at first did not do well at the box office, but was hailed by critics and wound up with two Academy Awards (best supporting actor and best makeup). In fact, when *Ed Wood* was being shown in theaters during 1994, the VCR tape of *Plan 9 From Outer Space* was among the top ten in video sales. And a re-mastered version of that 1956 flick—complete with a two-hour documentary—was released in 2001, much to the delight of Wood aficionados. So even though he never won any awards, Ed Wood lives on as both a Hollywood and Hudson Valley legend.

26. "Sin Finds Out the Criminal"— The Strange Case of Richard Jennings

THICKENING CLOUDS THAT THREATENED SNOW ON THE MORNING OF December 21, 1819 made 70-year-old Richard Jennings reluctant to leave his home in the Orange County hamlet of Sugar Loaf. It would be a long, cold walk to his woodlot, but past experience had taught him he'd better keep an eye on it, so he set out at a brisk pace that belied his advanced age.

As he passed James Teed's house, Jennings may have noticed someone watching from the window. If he did, he apparently made no connection with that and the figure soon following behind him. Or maybe hurry took precedence over suspicion, for the first flakes were already beginning to fall.

The snowstorm did not intensify until later that day, but Richard Jennings never made it home. A week later his frozen remains were found in the woodlot, the bullet-shattered skull and brutally beaten body immutable proof of a murder that was to become one of the Hudson Valley's most bizarre cases, and New York's first homicide-for-hire.

It was no secret in the close-knit community that Jennings had fomented a family feud when he allegedly cheated his nephew James Teed out of a 50-acre parcel of land. Teed had later signed over the contested property to his brother-in-law David Conkling, and a series of bitterly fought court cases ensued—not only over the property on which Teed continued to live with his wife and a tenant named David Dunning, but also the woodlot that Jennings contended was being regularly raided by his warring relatives. Investigators, therefore, figured they had the motive for Jennings' murder, if not the perpetrator. Then someone recalled having seen David Conkling's hired man, Jacob "Jack" Hodges, on the same road Jennings had taken that fateful day.

A crude ex-sailor overly fond of alcohol, Hodges was known to have a dog-like devotion for his employer— "would do anything for Conkling," he once had vowed. So the finger of suspicion was pointed at Hodges. The only trouble was that the hired man had taken French leave.

What followed next was a chase scene to rival any Hollywood western. Acting upon tips that Hodges was headed for New York City, four citizens formed a posse and went thundering off on horseback toward Newburgh, only to miss their quarry by minutes at the ferryboat landing. Hodges, they learned, had crossed the Hudson on his way to the Putnam County port of Cold Spring. Following on the next ferry, they arrived in Cold Spring a few hours after a New York-bound sloop had set sail with Hodges aboard. Disappointed but undaunted, the possemen galloped south along the Post Road. When their horses gave out at Peekskill in Westchester County, they hired a team and wagon to take them the rest of the way, and were waiting on the Spring Street landing in lower Manhattan when Hodges stepped ashore.

The surprised suspect initially proclaimed his innocence, but gradually wilted under the pressing questions of the posse. Thereupon, they hustled Hodges aboard the next upriver sloop, which only went as far as the Rockland County port of Haverstraw. This meant that the now exhausted posse still faced a long haul by hired wagon over snowy roads. Yet they delivered their prisoner to the Orange County jail in Goshen in record time, and Hodges was just as expeditiously indicted.

As shocking as the murder was, the story Hodges told was even more so. The homicide, he confessed, had been plotted at the home of his employer David Conkling, who offered Hodges and David Dunning $1,000 to do away with that "worthless, trouble-making man Richard Jennings." Upon their agreement, Conkling had loaded a musket and handed it to Hodges, saying he should stay with Dunning at James Teed's house, where they could more easily monitor the movements of the victim-to-be. Meanwhile, Mrs. Teed was pressed into service, since Hodges set great store by what she said. So when he asked whether "it would be right" to murder Jennings, she stated, "Yes, for if the old man is not put out of the way, he will ruin my husband and brother." (Hannah Teed was David Conkling's sister.)

On the morning of December 21, Hodges was eating breakfast when Dunning spotted Jennings passing the house. Hodges later recalled he was still hesitant and looked up at James Teed's wife, asking if it was "necessary to proceed with the business." Handing him a mugful of whiskey, she replied, "Yes, it's time the old savage was out of this world!"

Fortified by the fiery drink, Hodges picked up the musket and followed Dunning out of the house. They caught up with their quarry at the woodlot, where from a distance of 10 feet Hodges shot Jennings in the face near the eye, with the careening bullet cutting off part of the old man's ear. The wound was not immediately fatal, however, and as Jennings writhed on the ground, Hodges again hesitated—at least that was his version of what happened next. Dunning, he swore, then tore the gun from his grasp and beat Jennings with it until the musket shattered and the victim was a bloody pulp.

The falling snow covered their return tracks to the Teed house in Sugar Loaf, where Hodges proceeded to embark on an applejack bender. Fearful lest he drunkenly babble about the crime, the other conspirators urged him to go to New York. Conkling promised to meet Hodges there, at which time he would pay the hired man his half of the $1,000, plus the wages due him; for the present Hodges had to be satisfied with $10 and a letter in which Conkling recommended him to a prospective employer in the city as being "faithful and honest"! James Teed then escorted the besotted Hodges to the Newburgh ferry.

Within two months of the grisly discovery in the woodlot, all five conspirators were brought before the bar at Goshen. Hodges pled guilty and testified for the prosecution, while the other three men—Conkling, Dunning and Teed—maintained their innocence. Hannah Teed at first said she was not guilty, then later changed her plea, throwing herself on the mercy of the court.

It was an event so singular and sensational that winter roads did not deter hordes of out-of-towners from converging on the courthouse, where none other than Attorney General Martin Van Buren opened the proceedings by declaring that Jennings' death was "the first instance in the criminal records of our state of murder by a hired assassin."

Supreme Court Justice William W. Van Ness presided over the five separate trials, bringing them to an unprecedented speedy conclusion by holding sessions often lasting until late at night. By March 11, 1819—less than three weeks after the court was convened on February 23—the defendants had all been convicted, with the four men sentenced to death by hanging. Yet after the execution, only Hodges' body was to be brought to the Orange County Medical Society for dissection—a decision based perhaps on the fact he had no family, though his African-American ancestry may well have played a part. (The three other male defendants were white.) As for Hannah Teed, she not only was pregnant and had several small children at home, but the judge felt she could have been coerced by her "stern and inflexible husband." Therefore, the charges against her were reduced, and she served just 30 days in the Goshen jail.

More surprises were in store. Shortly after the trial, Conkling's sentence was commuted to life imprisonment; that of Hodges to 20 years. This left only David Dunning and James Teed to face the hangman on April 16, 1819.

Announced on handbills posted throughout the county, the public execution brought thousands of people flocking to Goshen. Sheriff Moses Burnett had anticipated this influx and changed the site of the gallows from the green near the jail in the center of Goshen to a more spacious natural amphitheater on the southern side of the village. But the spectacle still began in front of the jail, where "two companies of dragoons and several infantry" spent an hour parading for the public on the morning of the execution, after which the prisoners were escorted to "the place of death" nearly a mile away. Nor was there a quick conclusion when they arrived. With nooses around their necks, Dunning and Teed were made to kneel on the gallows trapdoor for two long hours while a quartet of clergymen held services. The sermon best remembered is that of the Reverend Ezra Fisk, whose subject was "Sin Finds Out the Criminal." And it can only be wondered how this affected David Dunning, who denied killing Jennings until the very end.

The strange circumstances of the Jennings case didn't end with the executions either. A local tradition holds that because convicted murderers were not allowed burial within the bounds of any cemetery, the bodies of Dunning and Teed were interred beyond the pale of a private plot on the outskirts of Sugar Loaf—graves marked only by sharpened stakes that had been superstitiously driven deep into them. If true, those Dracula-type doings almost surely contributed to the derangement of Hannah Teed, who survived her husband by a mere four years. In August 1823, her body was found floating in the Hudson off New Windsor—a suicide.

Hannah's brother, David Conkling, developed a debilitating case of rheumatism in prison, which prompted Governor William Marcy to grant him a pardon after he had served more than 13 years of his sentence. But the pain-wracked Conklin died shortly after his release.

Incredibly, Jacob Hodges emerged phoenix-like from the ashes. Having been influenced by the aforementioned Reverend Fisk while awaiting trial, the alcoholic ex-seaman became a model inmate at Auburn Prison in Cayuga County where he learned how to read, and he was pardoned after serving 15 years. Hodges then spent about a year at the Auburn Seminary, during which time he lived in the home of William H. Seward. (An Orange County native, Seward—of Alaska purchase fame—just happened to be the nephew of Richard Jennings!)

Remaining in the Finger Lakes region, Hodges went on to become a celebrated evangelist in the Ontario County community of Canandaigua. And it is there in the Pioneer Cemetery on West Street that a monument to him can be found:

JACOB HODGES
An African Negro,
Born to poverty and ignorance:
Early tempted to sin by designing and wicked men:
Once condemned as a felon:
Converted by the grace of God, in prison:
Lived many years as a consistent and useful Christian:
Died Feb. 1842,
In the faith of the gospel:
Aged about 80 years.

Did sin, indeed, find out the criminal? You be the judge.

V. Making Their Mark

27. The Last of the Log Cabin Presidents

Traveling the steep route across Rensselaer County's Taconic range could be tricky in any season, but a rash of ice storms during the winter of 1855-56 made it particularly treacherous. That was why the Reverend Myron J. Streator and Matthew Moody insisted on driving their young visitor back across the mountains to his room at Williams College. They did fine for awhile after leaving Poestenkill, with the horse easily pulling the sleigh up the western slope of Berlin Mountain. Ice, however, was accumulating as they crossed the state line into Massachusetts, and by the time they began their descent toward Williamstown, the lightly shod horse was sliding all over the road.

Figuring they must either forge ahead on foot or freeze, the clergyman was about to climb down from the cutter when the student stopped him. "You've been ailing, Rev. Streator," he said, "and shouldn't be walking in such weather. Please stay seated." With that, the young man quickly unhitched the horse, which he handed over to the other traveler to lead. Then placing his own burly body in the traces, future president James A. Garfield slowly pulled the cutter the remaining miles to safety.

That little-known local link with the last of America's log cabin presidents likely comes as a surprise to anyone aware of Garfield's lifelong Ohio associations, let alone those of us who may have regarded him as a fairly colorless character. Yet the political career of our 20th president not only began right here in the Hudson Valley, it also ended as he was returning to the region. And in between there was rarely a dull moment.

As for the early life of James Abram Garfield, that was Lincolnesque, to say the least, starting with his birth in a rural Ohio log cabin on November 19, 1831. Eighteen months later, his father died, leaving James and his three surviving siblings to experience a childhood bereft of material wealth, but rich in the moral strength of their religious mother. It was this strength that helped sustain young James in his struggle to achieve an education—schooling he paid for by working a variety of jobs, including a stint on the Ohio & Erie Canal during 1848.

The summer of 1854 found 22-year-old Garfield heading east, determined to attend Williams College, despite the fact that he had no definite means of funding a full course of study. Nor did a lean wallet deter the handsome, sandy-haired six-footer from a brief Hudson River detour before buckling down in the Berkshires, and on July 5 he boarded the steamship *Hendrik Hudson* at Albany for the evening run to Manhattan. Garfield's diary for that date reveals how he was instantly ensorcelled by the watery "necklace of New York strung with cities more valuable than pearls or diamonds." So it is not surprising that after a week spent in and around Manhattan, he again chose the river for his return north; this time taking the steamer *Rip Van Winkle* to Troy, where he debarked on the morning of July 11. Then after breakfasting (for all of 38 cents) at the Fulton House, he set out on the final leg of his journey.

The distance from Troy to Williamstown is less than 30 miles as the crow flies, but mid-19th century travelers dependent on public transportation had a much more roundabout route. First Garfield took the Troy & Boston Railroad north to Hoosick Junction, where he got a horse car down to Hoosick Falls, and from there a stagecoach southeast to Williamstown. Arriving at midday, he reported at once to Williams College president Mark Hopkins, who then arranged for his examination by several professors. And though he must have been woefully travel-worn, Garfield tested so well in Latin, Greek and trigonometry that he was told he could enter Williams as a junior. (His dormitory room, by the way, was #23 in what is now called the old East College building.)

The new semester didn't start until September, but the intervening months were not idle ones for Garfield. When he wasn't monitoring a couple of summer classes, he went exploring in the mountains, and in the meantime triggered a minor scandal. It all began on August 23 when Garfield was visiting Great Barrington and happened to pick up a copy of the *Berkshire Courier* containing a poem by Hattie A. Pease. Impressed, Garfield sent off an answering verse "To Hattie," signing it simply "A Stranger." The newspaper published it, and there allegedly followed a "long and pleasant correspondence" between the poetess and the future president.

The one person who did not consider the poetizing so pleasant was Lucretia Rudolph, the girl with whom Garfield had an "understanding" back home in Ohio. Apparently Lucretia was alerted to the affair by someone in the area, for during November the *Courier* ran a poem by "Ohio's Daughter"

During the 1850s, future president James A. Garfield was a familiar figure in the Taconic foothills of Rensselaer County, where he left behind more than one local legend.

in which the "Stranger" was melodramatically reminded of his romantic responsibilities. As for the identity of Lucretia's informant, it could have been any one of a number of people, since Garfield not only had cousins living in the Berkshire County town of Monterey, but many of his New York friends had Ohio ties. Among the latter group as Myron J. Streator, a Disciples of Christ preacher from Ohio who was then pastor of that denomination's church in Poestenkill. Garfield, of similar religious persuasion, had also done some preaching, and during that first summer began participating in the prayer meeting Streator conducted in such outlying Rensselaer County communities as Eagle Bridge.

Poestenkill, however, became the fulcrum of Garfield's religious and social life away from school. He was often invited to give the Sunday sermon at the Church of Christ, and after hiking over the mountains from Williamstown on Saturday, he would settle in as a welcome guest in one of the parishioners' homes. (Although the church where he preached is no longer standing, its replacement—the Poestenkill Christian Church at Snyders Corner Road and Route 351—boasts a commemorative bas relief, as well as the wooden "desk" pulpit used by the future president. And to get some idea of the route he took back to college, drivers can try the Plank Road—Route 40—heading east from the village toward Berlin.)

Without a doubt Garfield's favorite refuge was the comfortable dwelling of Maria and Charles Learned, whose many kindnesses to the struggling student included gifts of clothing. Garfield liked being at the Learned house for other reasons too, not the least of which was the frequent presence of his hostess' close friend, Rebecca Jane Selleck. Witty and pretty, the charming Rancie (as Rebecca was known) eventually had Garfield rethinking his commitment to Lucretia, especially after he spent a springtime vacation at the Selleck home in the Westchester County town of Lewisboro. But that was as far as it went, and the result was a rather strange relationship in which

Rancie—who unquestionably loved him—remained a close companion even after Garfield married Lucretia in 1858.

Getting back to those all-important college years, Garfield had come east with about $350 in savings—certainly not enough to see him through graduation, despite the aforementioned generosity of his Poestenkill friends. Nor was he one to rely on the charity of others, as was evident when Troy tailor E.P. Haskell agreed to supply the needy student with a new set of clothes. Garfield reportedly assured the seamster that although "he could not fix the date," he would pay for the suit as soon as possible. Garfield was aided in keeping his promise by the advent of some teaching jobs. It has been said that he was so proficient in the classics, he could simultaneously write Greek with one hand and Latin with the other. Be that as it may—and such ambidexterity may well be pure myth—it was by giving lessons in English penmanship during school vacations that Garfield managed to stay solvent.

His talent as a teacher is well remembered in Eagle Mills (then known as Millville), where he also preached in the local church and was a frequent guest of the Joseph H. Allen family. (County Route 137 north of Poestenkill is called Garfield Road. At its junction with State Route 2 in Eagle Mills can be found a historic marker designating the site of the school where Garfield taught. A short distance to the west, at the corner of Creek Road—Route 139—stood the house where Garfield enjoyed the hospitality of the Joseph Allen family.)

The writing classes Garfield conducted at Poestenkill are significant due to their association with a character-illuminating anecdote. For it was after arrangements had been made for him to use one of the Poestenkill Academy's classrooms, the principal unaccountably refused him access. Though the rebuff must have hurt, Garfield remained unruffled and simply moved his students to the ballroom of the nearby Union Hotel. The tables were turned a short time later when Principal Martin was participating in a public debate and wound up so outclassed that he was forced to recruit Garfield's help in rebutting the opposition's arguments. Instead of exacting revenge, the young gentleman from Ohio genially joined the principal's side, winning the debate as well as the other man's promise to make amends.

Garfield's verbal victory was no accident. In addition to his preaching, teaching and poesy, he had ample opportunity for perfecting his persuasive powers during literary debates at Williams, and as editor of the school *Quarterly*. It was also during his college years that Garfield first evinced an interest in politics, fostered in part by a trip he took to Albany during the winter of 1855, when he attended legislative sessions as the guest of State

Assemblyman Edmond Cole. (Married to the sister of Maria Learned, Edmond Cole was then representing Rensselaer County's 3rd District, and belonged to the Poestenkill Church.)

Just before graduating from Williams on August 6, 1856, Garfield made his first political speech in public—at a student gathering to support the new Republican Party's nomination of John C. Frémont. At that time, though, the 25-year-old had no other plans than to return to Ohio, where he had accepted a teaching position at Hiram Institute. (Earlier in the year, he had been offered the directorship of Troy's public schools at a much higher salary, but rejected it after a soul-searching walk atop a nearby mountain.)

In comparison to his later life—school administrator, state senator, Civil War general, congressman, and dark-horse president not nominated by his party until 36th ballot (!)— Garfield's two-year residence in the region may seem minor. It meant a lot to him, however, and he returned to Williams and Rensselaer County whenever he could. That was what he was looking forward to on July 2, 1881, when he arrived at Washington's Baltimore & Potomac Railroad station. But before he could board the train, a disappointed office-seeker named Charles Guiteau rushed up to him. A shot rang out. Garfield slumped to the platform, a bullet in his spine. He had been in office a mere four months.

For once Garfield's prodigious strength worked against him. The prognosis was hopeless, yet he lingered in agony through the sweltering summer, finally succumbing on September 19 to infection and internal hemorrhage. It was the anniversary of the Civil War Battle of Chickamauga where he had performed heroically, yet Garfield died wondering about his place in history.

Helping to preserve that place have been the people of Rensselaer and Berkshire counties, where a Garfield Memorial Association once operated, and the Poestenkill and Brunswick Historical societies host programs concerning the 20th president. And surely the martyred man would have been particularly pleased that one of the presidents of Williams College turned out to be his son, Harry A. Garfield.

28. Santa Claus: Home-Grown Hero of the Hudson Valley

WERE YOU AWARE THAT SANTA CLAUS WAS BORN ALONG THE BANKS of the Hudson? While it's true that his ancestry is rooted in the Old World, the jolly, red-coated gift-giver we know today is strictly a product of regional writers and artists.

It all started in 1809 when Washington Irving published his *History of New York*, a tongue-in-cheek account of the city when it was under Dutch rule and known as New Amsterdam. Although of Scottish parentage, Irving's childhood was spent in Manhattan and the surrounding Hudson Valley, where the Dutch influence was still strong, and he grew up absorbing their traditions. Among these was a deep regard for St. Nicholas. Not only had a figurehead of St. Nicholas decorated the *Goede Vrouw* which had brought the first Dutch settlers safely to New Amsterdam, but the holy man was considered the protector of the city and the settlers' first church was named for him. All this in addition to a belief in St. Nicholas bringing gifts to good children on December 5, the eve of the day set aside to honor him.

That belief was grounded in the most popular of the many legends concerning the generosity of St. Nicholas, who was no myth but a very real man. As a bishop in Asia Minor during the fourth century, Nicholas heard about an impoverished nobleman who could not provide a dowery for the eldest of his three daughters. Knowing that a dowerless girl had little hope of marriage, Nicholas crept up to the nobleman's house late one night and, undetected, tossed a bag of gold coins through the daughter's bedroom window. According to one version of the story, the money landed in a stocking that had been hung near the fireplace to dry—which resulted in the custom of hangng up stockings in hopes of receiving presents. (Among the Dutch, wooden shoes were substituted.)

The nobleman's daughter subsequently married well, and Nicholas repeated his secret generosity when the second girl came of age. However, when the third daughter was ready for marriage, her father was waiting when the bishop threw the bag of gold through the window. Nicholas asked to remain anonymous, but the grateful nobleman couldn't resist telling others, and eventually Nicholas became known as the patron saint of marriageable girls. The three bags of gold, it might be added, were usually depicted in paintings and statues of Nicholas, and when early bankers in northern Italy adopted him for their patron saint, they hung a representative trio of golden balls over their doorways—a symbol still seen in pawnbrokers' signs.

Nicholas also became the patron saint of sailors, due to several miracles he is said to have performed that saved men on the high seas, so it was not unusual that the Dutch chose his likeness for the *Goede Vrouw's* figurehead. What was unusual was the way Washington Irving described that figurehead. Instead of the traditional image of a patriarchal St. Nicholas in long bishop's robes, Irving had the ship's figurehead sporting "a low, broad-brimmed hat, a huge pair of Flemish trunk hose, and a pipe that reached to the end of the bow-sprit." That Dutch-attired figurehead of Nicholas, he further added, was placed in front of the first church the settlers built in New Amsterdam, where "divers miracles" were "wrought by the mighty pipe which the saint held in his mouth; a whiff of which was a sovereign cure for an indigestion."

Nor did the fun-loving Irving abandon such flights of fancy. Throughout *The History of New York*, in which he mentioned Nicholas dozens of times, the author drew a playful portrait of the saint, who went "riding over the tops of trees in the self-same wagon wherein he brings his yearly presents to children." And so began the Americanization of St. Nicholas or, more properly, the emergence of Santa Claus.

The name Santa Claus derives from the Dutch "Sanct Herr 'Cholas" (Saint Sir Nicholas), which the New Amsterdamers soon shortened to "Sinter Claes" or "Sinter Klas." Then when the British took over the city in 1664, the name was anglicized to "Santa Claus," and became associated with the English "Father Christmas" figure. Aspects from other nationalities crept in too, including the German equivalent of Kris Kringle, and in time Santa's visit was switched to Christmas Eve, although many Dutch families held on to the December 5 date well into the 1800s.

Santa's mode of travel was changing as well—a subject addressed by author James Kirke Paulding, who was born in 1778 at Great Nine Partners in what is now Putnam County, and lived most of his long life in the region. In his humorous sketch called "The Revenge of Santa Claus," Paulding recounted that "Some say he comes down the chimneys in a little Jersey wagon; others, that he wears a pair of Holland skates," while still others "maintain that he has lately adopted a locomotive, and was once actually detected on the Albany railroad . . . .My own opinion is that his favorite mode of travelling is on the [Erie] canal, the motion and speed of which aptly comport with the philosophic dignity of his character."

Oddly enough, Paulding didn't mention Santa's oldest known means of transportation (by foot, or on the back of a white horse), or the reindeer that had appeared two decades earlier in an 1823 poem attributed to Clement Clarke Moore called "A Visit From St. Nicholas"—a poem already famous when Paulding wrote his sketch. It's possible, of course, that Moore's "right jolly old elf" didn't jibe with Paulding's idea of a more dignified Santa. Whatever the case, Paulding's sketch is little known today, while Moore's poem became one of the major molders of our modern Santa Claus image.

Born in the Chelsea section of Manhattan in 1779, Clement Clarke Moore seems an unlikely candidate for authoring a whimsical poem, since he was a Hebrew scholar and a professor at the General Theological Seminary, plus something of a curmudgeon. But Moore was a loving father too, and in 1822 he supposedly penned "A Visit From St. Nichlas" as a Christmas gift for his children. Tradition tells of a guest being present the night he read it to the youngsters, and she enjoyed it so much that she copied down the rhyming couplets. The following year, she sent it to the Troy *Sentinel,* where it was published anonymously on December 23.

Moore's authorship was soon made known, though the scholar hmself did not immediately acknowledge the poem, perhaps because he felt it conflicted with his role as a teacher of the Bible. Indeed, the poem—better known to some people for its opening line, "'Twas the Night Before Christmas"—makes no mention of the nativity, and is totally non-religious in nature. In time, however, Moore did include it in a collection of his poetry, and even discussed its genesis.

Reportedly, Moore had heard stories about St. Nicholas from an old friend—a white-bearded, rotund Dutchman who possibly served as model for the poem's round-bellied Santa with beard "as white as snow." But other influences surely came into play, including Washington Irving's *History of New York*, which may even have been responsible for the names of two of the reindeer in Moore's poem. For "Donder" and "Blitzen" sound very much like the common Dutch expletive "dunder and blixem," loosely translated as "thunder and lightning" and mentioned by Irving, although Moore could have heard this oath elsewhere, considering he was a New Yorker.

That Moore might even have taken credit for a poem penned by some-one else has been the contention of various researchers down through the years, with Dutch-descended Henry Livingston Jr. the most favored candi-date. A poet and jurist as well as entrepreneur and the father of a dozen chil-dren, Livingston certainly had the kind of style and whimsical humor seen in "A Visit From St. Nicholas." But so far no concrete proof has been prof-fered that he composed the poem, which had first appeared five years before his death at the age of eighty in 1828. (The site of Livingston's home can be seen on the grounds of Locust Grove, the Samuel Morse Historic Site on South Road—Route 9—in Poughkeepsie.)

Clement Clarke Moore has also been credited with the first use of a rein-deer-drawn sled for Santa Claus, but the idea did not originate with him. A year before he wrote his poem, the 1821 edition of *The Children's Friend* was published in New York, featuring pictures of "Santeclaus," along with a verse about his sleigh and reindeer, and Moore may have come across this when reading to his children. As for his elf-like Santa, it is possible that the schol-ar knew of Nisse, the Norwegian nickname for Saint Nicholas, and a word that means "imp."

Whatever its sources, and despite its title, "A Visit From St. Nicholas" presented a new and thoroughly American Santa Claus—a lovable Christmas character who soon became the country's most familiar folk hero. St. Nicholas, it should be noted, did not entirely disappear from the scene. As mentioned earlier, nineteenth-century Dutch families continued to cele-brate his feast day, and in 1835 Washington Irving organized a St. Nicholas Society. Members—primarily Hudson Valley residents descended from early Dutch settlers—met on December 6 each year to follow old Dutch customs, including the smoking of long clay pipes. And even today St. Nicholas Day is celebrated at Philipsburg Manor, an eighteenth-century Dutch dwelling off Route 9 in North Tarrytown, maintained by Historic Hudson Valley and open to the public.

Following the publication of Moore's poem in 1823, American artists began devoting more attention to Santa Claus, including John Gadsby Chapman (best remembered for his Pocahontas painting in the Rotunda of the nation's Capitol), who in 1847 showed Santa dressed in a fur-trimmed outfit and high boots. Other artists, though, followed their own instincts or Old World ideas, and it was not until 1863, when Thomas Nast began contributing a series of Christmas drawings to the New York *Harper's Weekly*, that the pictorial image of the American Santa was for-malized.

Most Americans may think of Santa Claus as described in an 1822 poem attributed to Clement Clarke Moore. But did the verses really come from the pen of a Hudson Valley father of twelve? (Thomas Nast's "Coming of Santa Claus" via Dover Publications)

Nast had come to New York as a six-year-old boy from Bavaria, where Pelze-Nichol (Nicholas with Fur) brought gifts to children. This, plus the image evoked by Moore's poem and the work of other artists, influenced Nast in his drawings of Santa's fur-trimmed clothes, and he was to supply *Harper's Weekly* with a Santa drawing nearly every holiday season for the next twenty years. There were Santas making toys, decorating a Christmas tree, flying across the housetops in a sleigh, and even looking through a spyglass to discover which children deserved presents, but Nast's most memorable contribution to the figure of Santa Claus was to add an aura of patriotism.

With the Civil War still raging in 1864, Nast's Christmas drawing for the cover of *Harper's Weekly* that year showed Santa wearing a stars-and-stripes suit as he handed out presents to Union soldiers. And in another Nast illustration, a Union soldier unexpectedly arriving home on Christmas furlough catches Santa in the act of leaving gifts for the family. But after Appomattox, Nast's Santa didn't take sides, except for keeping a list of who had been good or bad—a touch the artist included in one of his later Christmas illustrations. Nast also is credited with inventing the letter to Santa Claus, though he may only have been reflecting a trend already in progress, and one still very popular, as harried postmasters attest every holi-day season.

The most favored of all Santa letters, however, was not written to, but about him—the poignant query of an eight-year-old, upper Manhattan girl named Virginia O'Hanlon, who in 1897 wrote to the editor of the New York *Sun,* asking whether there really was a Santa Claus. The *Sun's* Francis P. Church replied affirmatively in a moving editorial that was annually reprinted in the newspaper for many years thereafter, and which said in part that Santa "exists as certainly as love and generosity and devotion exist."

The simple beauty of Church's words later found echo in a little-known incident that occurred in our region during the dark days of the Great Depression. It seems that a destitute man and wife were facing a dreary Christmas, with no gifts for their six children, and very little to eat. On Christmas Eve, the family retired early, the children hopeful, but the parents depressed over the disappointment they were sure they would see on the youngsters' faces the following day. They were wrong, though. When the couple opened their front door on Christmas morning, they discovered a large box sitting on the snow-covered steps. It was brim full of holiday good-ies. The astonished parents rushed outside and looked around, but saw no one. Nor were there any fresh footprints leading up to the house. Then, by chance, they glanced upward to the roof. There, in the crusted snow near the chimney, were two long grooves—just like the tracks a sleigh would make!

Practical-minded people who heard the story insisted that charitable neighbors not wanting to reveal their identity must have made the grooves with a long pole, after depositing the box of presents on the steps. But that didn't solve the mystery of the missing footprints, and by way of explanation many fok merely repeated the words of Francis Church: "Yes, Virginia, there is a Santa Claus. . . ."

29. God's Own Gardener

IT HAD BEEN MORE THAN EIGHT MONTHS SINCE THE BRITISH WERE defeated IN the Battle of New Orleans, but when a son was born in October 1815 to an Orange County nurseryman and his wife, they named the baby after the victorious American general, perhaps in the hope that their child would also rise from humble beginnings to become a national hero.

Andrew Jackson Downing did just that, though he grew up preferring pruning hooks to spears, and for awhile it looked as if he expected nothing more than to help his older brother Charles run the family's horticultural business in Newburgh.

When their father Samuel died in 1822, he left his nursery to Charles, while the education of seven-year-old Andrew was entrusted to another older brother, Dr. George Downing. Soon enough the youngster with the flashing dark-brown eyes and even brighter intellect was excelling at one of the city's primary schools—so much so that in 1829 Andrew was sent to board at the respected Montgomery Academy, located about a dozen miles west of his Newburgh home. There, in the Federal-style brick building that is now a National Historic Landmark serving as Montgomery's Village Hall on Clinton Street, Downing readily absorbed Greek and Latin as well as one seemingly prophetic course called "Drawing, Landscape and Perspective." But there was no money for him to attend college, and after a couple of years Andrew left the Academy to work at the Downing nursery near Newburgh's Broad and Liberty streets.

This decision did not coincide with his mother Eunice's belief that he'd do much better as a dry-goods clerk. She was forced to change her mind, however, when the business flourished to the point that the brothers were offering their customers over one hundred varieties of apples and even more kinds of pears. Much of this success was due to Charles' expertise, plus a surge of public interest in pomology. Yet part of it surely derived from Andrew's association with some of the region's wealthy families.

All things in nature interested Downing, so as a teenager he was wont to roam the Hudson Highlands—from Cedar Cliff on the north, to Cronomer

Hill (now an Orange County park) on
the west, and south to Plum Point (present-day Kowawese Unique Area)—observing the flora and fauna as he collected
mineral specimens. And it was on one of
these excursions that Downing encountered a fellow-collector, Baron Alois Freiherr
von Lederer, the Austrian Consul-General
in New York City, who had a summer
home in Newburgh.

The Baron took a liking to the young
naturalist, with the result that Downing was
soon socializing with the city's intelligentsia,
among them the English-born, Newburgh-
based landscape painter Raphael Hoyle.
Despite a decade's difference in their ages,
Hoyle became Downing's close friend, as
did the Armstrong family of Danskammer
Point, just north of Newburgh.

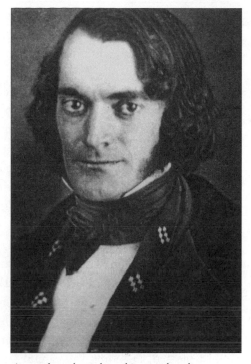

*As courtly and comely as he was talented,
Andrew Jackson Downing rewrote many of the
rules regarding regional architecture and landscape gardening during the years before his
tragic death at age 36.*

Downing was already developing ideas
as to what type of housing best suited the
Hudson Valley, and the Armstrongs' recently constructed (1834) Greek temple of a
mansion certainly didn't fit the bill, but these differences in no way dampened
their relationship. In fact, Downing's career as "America's first professional landscape architect" may have had its start when Mrs. Armstrong accepted his suggestion that a double line of locust trees be planted along the lane leading to her
many-columned mansion. (Those columns, by the way, now grace the grounds
of Storm King Art Center in the Orange County community of Mountainville,
and granite blocks salvaged from the Armstrongs' Danskammer mansion—
demolished in 1932—were used in the Center's museum building.)

Downing had a talent for verbal composition too, and before his twentieth
birthday, the *New-York Mirror* had published two of his essays extolling local
scenes. In "American Highland Scenery. Beacon Hill," he referred to Dutchess
County's Mount Beacon as being among nature's "most majestic thrones," meanwhile calling the Hudson "the prince of rivers." Then he turned his attention
westward to discuss a legendary Indian ceremonial site in "The Dans Kammer: A
Reverie in the Highlands," expressing sadness over the expulsion of the indigenous people, yet seemingly satisfied that such was the price of civilization.

How men might most contentedly reside in that civilization became one of his chief concerns, and Downing traveled up and down the river studying the architecture of the Hudson Valley, often as a guest in one of its shoreside houses.

A house that especially attracted him—albeit not solely for is architectural attributes—was Locust Grove at Fishkill Landing in what is now the city of Beacon. (This Locust Grove should not be confused with the same-named estate of inventor/painter Samuel F. B. Morse, farther upriver in Poughkeepsie, which has become a house-museum open to the public.) For the Fishkill Landing house was where Downing fell in love with the wealthy owner's daughter, Caroline DeWindt.

The house Downing loved the most, however, had to be his own Highland Gardens, the turreted Gothic villa overlooking Newburgh Bay that he designed for Caroline shortly after their wedding in June 1838. During the months of construction, the newlyweds lived with Caroline's parents at Locust Grove; Downing commuted across the Hudson each day to supervise the building, while also conducting business at the nearby nursery. He had taken over his brother Charles' interest and was free to do as he pleased, including the careful landscaping at his 6-acre estate so that the nursery was hidden from view but not the river vista to the east.

By this time, Downing had defined his own landscaping philosophy, with Highland Gardens demonstrating that such designs could be both practical and picturesque—two points that figured prominently in his *Theory and Practice of Landscape Gardening* (an abbreviation of the paragraph-long title Downing gave his first book, published in 1841). But the linchpin was his idea of a building blending perfectly with its setting—something Downing believed could be achieved on even the most modest scale, and by respecting the natural landscape as opposed to reconstructing it.

The *Theory and Practice of Landscape Gardening* was an immediate and international success, influencing a wide range of readers, among whom was author Edgar Allan Poe. A year after Downing's book appeared, Poe published a serenely lovely sketch "The Landscape Garden" (later expanded into a tale called "The Domain of Arnheim"), in which he admiringly quoted the Newburgh horticulturist. In addition, Downing's inspiration can also be seen in "Landor's Cottage," Poe's 1849 sequel to the two earlier stories. As for a more material approbation, in December 1845 newspapers were reporting how "the Queen of Holland" had sent Downing "a magnificent ruby ring encircled by three rows of fine diamonds in acknowledgment of the pleasure she had derived from" reading his "most charming book on landscape gardening."

Highland Gardens, the turreted Gothic villa that Andrew Jackson Downing built for his bride, demonstrated his belief that such designs could be both picturesque and practical.

Downing soon followed his first book with *Cottage Residences* (1842) and then *The Architecture of Country Houses* (1850). As the names of the volumes indicate, Downing expanded his interest in architecture, designing a number of Hudson Valley estates, such as Springside, the never-completed summer home of Matthew Vassar in Poughkeepsie. (Now a National Historic Landmark open to the public, Springside is located off Academy Street in the southwestern part of the city.) The grounds of Blithewood—presently owned Bard College in Annandale—were Downing's work as well. He was also a staunch supporter of the movement to site new insane asylums on large peaceful tracts, where it was thought patients would be subjected to less stress than in an urban environment. Accordingly, he designed landscapes for state facilities at both Utica, New York, and Trenton, New Jersey.

One design that was *not* Downing's work, though at first attributed to him, was the village of Dearman—now Irvington—in Westchester County. Hoping to attract buyers to their uninspired, gridiron-like plat of small same-size lots, developers of Dearman—without Downing's prior knowledge or permission—dared to illustrate their offering maps with engravings from *Cottage Residences,* as if Downing endorsed their scheme. Nothing could have been further from the truth; the Dearman plan went against everything Downing felt necessary for suburban living and in an article called "Our County Villages" he witheringly condemned all such crammed developments.

The aforementioned article appeared in *The Horticulturist,* a popular periodical that Downing began editing in 1846, a year after publishing a book on *The Fruits and Fruit Trees of America.* The editorship was a job he thoroughly enjoyed, for he was ever the nurseryman, championing native plants, urging the establishment of agricultural colleges, and even linking landscape beautification to patriotism. Indeed, Downing had already been acknowledged in Asa Gray and John Torrey's monumental study of the *Flora of North America,* and Torrey (whose Rockland county home is now part of the Lamont-Doherty Geological Observatory in Palisades) later named a newly discovered plant species in Downing's honor.

Of all his many talents, managing money wasn't one of them, and in 1846 Downing found himself in such financial straits that he had to sell his nursery. Even worse, his father-in-law accused him of fraud—a charge that alienated Caroline Downing from her parents, and resulted in a lawsuit that dragged on until April 1849, when an agreement was finally reached. According to Downing biographer David Schuyler, lawyers were confident that Downing would have won a large award if the case had gone to trial, but he was satisfied with a settlement in his favor, because it would hasten the reuniting of his wife with her family.

That Caroline had steadfastly remained at Downing's side throughout the long ordeal was not surprising since they seemed to share a singular devotion to one another. They made a striking couple too: the quiet and courtly Downing, tall and handsome, with wavy dark hair barely brushing his shoulders, and gentle Caroline, "charming, merry and amiable," with eyes "as blue as . . . Swedish violets."

The description comes from the Swedish novelist Fredrika Bremer, who in 1849 stayed with the Downings at Highland Gardens before embarking on a tour of the United States. The two writers had become friends via an exchange of letters, and shared similar views regarding women. A staunch feminist, Bremer applauded Downing's concern for the well-being of women, as seen in his determination to wage "a successful war against perpetual *stitchery.*"

He was equally committed to being a perfect host, and the 48-year-old Bremer was treated to a round of socializing—from a picnic atop Mount Beacon to a party at Blithewood that culminated in a moonlight sail past South Cruger Island (presently part of Tivoli Bay Estuarine Research Reserve in Dutchess County), where "ruins" had been built to house Mayan artifacts brought back to America by explorer John Lloyd Stephens. Downing also took Bremer downriver to dine at Nevis, a Westchester County mansion today owned by Columbia University, but then the home of Alexander Hamilton's son James. There Bremer basked in the company of elderly writer Washington Irving, who lived nearby at Sunnyside (a National Historic Landmark now open to the public). The only place Downing would not take her, respite Bremer's expressed interest in it, was Manhattan's infamous Five Points slum—that simply wasn't his idea of civilized society.

After Bremer took off on her American tour, in 1850 Downing turned his attention to a trip of his own: a six-week sojourn in England and France, during which he would study estates, obtain illustrations for *The Horticulturist*, and hopefully find an associate for his own burgeoning design business. He had long been working with Alexander Jackson Davis, who did many of the drawings for Downing's *Cottage Residences* as well as the *Architecture of Country Houses*, and today is honored as architect of the Knoll (the original name of Lyndhurst, a National Historic Site in Tarrytown open to the public). But Downing and Davis apparently could not—or would not—agree on an official partnership, so Downing was forced to look elsewhere.

It was in London that he discovered Calvert Vaux, a 26-year-old landscape architect who was so impressed by Downing that he readily pulled up roots and came to America. Their first cooperative effort was a new two-room office at Highland Gardens—much needed space, considering that within two years Downing was so besieged by clients, he signed on still another English-born architect, 24-year-old Frederick Clarke Withers.

Among those clients was the U.S. government, for Downing had been appointed by President Millard Fillmore to design and oversee the construction of a "public grounds" around the Capitol in Washington, D.C. He also had been campaigning for a spacious public recreation area in New York City—what was to become Central Park, the country's first landscaped public park. But Downing was not destined to see the completion of either project, as was eerily augured during a sail on the Hudson one evening in June 1852.

According to the noted historian/folklorist Carl Carmer, it was during a party at Highland Gardens that Downing rowed his guests across the river to the Verplanck house in Beacon, where they were shown the room in which the Society of the Cincinnati had been formed at the close of the Revolutionary War. (Known today as Mount Gulian, the Verplanck home is open to the public.) While on the water, Downing related how he used to swim across the river and back as a boy, that he thought he might even be able to do it still; then strangely adding that if he had a choice in the way he was to die, it would be by drowning.

Downing was due to direct construction of a villa at Newport, Rhode Island, that summer, so on July 28 he embarked from Newburgh landing on the *Henry Clay*, bound for New York City. Accompanying him were his wife Caroline, her mother Mrs. Peter DeWindt with two of her children, and a widowed friend named Matilda Wadsworth—all of them looking forward to the downriver run on one of the Hudson's newest and fastest steamboats.

What they didn't know was that the *Henry Clay* had been in a hell-bent-for-leather race with the *Armenia* ever since the two steamers left Albany earlier in the day—a contest which should never have taken place in view of the fact that the rivalry between the crews was well known, and an agreement had been made to keep the two vessels on different schedules to prevent any racing. However, on July 28 fate intervened. Another steamboat, the *Reindeer*, had been slated to leave Albany at the same time as the *Henry Clay*, but when it was determined that the *Reindeer* needed repair, the *Armenia* replaced her.

Shortly after 7 a.m., the two sleek steamers started speeding down the Hudson, black clouds and red-hot cinders billowing from their smokestacks. Neither boat stopped for passengers at several landings below Albany. Then at the Columbia County city of Hudson, the *Henry Clay* docked to pick up passengers, while the *Armenia* shot ahead—a lead she maintained past Catskill. But at Bristol the *Henry Clay* caught up with her. Side by side, their throbbing white-painted hulls cut through the ebbing Hudson until approaching Kingston. There the *Henry Clay* careened into the *Armenia* in an attempt to strand her on some shoals. All that was accomplished was the splintering of both boats' wooden side guards, but it was sufficient for the *Armenia's* captain to order a temporary lay-by, during which he relieved pressure on the overheated engine by "blowing steam."

Later reports revealed that no such safety measures as venting steam occurred on the *Henry Clay*, even though she remained far ahead of the *Armenia* for the rest of the trip, including docking time at Poughkeepsie. While there, a number of frightened passengers disembarked, preferring to continue their journey south by train, rather than rely on the assurances of the steamer's owner Thomas Collyer that "There is no danger whatever."

Nor did there seem to be any peril when Andrew Jackson Downing and his party boarded the *Henry Clay* at Newburgh. With the *Armenia* now many miles behind, the race was surely over—or was it? For some reason the *Henry Clay* maintained its hellish speed, and it wasn't long until one passenger found the deck so hot near the boiler room that he had to cover his face as he passed. But still there as no letup.

Then around 2:45 in the afternoon, as the *Henry Clay* passed Yonkers, there came the horrifying cry of "Fire!" At first passengers were assured the blaze was out—something quickly disproved by screams below decks and flames that shot skyward from the miships boiler area. A bucket brigade was formed. The effort proved futile.

Convinced the fire was out of control, the steamer's pilot spun his steering wheel sharply to the left, aiming for the east bank of the Hudson, near where State Assemblyman Russell Smith's estate was located in Riverdale. The pilot's intent was to beach the vessel bow-first so that passengers might have the best chance of reaching dry land. But things didn't turn out that way.

The *Henry Clay* was going so fast when she struck the riverbank, a few passengers on the bow were literally thrown ashore, while others landed in the water. Even worse, having been told to go to the back of the boat so their weight would help elevate the bow as it grounded, many passengers were now caught between the worsening midships fire and the deeper water off the *Henry Clay's* stern. And most of them couldn't swim.

Downing was among those who could. After calmly giving instructions to his family, he proceeded to throw wooden deckchairs in the water to serve as makeshift rafts, then jumped in to help whomever he could. When last seen alive, he was struggling to support the widowed Mrs. Wadsworth. She did not survive, nor did Mrs. DeWindt, whereas Caroline Downing and the two DeWindt children made it to shore. As for the heroic Downing, his body was finally found the following day, when it was laid in the long line of bough-covered bodies along the Hudson shore.

Whatever corpses remaining unclaimed or unidentified were buried at St. John's Cemetery on Saw Mill River Road in Yonkers, where a broken column of white marble memorializes their passing. But the majority of the estimated hundred victims of the tragedy lie in various graveyards throughout the region. Downing's remains, though at first interred at Newburgh's Old Towne Cemetery on South Street, were later reburied in an aboveground sepulcher—one end poignantly inscribed "Drowned"—at Cedar Hill Cemetery off Route 9W in the Orange County community of Middle Hope.

Within three months of his death at age thirty-six, Downing's dream house—his Highland Gardens—was auctioned off, and what was considered by many to be the best example of his work was remodeled by the new owner. The house changed hands steadily over the next half-century, suffering desuetude along the way, so that in 1920 its condition was so parlous that it sold for a mere $100 and subsequently was demolished. Only a small part of it sur-

This fanciful chimney was rescued during the demolition of Andrew Jackson Downing's Hudson-shore home, and is now in the collection of the Historical Society of Newburgh Bay and the Highlands.

vives: an ornamental chimney which can be viewed at the Historical Society of Newburgh Bay and the Highlands, on Newburgh's Montgomery Street. Nearby are two Downing-designed buildings—the City Club at 120 Grand Street, and the David Moore house at 55 Broad Street—while the historical marker near a Downing-like villa on Montgomery Street records his influence on the work of his disciples, Calvert Vaux and Frederick Clarke Withers.

Still another architect profoundly influenced by Downing was Frederick Law Olmsted, whose articles on parks first appeared in *The Horticulturist*, and who joined Calvert Vaux in submitting the winning design for New York's Central Park—a commission Downing surely would have been awarded had he lived. Both Vaux and Olmsted freely acknowledged their debt to Downing, and over the years they sought to stir public interest in some kind of memorial to the man who had been deemed "the apostle of taste"—first a memorial for Central Park (1860), and later (1882) for Downing's public grounds plan in Washington, D.C. Eventually a large vase similar to one that graced the lawn at Highland Gardens was installed on the grounds of the Smithsonian Insituion, with part of the inscription recalling that Downing had been "born and lived and died on the Hudson River."

Easily, the greatest tribute of all, however, was initiated in 1887 when Olmsted and Vaux offered to design a park gratis if the city of Newburgh would name it after Downing. Located along Robinson Avenue (Route 9W/32), between Third and South streets, the 35-acre Downing Park was completed in 1896, with a design that embraced the principles of its namesake—from a pergola-crowned scenic overlook and curving woodland walks to play areas, lush flower beds, and a Polly Pond (the latter named for the pollywogs—or tadpoles—found there in springtime).

The "apostle of taste" would well have been proud, especially so since construction of the park had been supervised by Calvert Vaux's son, who just happened to be named Downing.

30. *Ever a Pathfinder, Never a President*

A COLD WIND OFF THE TAPPAN ZEE SWEPT THE SUMMIT OF MOUNT Nebo, causing some of the assembled mourners to shiver. Not the middle-aged man in the naval officer's uniform. Seemingly unaware of the late-November chill, he stood facing east, his sad eyes seeking a familiar roofline on the distant Westchester County shore. His father had wanted to be buried within sight of the family's beloved North Tarrytown home called Pokahoe. So on this day in 1894, John C. Frémont Jr. was able to temper his grief with gratitude for the autumn-denuded trees that afforded him a far-reaching view from the cemetery high above the Rockland County village of Sparkill. But perhaps most of all, he could be thankful that after four long years of non-interment, the body of his father—America's famed and defamed Pathfinder—would finally be laid to rest.

The difficulties that delayed the burial of John Charles Frémont were typical of his star-crossed life that began on January 21, 1813 in Savannah, Georgia. It was there that his mother briefly settled after abandoning her prominent but elderly husband for a handsome if impoverished young French émigré. The runaway lovers then roamed the South, living together as man and wife. But the scandal of their illicit union followed them from town to town, just as the stigma of his bastardy shadowed their firstborn son throughout his life.

That is not to say Frémont was generally treated as a societal dreg. Far from it. His father having died when Frémont was five years old, the handsome and precocious blue-eyed lad with the black wavy hair and

Twice nominated for the presidency, and hailed as the "Great Pathfinder" for his western expeditions, General John Charles Frémont nevertheless authored his own misfortune. (National Archives photo via the Rockland County Historical Society)

winning way was befriended by some wealthy Southerners, including South Carolina statesman Joel Poinsett (for whom the ornamental plant is named). They saw to his education and eventual appoointment as a second lieutenant in the Army Corps of Topographical Engineers.

It was the eve of America's great westward expansion, and Frémont's mapping duties took him first to the Upper Mississippi plateau (1838-39), and then along the Des Moines River in Iowa Territory (1841). The latter expedition was ostensibly the brainchild of Frémont's old friend and now Secretary of War, Joel Poinsett, but the idea actually had been birthed by Thomas Hart Benton, the powerful U.S. Senator from Missouri. Unhappy about a budding romance between his favorite daughter Jessie and the charismatic explorer with "the carriage of a soldier and the face of a poet," Benton had hoped for an out-of-sight, out-of-mind solution. It didn't work. Frémont returned from his western expedition a nationally known figure, and the determined 17-year-old Jessie eloped with him on October 19, 1841.

Without his well-educated and devoted wife, it is doubtful that Frémont would have gotten as far as he did—quite definitely not on his 1843 expedition with Kit Carson to the Oregon Territory. Jessie, it seems, kept secret a War Department directive that came for Frémont canceling the trip, and she even urged her husband to hasten his departure. She also managed to ignore—at least outwardly—Frémont's weakness for women. His enemies were not so kind though, and when Frémont became the first presidential candidate of the newly formed Republican Party in 1856, stories of his indiscretions were bandied about.

By that time, Frémont had completed five major Western expeditions and was hailed as the "Columbus of the Plains" or the "Great Pathfinder" primarily for mapping such essential immigrant routes as the Oregon Trail. Lesser known but also of great importance were his studies of the region's geology, flora and fauna, with the famed botanist John Torrey of Palisades in Rockland County authenticating the plant specimens Frémont collected. (Incidentally, Frémont named the California Torrey pine after the botanist.) Frémont had managed to become a millionaire as well, mainly due to gold discovered on land he owned in California—a state he had helped to create, then served as one of its first senators.

Campaign opponents in 1856 had a field day finding fault with those California connections, including Frémont's part in the Sacramento Valley's 1846 Bear Flag Revolt, and his 1847-48 court-martial following a jurisdictional dispute with General Stephen Kearny. The mud-slinging didn't end there either. Frémont was additionally accused of abandoning helpless men during a mid-winter mountain expedition that resulted in cannibalism, and of course there were nasty references to his illegitimacy. But most of his biographers believe the major factor in Frémont's loss to Democratic candidate James Buchanan was his stand against slavery.

Never once wavering in his belief that slavery was wrong, five years later when he was appointed a general in the Union Army's Western Department during the Civil War, Frémont issued his own emancipation proclamation—a full 16 months before Abraham Lincoln's edict. Needless to say, this didn't endear Frémont to the President, and his premature pronouncement may even have had something to do with his Manhattan mansion at 21 West 19 Street being marked for burning during the July 1863 draft riots in New York City. (Some rioters feared that freed slaves would flood the job market, resulting in unemployment for draftees returning from the war.) On the other hand, Frémont's anti-slavery action was applauded by abolitionists like New York newspaperman Horace Greeley, who in May 1864 joined with other Republican Party dissidents to nominate Frémont again for the presidency. The Republican Party was thus split between the Pathfinder and the incumbent President Lincoln, assuring almost certain victory for Democratic candidate George McClellan. That was enough to convince Frémont to step aside in favor of Lincoln, since McClellan "had declared in effect for the restoration of the Union with slavery." And so it was that Abraham Lincoln won his tragic second term.

The end of the Civil War found the Frémonts at their newly purchased country home overlooking the Hudson in the Westchester County community of North Tarrytown. Covering more than 100 acres northwest of Sleepy Hollow Cemetery and boasting a many-gabled gray-stone mansion set at the end of a winding drive through a walnut grove, the estate was called Pokahoe. (Spellings vary, but the name must come from Pockerhoe, which is what Indians called the area where the nearby Pocantico River empties into the Hudson at present-day Kingsland Point Park.)

Of the many places the Frémonts had lived during their long marriage, they were probably happiest at Pokahoe, with Jessie calling it "our true home" in an 1865 letter, and delighting in the fact that their two sons could attend school only a dozen miles away at the prestigious Peekskill Academy. Three years later John Charles Jr. (called Charley) was accepted at the Naval Academy in Annapolis, and eventually rose to the rank of admiral, while his younger brother Francis P. (Frank) went on to West Point. The Frémonts' only other child to survive infancy was firstborn Elizabeth (Lily), who helped her mother manage the plantation-like Pokahoe.

The Frémont Fountain along North Broadway in Sleepy Hollow replaced the natural spring where the General refreshed himself during walks near his Pokahoe home.

Despite his wealth and lavishly appointed home, Frémont was no sybarite. He dressed modestly, ate sparingly, drank little, smoked not at all, and when queried about his preferences promptly listed "old garments, old books, old friends." And although the family might winter at their Manhattan town house and spend part of the summer at Saratoga Springs or some other fashionable resort, Pokahoe remained a refuge where a young house guest named Nellie Haskell observed, "The general . . . usually read quietly or took evening walks with Mrs. Frémont." At other times, he enjoyed "long rides through the woods and along the post roads," frequently stopping to refresh himself at a spring along North Broadway—a spot later chosen by William Rockefeller for the fountain he erected in Frémont's memory. (The fountain is on the east side of the road just north of the entrance to Sleepy Hollow Cemetery.)

If at all possible, Frémont avoided late hours and large social functions, opting instead for the simple pleasures of entertaining house guests and listening to what he called "home-made music." Nellie Haskell recalled that he also liked "to play chess or chat with the neighbors, the Phelpses, Schuylers, Aspinwalls, or Beechers, who dropped in often." Their host, however, was frequently away on business.

Intrigued by the vast potential of trains ever since 1836 when as a 23-year-old he helped survey a route from South Carolina to Ohio, Frémont was inevitably caught up in the post-Civil War boom in railroad building. He unwisely invested his whole fortune, only to lose it all, along with his reputation. Accused of selling railroad bonds under false pretenses, Frémont was subsequently shown to be more careless than corrupt, but his life was a shambles. The Frémonts were forced to sell off their possessions, with Pokahoe being one of the hardest to part with, and late in 1875 they moved into a rented house on Manhattan's Madison Avenue that Jessie jokingly dubbed "Poverty Flat." It was no laughing matter though, and when their situation continued its downhill slide despite Jessie's newfound career as an author, President Rutherford B. Hayes came to the rescue by appointing Frémont territorial governor of Arizona in 1878.

Frémont was about as good a governor as he was a railroad financier, and in October 1883 he was pressured into resigning his post. The family then moved to Suffern in Rockland County, where Frémont renewed his friendship with railroad man William H. Whiton of Piermont. It was during one of his visits to the Whiton house—almost directly across the Tappan Zee from Pokahoe—that Frémont expressed a wish to be buried within sight of his old home. And Whiton recalled that remark nearly a decade later when word reached him of Frémont's sudden death in a New York City boarding-house on July 13, 1890.

Ironically, the future had only recently begun to look brighter for the Frémonts, who were then living in California. Three months earlier, Frémont had been awarded an Army pension long denied him, and he had come East on business. Also wanting to honor a promise to place a birthday bouquet on the grave of a friend's child, he headed out to a cemetery in Brooklyn, even though the weather was torrid. That night, Frémont became violently ill. A doctor was summoned, then a telegraph sent to the nearest relative, John Jr., in Ossining. Frémont's son soon arrived from his Westchester County home, but there was little that could be done to save a 77-year-old man suffering from peritonitis. The Pathfinder died a few hours later.

With Jessie still in California, Frémont's body was placed in the Trinity Church vault at 135th Street in Manhattan until burial arrangements could be made—a seemingly simple task, especially since William H. Whiton had offered a mountaintop plot in the Rockland County Cemetery near his home, and Jessie had accepted. Yet after the body was transferred to the Rockland Cemetery vault, it remained there for nearly four years while various factions debated a suitable monument! Finally in November 1894, at Jessie's request, Frémont's remains were interred atop Mount Nebo, even though the design of the monument was still undecided. Nor had one been installed by 1903, when Jessie's ashes were buried beside her husband.

It as not until 1911 that a graceful granite monolith—courtesy of New York State—crowned the site, with a large plaque on the back of the monument listing Frémont's numerous accomplishments. But for many people the best summation can be found at the entrance to Rockland Cemetery, where in 1989 a boulder was placed bearing Jessie Benton's Frémont's brief tribute to her husband:

*"From the ashes of his campfires
have sprung cities."*

31. Man of a Million Words

I T WAS MORE THAN 40 SPINE-JOLTING MILES FROM NEW HAVEN TO
Katonah, and the raw autumn wind smelled of snow, but 70-year-old
Noah Webster wasn't about to be deterred from this long-awaited journey. Nor was Chief Justice John Jay overly surprised when a carriage arrived
at his Westchester County home later on that cold November day in 1828,
and Webster climbed down carrying a pair of brand-new books. For Jay
knew just how determined his friend could be—a determination which had
allowed Webster to accomplish such seemingly impossible tasks as the two-
volume dictionary he now presented to the retired jurist.

That determination had been evident almost from the time Webster had
been born into a family of Connecticut farmers on October 16, 1758.
Although named for his father, Noah was the youngest of three sons, and
hence without hope of inheriting any land in those days of primogeniture. He
probably wouldn't have wanted the farm anyway, for as he later told George
Washington ". . . books and business will ever be my princpal pleasure."

What Webster wanted was an eduction, and by the time he was ready
for college in 1774, the 16-year-old had convinced his less-than-wealthy
father to fund four years at Yale by mortgaging the farm. Webster went on
to study law and by 1781 he had passed the bar exams. But with the
Revolution still raging, job prospects were poor, so he decided to start a
school, having previously tried his hand at teaching as a means of supporting his own studies. He had developed definite ideas about education too,
and four essays he wrote at this time demonstrate how decidedly modern was
his thinking in that "The pupil should have nothing to discourage him,"
especially not the then-championed practice of corporal punishment. Small
classes, attention to student health, availability of books, qualified teachers
and reward incentives were other principles Webster would fight for the rest
of his life—precepts he brought along with him to Sharon, Connecticut,
where he opened a school on July 1, 1781.

Located just over the Westchester County border, Sharon had become a
haven for several influential patriot families forced to flee their Manhattan
homes when the British captured New York City. They welcomed the well-

educated new schoolmaster, with his similar politics and prior service in the militia, and Webster soon had a full class, including three daughters of Robert Gilbert Livingston. None of these young ladies was responsible for Webster's eventual decision to close down his successful school, though a case of unrequited love seems to have been what caused him to leave Sharon and retreat to the Orange County village of Goshen in the spring of 1782.

Why Goshen? In addition to it being far enough away from the scene of his failed romance, the busy county seat of government offered employment to the young lawyer-turned-teacher. Moreover, Webster was no stranger to the region, having penned some pro-American articles that had appeared in Dutchess County's Fishkill-based *New-York Packet* the preceding winter. And earlier in the Revolution, inspired by the essays of Thomas Paine, he had joined his father's regiment when those Connecticut volunteers marched up the east bank of the Hudson, hoping to halt British General John Burgoyne's advance southward.

Part of present-day Goshen Town Hall, the 18th century Farmers Hall Academy was where Noah Webster taught school and, in his spare time, compiled his famous "blue-back speller."

"Gentleman Johnny" had surrendered at Saratoga before the Nutmeggers drew near, but not before they witnessed the burning of Kingston on October 16, 1777—a sight which must have been in Webster's mind when he later wrote of the "terror and destruction" experienced on that march. Even worse, there came a time when "half the soldiers were sick with dysentery and fever, so that the very air was infected."

Webster's description of his arrival in Goshen was similarly somber: with no more than 75¢ in his pocket and initially knowing not a soul, for several months he "suffered extreme despression and gloomy forebodings." But like its biblical namesake, Goshen proved providential. Webster was soon teaching at the Farmers Hall Academy—what is now part of the Town Hall on Webster Avenue—and in his spare time compiling the volume that has been called "the best-seling book ever written by an American."

Now popularly known as the "blue-back speller" because of the paper cover contractually required on most of the more than 400 editions produced during his lifetime, the book was the first in Webster's projected three-part series titled *A Grammatical Institute of the English Language*. The speller was to be followed by a reader and a grammar, with which Webster hoped to introduce a new system of education. It was a system designed to standardize the language and foster American nationality, while freeing the fledgling republic from its cultural reliance on Europe—most especially England. For Webster believed that the American language was—and must ever be—distinct from British English. And it is largely through his efforts that today the two tongues officially differ so markedly in such things as spelling and syllabification. For example, he eliminated the "u" in words like "favour," substituted an "s" for the British "c" in such words as "defence," dropped the "k" from words like "musick," and instead of "re" used "er" in "theatre" and similarly ending words. When it came to suffixes like "tion" and "sion," Webster thought they should be treated as a single syllable instead of two; in fact, he felt that dividing any word into syllables (syllabification) should depend on pronunciation, rather than derivation (the latter being the British method).

There is a local tradition that tells of Webster being aided in the preparation of his speller by one of his Goshen students. Reptuedly Hezekiah Howell possessed such a "good voice" that Webster had the lad "give him the sound of the different vowels." Webster also is said to have asked the pupils' parents what they thought of his ideas, and was encouraged by their "universal approval." However, the only help that can be firmly documented is an August 1782 letter from Henry Wisner, whose children attended the Farmers Hall Academy. Wisner wrote that Webster had "taught a grammar School . . . much to the Satisfaction of his Employers," and "is now doing business in the liturary way which will in [the] oppinion of good Judges be of service to postarity." Hence, "any favours which you may do him will be Serving the public. . . ." (Spelling and capitalization follow the original.) As a respected statesman and signer of the Declaration of Independence, Wisner's words carried weight, and in the late summer of 1782 when Webster set out to secure copyright protection for his aborning book, Wisner's letter of recommendation opened some important doors for him. It might also be pointed out that in the new nation authors did not enjoy the copyright privileges now guaranteed by the federal government. Webster's efforts begun on his own behalf in 1782 became a campaign for the rights of all authors, and he is championed as the "father of copyright legislation in America."

The spring of 1783 found Webster leaving Goshen for a home in Hartford, Connecticut, where history was made that October with the publication of his speller—price 14 pence. (The grammar book and reader followed in 1784 and 1785 respectively.) Much more than just an ABCer, the little book (a mere 119 pages) was filled with simple yet fundamental maxims still familiar today: "He that lies down with dogs must rise up with fleas," "When wine is in, wit is out," and "Let not your tongue cut your throat," to quote only three. Fables were added in subsequent editions, including that old chestnut about the boy stealing apples (not original to Webster): an old man first politely asks the boy to come down from the apple tree, then he pelts the thief with soft sods, and finally gets the boy to mind hm by hurling rocks at him, the moral being "If good words and gentle means will not reclaim the wicked, they must be dealt with in a more severe manner." (One can only wonder how that would go down in today's society.)

By and large the speller received commendatory reviews, but Webster didn't mind unfavorable ones either so long as they stirred up publicity. Indeed, he cannily perceived the value of promotion, and presented copies to whomever he felt might help his book sell, in addition to writing "puffs" that he submitted to newspapers, using a variety of pseudonyms. News of the speller thus spread quickly, and in the autumn of 1783, when Colonel Timothy Pickering heard about it while serving as Quartermaster General with the Continental Army then encamped at New Windsor in Orange County, he ordered a copy, for he was concerned about the education of his son while he was away at war. So taken was he by the text that Pickering reportedly stayed up all night perusing the speller, whose author he later lauded as "ingenious," saying Webster wrote "from his own experience as a schoolmaster as well as the best authorities; and the time will come when no authority, as an English grammarian, will be superior. . . ."

After 1783, Webster never did return to the Hudson Valley for any extended stay, although regional threads run through the remaining fabric of his life. Some are mere snippets of local color, like Webster being warned in 1786 that he wouldn't make any money lecturing in Albany because the resident Dutch regarded the English language as "disagreeable." But there is also the long strong strand of Webster's association with John Jay.

During the decade following the publciation of his speller, Webster learned that the reciprocal of renown is not necessarily financial reward. He attempted to augment his auctorial income by returning to teaching, then tried editing a magazine, and following his marriage in 1789 Webster even went back briefly to being a lawyer. Debt was still dogging him though in

1793 when he was approached about starting a Federalist newspaper—*The American Minerva*—in New York City. It was an opportunity too good to be true, for Webster's advocacy of a strong central government dovetailed perfectly with the policies of the Federalist leaders willing to put up the cash to start the newspaper. Among those men was John Jay, then Chief Justice of the U.S. Supreme Court, who settled the matter with Webster over dinner on August 16, 1793.

Their cordial relationship continued until the Chief Justice's death in 1829, much to the benefit of both men. For when there arose a public outcry over the 1794 treaty Jay negotiated with England, Webster came to his rescue by publishing a dozen essays under the pen name of "Curtius" in which he explained the terms of the agreement and allayed people's fears. And had it not been for Jay's moral—and occasionally financial—support, Webster's most monumental project might never have been completed.

Whereas his straight-backed stance, ruddy complexion and level gray eyes gave the impression of good health, Webster's constitution had been compromised by a 1777 bout with smallpox and subsequent neurological disorders. Hence, his family and friends worried when in 1807 he announced his intention to compile an unabridged *American Dictionary of the English Language*—a magnum opus which he figured would take him at least 20 years, along with the mastering of an equal number of languages.

At first John Jay tried to dissuade his friend from taking on such an ambitious task, but eventually he acquiesced to Webster's bull-dog determination, and their subsequent correspondence shows the ongoing interest of the Chief Justice—a concern that accounts for Webster's triumphant ride to Westchester County on that snowy November day in 1828. (The two-volume dictionary he delivered can be seen at the John Jay Homestead State Historic Site at 400 Route 22 in Katonah.)

Considering Webster's great contribution to this country and its language, it may seem strange that his story is not better known. Indeed, he is often confused with Daniel Webster (no relation), and few people are aware of just how much else he accomplished—from acting as the first U.S. postal inspector, to his pioneering work in such fields as demography, epidemiology and climatology—before his death in 1843. But he will never be forgotten so long as "Webster's" remains a synonym for "dictionary"—and perhaps that is the greatest homage of all.

32. The Wasp and the Bee

If perchance there comes a Bee,
A wasp shall come as well as he.

I T WAS IN JULY 1802 THAT A YOUNG EDITOR NAMED HARRY CROSWELL used that seemingly innocuous front-page rhyme to premiere his newspaper the *Wasp* in the Columbia County city of Hudson. The couplet, however, was really a challenge, and the political hornets' nest soon stirred up not only resulted in one of the country's most important trials, but also factored into its most infamous duel.

To set the stage, it's necessary to turn back in time to another famous court case—the 1735 trial of John Peter Zenger, a printer whose newspaper accounts of a Westchester County election got him indicted for seditious libel. The common conception that the Zenger case firmly established freedom of speech and press isn't correct. Whereas the New York City jury may have returned a verdict of "not guilty," that did not alter the law. Seditious libel continued to be defined as the broadcasting of any information unfavorable to the government, *whether it was true or not.*

Despite the passage of the Sedition Act of 1798, plus punishments for libel of fines, imprisonment, or both, journalists remained largely undeterred. For the post-Revolutionary period was one of a

A simple rhyming couplet by newspaper editor Harry Croswell was to play a part in a precedent-setting trial as well as an infamous duel.

partisan press, when practically every newspaper was the conduit of a particular political faction, and mud was slung by most. That included the country's two most powerful parties at the turn of the 18th century: the Federalists, founded by Alexander Hamilton, and the Republicans (not to be confused with the same-named party formed in 1828), headed by Thomas Jefferson.

Jefferson's election as president in 1800—with Hamilton's arch rival Aaron Burr becoming vice-president—forced the federalists to find or fund additional press coverage favorable to their cause. And no newsman was more sympathetic than Harry Croswell, who had honed a stiletto style of writing at the Greene County office of the *Catskill Packet*, then edited by his older brother Mackay.

In May 1801, 22-year-old Harry moved across the river to Hudson, where he joined Ezra Sampson and George Chittenden in publishing the *Balance and Columbian Repository*. Located on the upper floor of a Warren Street store near Second Street, the *Balance*—printed on "coarse, dingy paper, but . . . edited with ability"—began as a neutral paper. Before its first anniversary, however, with the backing of prominent local politican/attorney Elisha Williams, it became fully Federalist, refunding money to any subscribers who did not care for the switch in policy.

An avalanche of anti-Republican editorials in the *Balance* prompted local Jeffersonians to respond in kind. A Connecticut newsman named Charles Holt had recently been imprisoned and fined for libeling Alexander Hamilton, so he was easily persuaded to move to Hudson, where his pro-Republican paper, the *Bee*, could do battle with the Federalist *Balance*. Hearing this, Harry Croswell convinced the *Balance's* senior editor to let him produce a small letter-sized sheet he called the *Wasp*, and a venomous war began.

Choosing the pen name of "Robert Rusticoat"—possibly a double play on "rusticate" and the red uniform jackets worn by musicians of the Federalists' instrumental band in Hudson—Croswell embarked on a crusade to "Lash the Rascals naked through the world," as his masthead motto proclaimed. The "Rascals" of course were the Republicans, who the *Wasp* would "strive to displease, vex and torment . . ." even if it meant wading "knee deep in smut before he can meet his enemies on their own ground."

The smut heaped deeper than any insect's knee as the *Wasp* and the *Bee* attacked both local and national leaders, often at the personal peril of either editor. On the streets of Hudson, Croswell fared much better, since he stood a hefty six feet tall and could stare down even a horsewhip-wielding judge named Hagedorn, who thought a *Wasp* report of a tavern deadbeat referred to him. Holt, on the other hand, was small and crippled. When his *Bee* stuck a verbal stinger into Federalist Elisha Williams, the lawyer and some of his friends ambushed Holt on the street—a pummeling that nearly provoked a riot between the city's rival political parties.

The national scene was something else, and when the *Wasp* added to its attack on the President's policies by repeating some of the scandals surrounding him—Jefferson's sexual indiscretions, as well as his alleged subsidizing of a pamphlet slandering George Washington—Croswell was in deep trouble. By no means was the *Wasp* the only Federalist paper to be printing such things, but as Jefferson later wrote to Pennsylvania Governor Thomas McKean: "I have . . . long thought that a few prosecutions . . . would have a wholesome effect in restoring the integrity of the presses. Not a general prosecution, for that would look like persecution: but a selected one. . . ."

That the *Wasp* was one of those selected to be swatted may have had as much to do with its location as its content. Since the paper was published at Hudson, its editor would be tried for seditious libel at the county seat of Claverack—a nearby community not large enough to elicit much publicity, but where a guilty verdict would still set a precedent.

On July 11, 1803, Croswell's trial began in the courthouse that stood at what is now the intersection of Route 23B and Old Lane in the hamlet of Claverack. During the six months since he had been indicted for "deceitfully, wickedly and maliciously devising, contriving and intending . . . to detract from, scandalize, traduce, and villify" the President of the United States, Croswell had attracted an impressive—and pro bono—defense team made up in part of such legal luminaries as Columbia County's William Van Ness, the aforementioned Elisha Williams, and Abraham Van Vechten of Albany. Yet there was little hope of exonerating Croswell in what Hamilton biographer Robert A. Henrickson called "a political trial if there ever was one."

Adding weight to the prosecution's pan on the so-called scales of justice was anti-Federalist Morgan Lewis, who temporarily set aside his role as Chief Justice of the New York Supereme Court to act as trial judge. In addition, another non-Federalist, State Attorney General Ambrose Spencer, personally conducted the prosecution, instead of District Attorney Ebenezer Foote, who merely assisted. It therefore was no surprise that Croswell was denied a written copy of the indictments against him, and a defense request for a delay in order to obtain testimony from an out-of-town witness was refused on grounds that "truth of the matter published cannot be given in evidence." (The witness soon after died

Alexander Hamilton's talent as a trial lawyer was never more evident than in his eloquent argument before the New York Supreme Court regarding libel laws, voiced only months before his death.

under suspicious circumstances.) Nor was it surprising that the jury returned a verdict of "guilty" after Judge Lewis instructed them that their *only* duty was to decide whether Croswell had published the statements in question!

The defense team used that instruction to appeal for a new trial, and on February 13, 1804, the case was brought before the New York Supreme Court then sitting in Albany at the old Capitol building on Broadway near Hudson Avenue. This time the defense was headed by Alexander Hamilton. The services of the brilliant Federalist lawyer had been sought for the earlier Claverack trial, with Croswell supporters even asking Albany patriarch Philip Schuyler to petition his son-in-law Hamilton to take the case. But Hamilton had been too busy then with other lawsuits, though he may have contributed occasional counsel. Now he was free and ready to mount what one trial-goer called "the greatest forensic effort that he ever made."

It is said that state legislators abandoned their chambers and packed the courtroom in order to hear Hamilton's six-hour-long argument focusing on the role of truth in determining libel, and the right of the jury to take into consideration the intent of the accused. His impassioned words reportedly brought tears to the eyes of many, especially when he closed with a warning that "Never can tyranny be introduced into this country by arms. . . . It is only by the abuse of the forms of justice that we can be enslaved. . . . By devoting a wretched but honest man as the victim of a nominal trial."

No matter the eloquence of Hamilton, his logic, his appeal to all who loved liberty, the Supreme Court still voted along party lines. The 2-2 decision it rendered three months later meant there would be no new trial, and Croswell still faced sentencing. Yet no move was made in that direction. Croswell remained at large, continuing his career with the *Balance*, the *Wasp* having ceased publication with the twelfth issue, shortly after its editor's January 1803 indictment.

Croswell was not home free, however, The final issue of his *Wasp* had contained attacks on Attorney General Spencer and District Attorney Foote, both of whom sued separately for libel at Hudson. Eventually Spencer was awarded $126 in damages, while Foot got a mere 6¢, thanks to witnesses attesting to his less than sterling character. As for the original case, Croswell finally was granted a new trial, but it never took place, and in 1809 he moved the *Balance* from Hudson to Albany. Once there, the Federalist support he had been promised did not materialize, and within two years Croswell wound up in debtor's prison, having defaulted on a loan. That finished him with newspapering—and Federalists—forever.

On May 8, 1814, Croswell was ordained an Episcopal deacon, and the following Sunday he took charge of Christ Church in Hudson. A year later he moved to New Haven, Connecticut, where he served as rector of Trinity Church until his death in 1858—a period of more than four decades during which he never again attended a political meeting, nor voted in any election, and restricted his writing to diary entries and sermons, the latter of which he is said to have found a tad tedious to compose.

In regard to the legal principles that Alexander Hamilton had so passionately promoted in his appeal to the Supreme Court, on April 6, 1805, the New York State Legislature passed a bill recognizing the right of juries to decide criminality in libel cases, and allowing truth as a defense if the material in question had been published "with good motives and for justifiable ends."

Hamilton did not live to see this happen. While at Albany for the Supreme Court appeal in February 1804, he had dined one evening at Judge John Tayler's house and during the course of the meal made some caustic remarks about Aaron Burr. At least that was the contention of Judge Tayler's son-in-law, Dr. Charles D. Cooper, who had been present at the dinner, and on April 12, 1804 wrote about it in a letter to Andrew Brown of the Albany County town of Berne. Somehow Cooper's letter was "embezzled and broken" open, with the contents made public—including a reference to Hamilton denouncing Burr as a "dangerous man" who "ought not to be trusted."

At any other time all of this might have blown over. But Burr was then running for Governor of New York against Morgan Lewis, and the election was less than two weeks away. Meanwhile the story was kept simmering in printer's ink as newspapers published a letter of Philip Schuyler, who attempted to shield Hamilton by stating that his son-in-law never said such things about Burr. This was rebutted in a letter by Dr. Cooper that appeared on April 24. Voters went to the polls the next day, April 25, with the result that the seemingly shoo-in candidate Burr ws roundly defeated by Lewis.

A copy of Cooper's letter accompanied the demand for satisfaction that the embittered Burr sent to Hamilton on June 18, 1804—a challenge not conducive to any conciliation attempts, thus making a duel inevitable. Three weeks later, on the morning of July 11, the two men met along the shore of the Hudson at Weehawken, New Jersey, and only one walked away.

Fatally wounded, the 47-year-old Hamilton was rowed across the river to a friend's house at 80 Jane Street in lower Manhattan, where he died the following day. But his contribution to our civil rights through the Croswell case lived on to become part of the New York State Constitution adopted in 1821. And in that passage, which has served as a model for other states, you can almost hear Hamilton's courtroom declamations in the guarantees that "every citizen may freely speak, write, and publish his sentiments on all subjects . . . and no law shall be passed to abridge or restrain the liberty of speech, or of the press." What's more, "In all criminal prosecutions or indictments for libels . . . the truth may be given in evidence to the jury . . . and the jury have the right to determine the law and the fact."

No wonder then that the epitaph on Hamilton's monument in New York City's Trinity Churchyard on lower Broadway promises admiration by a "grateful posterity long after this marble shall have mouldered into dust."

33. Doing It for the Gipper

THE HUSHED ATMOSPHERE OF APPROACHING DEATH WAS BELIED BY the healthy-looking body of the college athlete lying in the hospital bed. Then a rasping cough came from his pneumonia-ravaged lungs, and 25-year-old George Gipp glanced resignedly at his visitor, Knute Rockne. As coach of the Notre Dame University football team, Rockne took a personal interest in all his players, but this young man had been special from the very start. And as he searched for something reassuring to say, Rockne recalled the day in September 1916 when he first caught sight of Gipp at the South Bend, Indiana, school.

It had been right after football practice and the Notre Dame playing field was deserted except for an unfamiliar figure in street clothes drop-kicking a ball for an incredible number of yards. Rockne knew a natural athlete when he saw one, but the slim six-footer—who introduced himself as freshman George Gipp from northern Michigan—seemed disinterested in the older man's suggestion that he try out for the team. He hadn't played much football, Gipp explained. Baseball was more his game.

Nevertheless, Gipp showed up at the practice field a few days later, and within a month he had won a freshman game for Notre Dame with a 62-yard drop-kick that demonstrated both his exceptional talent and a distinctly unconventional nature. The quarterback, it seems, had specifically instructed Gipp to punt.

A similar event occurred the following Spring when Gipp took a seasonal shift from the gridiron to the baseball diamond. Brought up to bat in one of Notre Dame's games, he was signaled to bunt. Instead, Gipp hit a home run because, as he later explained, "It was too hot to be running around the bases after a bunt." On the other hand, Gipp sometimes worked harder than he had to, as was the case when the financially pressed freshman asked Knute Rockne's help in securing a part-time job. Rockne's mention of possibly arranging "something not too demanding" was rejected by Gipp, who politely but firmly said it was real work he wanted, and wound up waiting on tables.

Gipp was less conscientious about things he deemed he could do without, such as certain studies and sports practice. Whereas Rockne went along with the latter absences so long as they didn't affect Gipp's performance on the playing field, university officials were not so lenient when it came to academics. In the Spring in 1919, Gipp was dismissed for cutting his law school classes. This only added to his growing reputation though, for he promptly proposed that the professors give him an oral exam, and if he passed, then he would be reinstated. A grueling two-hour test was subsequently set up— one that Gipp passed with flying colors.

That Gipp didn't always follow the rules didn't seem to bother his teammates, who respected his rarely erring instinct for the right play, coupled with the ability to accomplish it. Plus that, Gipp was genuinely pleasant to be around, and never sought personal publicity. In fact, when Notre Dame played Army at West Point in the autumn of 1920, the Gipper, as he was then being called, evaded New York City journalists who had come up the Hudson to interview him. He didn't like posing for pictures either, with the result that very few photographs can be found of him in uniform. The images that do exist show a lean and graceful halfback, who first played against the cadets at West Point's Cullum Hall Field (now The Plain) on November 3, 1917.

By that time, a strong rivalry had developed between the two teams—a rivalry which would bring about some of the finest moments in football history—all of it stemming from their very first contest in 1913, when underdog Notre Dame trounced the Cadets 35-13. The contest also contributed to the canon of legends linked to the U.S. Military Academy. For when the Notre Dame players arrived at West Point and went to eat at the Washington Hall Cadet Mess, they mistook the kitchen door for the entrance, much to the amusement of the host team. Undaunted, the visitors went on to win the game, after which they decided their back-door faux pas might well have been a good-luck token worthy of repetition. The tradition was then continued until 1916, when one of the team members insisted they enter the cadet dining room via the front door. Notre Dame nosedived that game 30-10, reportedly prompting the resumption of their kitchen entrance when next they played West Point. And this time they also had the Gipper.

Despite a gusty wind and muddy field that November Saturday in 1917, Gipp demonstrated an effective if unorthodox style that not only helped his underdog team beat Army 7-2, but hinted of the hero he was to become. Such recognition, however, was put on hold when he broke his leg in a game the following week. But no fracture could cause Gipp to forfeit football, and both he and Knute Rockne were delighted when the 1918 college gridiron season was declared unofficial due to World War I. For this meant Gipp was eligible to play varsity football an extra year.

What sports spectaculars the following two seasons proved to be—particularly when Notre Dame's "Fighting Irish" traveled east to meet their arch rivals on Army's home turf high above the Hudson at West Point. Though far from home, the visiting team never lacked for supporters, thanks in part to a special train arranged for by a Notre Dame alumnus named Angus MacDonald, who just happened to be a railroad executive. So it was that many of the 15,000 attending the game at Cullum Hall Field on November 8, 1919 were cheering for the Gipper and his teammates. Nor were those rooters to be disappointed.

The game was almost half over, with Notre Dame trailing Army 9-0, when Gipp pulled off one of the most surprising plays of his career. Seeing that the timekeeper was just about to call an end to the second quarter—and well aware that the rules allowed any play started before the whistle sounded to be completed—the quick-thinking Gipp didn't wait for the Notre Dame quarterback to signal the next move. Instead, Gipp shouted for the pigskin to be passed to him. A startled teammate complied. Gipp was over the goal line before any opposing player could react. And it was this touchdown that turned the tide: Notre Dame wound up winning 12-9.

The following year found Gipp bettering his already dazzling performance on the gridiron—so much so that writer Ring Lardner reportedly quipped that Notre Dame's game plan had been reduced to a single strategy of passing the ball to Gipp and having him "use his own judgment." That wasn't too wild an exaggeration either, considering Gipp's pre-game demonstration at West Point's Cullum Field when Notre Dame played Army on October 30, 1920. After besting a cadet in an impromptu drop-kicking contest, Gipp had four footballs set up on the midfield line—fully 50 yards from either goal. Then seemingly without any effort, he executed four perfect kicks: two pigskins for one goalpost, and two for the opposite end of the field.

This extraordinary exhibit only spurred Army to fight harder when the starting whistle sounded, causing the subsequent competition to be called one of the greatest college football games ever played. Certainly it was Gipp's greatest as he racked up a total of 357 yards—much of it from risky plays that prompted one sportswriter to call him "the cool gambler responsible for the [Notre Dame] victory of 27-17." It wasn't the first time Gipp had displayed his willingness to take chances either, and once when an interviewer asked Knute Rockne if he approved of such gambles, the Notre Dame coach responded, "I simply approve of George Gipp."

Rockne may have been thinking of this six weeks later as he sat beside Gipp's hospital bed in South Bend. A smile might even have crossed his lips as he recalled the young man's often hilarious tactics for delaying a game, especially the time Gipp let himself be flattened by a tackle, then purposely hung on to the other player as he (Gipp) hollered, "Let me up!" On still another occasion, his attempts at stalling for time caused the exasperated coach of the opposing team to demand what Gipp was majoring in at Notre Dame. "Clock repair!" was the quick response.

Most of all, Rockne would have been reviewing the weeks since the student he considered a "football genius" first complained of a sore throat following a foul-weather practice session in November. Sent to the school infirmary, Gipp allegedly snuck away from his sickbed a few days later in order to play in Notre Dame's game with Northwestern. That landed him back in the infirmary, where his condition worsened, there being no antibiotics in those days which might have stopped the streptococcal infection from spreading throughout his system.

At the beginning of December news came that Gipp had been named All-American fullback, as well as the country's outstanding college player—accolades which guaranteed him a bright future in football. He could also count on a contract with the Chicago White Sox if he preferred to go into professional baseball after graduation. But it was soon obvious to everyone, including Gipp, that he had played his last game.

Instead of reacting with bitterness, Gipp faced reality and asked a final favor of the coach who had done so much to further his career. "Sometime," he managed to whisper to Rockne, "when things are wrong and the breaks are beating the boys, tell them to go in there with all they've got and win just one for the Gipper. I don't know where I'll be then, Rock, but I'll know about it, and I'll be happy."

George Gipp died shortly afterward, on December 14, 1920, and for nearly eight years Knute Rockne never acted on the request. Then in November 1928, he found himself facing an undefeated Army team, while his own injury-prone players had yet to reach their full potential.

As Jerry Brondfield pointed out in his 1976 biography of *Rockne*, playing Army had a particular importance, in that the coach felt "Notre Dame's rise to national prominence could be traced, in great part, to the series with the Cadets—beginning with the seminal game on the [West Point] Plains in 1913." It had also been Rockne who in the 1920s convinced officials to shift the contest from West Point downriver to New York, where for many years it was the city's "biggest annual sporting event."

In the 15 years since their first game, Notre Dame usually had bested Army. However, when he and his team settled in at the Westchester (County) Country Club in the town of Harrison prior to the Saturday, November 10, contest at Yankee Stadium, Rockne was far from optimistic. Nor did it help when the

Army players—on their way to pre-game quarters at Manhattan's Astor Hotel—just happened to stop off for workout displaying their winning-streak form at New Rochelle's Travers Island, not far from where Notre Dame was staying.

On Saturday morning, as the Notre Dame players suited up in a near-silent locker room at Yankee Stadium, Knute Rockne knew the time had come to honor Gipp's request. However, he waited until almost game time before beginning, "You've all heard of George Gipp, of course. . . ."

Without resorting to his traditional pep-talk tactics, Rockne quietly told his players what the dying athlete had said about winning one for him, and it was an equally quiet team that left the locker room a few minutes later. But it was a team "ready to play the game of their lives," as halfback Jack Chevigny recalled afterwards.

They certainly did play that way, notably Chevigny. He made the initial touchdown for Notre Dame after a scoreless first half, literally flying over the Army defenders to shout from the end zone, "That one was for the Gipper!" So was the rest of the game, with the Notre Dame underdogs defeating Army 12-6 in a contest some observers called "the greatest demonstration of inspired football ever played anywhere."

The cynics among us—especially those who have viewed the somewhat maudlin 1940 movie, *Knute Rockne, All American*, which features Ronald Reagan as George Gipp—may well wonder if the deathbed request really occurred, or whether it was a bit of hype dreamed up by a coach with a well-known flair for the dramatic.

A revealing clue could be the reaction Rockne had to a report by sports-writer Francis Wallace that appeared in the New York *Daily News* a couple of days after the game. Headlined "Gipp's Ghost Beat Army," its repetition of Rockne's locker-room speech thoroughly upset the Notre Dame coach, who berated Wallace for betraying a confidence. Clearly the pain of Gipp's passing was still fresh for his mentor, and it is hard to imagine Rockne ever taking liberties with that tragic event.

The rift between Rockne and the reporter was resolved by Wallace's explanation that he had not intended any personal insult, but believed Gipp's words—like the beloved athlete who uttered them—belonged to posterity. How right he was.

Voted into the National Football Hall of Fame in 1951, Gipp's career total of 2,341 rushing yards was not surpassed until 1978, and some of the other records he set at Notre Dame still stand. Meanwhile, to do something "for the Gipper" has gone beyond the bounds of football phraseology to become an inspiration for anyone facing overwhelming odds.

34. The Great Granddaddy
of 'Em All

B UTTER-COLORED CLUSTERS OF BLOSSOMING SPURGE RIVALED THE RAYS of the early May sun as the farmhand made his way across the meadow to a tree-covered knoll. Savvy to the ways of horses, William Rysdyk had a hunch his employer's missing mare might have sought the privacy of the copse, since her pregnancy was near term. A low whinny validated Rysdyk's intuition, and he followed the sound to where the mare stood watch over her newborn foal. Spindly legs splayed, it was struggling to stand up, but its spunky determination and eventual success did not bring a smile to the farmhand's lips. Instead, Rysdyk frowned at the newborn's swaybacked scrawniness. Could that underdevelopment have anything to do with the mare being crippled a couple of years earlier during a race on Manhattan's Third Avenue?

Rysdyk recalled that his employer, Jonas Seely, had felt sorry for the injured mare. Purchasing her from an abusive New York butcher who had been working her as a lowly cart horse, Seely brought the mare back to his farm in the Orange County town of Chester. To everyone's surprise, the mare recovered to such an extent that in June 1848 Seely decided to breed her to a champion stallion named Abdallah, since she too had fine bloodlines. The result was the foal Rysdyk had found.

As he brought both horses back to the barn that morning of May 5, 1849, Rysdyk looked at the bony newborn's white hindfeet and was reminded of an old farmer's superstition about "One white leg, inspect him; two white legs, reject him." Altogether not very promising, Rysdyk concluded. Yet there was something about that foal . . . .

Within three months, Rysdyk had approached his employer about buying the horse. Seely's asking price of $125 included the mare too, but it was still a fortune for the farmhand. Somehow Rysdyk managed to borrow the money, and late in September he proudly showed off his acquisition—with snow-white bridle, girth and martingale complementing the colt's dark reddish-brown coat—at the Orange County Fair in Goshen. Onlookers were not overly impressed,

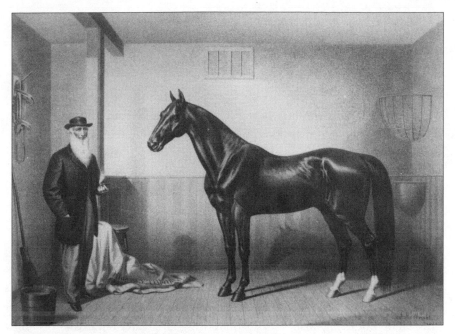

William Rysdyk, shown here with Hambletonian in a Currier & Ives print, never suspected that the scrawny foal he found in an Orange County meadow would one day earn him a fortune. (Photo courtesy of Phil Pines)

despite the fact that the colt was beginning to show signs of the massiveness he would achieve in maturity, and there were those who joked about him being "Bill Rysdyk's bull." Even his name—Hambletonian—was joked about, with some people insisting Rysdyk had really meant to call his horse Hamilton, but was too poorly educated to spell it correctly. In truth, the colt was the latest in a long line of similarly dubbed horses, which made his full name Hambletonian 10. He would, however, always be known as Rysdyk's Hambletonian.

As a yearling, Hambletonian remained unremarkable and when the financially strapped Rysdyk tried to sell the colt in 1850, not even $30 was offered. Still in need of funds the following year, Rysdyk tried an auction. Not a single bid was made, so he appealed to a friend, John Minchin, one of the few people who thought favorably of Hambletonian. Minchin, in turn, asked his fellow auction-goer, the wealthy New Yorker George Payne, if he would go halves with him in the $1,000 Rysdyk wanted for the horse. Payne only snorted, "Who ever heard of $1,000 for a two-year-old colt?"

Those nine words may well have been the costliest Payne ever uttered, for Hambletonian was to earn his owner a fortune. And thanks to Payne's frugality, that owner remained William Rysdyk, who never again put his beloved horse up for sale. Instead, Rydkyk decided to offer Hambletonian as a stud—at first for free, then for a fee of the horse proved to be a good breeder. Meanwhile, it was in Rysdyk's best interest to demonstrate just how fine a trotter he felt Hambletonian to be. The opportuniaty came in 1852, when Rysdyk raced his 3-year-old horse at the Union Course on Long Islnad. Competing against his half-brother, Abdallah Chief, Hambletonian trotted around the track in a then-record 2 minutes, 48½ seconds—the first and last time he ever raced.

In those days when horse racing was more a game than a money-maker, Rysdyk rightly figured that once was enough for Hambletonian to prove his speed, since there was no sense in risking injury to what might be a valuable stud. But there was no way Rysdyk could have imagined just how great a horse he had—not even when Hambletonian won first prize at the Orange County Fair in September 1853 and two Virginia men wanted to buy him for $10,000. Rysdyk, who had never really wanted to part with his horse, turned them down, just as he did trotting enthusiast Robert Bonner, when the publisher of the New York *Ledger* later upped the ante to $20,000. It is said that Mrs. Rysdyk stayed up all night trying to convince her husband to accept Bonner's offer. Rysdyk was adamant, however, convinced that Hambletonian's prowess in producing quality foals would bring far greater rewards.

Once again, Rysdyk was right on the money. From a $25 stud fee in 1853, the rate for Hambletonian's siring services steadily rose to $500, so that when Rysdyk bought some Chester property in April 1865, he was able to say, "The farm cost me nearly $22,000 and Hambletonian earned the purchase price in three months." This was also the year Rysdyk drove the 16-year-old stallion to a skeleton (stripped down) wagon past applauding fans filling the grandstand at the Orange County Fair in Goshen. Though Hambletonian's Roman-nosed head with its vague white star was more homely than handsome, he possessed a certain majesty enhanced by his peak condition and perfect grooming. His annual appearances at the fair were therefore considered highlights, especially when some of his by now numerous progeny were exhibited with him, or when he was put on a long lead and allowed to show his speed.

Among Hambletonian's many admirers was none other than Ulysses S. Grant, who was an avid horseman and attended the races in Goshen during the 1870s. In fact, it was the sharp-eyed Grant who has been credited with spotting a distinctive trait in Hamletonian's offspring, which apparently contributed to their trotting speed. Their hips were higher than their withers (the ridge between the shoulder bones)—something Grant reportedly named the "trotting pitch." It was not long, therefore, until Hambletonian's speed was bested by some of those descendants, including such standardbred legends as Dexter, Goldsmith Maid and St. Julien. But far from diminishing Hambletonian, these record-setting accomplishments only added to his renown, and he remained in great demand as a stud, much to the financial delight of his owner.

When William Rysdyk died in 1870, he is said to have left an estate of nearly a quarter-million pre-income-tax dollars, along with an interesting anecdote. According to Marguerite Henry's book, *One Man's Horse*, shortly before he expired in his Chester home, Rysdyk asked that Hambletonian be brought up to his first-floor bedroom window so he could see the stallion one last time. But Hambletonian somehow sensed what was happening, and appeared outside the window before anyone went to fetch him.

Hambletonian survived his owner by six years, finally succumbling to old age on March 27, 1876. During his nearly 28 years, he had fathered more than 1,300 foals whose championship qualities ensured the continuation of standardbred excellence when other bloodlines faltered, and it is estimated that most of today's trotters and pacers are directly descended from Hambletonian—which is why he is called the "Granddaddy of 'em all." This importance wasn't lost on people of his day either. Hambletonian's death was front-page news, with both schools and businesses closing for the funeral. Youngsters filing past the bier even "took hairs from his tail to weave into braids of memory," and his original owner, Jonas Seely, is remembered as intoning, "Gentle peace to him that sleeps in the mystery of death, but lives in the heartbeats and hoofbeats of his sons."

Nor was the big bay stallion forgotten after he was laid to rest in his home pasture off High Street in the village of Cheser. It was there, on what is now Hambletonian Avenue, that a tall shaft of pink Ozark granite was erected to his memory in 1882. The cost had been covered by contributions from horse-lovers across the country, including California Governor Leland Stanford, a Hudson Valley native born in the Albany County community of Watervliet, who just happened to own Hambletonian's son, Electioneer. The shaft, by the way, was sited specifically so that train passengers on the nearby Erie tracks (now a public rail trail accessible from Winkler Place in the downtown business district of Chester village) would be able to see it as they chugged by. Hambletonian's birthplace is also duly marked, with a bronze plaque on a boulder easily seen from the road that is named for him (not to be confused with the avenue in Chester village) just west of the hamlet of Sugar Loaf. But the best-known commemoration continues to be the annual Hambletonian Stake, first run in 1926, and described by the late Goshen historian Elizabeth Sharts as "the greatest of harness races, memorializing the greatest of harness racing sires." After all, it's almost always one of his descendants that wins it!

THE HOUSE THAT HAMBLETONIAN BUILT

If Hambletonian is the king of standardbred horses, then the Harness Racing Museum and Hall of Fame on Goshen's Main Street surely is his palace—a palace as pleasing and public-oriented as perceptive planning, plus state-of-the-art technology can make it.

Originally called the Hall of Fame of the Trotter when it was established in an elegant Tudor-style stable back in 1951, the museum—much enlarged in the late 1990s—still encompasses that stable, with exhibit-filled stalls offering an intriguing time-line of standardbred history, from Hambletonian's stud book to sulkies, silks and sweat-scrapers. And since the stable is usually the first stop for museum-goers, every effort has been made to retain its realism while enveloping visitors in the world of horses. A bale is in the process of being hauled up to the hay loft; stall doors still show "cribbing" scars made by horses gnawing on them, and even an original floor of macadam bricks— easier on horses' feet than the more usual cobblestones or regular brick—

has been retained. Meanwhile in the background, one hears an occasional recorded low whinny, the crunch of hay being chewed, the clip-clop of hooves, or the chirp of birds outside in the yard. Only the smell of a stable is missing.

Duly initiated, visitors go on to gallery after gallery of what must be the most comprehensive collection of harness racing memorabilia ever compiled, including a statuette hall, extensive library, and an impressive assemblage of horse-related Currier & Ives prints. On view, too, is the second-floor, wood-paneled clubhouse, where in the old days the wealthy were wont to gather, watching races from the porch overlooking what is now Historic Track in

Although part of it is housed in an old Tudor-style stable, the Harness Racing Museum and Hall of Fame in Goshen utilizes state-of-the-art technology to present the colorful history of standardbred horses.

back of the museum. Often among those onlookers was railroad magnate E. H. Harriman, who owned the property during the early part of the 20th century, and whose family provided the horsehead-decorated fountain in the nearby village square.

Far from being a stodgy, too-serious place, the museum offers a number of innovative and fun displays for both young and old to enjoy. For example, there's a talking horse, as well as a frame of movable blocks so smallfry can assemble their own trotter. Visitors may also try judging a horse or calling a race, and then relax in a mini-theater showing scenes from harness-racing movies, before finding out how it feels to sit in a sulky behind a life-sized but inanimate trotter. The greatest thrill, however, has to be the 3-D Simulator—a movie theater where visitors experience just what it's like to drive in a race, with the wind in their faces, noise in their ears, clods of mud flying past them, and seats that vibrate on bumpy ground, or tilt as the horse goes around a turn!

To see real-life horses, all one has to do is walk around the museum building to Historic Track—a half-mile-long dirt oval with associated buildings, including a quaint old judge's stand, all of which are on the National Register of Historic Places. The first site in America to be so designated, the race course is also the oldest active harness track in the country, having been built in 1838. At the time of this writing, the track hosts races only during Matinee Days held on three Saturdays in June, and Grand Circuit Week in July, but it is open year-round and visitors are welcome to stroll past the stables where horses are boarded, or watch as the animals are exercised on the track. And who knows, you just might spot a big bay stallion leading all the rest.

VI. CORNUCOPIA

35. Go With the Flow—Celebrating the Region's Waterfalls

SEPTEMBER HAD BARELY BEGUN, BUT A CHILL WIND CAME WHIPPING across the mountain meadow's twin lakes, causing botanist John Bartram to shiver uncontrollably as he reached the shore. Having recently risen from a sickbed, he had debated the wisdom of traveling from his Philadelphia home to this section of the Catskill Mountains. His livelihood, however, depended on overseas clients who were awaiting seeds that could be gathered only at this time of year—clients who, Bartram felt, would be equally interested in an "amazing waterfall" he had heard about and hoped to find.

So on that September day in 1753, despite being enfeebled by fever, 54-year-old John Bartram determinedly followed a stream flowing from the twin bodies of water now known as North and South lakes, in the Greene County town of Hunter. Accompanied by his 14-year-old son William and a hired guide, the botanist eventually managed to bushwack to the brink of the falls, where he gasped at the "great gulph that swallowed all down"—a two-tier cascade that at 260 feet was higher than Niagara Falls. Indeed, Kaaterskill Falls—the name it came to be called—turned out to be the tallest in all New York State, as well as a great tourist attraction praised by poets and painters alike. At the time Bartram saw it, though, New York was still a British province, and waterfalls generally were valued more as an energy source than for any scenic grandeur.

Thanks to its mountainous terrain that tumbles countless tributaries toward the mighty Hudson, our region was ideally suited to the water-driven mills and forges necessary for developing the land. And although the passing centuries have largely done away with those initial industrial structures, most of the waterfalls survive, often having served later factories or power plants. For instance, the large falls on the Wallkill River (best seen from the

West Main Street bridge in the Orange County village of Walden) now helps generate electricity; similarly, Honk Falls hosts a powerhouse, both of which are visible from the Route 55 bridge just west of Napanoch in Ulster County. Another fine example can be found along Fishkill Creek in the Dutchess County city of Beacon, where Madame Brett Mill Park (located on South Avenue between two old factory complexes) offers views of the water-fall that once powered a 1708 operation.

Stuyvesant Falls in Columbia County also hosts a creek-side park (on Kinderhook Street) overlooking one of the cascades that made this an impor-tant mill town in the 19th century. Its mill district is now listed on the National Register of Historic Places, as is the Harmony Mill site near where the Mohawk River enters the Hudson at Cohoes in Albany County. Helping to power the vast Harmony complex were the 600-foot-wide Cohoes Falls, which can be observed from Overlook Park on School Street, off Cataract Street. Lovers of superlatives should take note that in 1872 Harmony Mill #3 (also called Mastodon Mill for the skeleton of a prehistoric beast unearthed nearby) was considered the country's largest cotton-producing factory. Meanwhile, on the western side of the county, what may have been the first felt mill in North America was built in 1870 at Rensselaerville Falls. Located in the Edmund Niles Huyck Preserve off Main Street in Rensselaerville, the top of these lovely falls may be seen from the upper bridge, whereas the lower bridge just north of the parking lot provides the best view, including the mill ruins.

We cannot forget water-dependent tanneries either, with two different Red Falls in Greene County—one on the Schoharie Creek at Hunter and the other on the Batavia Kill east of Prattsville—supporting the 19th century leather industry. Several pull-offs along the south side of Route 23 have short trails leading to the Batavia Kill's Red Falls, which were named for the local rock, rather than for the color of the water.

The early iron industry was powered by water too, and Foundry Brook Falls are now part of an 85-acre preserve off Chestnut Street in Cold Spring, Putnam County, where the West Point Foundry produced deadly Parrott cannon during the Civil War. As for a site from the preceding cen-tury, an historic marker in the Columbia County town of Ancram lays claim to New York's first ironworks, situated where Route 82 crosses the falls on the Roeliff Jansen Kill (Ancram Creek), presently the home of a modern paper mill. Paper production in our region is perhaps more close-ly associated with Glens Falls, on the northern border of Saratoga County, where Route 9 spans the Hudson. The Indian name for the cascade meant "difficult place to get around," but it was later called Wings Falls for an early settler, Abraham Wing—that is, until the settler's son attended a tavern gathering one night. Tradition tells of young Wing offering the name of the cascade in exchange for fellow party-goer John Glenn picking up the tavern tab, and it's been known as Glens Falls ever since.

From the foregoing, it's easy to see that the region's waterfalls frequently bear names of people or places, yet the connection is not always readily apparent. A case in point is the Columbia County village of Valatie (pronounced Va-lay-sha), which is Dutch for "little falls." By the same token, the name of Purling in Greene County reflects not knitting, but water riffled by several falls along the Shingle Kill. Such descriptive terms are common throughout the region, with "Buttermilk" an all-time favorite. Not only is there a Buttermilk Falls in the Kaaterskill Clove of Greene County, but one spouts

Named for the color of the sandstone ledges over which if flows, Red Falls once supplied water to power a variety of industries on the Batavia Kill in Greene County.

from an underground source off Peekamoose Mountain Road in the Ulster town of Denning, and a third froths into the Hudson at Orange County's village of Highland Falls. Still another has given its name to a Rockland County park on Greenbush Road in West Nyack, where a short walk from the trailhead at the north end of the parking lot takes visitors to a scenic ravine reputedly favored by Theodore Roosevelt.

Aside from Wappinger Falls (recalling the Munsee band that once inhabited parts of Dutchess County), the aforementioned cataract at Cohoes (an Indian word of various definitions), and Broadstreet Hollow's Nannette Falls (recognizing a 19th century Indian woman who sold souvenirs to Catskill tourists) near Shandaken in Ulster County, the native American presence has been largely overlooked when it comes to naming regional cascades. Even the tall ribbons of water falling from the escarpment at John

Boyd Thacher State Park (off Route 157 west of Albany) bear mundane labels unrelated to the awesome Indian Ladder Trail (some of it still walkable) that indigenous travelers took to reach the top of the cliff.

On the other hand, there's a sufficiency of fanciful stories about lovelorn Indians plunging over waterfalls. Like as not such tales were trumped up as tourist lures, or perhaps worried parents concocted a plot or two to keep youngsters from roaming, but some stories may well have grown from a grain of truth, which is more than enough reason to retell a few here. One of the oldest concerns Indian Brook Falls, near Constitution Marsh Sanctuary south of Cold Spring. (Follow signs from the sanctuary parking area on Indian Brook Road.) Somehow a Dutch sailor from Henry Hudson's crew was left behind when the *Half Moon* sailed back to Europe in 1609. Making the most of things, the sailor dallied with the daughter of a local Indian chief until another ship came up the river. Thereupon the qualmless Dutchman swam out to the vessel and sailed away, leaving his heartbroken Indian lover to leap from the top of the falls and drown in the pool below— a tragedy commemorated by the white flowers said to still bloom wherever her tears fell.

Up in Rensselaer County there's a slightly different spin to a story set in Troy's Poestenkill Gorge, where Mount Ida Falls (accessible from a trail off Linden Avenue) once powered a host of industries. Long before that, when the Dutch still ruled the region in the early decades of the 17th century, legend says a fair maiden named Elsie Vaughn leaped over the falls rather than submit to the lustful advances of a local warrior. Retrieving her broken body from a boulder, the mournful Indian brought it to a cave beneath the falls, where he kept vigil until he, too, died. And for those who might doubt the truth of the tale, it was reported that many years later human bones were discovered in the cave, along with a ring inscribed "Elsie."

Traveling north on Route 47 toward Oliverea in Ulster County, just past Winnisook Lake there is a series of cascades on Esopus Creek, including one called Blossom (or Crazy Nell) Falls. It is there that two star-crossed Indian lovers supposedly are still seen jumping to their death from the flat rock above the falls, whereas the spirit of an Indian wife who died at Bash Bish Falls is said to appear in its spray. Located across the Columbia County border in the Berkshires, ever-popular Bash Bish Falls is included here since a main trail leading to it originates along Route 344 in the Copake Falls area of Taconic State Park.

Waterfall haunts are by no means limited to the Indian population, as can be seen—better yet, heard—at Barberville Falls in the Rensselaer County town of Poestenkill. Now part of a 119-acre Nature Conservancy preserve, the 90-foot falls can be reached from a trail by the bridge on Route 79 (Ives Corners Road) just west of its junction with Route 40 (Plank Road). Faint sounds may reach you too—ghostly reminders of a poor peddler and his horse that were washed over the falls by a flood a century or so ago.

That Captain Kidd buried some of his booty at Barberville Falls is about as believable a local legend as one touting Rip Van Winkle's 20-year snooze to have taken place at the foot of Kaaterskill Falls. (The latter is reached by a yellow-blazed trail from the horseshoe curve at Bastion Falls on Route 23A, west of Palenville.) But credence can certainly be accorded the story about an illegal whiskey still along Hannacroix Creek causing quite a commotion during Prohibition. (The falls are near the entrance to the Nature Conservancy's Hannacroix Ravine Preserve, on Cass Hill Road, west of Clarksville in Albany County.) And it is only too true that the 1961 movie, *Splendor in the Grass*, has a strangely prophetic scene showing actress Natalie Wood nearly drowning at the base of Rondout Creek's High Falls. Twenty years later, Miss Wood died in a boating accident. (The cascade can be viewed from the linear park in the hamlet of High Falls; entry is from Route 213, at the eastern end of the bridge crossing Rondout Creek.)

We are fortunate that so many of the region's loveliest waterfalls lie in parklands and otherwise protected areas the public may visit. Among the most extensive are the contiguous Harriman and Bear Mountain State parks, covering parts of Orange and Rockland counties, and featuring such spots as Hell Hole Falls on the red-blazed Popolopen Gorge Trail just north of the Bear Mountain traffic circle, Gray's Dam on Doodletown Brook west of Route 9W, the stone-stepped fall where the Beech Trail heads northwest from Tiorati Brook Road, plus the wonderful Cascade of Slid, located along the white-marked Kakiat Trail east of the Reeves Meadow Visitors Center on Seven Lakes Drive. The latter falls were named for a mythical character, the god of all waters, created by Anglo-Irish author Edward Plunkett, Lord Dunsany. But a literary source doesn't seem to be the case for the label placed on another falls in the southeastern corner of Rockland County, near the New York-New Jersey border. Around the turn of the century, when Snedens Landing sculptor Mary Lawrence Tonetti developed the site as a private garden, complete with stone steps and columned pergola, the flume was called simply The Cascade. Today the place (reached by an unmarked trail off the turquoise-blazed Long Path, south of the Lamont-Doherty Observatory) is maintained by the Palisades Interstate Park Commission and has been redubbed Peanut Leap Falls.

Such singular sites are not a rarity either. Vernooy Kill Falls has long been a family favorite on hot summer days, with its series of small cascades, a rustic footbridge, and the ruins of a centuries-old gristmill. (The falls are part of Sundown Wild Forest, with a trailhead on the west side of Upper Cherrytown Road in the Ulster County town of Rochester.) Another favorite—as much for its flora as for Havermyer Falls—is the Mianus River Gorge Wildlife Refuge and Botanical Preserve, which was the first designated National Natural Historic Landmark, as well as the Nature Conservancy's pioneer project. (Trails begin at the parking area on Mianus River Road in Bedford, Westchester County.) The Nature Conservancy also helped preserve Mineral Spring Falls in the Orange County town of Cornwall. A small pull-off on Old Mineral Spring Road connects with a path to the falls, at the base of which is the natural font where a local farmer is said to have bottled the mineral water to sell to summer boarders.

A slightly more strenuous hike—but one well worth it—is required to reach Fishkill Ridge Falls, about a mile from the trailhead off East Main Street in the Dutchess County city of Beacon. But those seeking a more civilized cascade might do better to continue north to Poughkeepsie, where a small fall charms visitors to Locust Grove, the former estate of Samuel F.B. Morse on South Road (Route 9). There are many other such easy-to-reach places. From the point where the Appalachian Trail crosses Lakes Road in the Orange County town of Warwick, it's a 15-minute stroll east along the white-blazed path to the eye-pleasing Fitzgerald Falls. An even shorter walk can be taken to the cascade in a scenic glen on the west side of Hurley Mountain Road, just south of its junction with Route 28 in Ulster County.

Over in Dutchess County, at the bottom of Hyde Park's Teller Hill, it's just a few minutes from the parking area on the east side of Route 9 to the small waterfalls on the Maritjekill (Margaret's Creek). Even better, you don't have to get out of your car to marvel at the magnificent 200-foot stepped spillway of the Cornell Dam at Croton Gorge Park, off Route 129 in the Westchester County town of Cortlandt. The same holds true for the spillway at the Erie Canal's Lock #5, along the Canal Park road west of Waterford in Saratoga County. And you won't want to miss the water-carved ravine that serves as a spillway for the Ashokan Reservoir, near the junction of Beaver Kill and Stone Church roads in Ulster's Marbletown. While in the vicinity, you might want to continue west on Beaver Kill Road to the Ashokan Field Campus of the State University of New York. A small day-use fee provides access to trails in a beautiful area containing both Winchell Falls (a former mill site) and the pristine Cathedral Falls.

Driving tours featuring waterfalls frequently focus on the Kaaterskill Clove, with cars taking Route 18 east from Haines Falls, and ascending to the DEC-operated North-South Lake Campground (day-use permits available). From there, strollers can reach the top of Kaaterskill Falls or head for Ashley Falls in Mary's Glen. But not so well known—or traveled—is a sister clove to the south, where a mountain stream has carved an equally awesome ravine with numerous cascades, best appreciated by taking the Platte Clove Road (Route 16) west from the Ulster County community of West Saugerties. The steep curving road is only open between April and November, and cars should be in good working order to attempt the ascent—but ah, what an experience! Part way up you can park by the bridge above the aptly named Hell Hole Falls (not to be confused with the Orange County version). And at the top can be found the

Rainbows sometimes dance in the spray from the Cornell Dam's 200-foot stepped spillway. Also called the New Croton Dam, it forms a fine backdrop for the Westchester County park at its base.

Catskill Center's Platte Clove Nature Preserve (look for the sign near a red cottage on the left), with trails leading to sites like Plattekill Falls.

No celebration of regional cascades could be complete without mentioning the Shawangunk Mountains, and most especially Minnewaska State Park, on Route 44/55 west of New Paltz. First in alphabetical order and by far the best known—possibly because it's the easiest to reach (via the carriage road just south of the main tollgate)—is the breathtaking Awosting Falls, as beautiful in winter as it is in summer. Next is Rainbow Falls, on the Long Path where it crosses the Peterskill. Also on the Peterskill is Sheldon Falls to the north of Route 44/55. And farther west is Stony Kill Falls, its top reached via a carriage road that banches off from the Old Smiley Road near Lake Awosting. The bowl-like base of the falls (often down to a drip in dry summers) can be reached from a trail at the end of Shaft Road, south of Kerhonkson. As for the Verkeerder Kill cascade (sometimes called Katykill

Falls), that well-loved Shawangunk Ridge site can be approached from Sam's Point Dwarf Pine Barrens Preserve (off Route 52 at Cragsmoor), where hikers follow a green-blazed trail through acres of huckleberry bushes and some of the grandest views to be had.

The preceding sampling of places—and it's only a sampling—goes to show why, since the time John Bartram first viewed the Kaaterskill's "great gulph," there have been people who "collect" regional cascades. Obviously this writer is one of them, and anybody is welcome to join. Nor does it matter if you seek out waterfalls because of their scenic beauty, for their history and legends, or simply for the relaxing sound of their "white noise"—it's a satisfying pastime with a seemingly endless supply.

36. Vino, Vitis, Vinifera . . .
A Tale Divine

URING THE WEEK THEY HAD BEEN SAILING UP THE UNCHARTED river, a September heat wave had plagued these mariners accustomed to the cooler climes of northern Europe. Hence, when the *Half Moon* anchored off what would one day be called Albany, the crew welcomed the thirst-quenching wild grapes brought to them by "the people of the countrie . . . flocking aboard." That quote comes from Robert Juet, the chronicler of Henry Hudson's 1609 voyage, and is perhaps the earliest printed reference to the native grapes that eventually helped foster the region's fame. But between those two events lay a long trail of trial and error, its main milestone being an amazing—sometimes amusing—vinicultural craze that swept through our valley during the 19th century.

Fueling that fire had been the glowing reports of colonists like New York Governor Richard Coote, Earl of Bellomont, who in 1700 wrote to London about the "wild grapes . . . in very great abundance . . . especially above Albany on the side of the Hudson river . . . where the vines all along twine around great trees." Similarly, the French writer, J. Hector St. John de Crèvecoeur—who prior to the American Revolution resided at his Pine Hill farm on what would become Route 94 between the Orange County villages of Chester and Washingtonville—mentioned in *Sketches of 18th Century America* that he had "often been astonished at the great quantity of grapes which grow," and "I verily believe that I have grapes enough some years in my south swamp to make a hogshead [around 63 gallons] of wine. . . ."

Yet initially little effort was made to cultivate the wild varieties that grew in such profusion. One group of people that reportedly did pioneer in planting native grapes were the French Huguenots who settled around Ulster County's New Paltz in 1677. But for the most part, early attempts at grapegrowing—both amateur and professional—involved Old World vines of the *Vinifera* family, even though these imports generally did not fare as well in the Valley soil as did the indigenous *Vitis*.

Famed physician Samuel Bard, for instance, tried his hand at cultivating Spanish vines from Madeira when in 1798 he retired to his Hyde Park estate (now the site of the Vanderbilt Mansion National Historic Site on Route 9). And farther downriver, Robert Underhill of Westchester County's Croton Point used European grapes when he began what has been called the Valley's first commercial vineyard around 1827. The foreign fruit died, but not Underhill's determination. Aided by his two sons Richard and William, Underhill next tried a combination of American Catawba and Isabella grapes, with the result that his riverside vineyards eventually encompassed 75 successful acres.

Present-day Croton Point Park, east of Route 9 in the town of Cortlandt, hosts remnants of Underhill's estate, including two brick wine cellars. The latter are featured in guided tours and are a favorite for Halloween programs since a ghost reportedly haunts the depths. Legend tells of a time when the Underhills were bothered by thefts of wine and equipment, and in order to catch the criminal they stretched a wire across the lane leading to the wine cellars. Unfortunately on his next raid the thief—some say it was a family member—must have been going too fast. He was decapitated when he hit the wire, and supposedly his headless body still roams the vaults.

Croton Point isn't the only site of viticultural starts in the 1820s. During that decade Rufus Barrett of New Paltz began shipping the native grapes he'd grown to New York City, while in Greene County a man named Wilkes Hyde developed a new variety of grape from a vine he had found growing on his farm near Catskill. But even more significant was John Jaques' decision to plant a few grapevines in back of the general store he owned in Washingtonville.

Contrary to popular tradition that tends to Gallicize his name, Jaques was neither a Frenchman nor a trained vintner. Instead, this resourceful Scotch-American taught himself viniculture via a set of books that were later passed down to his descendant, Washingtonville author-historian Edward J. McLaughlin III. In *Around the Watering Trough*, McLaughlin related how his great-great-grandfather initially tried selling his backyard harvest on the Manhattan market, but the price paid was so small that Jaques began pressing the grapes and making his own wine. This proved much more profitable, and in 1835 he purchased nearby land for a large vineyard. His first commercial vintage followed four years later.

The wine cellars Jaques excavated can still be seen on the property at 35 North Street in Washingtonville. Wine is still produced there too, supporting a claim that this is the country's oldest continuously operating winery.

Only now the place is called Brotherhood. And behind that name lies another little-known tale. It seems that when the Jaques family sold the business to Edward Emerson around 1885, the new owner wanted to change the winery's name to his own. However, Emerson had also been dealing with a winery run by the Brotherhood of New Life in the Dutchess County town of Amenia, and he was supposedly better known as "the Brotherhood man." So no matter how hard he tried to get "Emerson" across, "Brotherhood" was the name that stuck.

As for the Amenia operation, that was part of a utopian community established in 1861 by the charismatic spiritualist Thomas Lake Harris. The wine produced there was touted as divinely blessed, and even teetotalers were told they could safely drink it! Actually, the Amenia Brotherhood claim was not all that curious when taken in the context of its time—a period of keen competition when even established growers like the Underhills of Croton Point might call upon a Board of Health commissioner to attest that their wines were "pure and can be relied on as a tonic in sickness and for table use."

The catalyst for this competition was the Valley's golden era of viniculture, which spanned roughly half a century, starting in 1845. In that year a Long Island man accomplished what Newburgh pomologist Charles Downing deemed "the first genuine cross between foreign grapes and our natives." This opened the door to hybridization, and for a while it appeared that practically every Valley dweller was determined to grow—if not personally develop—the perfect vine.

By the time U.P. Hedrick compiled his seminal study of *The Grapes of New York* in 1907, the number of Hudson Valley varieties hovered around the hundred mark. Most of them had been developed through careful scientific selection, but some are simply serendipitous. The Alice grape, for instance, was found growing near an old stone wall by Ward D. Gunn of Clintondale in Ulster County, whereas the Denniston was discovered on an island in the Hudson just south of Albany by Isaac Denniston, and the Rebecca was first spotted growing in the garden of E.M. Peake at Hudson in Columbia County. The foregoing is not meant to imply that new varieties were almost exclusively named after people. Geographical locations were popular too, and can be a good clue to a Hudson Valley origin. Take the Dutchess, Hudson, Poughkeepsie, Ulster and Modena grapes: these were all developed by Andrew Jackson Caywood, some of whose fields became part of Mark Miller's Benmarl Winery on Highland Avenue in Marlborough, Ulster County.

Not surprisingly, the Croton grape came from the aforementioned

Underhill vineyards. And even more localized landmarks are apparent in Orange County grapes like the Storm King, developed by Cornwall's Edward Payson Roe; the Schoonemunk, or Skunnymunk, named for another mountain close to the Mortonville (Vails Gate) home of W.A. Woodward; as well as the Quassaic, which is a stream in the northeastern part of the county.

The Iona was different in that the island off the Rockland County shore reportedly got its name from the grape, rather than the other way around. This finely flavored purple grape was the product of C.W. Grant, a Newburgh dentist who in 1856 gave up his practice to devote full time to the commercial nursery he'd started on the island. Sad to say, Grant was a poor businessman and even worse at planning parties. An 1864 fruit-growers' convention he organized on the island was an utter fiasco, and there was also widespread criticism when his delicate Iona grape was awarded the $100 prize offered by newspaperman Horace Greeley for a variety best adapted to general cultivation. Grant was persuaded to return the prize, and he retired from grape-growing a few years later. Today only some errant vines hint at Grant's 20-acre vineyard on Iona Island, most of which is not open to the public, even though it is part of the Palisades Interstate Park system.

Financial failure was a fairly common fate among the Valley's 19th century viticulturists, including the most prolific of them all—Newburgh's James H. Ricketts. During the 1860s and '70s, Ricketts bred dozens of different varieties, among which the Downing, Empire State, and the Highland are three of the best known. The Downing, by the way, was named after Charles—not his younger brother, the landscape architect Andrew Jackson Downing. (See the chapter on "God's Own Gardener.") Both of these Newburgh brothers raised and wrote about grapes, but it was Charles who was considered the country's foremost pomologist.

Farther up the Valley in Columbia County, the ever-enterprising Shakers of New Lebanon had early climbed aboard the viticultural bandwagon when two of their members introduced the Northern Muscadine grape around 1852. Alas, the fruit proved unprofitable since it tended to split as soon as it ripened. But that didn't deter the Shakers, who went on to develop several other varieties, including the Mount Lebanon grape.

Perhaps the most unusual viticultural tale also comes from the Shakers, though this one is set across the river in the Watervliet community of Albany County. It was there in the Spring of 1878 that, according to the journal of Elder David Austin Buckingham, "grape potatoes" were inadvertently invented by him. In an effort to staunch the "bleeding" of a cut grapevine,

Buckingham "put on a potato tightly pressed." The following fall he found the host plant had produced young potatoes "about the size and color of the Delaware Grape." When planted, these yielded plum-size potatoes, and by 1881 Buckingham was getting "grape potatoes" weighing almost 2 pounds!

At other Valley vineyards, the yield was certainly not as enormous. Viticulture was at best an uncertain business, with long days of back-breaking labor subject to invalidation by some whim of nature. And anyone interested in a frank first-hand account should be sure to read the short chapter Julian Burroughs included about it in his *Hudson Valley Memories*. The author's father was the famed naturalist, John Burroughs, who operated a fruit farm at his Riverby estate in Ulster County's West Park.

The Burroughs family was fortunate in that it grew mostly "fancy" or "table" grapes, for the bottom fell out of the vintner's vat toward the end of the 19th century. The decline of the valley's wine industry was all the more deadly because it was due to a combination of factors: diseases of eastern grapes that had not yet been addressed by modern science, overproduction in California that flooded the market with low-priced western wines, and a growing temperance movement with such song lines as "No, sir. No, sir. Not with the wine/Lips that touch liquor must never touch mine." Prohibition struck the final blow, and only a few vintners survived the "noble experiment" by producing sacramental wines.

There's something magic about this Valley, though. In the latter part of the 20th century there was a virtual vinicultural revolution. New vineyards were planted, new wineries built, and new grape varieties developed. Modern merchandising techniques were brought into play as well: wine tastings, grape stompings, art shows and other entertainments have been introduced to lure tourists, along with touting the spectacular scenery of hillside vineyards. Aiding all this was a 1999 state law creating a "Winery Trail," and in 2001 a store opened in Manhattan's SoHo district devoted solely to New York wines—200 kinds from 52 different wineries. Two years later, about 170 wineries were in operation state-wide, dozens in the Hudson Valley alone. And with numbers like that, there's no doubt the grape is here to stay.

37. Orange County's Ice-Age
Time Capsule

Unmindful of the human eyes monitoring its every move, the mastodon lumbered through the swamp, intent on reaching the lush vegetation bordering a nearby lake. But as it passed below the hillside cave where the hunter crouched, the beast bogged down—a perfect target as each thrash of its multi-ton body caused it to sink more securely in the mud. The hunter dropped the caribou bone he had been gnawing and grabbed for his spear. Then just as quickly he set the weapon aside. Enmired though it might be, the mastodon's long and curving twin tusks made it more than a match for the lone man. Far better, the hunter decided, to get help from other members of his clan. And so anxious was he to find them that he hurried from the cave, unaware that one of his spear points had fallen from his belt . . . .

The foregoing may well have been the way a distinctive fluted point was deposited in an Orange County cave at the end of the Ice Age, but no one knows for certain. The only surety is the sensation that spear point caused many millennia later. For the presence of that artifact, along with associated finds of stone and bone, make the place where they were discovered one of the most important archeological sites in the northeastern United States— and one of the most endangered.

It is also a site that has changed dramatically in the hundred or so centuries since the last of the great glaciers retreated and mastodons roamed the region. Located on the northern face of a limestone hill in what is now the town of Goshen, the cave visited by the aforementioned Paleo-Indian hunter was only one of several shelters in the rock that were utilized by succeeding native American cultures—the Archaic (dating from around 8000 to 1000 B.C.), as well as Woodland people (c. 1000 B.C.-A.D. 1650).

But by the time European settlers arrived in the area at the beginning of the 18th century, rockfalls and the silting-in of some cave openings had pretty much masked the presence of those prehistoric people.

The newcomers soon found their own uses for the hill, which they called

Mount Lookout. A local tradition tells of beacon fires being lit there during the Revolutionary War, but the name may merely reflect the spectacular view from the summit, or the fact that early land surveyors used it as a focal point. Whatever the case, the promontory later lent its name to the adjoining Mount Lookout Farm, part of which Judge William Thompson sold to the county on January 29, 1830. The purpose of the purchase was to establish a county-run home for paupers, with the contract for construction awarded to John H. Corwin and Samuel Bull of Wallkill. The Bull family was noted for its sturdy stone houses, examples of which are still extant, including Hill Hold, a 1769 house-museum on Route 416 in the town of Hamptonburgh. So it stands to reason that stone was the material Samuel Bull selected for the new structure. Nor did the builders have to go far; they simply quarried the lead-colored limestone of Mount Lookout.

While this stone was not considered very good for lime-burning, it did make fine building blocks, and during the ensuing decades it was chosen for various buildings, including such Goshen churches as St. James' Episcopal (1853) on South Church Street, and the First Presbyterian (1871) on Park Place. As for the Poor House completed in 1831, that 4-storey building stands on the grounds of what is now the Orange County Residential Health Care Facility just off Quarry Road (County Route 68).

It was a problem with the Poor House water source that first hinted of a network of subterranean tunnels in and around Mount Lookout. Writing about the 660-foot promontory in his 1846-47 *Outline History of Orange County*, Samuel W. Eager noted that not only was it "cavernous," but that in times of flood a stream on the *east* side of Mount Lookout "vents itself through the base of the hill." Then emerging on the *west* side, the stream "discolors and muds the [Poor House's] fine large spring." It was not until a dozen decades later, though, that the possibility of a cave system was scientifically explored. In the meantime, what seemed like merely a series of shallow rockshelters attracted generations of local sightseers. The late Amy Bull Crist, for instance, fondly recalled the day her father Bartow Bull took time off from their Stony Ford farm in the town of Wallkill and drove the family down to a place locally known as Dead Dog Rockshelter. That 1919 outing proved so enjoyable that years later when she became a teacher, Amy regularly led Enrichment Program field trips to the Mount Lookout area.

An earlier teacher had not fared so well, yet that schoolmarm's misfortune may be the very thing which kept a vital location from being lost. It seems this rather hefty lady was teaching at the Old Stone Schoolhouse on Route 17A (now maintained by the DAR and occasionally open to the public), when she decided to take her class for a springtime nature walk on nearby Mount Lookout, and wound up getting wedged in the narrow entrance of a cave. The thoroughly flustered teacher was freed within a few minutes, thanks to the tugging of her students, but it is safe to say that few of them ever forgot what happened—at least not a Durlandville boy named Gustav Havrenek, who was present that day.

More than a half-century later, in May 1964, Havrenek described the incident for two members of the Orange County Chapter of the New York State Archaeological Association, who were then conducting a survey of Indian sites. Even more importantly, Havrenek was able to tell them where to find the cave. Fortunately, it was located on the northwestern face of Mount Lookout, and therefore had escaped damage from the still-active quarry at the southern end. For according to a Middletown man named Henry Malley, who had played there as a boy, another larger cave on the quarry side of the hill had yielded numerous Indian artifacts before being obliterated by blasting in the 1930s.

Both of the amateur archeologists—George R. Walters of Otisville and William F. Ehlers, Jr. of Middletown—felt that Havrenek's cave merited investigation. Enlisting the aid of other chapter members, they soon unearthed enough evidence of human presence there to mount a full-scale excavation in March 1965. But by no means did any of them dream how far back in time their discoveries would take them, or how much dedication would be demanded. The first major hurdle was a massive amount of fallen rock that had nearly closed off the cave entrance, leaving an opening a mere 31 inches high. (No wonder the hefty schoolmarm got stuck!) It took three weekends of back-breaking labor just to clear away the tons of rubble. And it wouldn't have been accomplished in that time had it not been for a cadre of Middletown High School student volunteers led by their science teacher, Ralph Robinson. Yet the work had just begun. Many more tons of dirt and stone remained to be sifted or shifted as the amateur archeologists carefully studied the 60-foot-deep cave.

The effort was well worthwhile. Within two months of the project's start, chapter member Bill Vernooy discovered a fluted Paleo-Indian spear point not far from some caribou bones. ("Fluted" denotes a spear point with a carved channel down the middle for attaching a wooden shaft. Interestingly enough, tools made by the earliest—or Paleo—Indians tend to be more skillfully crafted than artifacts of later cultures.) Either find would have been remarkable by itself, in that caribou remains are extremely rare as far south as Goshen, and fluted points almost as uncommon. But taken together, the stone artifact and the bone—the latter of which could be carbon-dated and showed signs of having been broken by humans to extract the marrow—constituted some of the earliest evidence of man ever found in the Northeast, possibly dating back as far as 12,500 years.

In all, the excavation yielded nearly 5,000 pieces of bone, ranging from ancient elk to the now extinct passenger pigeon, and even some scales from a giant sturgeon. The fish was likely obtained locally too, for in the far distant past a large lake—dubbed Halcyon by scientists—once covered what is now the black-dirt farmland at the base of Mount Lookout.

The discovery of over 30 prehistoric tools, most of which are now housed at the State Museum in Albany, also helped to give investigators a fairly good idea of how native Americans used the cave: mainly as a temporary shelter while hunting during the warmer months. But countless questions remained, and in an effort to protect the county-owned site for future study, the archeological group sought to have it declared a historic preserve. By this time, the shelter was being called the Dutchess Quarry Cave, due to the mining company of that name which had been leasing much of Mount Lookout from Orange County since 1938. And during those decades, their quarrying had come closer and closer to the escarpment containing the caves.

Archeologists' marks on the interior wall of Dutchess Quarry Cave indicate the height of the dirt and rock that nearly filled the chamber during the hundred or so centuries since Paleo-Indians first camped here.

A preseve of slightly more than 2 acres was listed on the New York State Register of Historic Places in 1970, followed by national landmark status in 1974. That was the year the site came to the attention of Dr. J.S. "Steve" Kopper, a Long Island University professor of anthropology, who was also an experienced spelunker knowledgeable in karst formations (those features associated with cavernous regions). Kopper immediately suspected the site was part of a single large cave system, and by using an electrical resistivity meter he discovered seven other entrances buried by rock debris. Three of them proved to contain archeological evidence, including several more fluted points and some mysterious spear tips that Kopper could not match with any previously known types. This, naturally, spurred him to further study, and he continued to visit Mount Lookout periodically until his premature death in 1984.

That tragedy heralded tying time ahead. Kopper's excavated material wound up missing, along with his field notes. Those notes were never found, but State Archeologist Robert E. Funk and paleontologist David W. Steadman eventually manged to track down some specimens, which were then brought to the State Museum in Albany for examination. And whenever time permitted, Funk and Steadman joined archeological chapter members in carrying on work at Mount Lookout—work that turned up still another fluted point and the possibility of at least a couple more buried caves.

The two scientists eventually produced a study of the Dutchess Quarry Caves—purportedly the only monograph the New York State Museum has ever published about an Orange County archeological site. But perhaps an even greater contribution was Funk and Steadman's involvement in the crusade to save the caves from threatened demolition. Simply stated, the controversy commenced when the quarry company sought permission to expand its activities at Mount Lookout during the late 1980s. The Department of Environmental Conservation then required a cultural resources survey be made. The survey was funded by the quarry company and completed in 1992.

It should be noted that the quarry company had a reputation for respecting preservation efforts. In fact, at one time the company committed some of its equipment to help the archeological chapter in recovering a mastodon skeleton at another site. Nevertheless, there was fear for the safety of the caves—a fear further exacerbated by talk in the county legislature of selling the property outright to the lessee for mining. No action was taken, but $555,000 for 46 acres was no small sum in financially stressed times, especially when the quarry company promised to reclaim the land following its depletion, then return it to the county.

It sounded like an offer too good to refuse, yet that is exactly what the opposition demanded. For while the 2.1-acre preserve could not be touched, reverberations from nearby dynamite charges could cause damage. Once disturbed, let alone destroyed, an archeological site can never be reclaimed, the activists argued. And there was still much work to be done, considering that none of the caves had been fully excavated. What's more, studies had shown there were significant spots extending beyond the boundaries of the original preserve. How far? That was not fully known, which was why some people insisted that all of the county-owned land at Mount Lookout should be protected, or at least that the boundary of the historic preserve be expanded to 13.2 acres. The latter was accomplished in the mid-1990s with the enlarged site receiving state—but not national—registration. That does not mean this Ice-Age time capsule is secure, but it's a step in the right direction—the direction being a greater understanding of our ancient heritage.

[Note: The preceding chapter is dedicated to the late William F. Ehlers, Jr., who was ever generous in sharing his vast knowledge of archeology, and who did so much to preserve the state's prehistoric sites.]

38. Passing Marks

CHECK ANY LIST OF LEISURE-TIME ACTIVITIES IN THE HUDSON VALLEY, and you're not likely to find mention of cemetery touring. Yet this little-publicized pursuit by people other than mourners has grown increasingly popular, particularly among genealogists who rely on tombstones to provide information missing in old records. As for art lovers, history buffs, and anyone simply seeking an enlightening outdoor adventure, lessons abound in these silent classrooms of the past.

Although native American burials date back thousands of years, it was not until the 17th century arrival of European settlers that the Valley hosted its first true epitaphs. Even then, not everyone was represented, for life was harsh and literacy a luxury. But most families managed some kind of memorial to their deceased loved ones, if only a set of initials scratched on a slab of local stone, such as the rough-cut spears that make Ulster County's old Hurley burial ground so dramatic.

That many of those early settlers hailed from Holland is readily apparent too, not only from their Dutch surnames, but in epitaphs beginning (with variant spellings) "Heir leydr begraven . . . ." That Dutch equivalent for "Here lies buried," found in practically all the Valley's old cemeteries, is usually followed by the exact age—down to the number of "maenden" (months) and "dagen" (days)—of the person who "gestorven" (died). Not solely a Dutch tradition, this Bible-derived numbering of days initially reflected the religiosity of the times, as did tombstone design. Stark death's head images—generally carved in a semicircle at the top of a fieldstone slab—provided graphic reminders of human mortality, with its heaven/hell afterlife option. And if symbols were not enough, there were always epitaphs. Typical of these is one at St. Paul's churchyard in the Westchester County city of Mt. Vernon that goomily admonishes:

> Stop my Friend: O take another view—
> The dust that moulders here
> Was once beloved like you.
> No longer then on future time rely;
> Improve the present and prepare to die.

Gradually, gravestone symbols became less scary: skulls gave way to winged angels, and there were even stylized depictions of the deceased called portrait stones. It was a change largely due to the advent of the Enlightenment, as well as the religious revivals of America's Great Awakening, the latter predating by a decade or so the 1751 appearance of Thomas Gray's influential poem, "Elegy Written in a Country Church Yard." With more emphasis being placed on heavenly rewards, tombstones sprouted symbols such as rising suns (resurrection) and ropes (eternity), but the willow tree (introduced early in the 18th century and representing sorrow) easily became the favorite. So did lengthy biographical epitaphs, which ranged from poetic endings—

> The Boisterous Winds and Neptune's
> Waves have Tost me too and Fro.
> By God's decree you Plainly See
> I am harboured here Below"

to the endlessly puzzling—

> She died *happily* . . .

And ever the poignant—as in the single tombstone at Tarrytown's Sleepy Hollow Cemetery that records the death of three siblings, all under six years of age and within nine days of each other, during the autumn of 1794.

On the other hand, those 18th century epitaphs did not have to be lengthy to tell a tale. Take Berhard Zipling's tombstone in back of the Lutheran Old Stone Church north of Rhinebeck in Dutchess County. The crudely lettered column with its reversed "N's" suggests the problems faced by Zipling and other non-English-speaking Palatine Gemans when they were relocated to America in the early 1700s. Then there are the many markers of men killed in battle, though perhaps not as numerous as the infants that died, or the women who succumbed giving birth to them. Their epitaphs recall this tragic toll, while associated stones often reveal the fact that surviving spouses frequently were forced to remarry in a hurry simply to keep their families intact.

But by no means did everyone die young. Women who survived childhood diseases and childbirth were apt to live to a ripe old age—something attested to at the Hamptonburgh Cemetery in Orange County, where Sarah Wells Bull was buried in April 1796, a few weeks after celebrating her 102nd birthday. As for colonial men, at least two Westchesterites achieved the age of 103: John Wallace, whose grave is located in the North Salem cemetery, and Captain John Buckhout at Sleepy Hollow.

Getting back to the distaff side, it is interesting to note that women were rarely treated as individuals on tombstones. Instead, they were referred to as "wife of" or "daughter of," with their names usually below that of the male relative when a single tombstone was used. In cases of separate markers, invariably the lady's was littler. This practice has not entirely died out either, though today it is common to see the marital bond symbolized by a carving of clasped hands above side-by-side, equal-sized epitaphs. And speaking of hands, in earlier days, many a tombstone motif was that of an upraised finger pointing towards heaven, but on at least one occasion the stonecutter was paid to direct the finger downward!

The dawning of the 19th century saw great changes occurring in the region's cemeteries. Different architectural styles gained favor—Federal as well as Greek Revival—and marble became the preferred medium for mortuary art. Meanwhile, the lengthy biographical epitaph declined in popularity, supplanted by briefer tributes meant as much for the mourner as the mourned. A grieving husband in the Albany County town of Berne therefore might find comfort in the verse dedicated to his wife Fanny, dead at the age of 23 on August 5, 1829:

> The winter of trouble is past
> The storms of affliction are o'er
> Her struggle is ended at last
> And sorrow and death are no more.

But widowers were wont to vent their anguish too, as seen in the closing lines of an epitaph written for another August burial two decades later in Phillipstown, Putnam County:

> There's nothing left to care for now
> Since my poor Mary died
> Thou single hearted yet firm purposed creature.

And sometimes saddened families felt it necessary to record exact details of tragic accidents like the one which befell Isaac Tallman, whose remains were interred in Rockland County's Palisades Cemetery:

> Engineer, killed on the N.Y. & Erie R.R.
> Whilst running the night express with
> Engine no. 37, caused by a rock laying [sic.]
> On the track, April 4, 1853, Aged 30 years,
> 3 months & 26 days.

Yet the expression of parental sorrow was still the most moving of all:

> Ah death couldst thou not spare
> This youthful bloom
> But summoned him so early to the tomb . . . .

That epitaph, seen in the Westchester County village of Bedford's Old Burial Ground, belongs to one of three children killed by an explosion set off when some boys began "testing" gunpowder in a local store on June 24, 1818.

Discovering the little-known stories behind such stones is one of the lures of cemetery touring, but at times it can be a tad disconcerting when epitaph and evidence don't jibe. For example, a certain Putnam County preacher has a monument in the Southeast Churchyard lengthily lauding— and in Latin—his "pleasant" and "placable" nature. Public record, however, reveals his parishioners thought otherwise.

Much may also be learned from the mere location of a stone. Those purposely placed flat on the ground usually were done so as a demonstration of death being the great equalizer, while west-facing markers recall the universal last journey into the setting sun. And pebbles placed atop a headstone indicate an old Judaic custom whereby visitors always leave such "calling cards." In addition, tombstones frequently can be found outside the fence of an old graveyard, but rarely was this done because there was no room inside. Rather, it was a case of segregation. Executed criminals were not allowed in hallowed ground, while unwed mothers and other "sinners" generally weren't either. Slaves occasionally were accorded one corner, but more often were interred "beyond the pale"—see, for instance, the scattered slabs in back of the white-fenced Bronck family cemetery in Coxsackie, Greene County.

Most communities set aside space for paupers, though not always within graveyards, which is why an indigent wanderer known as the Old Leatherman wound up in an unmarked plot at the entrance to Ossining's Sparta Cemetery in Westchester County. Fortunately, the site was not forgotten, and more than six decades after his death in 1889, the Leatherman was memorialized with the stone seen there today. It is a marker too often overlooked by seekers of the cemetery's more famous Ladew tombstone. That brownstone slab set in the cemetery fence has a hole supposedly made by a cannonball shot from the British warship *Vulture* as she lay at anchor in the Hudson during September 1780, waiting to transport the traitorous Benedict Arnold to New York City.

Other traditions tell of tombstones purposely turned. One in Kingston's Old Dutch Churchyard reputedly belongs to a young fellow who died in a drunken fall, and his marker faces away from those of his disapproving parents. Likewise, in Rensselaer County's Sand Lake Cemetery, the tall monument of 19th century Anti-Rent leader Smith Boughton is said to have been shifted so it would not overlook an enemy's grave. But that is not Rensselaer's most legendary marker. A headless, handless statue in the town of Brunswick's Forest Park graveyard supposedly sheds blood when the moon is full, while a few miles to the west, an impregnable mausoleum in Troy's Oakwood Cemetery signifies the fear of financier Russell Sage's widow that miscreants might kidnap the corpse and hold it for ransom.

Mention of Oakwood—one of the most magnificent of the region's rural cemeteries— brings us to the mid-19th century and the trend toward spacious burial grounds outside urban areas. Aside from aesthetics, contributing factors to this trend included overcrowded older cemeteries, developers' needs for city land, and even sanitary concerns. For example, Platt's *History of Poughkeepsie* cites the cholera epidemic of 1842 as being the probable catalyst in the eventual establishment of the city's extensive rural cemetery.

Volumes could be written about these "silent cities of stone," but the important thing to remember is that rural cemeteries were designed as much for the living as for the dead. Hence, their parklike settings were studded with all sorts of homey symbols: from sculpted seats and flower pots, to life-sized pet dogs and fenced-in family plots. Books were a big item too, the largest one likely the lovely stone tome fronting the Burden mausoleum in the Albany Rural Cemetery, whereas Middletown's Hillside Cemetery in Orange County hosts a book-bedecked desk memorializing a local lawyer. All this elegance was counterpointed in some rural cemeteries by caches of simple stones from burial grounds that had been relocated to make way for progress. And there is no more impressive a collection than that in the Poughkeepsie Rural Cemetery, where long rows of tilted, back-to-back markers recall the old North Road graveyard of the Reformed Dutch Church.

The late Victorian period (c. 1880-1905) has been called the Age of Monuments in mortuary art due to its preoccupation with opulence. Two of the grandest examples stand side by side in the West Point Cemetery: that of Civil War General Daniel Butterfield, with 16 embellished columns commemorating the 43 engagements in which he took part, and the Egyptian pyramid guarded by two sphinxes that houses the remains of General Egbert Viele. Like many Victorians, Viele was a spiritualist, and the bell in the apex of the pyramid reportedly was placed there in case he wanted to send some post-mortem messages. There is no record of Viele ever tolling his bell, but another supernatural happening—this one associated with a statue called the Bronze Lady in Sleepy Hollow Cemetery—has been verified by more than one observer. Sitting in mournful

Left: called the Bronze, or Weeping, Lady, this larger-than-life statue in Westchester County's Sleepy Hollow Cemetery is said to shed tears in mourning for Civil War General Samuel M. Thomas.

Below: as befitting a burial ground devoted to creative people, the Artists' Cemetery in Woodstock contains some of the loveliest and most unique modern memorials to be seen.

reverie overlooking the grave of Civil War General Samuel M. Thomas, this larger-than-life statue is said to shed tears—indeed, stains can still be seen running down its cheeks—and that some people have heard sounds of weeping.

Legends of another sort are legion in other Westchester County cemeteries such as Kensico in Valhalla and Ferncliff in Hartsdale, where so many famous folk are buried—bandleader Tommy Dorsey, author Ayn Rand, comedian Danny Kaye, baseball great Lou Gehrig, Broadway showman Florenz Ziegfeld, and composer Sergei Rachmaninoff, to name a mere half-dozen. And those interested in Prohibition era gangster Dutch Schultz, homerun hitter Babe Ruth, or comedian Fred Allen can find them all at Gate of Heaven Cemetery in Hawthorne, along with a host of other celebrities. (Some cemeteries, it might be added, provide tour brochures.) Westchester County also hosts the country's oldest animal burial ground—the Hartsdale Pet Cemetery, where a variety of fauna have been interred, from alligators, monkeys and chickens to snakes, birds and a lion named "Goldfleck." Eccentric millionaire financier Hetty Green's dog—named "Money," naturally—is buried there as well. But the cemetery is best known for its impressive War Dog Memorial capped by a lifelike statue of a German Shepherd commemorating the K-9 Corps of World War I.

Around the time the Hartsdale Pet Cemetery was established in 1896, there was the aforementioned trend for bigger and bigger human sepulchres, while inscriptions got smaller—something evident in the following epitaph from the Albany Rural Cemetery:

Dyer Lathrop
born into immortal life
1803
born into life immortal
1882

That kind of verbal reticence was finally followed by a more reserved taste in monuments—a refinement that has more or less continued to the present day. It might even be said that some tombstone design has come full circle, with a common choice being the kind of unembellished rough boulder used in the Harriman family plot at Arden in Orange County. But with CAD (computer-assisted design) programs currently revolutionizing the stonecutter's art, who knows what tomorrow's cemeteries may hold. Hopefully they will be as tasteful as the modern-day Artist's Cemetery in the Ulster County community of Woodstock—a place with the type of tombstones that make our Valley such a class act when it comes to passing marks.

39. Logging Our Historic Trees

I T MAY STARTLE SOME READERS TO LEARN THAT THE DEPARTMENT OF Environmental Conservation has been busy logging the region's most remarkable trees. But not to worry. It's cataloguing—not cutting—that the DEC's been doing, and it has resulted in an ensorceling two-part survey of the state's arboreal treasures. As its name implies, the part called the Big Tree Registry lists only giants, whereas the honor role of Famous and Historic Trees designates dozens of individual trees that are in some way significant to the story of New York, with many of them located in the Hudson Valley—from the oldest bald cypress in America at Albany's Bleecker Stadium, to the infamous gllows oak of Peekskill in Westchester County.

The latter, called the Hanging Tree, stands apart from all other Hudson Valley honorees in that it is a grim reminder of the military executions that took place during the dark days of the Revolutionary War. A local man named Daniel Strang met his death there on January 27, 1777, having been tried at a court-martial presided over by Colonel Henry B. Livingston. Strang had pleaded innocent to the charge of being a British spy, but could not deny possessing a document that empowered him to raise recruits for the redcoats. That was enough to convict him, and he was soon swinging from a limb of this white oak, after which a party of mounted patriots paraded around the tree prior to burying Strang's body in an unmarked grave nearby.

The story doesn't end there though, nor does the Hanging Tree's military associations. In 1834 the Peekskill Military Academy was established at the site, and for more than a century the wide-spreading oak was a favorite gathering place for cadets, as well as the focal point of the school's commencement ceremonies. Doubtless the tragedy of the Tory recruiter was conversational fare from the very first day the academy opened, but the tale was given a fresh twist in 1843 when excavation for a new school building unearthed what were believed to be Strang's bones. This only added to the already deep regard for the Hanging Tree as a "living link to the Revolution," and it was carefully tended down through the decades—a towering history lesson on what is now the Peekskill High School campus, northwest of the junction of Wells and Elm streets.

Revolutionary War associations also figure in two other Hudson Valley trees being named to the state registry. Both are lovely old sycamores, and both shade buildings that served as George Washington's headquarters, with the best known being the one that stands by the old Miller farmhouse on Virginia Road in North White Plains. Presently maintained as a museum by Westchester County, the Miller dwelling is dwarfed by the centuries-old sycamore, whose roots have pushed up the floorboards, and whose branches brush the window of an upstairs bedroom used by the commander-in-chief during the critical battle of White Plains in October 1776. The farmhouse was small, so whenever the weather was warm enough, Washington met with his men in the shade of the sycamore. Alexander Hamilton, George Clinton and General Lafayette are three of the officers who conferred there, while in later years the renowned Methodist leader Francis Asbury preached beneath its branches.

The second sycamore can be found at the John Kane House on Main Street in the Dutchess County village of Pawling. Like Peekskill's Hanging Tree, it hints of the divided loyalties that made the Revolution America's first civil war. For the house it stands near—cared for by the Historical Society of Quaker Hill and Pawling—was owned by a Tory whose property was confiscated and he was forced to flee. Subsequently, George Washington moved into John Kane's home, using it as his headquarters during the two months he stayed at Pawling during the autumn of 1778.

The granddaddy of sycamores, however, is a double-trunked giant bordering Brown's Road in the Orange County town of Montgomery. Topping out at 154 feet and measuring 26 feet in circumference, it is the largest American sycamore in the state. No one knows exactly how old it may be, but in the 1800s, its already towering trunks were stabilized by a chain whose links are now so deeply embedded in the bark that the chain looks as if it grew out of the tree. Yet it was not size alone or preservation efforts that won the Wallkill Valley Sycamore its place on the state registry; it overlooks a council ground frequented by native Americans in the 1600s, and likely served as their landmark.

For anyone interested in such tribal traditions, Putnam County's Indian Oak is also noteworthy. Located on private property, but visible from a fieldstone marker on Andrea Drive at the northwestern tip of Peach Lake, this magnificent white oak—whose branches have a horizontal spread of over 95 feet—is an apt monument to the Wappingers who maintained a permanent summer camp there. (Acorns, of course, were an important food source for Indians during times of scarcity, but the white oak was particularly prized by them because of the astringent and antiseptic properties of its inner bark.)

From the foregoing it might appear that only sycamores and oaks have been named to the Famous and Historic Tree Registry. Indeed, these durable species do dominate the list, but they are joined by an assortment of other trees, each with its own interesting story that touches upon some aspect of our history. There are, for instance, Rockland County's Concklin Apple Trees, seen on the east side of Route 45, where it meets Pomona Road. Planted by Nicholas Concklin in 1711 and still bearing apples, these trees reportedly represent the oldest fruit farm in the United States, and the start of an important Hudson Valley industry.

Locusts were widely planted by 18th century settlers as well, since these thorny hardwoods were both utilitarian and ornamental. In addition to its wood—used for everything from fenceposts and furniture to animal traps— the locust's heavily scented May blossoms were irresistible to bees, providing farmers with bountiful harvests of much-needed honey and beeswax. And because of their deep and fast-growing taproots, locusts were considered natural lightning rods, as is evidenced by those at the Heermance-Bulkeley Homestead on West Kerley's Corner Road (Route 78) in the Dutchess County town of Red Hook. While viewing the venerable locusts that front the road, look beyond at the Dutch stone farmhouse they were planted to protect. Built by the Heermance family in the mid-1700s, it was—according to the registry—"a vital link in communication" during the Revolutinary War.

Folklore-fanciers, on the other hand, may find the Balmville Tree most fascinating. Early settlers believed it to be a balm of Gilead tree and named the surrounding community for it, along with the road on which it stands, but it is actually a cottonwood, whose origins are layered in colorful legends. One such tale tells of a riding crop that was thrust into the ground and miraculously took root, while another tradition says its branched trunk resulted from the young tree being cut for a cattle goad during colonial times. Whatever its beginnings, the Balmville Tree, just north of Newburgh in Orange County, has remained a beloved landmark whose traffic-island site is

New York's smallest state forest–population one–the Balmville Tree may also be the oldest and most legendary, having supposedly sprung from a riding crop that was thrust into the ground and took root centuries ago.

now preserved as the smallest state forest in New York. In addition, it has been listed on the National Register of Historic Places since 2001.

Two other historic Orange County trees were not so fortunate. Shortly after being named to the state's Historic Tree registry, storms terminally damaged both the Messenger Oak (named for a famous stallion) at Goshen's Historic Track, and West Point's Copper Beech, which legend has it was planted in 1802 by the U.S. Military Academy's first superintendent, Major Jonathan Williams. But the latter mishap may make for still another Hudson Valley legend, since the copper beech fell at the time Kristin Baker became West Point's first female First Captain of the Corps of Cadets—and some male wags there maintained that the old tree died of shock!

As for other regional trees listed in the registry, all deserve appreciative attention, though they are accorded only a brief mention here. From south to north, they include:

• English Yews (tip of Teller's Point, Croton Point Park, west of Route 9, Westchester County), planted in the mid-1800s by the Underhill family, whose nearby vineyard was reputedly the first such commercial venture in the United States. (See chapter on "Vino, Vitas, Vinifera . . . A Tale Divine.")

• Merwin Oak (Vassallo Park, Old Albany Post Road, Croton-on-Hudson), the largest of its kind in Westchester County, it was named for village engineer Ted Merwin, who saved it from construction damage.

• Bedford Oak (Route 22 and Hook Road, north of Bedford Village, Westchester County), estimated to be 500 years old, and preserved in 1977 by local donations.

• Sargent Ginko and Weeping Ponderosa Pine (off Wodenethe Drive, Beacon, Dutchess County), planted by the noted 19th century arborist, Henry Sargent, in the garden of his Wodenethe estate.

• Memorial Oaks (near the railroad station, Memorial Avenue, Pawling, Dutchess County), numbering 13 pin oaks planted in 1945 by men from the Pawling Army Hospital to honor local servicemen who died in World War II.

• Vassar Sycamore (near the main building, Vassar College campus, Poughkeepsie, Dutchess County), adopted as a class tree in 1906, and symbolizing the concern of the college's founder, Matthew Vassar, for landscape planning. (The Vassar campus, by the way, hosts over 200 arboreal species, from sweetbay magnolia and weeping hemlock to Korean hornbeam and Russian olive trees.)

• Klyne Esopus Tree (Klyne-Esopus Historical Society, Route 9W, Esopus, Ulster County), one of the last of the maples that were mature trees as the time the brick Dutch Reformed church—now a museum of lcoal history—was built in 1827. (Unfortunately, the tree was felled by tropical storm Floyd in September 1999.)

• Schuyler Walnut (The Grove, Route 308 and Miller Road, Rhinebeck, Dutchess County), planted in 1794 by Revolutionary War General Philip Schuyler on the lawn of his son's estate.

• Chatham's 1902 Arbor Day Oak (Middle School, Woodbridge Avenue, Chatham village, Columbia County), the oldest of the trees planted by the local school district, which has continuously celebrated Arbor Day since New York began the observance in 1889.

Arbor Day was the brainchild of a native New Yorker, Julius Sterling Morton, who introduced the idea in 1872. It soon became a national movement, backed by leading conservationists of the day, including the Hudson Valley's beloved "Sage of Slabsides," John Burroughs, and by the end of the 19th century Arbor Day was being celebrated in almost every state in the union.

The planting and preservation of trees has become even more important in the 21st century, as scientists seek to combat global warming with massive reforestation. In 1990, President George Bush proposed that a billion trees a year be planted across America during that decade, while the American Forestry Association hoped to have 100 million seedlings in place by 1992 through its Global ReLeaf campaign. Meanwhile, the National Arbor Day Foundation, in conjunction with the U.S. Forest Service and other related organizations, encouraged urban arboreal management through such programs as Tree City, USA. More than a score of communities in the Hudson Valley have been designated as Tree Cities: Millbrook (Dutchess), New Paltz (Ulster), and Port Jervis (Orange) among them. Some of these Tree Cities also host state champions honored in the DEC's Big Tree Registry. Hyde Park, for example, had the state's biggest honey locust, while Poughkeepsie's Vassar College could claim the largest Norway maple, and on nearby Forbus Street stands a champion butternut.

It has been over a century since Arbor Day was first celebrated in New York, and the Hudson Valley can well be proud of its role in preserving trees, as well as in some of the finest arboretums to be found anywhere. The oldest of these is the Mary Flagler Cary Arboretum—also known as the Institute of Ecosystem Studies—on Route 44A in the Dutchess County village of Millbrook. The youngest is the Orange County Arboretum on Route 416 in Hamptonburgh's Thomas Bull Memorial Park. And in between are Lasdon Park Arboretum on Route 35 in Somers (Westchester County), and the Mountain Top Arboretum on Route 23C just north of Tannersville in Greene County. All of them welcome visitors, and if you're not already a tree lover, these exceptional places are sure to make you one.

40. Castles in the Air

D URING THE 1800S IT WAS COMMON TO HEAR THE HUDSON CALLED the American Rhine, even though, as one Berlin University professor put it: "You lack our castles." That quibble wasn't correct, however. For our Valley had long boasted a bevy of castles—albeit some of a brand quite different from Germany's crag-top bastions—and many grander editions would be built before the century ended.

The oldest structures were the work of native Americans: palisaded, hillside strongholds that could contain dozens of dwellings, as did the Shawangunk Castle of the Esopus Indians, located near present-day Ellenville in Ulster County. Others like Maringomen's Castle, on the north end of Orange County's Schunnemunk Mountain, sheltered single families. (Much of the mountain is now public parkland open to hiking, but no trace remains of the castle.)

Across the Hudson, the name of the Westchester County town of North Castle reflects the fact that a large Indian fort once stood on the hill later occupied by IBM's Armonk headquarters. Likewise, aboriginal strongholds reportedly were why Dutchess County's Castle Point and Rensselaer's Castleton were called that. However, not all such old place names have Indian origins. Albany's Castle Island hosted several different colonial forts, the earliest believed to have been built by French traders, and already in ruins when the Dutch took over the site in 1614. At one time even ordinary dwellings might be deemed castles, especially stone homes that were thick-walled and portholed for protection. Coeymans Castle is one example, built around 1674 south of Albany. It was demolished in 1833, but another stalwart structure—the c. 1682 Philipse Castle—remains along Westchester County's Pocantico River in North Tarrytown. (Now part of Philipsburg Manor just east of Route 9, the house is open to the public.)

And while the 1767 mansion of the Cadwallader Colden family was not generally considered a castle, it was the reason for naming a nearby road in the Orange County town of Montgomery. (The ruins of the mansion can be viewed in back of the historic marker near the northeast corner of Route 17K and Stone Castle Road.)

Before leaving the subject of place names, it should be pointed out that they can be misleading. For instance, the source of Nyack's Castle Heights Road in Rockland County seems to have been nothing more than some developer's dream, whereas Newburgh's Castle Avenue was a name assigned "arbitrarily by some interested party." Nor will you find King Arthur's home at the end of Poughkeepsie's Camelot Road. It seems that when Peekskill-born Chauncey Depew was president of the New York Central Railroad in the late 1800s, he decided to re-dub the east-shore Milton Ferry station in order to avoid confusion with a similarly named stop on the west side of the Hudson. Supposedly Depew was also in the process of perusing Tennyson's then-popular poem, *The Idylls of the King*, so Camelot was the name he substituted.

Alfred, Lord Tennyson's long devotion to chivalric themes certainly stimulated interest in the Middle Ages, but even before he published his first widely acclaimed Arthurian poem in 1842, the medieval-type structures we most commonly think of as castles were already apparent in the Hudson Valley. The most prominent were at West Point, where in 1838 U.S. Military Academy Superintendent Richard Delafield deemed that Tudor towers and battlements best suited the new buildings then being planned. Also in that year, politician William Paulding contracted with architect Alexander Jackson Davis to design a retirement home for him in Tarrytown. It was the first of Davis' many Gothic Revival castles, and one so costly that a political rival of the owner referred to it as "Paulding's Folly." Paulding himself called it simply Knoll, but in later years, as it was enlarged by subsequent owner George Merritt, and then Jay Gould, it became known as Lyndhurst—nowadays considered by many to be the finest Gothic Revival residence still standing in America. (Today operated as a house-museum, Lyndhurst is located on Route 9 in Tarrytown/Sleepy Hollow.)

The rise of the Romantic Movement, with its emphasis on medievalism as opposed to classicism, was a catalyst for castle-building in the Valley, especially after the books of one of the movement's leading proponents—Newburgh-born Andrew Jackson Downing—began appearing in 1841. Within a generation, at least a dozen new citadels graced the Hudson shore, including the 1845 stone castle that Erie Railroad baron Eleazar Lord placed atop a Piermont palisade in Rockland County. Most, however, were built in Westchester County, among them the 1860s Belvoir, a Gothic manor on North Broadway in Yonkers that was later turned into the noted Abbey Inn, but is no longer standing; the Gothic Revival Ingleside of the 1850s, much altered in the years since 1881, when it became a Dobbs Ferry school on North Broadway; and Tarrytown's massive Herrick's Folly, built in 1854 on what is now Marymount Avenue. It saw long service (1895-1933) as Miss Mason's Castle School, but was destroyed in the 1940s.

Such commanding structures could also cast dark shadows. Due to a divorce, renowned actor Edwin Forrest never got to enjoy his magnificent multi-towered Fonthill, completed in 1852 at what was then the Yonkers hamlet of Riverdale. (Now part of the College of Mount St. Vincent on Riverdale Avenue, Fonthill is included on periodic walking tours of the campus.) And farther up the Hudson in the Dutchess County town of Rhinebeck, childhood visits to the gloomy, Norman-style brick bastion her aunt Elizabeth Jones built in 1853 left disturbing memories that author Edith Wharton would write about in later years. (See the chapter on "Wherefore Edith Wharton.") The 1860s Ophir Hall in the town of Harrison—said to have been Westchester County's largest castle-style residence, and named for a Nevada silver mine—had some ominous touches too, in that financial ruin was the fate of its first owner, and one month after it was renovated the building burned down. (Also known as Reid Hall, today the castle serves as the focal point of Manhattanville College, off Purchase Street.) Then there was Cunningham Castle, built about 1865 on an Irvington hillside. A local tradition that none but a Cunningham could live there seemed proven true when the castle was destroyed by fire in 1905, immediately after being sold out of the family.

Following a lull during the Civil War, a resurgence of castle-building resulted in some interesting "firsts." Westchester County's Ward Castle on Comly Avenue in Rye Brook is thought to be the "first [1876] building constructed throughout of reinforced concrete," while the painter Albert Bierstadt's 1866 Malkasten—built just west of Broadway in Tarrytown, and named after a German artists' club—was "one of the first Amrican studio-houses to receive extensive publicity."

It was, however, the studio-home of another Hudson River School painter that is better known today: Olana, the Persian-style palace Frederick Church erected on a prominence above Route 9G south of Hudson in Columbia County. Loosely translated, Olana is Arabic for "our castle on high," though "canvas" might be a more suitable noun, since "light, color, and vistas were carefully manipulated by the artist" in planning his home. Church also had a hand in Castle Rock, suggesting both the location and landscaping for the turreted hilltop home in the Putnam County village of Garrison that his childhood friend, William H. Osborn, built in 1881. (Olana is open to the public; Castle Rock is not, but can be viewed from Route 9D south of its intersection with Route 403.)

Scaled-down castles were also being built to fit into an urban setting, among them the 1891 home of inventor Charles La Dow on Albany's Thurlow Terrace, and the 1896 John Paine mansion on Troy's Second Street that is called The Castle. As elegant inside as out, the latter building now serves as the Pi Kappa Phi fraternity house, and was used for some of the scenes in the 1993 movie, *The Age of Innocence*. And for those who savor a spritz of spice, rumor has it that the chamber adjoining the second-floor master bedroom was occupioed by the owner's mistress, while his wife slept upstairs with the children. (Although not generally open to the public, tours of The Castle are held several times a year.)

Aside from residential castles, mention must be made of the region's other kinds of buildings with a medieval mien. Churches, of course, immediately come to mind since so many feature Gothic Revival architecture, and perhaps the most unusual is the Germanic castle otherwise known as the Summerfield Methodist Church on King Street (Route 120A) in Port Chester (Westchester County). As for armories, they are almost always medieval, with the picturesque example on High Street in Saratoga County's Ballston Spa the only one known to have been designed by architect Horatio Nelson White. And talk about beating swords into plowshares, this 1858 armory later became the parish house of nearby Christ Church.

"Castle-like" can also describe some of the later 19th century's large resorts, including Millbrook's Halcyon Hall on Route 44, and the Hotel Kaaterskill north of Tannersville in Greene County. Yet for sheer beauty of setting, nothing quite compares to the still-operating Mohonk Mountain House on Mountain Rest Road west of New Paltz. Nor can we ignore New Rochelle's Kleine Deutschland ("Little Germany")—a pair of beer-garden castles that were part of the amusement park John Starin built on Glen Island in the 1870s.

There are academic castles as well: notably the Emma Willard School on Troy's Pawling Avenue, boasting both Jacobean and Tudor Revival buildings. And among institutions of another sort, the red-brick bulk of Poughkeepsie's Gothic-style Hudson River State Hospital east of Route 9 well deserves notice, as does Napanoch's Eastern New York Reformatory (Eastern Correctional Facility) along Ulster County's Berme Road, featuring green-topped conical guard towers, which opened in 1900.

Diversity was the denominator of those castles constructed during the first few decades of the 20th century—ranging from the enormous, dark-gray granite Rockwood Hall that William Rockefeller finished building at Tarrytown in 1900, to the mere 30-by-80-foot Leeds Castle erected on

Greene County's Potic Mountain in 1913, and the hand-crafted, Depression-era complex which the eccentric philosopher-potter Charles Bouck White assembled atop the Helderberg Plateau west of Albany. (Concerning the latter, check the chapter on "A Maverick Among Us." As for Rockwood Hall, remains of it can be seen in the part of Rockefeller State Park west of Route 9 in Sleepy Hollow.)

Unfortunately, the dreams of some castle-builders never did fully develop. Dick's Castle, east of Route 9W in Garrison—modeled after an 8th century Moorish palace that had caught the fancy of Mrs. Evans B. Dick while touring Spain—was started in 1903 but remained unfinished for many decades. Neither did Charles F. Dieterich complete the various castles he envisioned for his vast estate called Daheim ("The Home") in the Dutchess County village of Millbrook, though one of the structures wound up as a cow barn. (Daheim is sometimes included in historic house tours of the area.)

Muralist Everett Shinn had better luck in making his dream castle come true, and his summer residence called Bailiwick still crowns a hill west of Catskill in Greene County. The 1915 summer castle that woolen manufacturer Julius Forstmann built along Route 47 in Ulster County is more impressive, however—not only because of its magnificent interior woodwork, but also for the ghost sometimes seen on the richly carved main staircase. (Frost Valley YMCA, which owns Forstmann Castle, conducts guided tours of the building.)

Not surprisingly, there have been supernatural sightings reported in other castles too, including the Norman-style Deming-MacGuffie residence in Rockland County's New City. But the bar-none spookiest spot has to be Bannerman's Island, in the Hudson just north of Cold Spring in Putnam County. The 7-storey Scottish castle that arms merchant Francis Bannerman built from discarded paving blocks in the early 1900s probably would be considered haunted even if it were not for the mysterious lights that occasionally flicker within its paneless windows. Ravaged by fire in 1969, the island with its castle complex is now part of Hudson Highlands State Park, and a group called the Bannerman Castle Trust has been waging a heroic battle to preserve the close-to-crumbling structures. (Access to the island is restricted, though fund-raising tours are conducted by the Trust.)

Happily, other Hudson Valley castles are being preserved by altering their purpose. Several have been incorporated into school complexes, as has Leland Castle at the College of New Rochelle. The 1870 Romanesque Revival Roe-Brewster residence in Orange County's New Windsor is now an apartment house, while other castles have been turned into restaurants, such

Not all of the Hudson Valley's numerous castles date back to the dim past. Peter and Toni Wing, for instance, began building their marvelous museum-home in 1969, using materials mainly salvaged from antique structures.

as Maze Castle, located at the Blue Hills Golf Course in Rockland County's Orangetown, which is now known as The Mansion. Still another residence-to-restaurant is Carrollcliffe—the tall gray stone structure also known as Axe Castle that can be seen dominating the eastern landscape as you cross the Tappan Zee Bridge from Rockland County. Opened as a luxury hotel and dining facility in the 1990s, it is now called The Castle at Tarrytown.

Nor has the era of castle-building come to a close, as seen in two contemporary examples a few dozen miles from each other in Dutchess and Columbia counties. Peter and Toni Wing's marvelous melange of recycled materials is located off the Bangall Road northeast of the village of Millbrook—and is straight out of a fairytale, with a museum-like interior (open to tours), while offering fabulous views from its hilltop setting. Scenic grandeur also distinguishes Roy Kanwit's Taconic Sculpture Park and Gallery on Stever Hill Road in Spencertown. But it is his mythology-inspired, monumental works of art—among them a giant "Head of Dionysus" containing interior stairs—that dominate the scene. The sculptor's fanciful fieldstone castle home can be viewed from the outside by visitors welcome to wander the 17-acre property.

By no means does this cover all the Valley"s castles; however, it should be more than sufficient to show that when it comes to the kind of riparian comparisons mentioned at the start of the chapter, our Hudson easily out-Rhines that other famed waterway in Europe.

41. April Gold and Purple Passion—
A Paean to Some Pests

A S WINTER WINDS GIVE WAY TO THE SOFT SHOWERS OF SPRING, THE greening Hudson Valley hills are soon studded with nuggets of floral gold—the first wave in a months-long deluge of dandelions that can be a boon or a bane, depending on your point of view. Many gardeners, of course, decry the dandelion as nothing more than a useless and unsightly weed that ruins lawns and should be eradicated at all costs. Such a harsh judgment horrifies some naturalists and health-food buffs, just as it would have shocked earlier societies, who anxiously awaited the appearance of this hardy perennial each Spring. For notwithstanding the lovers of velvety lawns, the much-maligned dandelion is a true "herbal hero," as author Euell Gibbons once lauded it, with its free-for-the-taking benefits ranging from meals to medicaments.

Exactly when the dandelion's many virtues were first recognized is not known, but an ancient Greek legend describes a nutritious dandelion salad served to Athenian King Theseus, and Chinese physicians have been prescribing dandelion decoctions and poultices for millennia. Nor can anyone say with any surety exactly what part of the dandelion is responsible for its name. While it has been called everything from an "Irish daisy" to an "earth nail," a "peasant's cloak," "priest's crown," "monk's head," and "blow-ball," nowadays the plant is most commonly referred to as a "dandelion"—a corruption of the French *dent de lion*, or "lion's tooth." But whether that describes the somewhat ragged petals, the fang-like leaves, or even the forked root is open to argument, as is the question of its origin.

Most botanists believe the dandelion began in Asia Minor and subsequently spread throughout the Old World, arriving in America along with early European colonists. Other scientists who have studied native American herb medicine are certain the dandelion was being used by Indians long before the 16th century, and one speculation is that trans-Pacific voyages by ancient Orientals resulted in the plant being brought to our shores.

Whatever way it reached the New World, the dandelion flourished and spread, eventually becoming part of the diet of practically every Indian culture across the continent. Some, like the Apaches, relished the slightly bitter leaves, and in springtime would travel long distances just to harvest this natural source of vitamin C for their winter-depleted bodies. Other Indian nations regarded the dandelion strictly as a "famine-food," to be eaten only when nothing else was available. But almost all Indians made use of the medicinal properties of the plant.

Dandelion poultices were thought to reduce swelling, ease bruises and even help mend broken bones, whereas a tea brewed from the blossoms was given as a mild sedative to people with heart trouble. Other parts of the plant provided potions that had a laxative or diuretic effect, and to a lesser degree the dandelion was used to treat respiratory disorders, hypochondria, and even venereal disease. Plains Indians also chewed dandelion stems to keep their mouths moist during dusty journeys or when water was unavailable. Contact between Indians and Caucasions brought about an exchange of ideas, so that today it is difficult to determine which dandelion remedies may have been adopted from or by early settlers. On the other hand, similar ideas could well have occurred independently in both cultures, considering the fact that sympathetic medicine has been practiced on either side of the Atlantic since primitive times. Formally designated as the "Doctrine of Signatures" by Medieval European scientists, sympathetic medicine is based on the belief that every plant has some feature (or signature) which reveals its healing properties. Thus, the color of the dandelion flower signified a cure for yellow jaundice, while the ubiquity of the plant was taken to mean that it was effective for a wide range of ailments.

Despite its genuine medicinal value, the poor dandelion simply couldn't live up to such broad claims, and as modern pharmacology shouldered aside the "Doctrine of Signatures," the once highly regarded plant was relegated to the category of a lowly weed. It was not totally forgotten, though, for it remains an effective treatment for certain disorders, and even today the dandelion is commercially grown for use in laxatives, hepatics and tonics. The cheapness and purity of these factory-produced pharmaceuticals argues against any chance of home-brewed dandelion potions regaining the popularity they once enjoyed. But more and more folk—fed up with food additives and chemical farming practices—are turning to the natural bounty to be found in the fields, and they are rediscovering the dandelion. Hudson Valley dwellers who feel this way—or those merely looking for a change-of-pace food—are in luck, for our region abounds with this easily identified and nutritious wild edible, which can be used in a variety of ways, including as a substitute for coffee.

Despite their propensity for popping up in people's lawns, dandelions are at their best in an untamed setting: "some place where they and the grass have been allowed to grow free" is the way Euell Gibbons described it in his book, *Stalking the Wild Asparagus.* The time of year is important too: dandelion leaves should be picked in early Spring, before the flower buds form, while the leaves are still tender and sweet. This is also the best time for harvesting dandelion roots to be used as a vegetable. However, when intended for a beverage, the roots are just as good if gathered in late summer or early autumn. For those who don't favor foraging the fields, it is possible to purchase commercially grown dandelions in the produce section of large supermarkets. In our region, much of the store-bought variety comes from the southern New Jersey town of Vineland, which calls itself the "Dandelion Capital of the World," and produces an annual crop worth hundreds of thousands of dollars.

Food and medicine are not the only ways the plant is useful. The rich gold of the dandelion's blossoms has been used for fabric dye, and during World War II some effort was made to cultivate the Russian dandelion from which latex could be extracted for the manufacture of rubber. And lest it be thought that the dandelion is an herbal hero only to humans, mention must be made of it as a food source for bees, as well as birds, who feast on the flowering plant's abundant seeds. Youngsters, too, find the dandelion's seeds a source of joy when the golden blossom evolves into a fluffy white ball, and a puff of wind scatters the seeds in all directions. Indeed, who hasn't played one of the many fortune-telling games associated with these delightful "blow-balls"? Depending on the locale and number of seeds remaining after a mighty blast of breath, the dandelion supposedly will reveal anything from the time of day to the number of children the blower may have or how many times that person will marry. As for group contests, these are based on the breaths it takes the player to divest the "blow-ball" of its seeds—old-fashioned fun for kids of all ages!

To sum up then, if you're a gardener given to grousing about the dandelions in your grass, take a moment to consider the other side of the coin—a coin that is, after all, pure April gold. Dandelions are mighty pretty too, though perhaps not as stunning as another plant that has been accused of being the Valley's number-one pest

New York's official state flower is the rose. But if that designation were based on sheer ubiquity as well as beauty, the title might well belong to loosestrife—that odd-named, unruly wildflower whose prolific plumes turn portions of the Hudson Valley into panoramas of scintillating purple each summer. First-time viewers have been known to gasp in awe at this phenomenon, while gasps of another kind emanate from ecological experts who view the beauty as a beast threatening wildlife and wetlands, along with other flora. In between is a legion of loosestrife-lovers, whose appreciation of the controversial wildflower encouraged at least one local newspaper columnist to headline its appearance each year. Yet despite all this attention, few folk know much about purple loosestrife, including the fact that it etymologically isn't. And since that constitutes a basic confusion concerning loosestrife, perhaps that is the best place to start its story.

Botanical legend traces loosestrife all the way back to ancient Thrace, where King Lysimachus was cornered by an angry bull one day while walking alone in a field. Weaponless and without shelter, the king frantically tore up a fistful of tall flowers, which he waved in the face of his four-legged foe. The bull was distracted long enough for the king to reach safety, and thereafter the plant was known as *lysimachia*—from *lysis*, meaning "a release from," and *mache* meaning "strife." The original English translation of *lysimachia* was "lose strife," as the Thracian king did when he escaped from the bull, but somewhere along the line the "lose" became "loose," and so we have "loosestrife."

Compounding this oddity is the fact that purple loosestrife is not *lysimachia* at all, but *lythrum salicaria*, or "blood willow," a name likely chosen to describe its willow-like tendencies and the color of its flowers. (Venal blood has a purplish tint, as opposed to the bright red of oxygenated arterial blood.) As for *lysimachia*, it is a member of the primrose family, and includes entirely different kinds of loosestrife, such as the yellow and whorled varieties.

Now, if all that is not confusing enough, it might be added that purple loosestrife occasionally is mistaken for "long purples" or "dead men's fingers"—a wetlands wildflower common in Elizabethan England, and one which Shakespeare uses to great effect in a scene where the fair Ophelia wears her funereal garlands. This passage in *Hamlet* has been cited by some students as proof that loosestrife and long purples are the same. Yet although the Bard of Avon does make mention of a willow, the long purples he alludes to are early orchids, as proven by his line about "liberal shepherds" calling the plant "a grosser name"—something best left for the reader to check in any unabridged dictionary under "orchis."

An English connection is not altogether erroneous, though, since it is believed that purple loosestrife was first brought to the Hudson Valley in a bale of British wool. The transplanting was totally unintentional: the loosestrife seeds, entangled in the raw wool, were washed into an adjoining waterway when the material was processed at an Orange County mill. Some historians say this occurred at New Windsor, since there are reports of purple loosestrife flowering along the banks of the Moodna Creek in Revolutionary times. Other accounts give loosestrife's starting point a later date and a different location: the seeds supposedly showed up at the old Crabtree Mill on the shore of the Wallkill, where the Montgomery Worsted Mills now stand off Route 17K. From there, loosestrife spread north and south along the river, which is why it is locally referred to as "Pride of the Wallkill."

Another name old-time farmers called it was "rebel weed"—possibly because of some association with the South (where loosestrife also grows), but more likely because even then they recognized its resistance to any form of control. This augury went unheeded, however. Loosestrife was simply too lovely to be considered a threat.

By the late 1800s loosestrife had gained enough of a foothold in the Hudson Valley for naturalist John Burroughs to describe patches of it as "purple bonfires" near his Ulster County home, and before long it was seen marching west along the Mohawk, sprouting up in places it had never been before—dry areas as well as wetlands. It began to extend its growing season too. Instead of just July and August, the purple plumes were appearing in late June and staying well into September.

That this amazing proliferation might one day become more of a worry than a wonder was not evident in the 1930s when Orange County journalist Mildred Parker Seese penned the first of hundreds of articles that eventually earned her the title of the region's "Loosestrife Lady." The diminutive journalist didn't plan it that way; it was just that once she started writing about loosestrife, her readers would not let her stop. Everyone, it seemed, had a question to ask, a story to share, or a photograph to send. And so Mrs. Seese's column in the Middletown *Times Herald* (later the *Times Herald-Record*) became a regular forum for loosestrife lore.

Reports arrived from such faraway places as Alaska and Ireland, and one time a California-based professor compiling a book about Central Park wrote to inquire if Mrs. Seese had ever seen loosestrife blooming in that mid-Manhattan bosk. There even evolved an informal "Loosestrife watch," with readers vying for the first local sighting of the year, the largest or loveliest patch, and new locations of the wandering wildflower. Nor was this a summer-only project, as is apparent in a March 1983 column that the late Mrs. Seese began by explaining: "This isn't the season to be writing about loosestrife, but it will get a couple of bulky file envelopes out of the way of my typewriter if I write about it now. . . ." Such accumulations of correspondence were common, for although "it seemed like everything that could be said about loosestrife had been said in years past," Mrs. Seese noted in another column, "it simply will not be ignored. Or, rather, its literally numberless admirers will not let it be ignored." Yet in time she became fearful of the plant's proliferation, and admitted she had come to dread rather than welcome it.

This was due mainly to reports from scientists studying the results of loosestrife's rampant spread. One of the most comprehensive and thought-provoking reports was compiled by R.A. Malecki and T.J. Rawinski, who published their findings in a Conservation Circular put out by Cornell University in the Spring of 1979. In it, the authors cited the example of

Montezuma National Wildlife Refuge at the tip of Cayuga Lake in central New York. A 1951 loosestrife survey had revealed only a few clumps in the entire 6,000-acre refuge. Five years later, loosestrife covered almost an acre; in 1959, 10 acres; in 1967, 200 acres; and by 1979, it had spread to 1,000 acres.

This might not be so bad if loosestrife did not crowd out vital wetland vegetation such as cattails, rushes and sedges. But its woody stalks are resistant to decay, and the buildup of dead plants adversely affects other kinds of flora and the wildlife that feeds on them. That is not to say loosestrife does not provide food and shelter for birds and small animals. It does, but not enough—some scientists believe—in comparison to the damage it does if left to its own devices. And that is why it has been called everything from the Purple Peril to the Purple Plague.

Adding to the problem is loosestrife's reistance to traditional methods of control (mowing and flooding, to name only two). The only sure-fire method is to pull out individual plants by hand, making certain the entire root system is removed—an impracticality in large areas where loosestrife already has a firm footing. This led the Nature Consrvancy to declare the plant one of America's least wanted species in 1996, and the following year saw a European weevil—one of loosestrife's few natural enemies—introduced into selected areas such as the buffer lands of Orange County's Stewart Airport. It was hoped that the weevil would attack the plant's roots, while an earlier introduced beetle would eat the leaves, the two insects together causing a drastic decline—if not total destruction—of loosestrife. But a cautionary finger was soon being waved by Erik Kaviat, Executive Director for the Annandale-based research institute, Hudsonia, who in 1999 maintained that "we should seek to understand the ecology of invasives [i.e. loosestrife] before killing them," and a 2002 newspaper article reported him as reminding the public that "the plant is not always the bane it's said to be."

Certainly it is not a "worthless weed" as some people contend. In these days of laboratory-produced pharmaceuticals, it is easy to forget that loosestrife was once a mainstay of the family medicine chest. And for countless centuries, a weak tea made from the dried flowers was used to control diarrhea and internal bleeding, while a stronger concentration provided an external astringent said to relieve skin rashes and mucosal inflammation. Currently loosestrife's greatest use—other than as a cut flower, which lasts better in a bouquet than most wild blooms—is as a honey. Its flavor is distinctive, and honey-fanciers who favor it have been known to journey far in order to procure some from the few bee-keepers who still pack it.

So it's not as pestiferous as might be supposed, nor is the lowly dandelion—which is why this paean was penned.

VII. WARFARE

42. The Many Bridges of Stephen Crane

THE MORNING SUNSHINE MITIGATED THE EFFECT OF THE WIND whipping across the nearby Delaware River still chill from its winter load of ice, but the young man with the tawny hair began to shiver as soon as he stepped down from the train at the Erie Depot in the Orange County City of Port Jervis. Pausing only to light a cigarette, he jammed one hand into the pocket of his threadbare ulster, then hurried along Jersey Avenue.

At the corner of Pike Street, the traveler turned north, dreading the long uphill climb toward Main Street that would surely activate his hacking cough. He was right: the cough was clutching at his chest by the time he was halfway up the hill. So he turned into the small park called Orange Square, which was dominated by the statue of a Civil War soldier. The benches abutting the statue were occupied by several men who glanced up curiously as the newcomer found a vacant seat. Some of them recognized him and their nods were an invitation to talk, but the young man remained silent, concentrating on catching his breath as he stared up at the tall memorial.

The statue hadn't been there, he mused, when, as a boy, he had lived on Sussex Street at the east end of the park. Yet even then, Civil War veterans who had served with the 124th New York State Volunteers (nicknamed the Orange Blossoms) had gathered here to exchange stories. And he remembered that occasionally a few of them had worn their old uniform jackets bearing the crimson diamond patch of the famed Kearny Division—an insignia that was known as the "red badge of courage." The only uniform in evidence this day was the one on the soldier's statue, which had been erected a few years earlier, in 1886.

The stories were still being told, though, for the young man overheard snatches of conversation: "Battle of the Wilderness . . . Chancellorsville . . . Gettysburg. . . ." He wanted to listen, as he had as a boy, but his brother William was expecting him.

Reluctantly rising from the bench, the young man consoled himself with the thought that he would be staying with William for awhile, and the park was not far from his brother's Main Street house. He'd come back soon, too, for a desire was stirring within him to do more with the veterans' stories than merely listen. . . .

That young man was Stephen Crane and what he did with those Civil War reminiscences became evident in December 1894, when *The Red Badge of Courage* was serialized in several newspapers, then published in book form the following year. An immediate success, and destined to be regarded as a classic of American literature—if not the finest war novel ever written—*The Red Badge of Courage* catapulted the then 23-year-old author to fame. It was a bittersweet fame, however, because that single slim volume overshadowed everything else Crane wrote, and he wound up calling it "that damned book." A seemingly unfair judgment, yet understandable in view of what has transpired.

Crane's personal favorite was his free-verse collection called *The Black Riders*, published in 1895, but few readers today are familiar with his poetry or the fact that much of his prose has a southeastern New York setting. Indeed, it is not generally known that his first published short story as well as the last volume he completed concern our region, and in between comes an assemblage of articles, tales and books so numerous that it seems impossible for Crane to have accomplished it all in the 28 years he lived.

That tragically short life began on November 1, 1871, in Newark, New Jersey, when the wife of Reverend Jonathan Townley Crane gave birth to their fourteenth child. They named him Stephen in honor of an ancestor who had signed the Declaration of Independence, but by the time the family had moved to Port Jervis in 1878, it was obvious the boy would neither follow in the footsteps of his namesake, nor in those of his father, who was then pastor of the Drew Church on Sussex Street. For the strict Methodism of his parents grated on young Stephen, even though he adored his gentle father.

In later years, Crane recalled how his father would take him along on his ministerial errands in and around Port Jervis, never driving the horse "faster than two yards an hour even if some Christian was dying elsewhere." It was from Jonathan Crane that the boy developed a deep love of animals, prompted in part by something that happened one day when his father was preaching in the Orange County city of Middletown. While waiting for the elder Crane to conclude his sermon, Stephen attempted to shoot a cow with a toy gun his brother William had given him. The incident is recalled in his short story, "Lynx Hunting," but not the reaction of Reverend Crane, who was distressed at his son's predatory display—almost as distressed as the day he and Stephen drove over to Slate Hill for a funeral and they found all the mourners drunk. On that occasion, the boy did not subscribe to his father's feelings, for already he was questioning the Methodist prohibition against drinking, theater-going, card-playing, smoking and dancing.

The divergent views of father and son might eventually have compromised their close relationship, but that never came to pass because the Reverend Crane died—from overwork, it was said—when Stephen was eight years old. The funeral traumatized the grieving boy, who later said, "We tell kids that Heaven is just across the gaping grave and all that bosh . . . then we scare them to glue with flowers and white sheets and hymns." In a way, it was his own declaration of independence, while at the same time touching upon what some people consider his greatest talent as a writer: the ability to convey with compassion and understanding the complex world of children.

Following the death of her husband, Mary Crane "lived in and for religion" (Stephen's words), and she was frequently away from home attending prayer meetings or lecturing on temperance and women's rights. This left her youngest son free to roam the streets, listening to the colorful tales told by the Civil War veterans who gathered in Orange Square on sunny days, and absorbing the sights and sounds he was to use in his many stories set in Whilomville—the fictional name he gave Port Jervis.

Life had never been economically easy in a large family subsisting on a clergyman's pay, but now it was almost impossible for Mary Crane to make ends meet. She struggled on in Port Jervis for two more years, then in 1882 moved her brood to Asbury Park, New Jersey, and enrolled Stephen in the Pennington Seminary, where his father had once been principal. The boy was an apt student, lovingly encouraged by his sister Agnes, a schoolteacher 15 years his senior, who served as his surrogate mother. For Mary Crane's concentration on religion had not lessened, and she was now covering Methodist events for various newspapers.

In 1884, Stephen was dealt another emotional blow by the death of his beloved sister Agnes. Perhaps it was then that formal education began losing its flavor for him, and in 1890, when he became a student at the Hudson River Institute in the Columbia County town of Claverack, Crane was more interested in fun and sports than in studying. Yet he loved the military regime at the institute, and when he left there six months later to attend Lafayette College in Easton, Pennsylvania, he wrote to a close friend that his heart remained in Claverack.

Whether Crane wrote any stories during the single semester he spent at Lafayette is doubtful, and the only noteworthy event of that period was his participation in a tug-of-war over a class flag that almost certainly inspired a similar scene in *The Red Badge of Courage*. But it was different at Syracuse University, where Crane enrolled in January 1891. Although dedicated to baseball (he played on the varsity team) and disinterested in classwork, he did devote some time to writing his first novel, *Maggie: A Girl of the Streets*.

The manuscript was still unfinished in June, when the dean suggested that Crane not return to Syracuse in September unless he decided to become "a less indifferent scholar." That was something the 19-year-old was not prepared to do, and if perchance he later changed his mind, the death of his mother that year precluded any continuation of his college education. So he turned his attention to journalism—a not surprising choice, considering that he used to write his mother's articles whenever she was too busy to meet a deadline. In addition, his older brother Townley operated a news bureau in Asbury Park, and Stephen regularly contributed material to Townley's column, "On the New Jersey Coast," which appeared in the New York City *Tribune*.

It was through Townley that in 1892 Crane was introduced to Willis Fletcher Johnson, day editor of the *Tribune*. Johnson liked the stories Crane showed him and agreed to publish them in his paper's Sunday supplement. The first to appear (on July 3, 1892) was "Four Men in a Cave," a fictionalized account of an underground exploration Crane made with three of his friends. Crane did not name a specific site, but from its description it could have been the extensive cave system beneath a Sullivan County limestone ridge in what is now the state-owned Bashakill Wildlife Management Area east of Route 209.

Crane's connection with the *Tribune* did not last long. In late August, Townley wanted to do some fishing at Sullivan County's Hartwood Club and asked his brother to write his weekly column. Crane agreed and included a sharply critical account of a local parade. It caused a public furor, with the result that both Crane and his brother were fired by the *Tribune*. Townley eventually got his job back, after explaining what had happened, but Crane remained persona non grata. The incident may have been a blessing in disguise, for it pushed Crane into pursuing fiction, as opposed to straight reportorial writing. Moving to New York City, he scraped together enough money to publish *Maggie: A Girl of the Streets*, using the pseudonym of Johnston Smith. The book did not sell, and for the next few years Crane lived in poverty, rooming with other struggling artists, while exploring the seamier aspects of the city, and writing . . . always writing.

Pale and thin, with a chronic cough exacerbated by his incessant cigarette smoking, Crane might have succumbed to illness much earlier than he did had it not been for the hospitality of his brothers. Though unaware of his destitution because Crane was too proud to tell them, both William (in Port Jervis) and Edmund (at Hartwood) encouraged him to visit as often as he liked. This Crane did, for home to him had always been Port Jervis and the surrounding hills where he had wandered with his Newfoundland dog, Solomon. These outdoor adventures formed the basis for some of his earliest stories, eventually collected in book form under the title *Sullivan County Sketches*.

Despite his love of the country, Crane felt drawn to the city during the mid-1890s—especially after *The Red Badge of Courage* was published and editors began clamoring for his stories—since New York offered a fertile field for his deep concern over social injustice. With the exception of brief visits out of town, including a trip to the West and Mexico early in 1895 as a correspondent for the Bacheller Syndicate, Crane remained in New York, churning out dozens of sensitive sketches—among them a haunting portrait of Westchester County's Sing-Sing prison, called "The Devil's Acre"—until a scandal sent him farther afield. That scandal began on September 16, 1896, with the arrest of a streetwalker named Dora Clark, who Crane had been interviewing for an article about the city's infamous Tenderloin District. When Crane protested that Dora had only been answering his questions and not soliciting, the arresting officer threatened to bring charges against him too. The incensed author then followed the pair to the Jefferson Market Court in Greenwich Village, where he vouched for Dora, and the presiding magistrate excused her. But Dora then pressed charges against the policeman for unlawful arrest, and the subsequent, much-publicized trial—at which Crane was called as a witness—left him with a besmirched reputation and a warning that the police were now out to get him.

While he had written brilliantly of war in *The Red Badge of Courage*, Crane had never experienced it at first hand, so with New York best abandoned for awhile, he decided to cover the rebellion then going on in Cuba. He got as far as Jacksonville, Florida, where he spent two months trying to arrange passge to Cuba. Finally, on January 1, 1897, he found a berth on a leaky old boat illegally carrying arms to the Cuban rebels. Only a few hours into the voyage, the boat sank, and for two days Crane and several other survivors were adrift on "waves . . . barbarously abrupt and tall"—an experience he related in his powerful story of "The Open Boat."

Giving up on Cuba, Crane turned his attention to the Greco-Turkish War, and in April 1897 he arrived in Greece as a war correspondent. Accompanying him was Cora Howorth Taylor, whom he had met in Jacksonville, where she ran a nightclub known as the Hotel de Dream. Whether the two of them ever married is controversial, but they lived as man and wife for the few short years Crane had remaining. Those years were full of frenzied writing by the author, who never had been adept at managing his finances and was always in debt. Nor did it help matters that he and Cora settled in a too-costly house in England—an expatriation perhaps brought about by the at-home scandal surrounding his liaison with what gossips declared was a shady lady married to someone else.

Whatever the legality—or lack of it—their relationship was a loving one, and Cora often tried to protect Crane from the hordes of visitors who descended on their country home in Surrey. He never could say no to company, however, particularly that of newfound friends and fellow writers like Joseph Conrad, Henry James and H.G. Wells. Yet he did find time for writing—he had to!—and his 1897 output included such stories as "The Bride Comes to Yellow Sky."

With the outbreak of the Spanish-American War in 1898, Crane returned to the United States, bent on enlisting in the armed services. He was rejected as being tubercular, but got to Cuba anyway as a war correspondent. He even took part in some of the action when he briefly served as a signalman at Guantanamo Bay—an exploit that earned him a citation for bravery from the War Department.

Crane was back in England by January 1899, and the following month he and Cora moved from their home in Surrey to a medieval mansion called Brede Place in Sussex. It was a foolhardy undertaking, for not only could they ill afford the added expense, but it was almost impossible to adequately heat the drafty old structure, and Crane was still weak from the malaria he had contracted in Havana. His hectic social life remained unchanged, though, as did his frantic writing, and it can be wondered if he even took the time to savor the publication of an anthology of his poetry, *War Is Kind*, or *The Monster*, a haunting novella set in the fictional community of Whilomville.

Readers familiar with Port Jervis and its history will find parallels in this tale of a black man whose face is horribly scarred while rescuing his employer's son from a burning building, and how public regard for him changes from hero worship to hatred. For the Bridge Street mentioned in *The Monster* has its counterpart in Port Jervis, and Crane knew an ash collector named Levi Hume, whose cancer-ravaged face frightened children. There was also a fire that reportedly trapped a child in the house next door to William Crane's home on East Main Street. As for the people in the novella turning against the protagonist, Crane certainly was familiar with the city's most shameful incident, when a mob hung a black man from a tree in front of the Baptist Church—said to be the only recorded lynching in New York State. And of course Crane wrote *The Monster* while still smarting from the hometown gossip generated by news of his coupling with Cora.

Despite any bitterness evident in *The Monster*, Crane remained fond of his boyhood home, and had written to his brother William that his "idea is to come finally to live at Port Jervis or Hartwood." But in 1899 that was out of the question, and the next best thing was to paint word pictures of remembered scenes. These became his *Whilomville Stories*, an autobiographical collection of tales about childhood in which Crane revealed himself as never before through the main character, a boy named Jimmie Trescott. (The same character appears in *The Monster*, as does the boy's father, Dr. Trescott, who is surely patterned after the Reverend Jonathan Crane.)

By November 1899, Crane had completed most of the *Whilomville Stories*, often working late into the night, trying to earn enough money to satisfy his creditors, while at the same time entertaining the many visitors to Brede Place. This exhausting pace finally took its toll, and on December 28, he collapsed with a lung hemorrhage. It was not a new problem—in past years Crane had twice been a patient of the famous lung specialist, Dr. Edward Trudeau, who operated a tuberculosis sanitarium at Saranac Lake in the Adirondacks—but this time it was complicated by a recurrence of malaria. Even so, Crane would not rest, until flattened by two more hemorrhages in April.

The following month brought no improvement and the doctors Cora consulted suggested that Crane be taken to a sanitarium in the Bavarian Alps. The journey was accomplished in several stages, for Crane was really too weak to travel, and it was not until the end of May that he and Cora arrived at their destination. A week later, he was dead.

As the world mourned what Henry James called "a brutal needless extinction," so did the people of Port Jervis, who had considered Stephen Crane a native, if somewhat wayward son. Yet strangely enough, a century after his death, the city boasts no monument to the man who was inspired to write one of America's greatest novels by the stories he'd heard in Orange Square. For a brief period in 1982, the square was designated the Stephen Crane Memorial Park, but the following year pressure from veterans' groups caused the Port Jervis Common Council to rename it Orange Square Veterans Park, so that today the author is mentioned only on a small plaque there.

Nevertheless, Crane's presence is still felt in Port Jervis, and anyone who goes there can visit several sites associated with him. In addition to Orange Square, the Drew United Methodist Church is at 49-51 Sussex Street, while a historic marker points out William Crane's house at 19 East Main Street. (During warm weather visits to his brother's home, Crane would do his writing while sitting in a wicker chair on the front porch, screened from pedestrian view by a large syringa bush growing in the yard.) There is also the restored Erie Depot on Jersey Avenue. It was from this depot that Crane often took the train to the Sullivan County town of Forestburgh, where a historical marker now points out his brother Edmund's home off the Hartwood Club Road, adjacent to Stephen Crane Pond.

But as interesting as all those sites may be, the most impressive memento of Stephen Crane's presence in the region is the wealth of stories he wrote about it—true badges of honor for a too little-appreciated writer.

43. Echoes of Big Thunder

ALTHOUGH STORM CLOUDS ARE APT TO HOVER OVER THE TACONIC foothills of Rensselaer County on hot summer afternoons, back in 1844 people weren't predicting the weather when word went around that the Fourth of July would bring big thunder to Hoags Corners. They were referring instead to the leader of a recently formed militant band, who in order to disguise his identity had been dubbed "Big Thunder." Nevertheless, there was a storm brewing—a man-made one that was to sweep across eastern New York from the Taconics to the Catskills, and eventually add new dimension to the meaning of Independence Day.

On that Fourth of July in 1844, farmers from all over Rensselaer County journeyed to the small crossroads community in the town of Nassau, having been prompted by posted handbills promising a "gala event" at the Hoags Corners parade grounds. What they got was a cacophonous extravaganza that began with the piercing call of a fife and a staccato drum roll echoed by the hoofbeats of dozens of horses galloping out from the surrounding trees. Astride each horse was a masked rider wearing a bright calico tunic over equally colorful pantaloons, and whooping like an Indian on the warpath. Between whoops, some of these ersatz Indians blew on tin dinner horns, while others rattled spears or banged on metal pans, as all circled the crowd, finally coming to a halt in front of a makeshift speaker's platform.

When the din died down, one of the horsemen dismounted to stand alone on the platform, a slight breeze stirring the feathers adorning his leather mask. "Brother serfs of Lord Van Rensselaer," he began, "these Indians have a battle cry that means your safety and your future: *Down with the rent!*"

The strangely garbed speaker did not have to elaborate. All assembled there were residents of Rensselaerswyck, the largest of the feudal-like manors that since colonial times had kept much of the Hudson Valley under the control of a few powerful families. Composed of two tracts totaling about 1.1 million acres, the manor covered most of Albany and Rensselaer counties, with as many as 3,000 tenant farmers tilling the land under a "freehold" lease that promoted perpetual servitude. For although farmers had been promised they could purchase their acreage after a certain number of years, this rarely if ever came about, and they were forced to continue paying the kind of rents that kept them in bondage. And woe to any tenant who, through illness or poor crops, couldn't pay his rent: he and his family would be evicted, their possessions sold at auction, and no recompense given for improvements they had made on the land.

This servitude had been made slightly more palatable during the long life of Stephen Van Rensselaer III, known as the "Good Patroon" because of his penchant for postponing payments due him or not collecting rents at all. But when he died in January 1839, leaving the east and west manors of Rensselaerswyck to his sons William and Stephen, he also left behind large debts that could only be met by collecting the $400,000 in back rents that tenant farmers owed him. Those who couldn't pay were to be forced out of their homes and their property auctioned off.

This new threat resurrected old grievances concerning the unfairness of the manor system, not to mention the questionable legality of some land titles, and an anti-rent movement was soon under way. It as not the first such protest—four decades earlier a tenant revolt on the 160,000-acre Livingston Manor in Columbia County had been put down by Governor John Jay— but this 1840s conflict proved to be the most effective, due in great part to an eloquent country doctor named Smith Boughton.

Born in 1810 on a Rensselaer County tenant farm, Boughton had grown up across the Hudson in the Helderberg Mountains west of Albany, where the anti-rent rebellion began shortly after the death of the Good Patroon. By that time, Boughton had returned to Rensselaer County and was a practicing physician in the hamlet of Alps, a few miles north of Hoags Corners. Boughton had always been a champion of the common man, and when he heard how his boyhood friends and family in the west manor of Rensselaerswyck were struggling to free themselves from feudalism, he vowed to organize the tenant farmers on the east side of the Hudson.

Boughton began his campaign in May 1844 and within two months had gathered enough supporters to stage the July 4 rally at Hoags Corners, where as Big Thunder he set forth his simple plan. No more rents would be paid, with participating farmers protected from eviction by a band of Calico Indians (called that because of the material used in their tunics) ready to ride the minute the blast of a tin dinner horn signaled the approach of lawmen.

While the idea of masquerading as native Americans was rooted in the Boston Tea Party of the preceding century, the Calico Indians went a step further in constructing costumes not only to disguise their identity, but to instill fear. Especially effective was the weird leather mask each Calico Indian fashioned for himself. Actually a hood, oftentimes with animal-like ears, it bore vivid streaks of warpaint and was frequently festooned with long hanks of horsehair or feathers—enough to scare the bejabbers out of anybody, friend or foe.

Another innovation was the tin horns that the Calico Indians used in place of bugles for rallying their members. Prior to the anti-rent rebellion, such tin horns had been used on upstate New York farms to summon field-hands to meals. But following their adoption by the rebels, no farmer dared announce dinner in this manner, lest he find his front yard full of Calico Indians, who were apt to be a bit angry over the false alarm.

The Calico Indians were counting on their wild appearance and superior numbers to scare off evicting sheriffs without any blood being shed. They were usually successful too, due in part to some lawmen sympathetic to the farmers' plight, and others who simply welcomed an excuse not to do their duty. This was Sheriff Henry Miller's choice five months after the Hoags Corners convocation, when he tried to auction off a tenant farmer's livestock in the Columbia County town of Copake. Accosted by Big Thunder and his Calico Indians, Sheriff Miller turned over the warrants he was carrying—which were later burned by Dr. Boughton—and was allowed to leave the scene.

Nonetheless, there were fatalities, including the death on December 18, 1844 of a Hillsdale lad named William Riffenberg, shot during an anti-rent rally at Smoky Hollow (now Hollowville) in the Columbia County town of Claverack. Since the boy was standing in front of Big Thunder, it is thought that the fatal bullet might really have been intended for the leader of the Calico Indians. But that mattered little to the outraged authorities, who by now had guessed the true identity of Big Thunder, and were determined to end his anti-rent activities. Boughton was arrested shortly afterwards, though not for the homicide, which never was solved. Rather, he was charged with stealing the eviction warrants from Sheriff Miller at Copake earlier in the month, and Boughton was then lodged in the jail at Hudson.

In this day and age, it might be difficult to believe the injustice of Boughton's two trials. Yes, two, for the first one—begun in March 1845—ended in a hung jury, with all the jurors voting for acquittal, except for a single holdout who just happened to be employed by another of the Valley's large landholding families, the Livingstons. What's more, despite the fact that in December 1844 Boughton had surrendered himself to the authorities after being assured that bail would be set immediately, bail was denied several times during his three-month incarceration. So when the hung jury necessitated another trial, Boughton was sent back to his dreary cell in the Hudson jail, with the only concession being that he was no longer shackled.

Worried about his wife and young son back in Alps, Boughton's health—never robust at best—began to decline, and plans were made to break him out of prison. It is said that the bars on his cell window already had been sawed through and relays of horses were waiting to take him to safety, when the prematurely gray physician decided he would "leave legally or not at all." That legality came in July, after large Independence Day gatherings of anti-renters across several counties convinced New York Governor Silas Wright that it might be politically advantageous to have bail set for Boughton and the two other men arrested with him: Samuel Wheeler and Mortimer C. Belden, the latter a Calico Indian known as "Little Thunder." And finally, after seven months in jail, Boughton was free—but only for a little while.

A few weeks later, on Dingle Hill in the Delaware County town of Andes, a sheriff's rent collection turned ugly, resulting in the death of a deputy named Osmond Steele. Big Thunder was nowhere near Dingle Hill on that fateful day, but in the rabid reaction to Deputy Steele's death—when dozens of innocent men were arrested simply because they agreed with the anti-renters—it was decided to make an example of Boughton by retrying him. And this time there would be no chance of a mistrial—not if Judge John Worth Edmonds had his way. Indeed, the judge was heard to say he intended to convict Boughton. One way of doing this was by making sure no juror disagreed with the tenant system, and Edmonds prejudicially assisted the prosecuting attorney in selecting a suitable panel. Edmonds also was not averse to publicly announcing his personal views, as when Sheriff Miller was on the witness stand. The judge interrupted the testimony to ask if Miller had been armed when Big Thunder relieved him of the warrants. The sheriff's denial elicited Edmonds' retort that "You should have been [armed], and shot the scoundrel dead!"

Such actions were sure to keep tempers short, and the opposing attorneys—35-year-old State Attorney General John Van Buren, son of President Martin Van Buren of Kinderhook; and 56-year-old Ambrose Jordan defending Boughton for the second time—wound up in a fistfight after exchanging insults one morning. A 24-hour contempt-of-court confinement did little to cool them, and while they didn't again resort to fisticuffs, the two attorneys kept at each other's throats, a prime example being the time Van Buren called a witness to testify he had seen Boughton dress up as Big Thunder, and Jordan called upon the witness' mother to aver her son had never been "right" since being hit on the head as a child.

The trial lasted until 8 P.M. on September 29, when Judge Edmonds made his charge to the jury, then retired to his hotel, confident their finding would be "guilty." But the next morning he was shocked to receive a note from the jury saying they were unable to reach a verdict, and should be dismissed. No way. Edmonds demanded they come to an agreement, then went off on a horseback ride, as if not caring how long their deliberations might take.

The jury got the message in more ways than one. A few hours later they handed down a verdict of "guilty." Thereupon Judge Edmonds assembled the 12-man sentencing court (not the same as the jury) and informed them that he wanted the maximum penalty. In those days, robbery such as Boughton was convicted of carried a sentence of anywhere from a minimum amount of time to life imprisonment, so there was plenty of discussion between the court members, but no agreement—that is, until dinnertime. According to Henry Christman, whose *Tin Horns and Calico* is deservedly considered the definitive history of the anti-rent rebellion, one hungry judge turned to the others, saying, "There's the dinner bell. You go for life and I will." And that was the way Smith Boughton—alias Big Thunder—wound up in Clinton State Prison at Dannemora in the northern Adirondacks.

As Boughton was being brought north to prison, crowds of anti-renters showed their support at Albany and then Troy, where there was an attempt to rescue him. But once again Boughton opted for legality, explaining, "I have made up my mind to go peaceably. It is for the benefit of our cause that I do so." His bravery also benefited the convicts at Clinton, for he was put in charge of the prison hospital, where so many unfortunate inmates were taken following accidents at their forced-labor jobs in nearby iron mines and furnaces. In addition, Boughton helped sustain the spirits of the other anti-renters incarcerated there, while they waited for a change in government that might bright about their release.

In January 1847, New York Governor Silas Wright was replaced by John Young, who had promised to free the anti-renters if elected. Actually it was a pardon that the prisoners received a month later—a pardon that meant Boughton and three other anti-renters would not regain their citizenship rights, since they had been sentenced to life imprisonment. But in September, when Governor Young again felt the need of anti-renter support, he restored those rights. The tide was thus turning for the oppressed tenant farmers on the large feudal estates, and by 1852 New York Supreme Court rulings pretty much confirmed their right to their land. There were still legal battles to be fought, but not by Big Thunder, who returned to Alps to resume his medical practice, content—as he said in later years—that "great good had risen from our struggles."

Nor was it a struggle that would be forgotten. For many years, Big Thunder Day was celebrated at Hoags Corners on July 4, and there still can be seen several sites associated with the anti-rent movement. These include the Hoags Corners Hotel at the junction of Route 66 and Dunham Hollow Road, where the Calico Indians met to plan their rebellion; Boughton's house, designated by a historical marker on Route 43 in Alps; and the Sand Lake Cemetery just north of Hoags Corners on Route 66, where Boughton's grave is located. The latter location is a must-see for legend-lovers, who will find Big Thunder buried near Willard Griggs, an anti-renter who reversed his allegiance to become a deputy sheriff, and was killed during an eviction attempt. Local tradition holds that Boughton's tall monument was purposely turned so he would not have to face the lawman; also, while flowers proliferate on the Boughton plot, none will grow on the grave of Griggs.

And so it is not unlikely that those who pause there on a summer's day, letting the little-known history sink in, just may hear echoes of big thunder off in the distance.

44. Enoch Crosby: Shoemaker–Spy of the Revolution

IF IT HADN'T BEEN FOR NOVELIST JAMES FENIMORE COOPER, THE Revolutionary War exploits of Enoch Crosby might have been forgotten. But the 1821 publication of Cooper's book, *The Spy*, not only brought instant fame to its author, it also insured that Crosby's role as one of the country's most daring espionage agents would not go unnoticed, though a mystery still persists to this very day.

Cooper, you see, never did acknowledge Crosby as the model of his novel's hero Harvey Birch, a country peddler who risked life and limb to supply the Americans with information about British activities in the Hudson Valley. The connection was put in print seven years after Cooper's book appeared, when H.L. Barnum published a slim volume called *The Spy Unmasked*, after interviewing the then-elderly Crosby at his farm in the Putnam County town of Southeast. The result has been a continuing controversy over the fictional Harvey Birch's resemblance to the real-life Enoch Crosby—a controversy which makes Crosby's story all the more intriguing.

That story began on January 4, 1750, when Enoch Crosby was born in Harwich, Massachusetts. He was not destined to stay there long, however. For even in the mid-18th century, land was scarce in that early settled Cape Cod community, and Crosby's father Thomas soon joined two of his brothers in migrating to what later became Putnam County. By 1754, Thomas Crosby had established his family on a farm south of present-day Carmel, and young Enoch spent a carefree childhood with no ambitions other than perhaps to follow in his father's footsteps. The elder Crosby's fortunes took a downswing, though, and at the age of 16, Enoch was forced to make his own way in the world.

A strong athletic lad, already nearing the 6-foot height of his adulthood, Crosby hiked north to the town of Kent. There he apprenticed himself to a local cordwainer, little knowing that the shoemaker's craft would provide him with a good cover during his eventual career as a spy. But the idea of war had not yet germinated from the dissatisfied grumbling of the colonists, and after his 5-year apprenticeship ended, Crosby settled in Danbury,

Connecticut. He was still there four years later, in April 1775, when the Battle of Lexington signaled the start of the American Revolution. Crosby lost no time in signing up with Colonel David Waterbury's militia regiment, and served out an 8-month enlistment that took him as far south as New York City and as far north as Montreal.

Returning to Danbury early in 1776, Crosby resumed work as a shoemaker, content to be a civilian once again—or so he thought, until reports of the faltering American cause convinced him otherwise. In August 1776, while visiting friends and family in his childhood home of Carmel, Crosby enlisted in Colonel Jacobus Swartwout's Dutchess County regiment, which had already left for Kingsbridge (then in Westchester County, now in the Bronx). Told to join his regiment there, Crosby headed south into the "Neutral Ground"— that part of Westchester County separating the British and American forces.

"Neutral Ground" is actually a misnomer, for many a battle was fought there, along with bloody raids and bitter retaliations by or on civilian sympathizers to either the British or American side. Throughout the war it was a place of danger, suspicion and intrigue—and it was there, on a late summer day near Pines Bridge, that Crosby, alone and on foot, was accosted by a stranger demanding to know if he was "going down." Since he was indeed on his way south to Kingsbridge, Crosby answered "yes," and was immediately glad that his reply had been brief. For "going down" meant something entirely different to the stranger, who asked if Crosby wasn't afraid to proceed alone, considering the fact that the countryside was infested with Rebels who would like nothing better than to waylay a Loyalist en route to British-occupied New York City.

Knowing better than to reveal his true mission to someone who obviously was a British sympathizer, Crosby cagily inquired if the stranger knew of any way he might "get through safely." The stranger took this to be a confirmation of Crosby's intention to join the British, and confided that a Loyalist company was being organized in the neighborhood; it would be far safer for Crosby to join that company and "go down" with them when they left in a few days. The stranger then introduced himself as Mr. Bunker and, pointing to a nearby house, said that Crosby was welcome to stay at his home until the captain of the Loyalist company could be contacted.

Somehow Crosby managed to sound sincere as he thanked Bunker for his kindness. Then adding that he preferred not to wait until recruitment for the company was completed, and that he would try to get through on his own, Crosby headed south on the Pines Bridge Road.

By nightfall, Crosby had reached the tavern of Joseph Youngs (at what is now Bradhurst and Grasslands Avenue, near the Greenburgh-Mt. Pleasant town line), and was given lodging. Youngs made no bones about his loyalty to the American cause, and when he mentioned that he was a member of the Westchester County Committee of Safety, Crosby revealed what he had learned from Bunker. Youngs questioned Crosby closely, then asked that he go with him the next morning to White Plains, where the Committee of Safety was scheduled to meet in the courthouse. Crosby readily agreed, thinking only that he would report on the Loyalist company, then go on to join Colonel Swartwout's regiment at Kingsbridge. But once the committee members heard how deftly he had handled his chance meeting with Bunker, they realized he was much more valuable as a secret agent than as a common soldier, and Crosby was asked if he would help in rounding up the Loyalist company.

A plan was quickly formulated: Crosby would be arrested as a British sympathizer and placed in the custody of Captain Micah Townsend, who commanded a company of rangers then stationed at White Plains. At the opportune moment, Crosby would "escape" his American captors, and make his way back to Bunker's house, where he would attempt to learn the identities and location of the Loyalists.

If Crosby had any misgivings about assuming the guise of a turncoat, his patriotism took precedence. He was turned over to Captain Townsend the very same day, and by midnight had made his "escape," thanks to the laxity of a guard who had to be in on the plan.

Crosby headed back to Bunker's house near Pines Bridge, where he regaled the Loyalist with details of his detainment by the Rebels. Bunker swallowed Crosby's story without a burp of doubt, nodding his agreement when the "fugitive" said he now wanted to join the Loyalist company. This was accomplished the next morning, and Crosby remained at the Loyalists' encampment until the eve of their departure to join the British forces. Then he slipped away under cover of darkness and went to the tavern of Joseph Youngs, where Captain Townsend was awaiting his report.

Lest the Loyalists become suspicious if they discovered him missing, Crosby was instructed to return to the encampment, which Townsend and his rangers would raid the following day. Crosby was to be captured along with the them, but would be released as soon as it was safe to do so. Unfortunately, "soon" was many days distant, and Crosby was forced to endure imprisonment first at White Plains, then at Fishkill in Dutchess County, where the captured Loyalist company was eventually taken.

Tradition states that, in order to maintain his Loyalist guise, Crosby was tried in a mock court proceeding held at the Van Wyck farmhouse (now headquarters of the Fishkill Historical Society, and open to the public), about a mile south of the village at the junction of present-day Route 9 and Snook Road. Requisitioned by the Continental Army in August 1776, the farmhouse also hosted sessions of the Committee for Detecting and Defeating Conspiracies, which recently had been established by the state legislature. Among its members was Westchester County statesman John Jay—a pivotal character in the later controversy over Crosby's relationship to Cooper's *Spy*—who concurred with the committee's request that Crosby continue his activities as a secret agent.

When Crosby reminded them that he was supposed to report for duty at Kingsbridge, the committee members assured him they would take care of that matter, along with arranging for him to be bailed out of prison following his mock trial. This would be done immediately too, for they alrady had in mind another assignment for their new spy.

This time Crosby was sent several miles northwest to the mouth of Wappingers Creek, where a local patriot named Nicholas Brewer was waiting to ferry him across the Hudson. Landing on the Ulster County shore, Crosby traveled by foot to the Marlborough home of John (or Jacob) Russell, who was suspected of being a Loyalist recruiter. Crosby introduced himself as John Brown, an itinerant shoemaker looking for work, and was readily hired by Russell.

That was the easy part. The hard part came as days passed by and Crosby learned little information from the reticent Russell, yet had to cross and recross the Hudson in order to report to the committee. His stealth must have been superior, however, for Crosby remained undetected, and eventually he made contact with a British officer headquartered at a cave in the Orange County town of Cornwall. (Although Crosby's biographer described this place as a man-made cave lying at the base of a mountain, others believe it was a natural cavern known as The Grotto, located on the southeastern slope of Crow's Nest Mountain, which had been used as a refuge since pre-Revolutionary times.)

The British officer, Captain Robinson, was indeed raising a Loyalist company and welcomed Crosby as a new recruit, even offering him the comfort of his cave headquarters. Nor is comfort an exaggeration, since Robinson reputedly had it stocked with fine wine and victuals, in addition to furniture. But there was little ease for Crosby, who was unable to learn the company's scheduled departure date until it was too late for him to get back to Fishkill with the report.

Another man might have given up at this point. Not Crosby. Drawing upon his knowledge of human nature, he suggested to his fellow recruits that, in the event of a Rebel raid, it would be safer for them to sleep in scattered locations so the whole band would not be taken unawares. Then after the others had scurried to secrete themselves behind various boulders and bushes, Crosby snuck off. He had heard the other recruits speak of a local resident as being a "wicked rebel," and it was to that man's home that Crosby sped, hoping his informers had not been mistaken. He was fearful about giving himself away to a stranger, but he felt he had no choice.

Reaching the house of the "wicked rebel"—a Mr. Purdy—Crosby relayed the news of the Loyalists' impending march, and entreated the man to warn the committee at Fishkill. Then trusting to fate, he returned to the Loyalist company and marched with them when they left their encampment near the cave.

Nightfall found the company billeted in a barn, with Crosby still wondering whether word had reached Fishkill. The answer came before morning, when a contingent of American troops surrounded the barn and the Loyalist company—including Crosby—was taken captive. Brought back to Fishkill, they were imprisoned in the Dutch Reformed Church on what is now Main Street. Once again, Crosby's escape was arranged, and he continued his double life as a shoemaker-spy. His contact was usually John Jay, who sent him all over the Hudson Valley—from Rensselaer County's Walloomsac, west to Albany, and south to Pawling in Dutchess County—ferreting out enemies of the American cause. Danger was a constant companion, close calls became commonplace, yet Crosby did not quit, even when it became evident that he had earned the enmity of former friends who thought he had turned traitor.

Finally it was the committee at Fishkill that called a halt to his activities. Crosby had survived nine months as a spy; to go on any longer would be too dangerous, and he was told to report to the paymaster in the Ulster County hamlet of Hurley, where he would be given a common soldier's wages for his service as a secret agent. (No hazard pay in those days!) Crosby did not consider this unjust, for he felt he had merely been doing his duty—a duty that he went on to meet by signing up for two more enlistments, and serving as a sergeant in regiments assigned to the Hudson Valley. Nor did Crosby ever make much of those dangerous days, and at war's end he returned to the scenes of his childhood, later buying a farm on what is now Enoch Crosby Road in Southeast. He augmented his pastoral pursuits by serving as a justice of the peace, an associate judge of common pleas, and deacon of the Gilead Church in nearby Carmel, but by and large his life was one of rural quietude, with his wartime spying only a dim and distant memory.

Then in 1821, James Fenimore Cooper—at that time living on the Angevine farm in Scarsdale—published *The Spy*, and readers wanted to know whether Harvey Birch had been an actual person. As mentioned earlier, Cooper declined to name the model for his ficitonal hero, but the public eye eventually focused on Crosby. An example of this occurred in the autumn of

1827, when the 71-year-old Crosby went to New York City to testify in a land-ownership suit. The Park Theatre was then presenting a dramatized version of *The Spy*, and when it became known that Crosby was in the city, he was invited to attend the play. The ovation that greeted his appearnce there showed that, in the eyes of the audience at least, he was indeed the real Harvey Birch.

The following years saw the publication of H.L. Barnum's book, *The Spy Unmasked*, which purportedly proved the Birch-Crosby connection. Unfortunately, the author took liberties with Crosby's story, sometimes drawing upon Cooper's fictional scenes, so that there was a confusing combination of fact and fancy. Questions thus remained, along with the mystery of why James Fenimore Cooper continued to deny ever having heard the name of Enoch Crosby prior to the time he invented Harvey Birch.

A solution of sorts has since been provided by researchers probing Cooper's papers and those of John Jay, whose Katonah mansion was not far from the novelist's home in Scarsdale. It was John Jay who told Cooper stories about a secret agent he had employed during the Revolution—stories that inspired Cooper to write *The Spy*. But John Jay never told Cooper the name of that agent, possibly because war-generated animosities were still rife in 1820 when he and Cooper talked. It is also possible that Cooper had heard local stories of other spies, for Enoch Crosby was not the only one who risked his life and reputation for little reward and even less recognition. Yet Crosby's activities most closely parallel the clandestine career of Harvey Birch.

Those activities were documented in a deposition Crosby made in October 1832, when he applied to the government for a war-services pension. The following September, he was awarded the sum of $100, which seems a pittance in comparison to the dangers he had faced. Even more so, considering an anecdote John Jay appended to the story he told James Fenimore Cooper. It seems that in 1780, when Jay was about to leave the country as Minister to Spain, he contacted his secret agent to meet with him in "a wood at midnight." The Continental Congress—likely at Jay's behest—had secretly voted a sum of money to be given to the selfless spy. However, the spy—assumedly Eoch Crosby—turned down the honorarium, saying he had only been doing his duty.

That phrase would have been a good choice for Crosby's epitaph. But in keeping with his unvaunted patriotism, his tombstone bears only the simple inscription: "In memory of Enoch Crosby, who died June 26, 1835, aged 85 years, 5 months and 21 days."

[Note: Enoch Crosby is buried in the northwest corner of the old Gilead Cemetery on Mechanic Street, off Seminary Hill Road, in Carmel. Appropriately, the cemetery is located on land once owned by Thomas Crosby, and the scene of Enoch's boyhood home.]

45. *"Come, Fill Your Glasses, Fellows"*

T HE SLIM WEST POINT CADET STOOD STIFFLY AT ATTENTION AS THE
verdict in his court-martial was announced. Absenting himself from
the post without permission on the night of July 31, 1825 had been
bad enough, but then imbibing "spirituous & intoxicating liquors" at a notorious off-limits tavern made matters even worse. So it was no surprise that,
having been found guilty, he was sentenced to be dismissed from the United
States Military Academy. The court, however, could be considerate. In light
of the 17-year-old cadet's previous good conduct, it recommended that the
sentence be set aside—which is how the later president of the Confederacy,
Jefferson Davis, remained at West Point to graduate with the class of 1828.

Whereas Jefferson Davis may also be the only cadet to have broken his
leg during a dark night's dash back to barracks, he was by no means unique
in sneaking off base for a bit of illicit elbow-bending. Such surreptitious for-
ays were fairly common among 19th century cadets, resulting in a legacy of
lore that makes it unlikely the now long-gone watering holes of West Point
will ever be forgotten.

The most legendary of those establishments belonged to Benny Havens,
a New Windsor-born native of Orange County, who set up shop in
Highland Falls around 1816 when the village at the southern end of West
Point was known as Buttermilk Falls. But Benny was not the first purveyor
of contraband booze to cadets. That dubious distinction belongs to a man
named Gridley, who supposedly became such a thorn in the side of Academy
officials that they purchased his place and turned it into a post hospital.

Gridley's departure left the field clear to Benny, who soon gained fame
for serving the best hot flip—a potent spiced drink of sweetened ale, beer
and cider sometimes mixed with milk and eggs. In fact, when the Marquis
de Lafayette visited West Point in 1824, he is said to have shown his appreciation for Benny's speciality by settling his bar bill with two gold buttons.

That his regular clientele of cadets couldn't afford to be so generous did-
n't bother Benny at all. (It was his place, by the way, that figured in Jefferson
Davis' court-martial.) Well aware that West Point fed its cadets as poorly as it

"If walls could talk. . . ." West Point's Old South Barracks could tell many a tale, such as one regarding the 1830 resident of Room 28, who bartered his blanket for some brandy and food—a cadet called Edgar Allan Poe.

paid them, Benny was not averse to trading his buckwheat pancakes for bits of clothing and equipment. He was even known to have accepted a batch of candles along with a cadet's only blanket in exchange for a bottle of brandy and a goose that was secretly roasted in Room 28 of the South Barracks.

The goose-bake occurred late in November 1830, and the Room 28 resident who bartered away his blanket was none other than Edgar Allan Poe. Unhappy at West Point, the 21-year-old poet lasted less than a year as a cadet, calling Benny Havens "the only congenial soul in this godforsaken wilderness." Indeed, Benny's place was all his surname suggested. And while a rumor persists that the tavern also offered accommodations for the clandestine coupling of lonely cadets with ladies of the night, it was Benny's genuine kindness and good humor, as well as his storytelling skill that made the place so popular. Plus that, his fine food and flip endeared him to his customers— so much so that in 1838 he was immortalized in a song beginning

> Come fill your glasses, fellows, and stand up in a row
> To singing sentimentally, we're going for to go;
> In the Army there's sobriety, promotion's very slow,
> So we'll sing our reminiscences of Benny Havens, oh!
> Oh, Benny Havens, oh! Oh, Benny Havens, oh!
> So we'll sing our reminscences of Benny Havens, oh!

Versions vary as to the authorship of that verse. It may have originated with Cadet John Metcalf, or been the brainchild of Dr. Lucius O'Brien when he was visiting West Point in 1838. However it came about, other stanzas were soon added, all of them sung to the tune of "The Wearin' O' the Green," with this paean to a publican winding up as the ever-popular cadet rallying song. And it is said that no one rendered it more mellifluously than Cadet George Pickett, who is better known for the tragic charge he led at the Civil War battle of Gettysburg on July 3, 1863.

According to John C. Waugh's absorbing study of *The Class of 1846*, Pickett was a regular customer of Benny Havens, though not solely for singing or sipping. The lack of palatable food in the West Point mess hall was still a problem, as a cadet named George Horatio Derby complained in a letter dated February 26, 1845: "India rubber boiled in Aqua forte [nitric acid] could give no idea of the toughness of our roast beef. . . ."

The promise of tastier fare therefore tempted many a hungry cadet to transgress Academy rules, including the artist James McNeill Whistler. A cadet from 1851 to 1854, Whistler "risked punishment by obtaining buckwheat cakes, oysters, ice cream, and other delicacies, at places out of bounds." More than likely, one of those places was Benny Havens' since the popular publican stayed in business until 1859. But by that time there was considerable competition.

Owing partly to Superintendent Sylvanus Thayer's policy of keeping the Academy in the public eye, West Point became a "must" stop for tourists, with a hotel built near the parade ground as early as 1829. Twenty years later, the magnificent Cozzens Hotel opened in Buttermilk Falls, followed by the equally posh Parry House, which occupied an adjacent promontory above the cascade that gave the village its name. The Cozzens burned down in 1869, but was immediately rebuilt into what the late Highland Falls historian Sidney Forman termed "the largest summer hotel between New York [City] and the Catskill Mountain House [above the Kaaterskill Clove in Greene County]." Subsequently called Cranston's, in 1900 the hotel became the site of Ladycliff Academy, where the West Point Museum is now located southeast of Thayer Gate on Route 218.

Those grand hotels were not frequented by cadets, of course, except perhaps when their families came for a visit. It was the cheaper, less-conspicuous watering holes that were chosen, preferably those with a sympathetic proprietor. Besides Benny's haven on the Hudson, there was the Eagle Valley Inn, conveniently situated at the foot of what is now Mountain Avenue, not far from the southern boundary of West Point. Convenient, too, was a pair of peepholes in the dining room door which protected cadets from being discovered by an officer entering the lobby. Once alerted, the young men could escape via a hidden panel in the taproom that led to a back door, or they might scurry up an enclosed stairway to the third floor.

Local tradition does not tell exactly who scooted through the secret passage, but of those cadets known to have frequented the Eagle Valley Inn, three names are of particular interest: Ulysses S. Grant (class of 1843), Philip Sheridan (class of 1853), and William Tecumseh Sherman (class of 1840). Many years later that famous trio was peripherally involved in one of the strangest and most unsavory scandals that ever rocked West Point—a case in which the Highland Falls tavern of Philip Ryan figured prominently. For it was there, on the night of April 5, 1880, that several cadets allegedly were overheard plotting an attack on a black upperclassman named Johnson C. Whittaker.

The subject of both a 1972 book (*Court Martial* by John F. Marszalek, Jr) and a 1994 television drama ("Assault at West Point"), Whittaker was accused of staging his own beating to cover up his poor grades, and was subsequently court-martialed and dismissed from the Academy. President Chester A. Arthur overturned the court-martial two years later, but Whittaker never graduated and therefore never got his commission—not until 1995, when he was posthumously awarded a second lieutenant's bars. As for the famous trio, they mainly were concerned in the controversy over how the case was being handled by West Point Superintendent John Schofield, a Civil War General and former Secretary of War, who had accepted the Academy post only upon the urging of Ulysses S. Grant and William T. Sherman. Neither was especially happy with Schofield's part in the scandal, then when a new post was created for him so that he could be replaced as Superintendent, an angry Sherman confided in his old friend Philip Sheridan. And that was the extent of the trio's involvement.

Returning to the tavern that figured in the Whittaker case, in 1880 Ryan's was already well known for catering to cadets. Not only could they take a concealed path from the post right to his pub, but Ryan reportedly provided a place where they could stash their uniforms if they wanted to change into civilian garb. And it went without saying that their presence would not be publicized. Ryan therefore denied under oath having ever served any cadet, let alone those on the night in question, with the result that the case became even more sensational, and the publican was eventually arrested for perjury.

Lest it be inferred that 19th century cadets were by and large a bunch of topers, it should be noted there was no way a cadet could carouse on a regular basis and still meet curriculum requirements. What's more, whole classes sometimes took a temperance pledge, though this was usually done—as Sidney Forman recorded in his history of *West Point*—"to save guilty classmates from dismissal."

When it came to relaxing in non-alcoholic surroundings, during the late 1800s cadets were welcome at the Constitution Island home of authors Susan and Anna B. Warner, just across the Hudson from West Point. There in a tent set out on the lawn, lemonade, cake and Bible lessons were liberally served by the sisters on summer Sundays. At other times of the year tea might be on tap, and the continuation of those Bible classes until after the turn of the century assured that they too became a West Point tradition. (Tours of Constitution Island and the Warner home, via boat from West Point's South Dock, are held weekly during the warmer months.)

The advent of the 20th century brought about many beneficial changes at the U.S. Military Academy, and few would be willing to trade modern times for the harsher life of earlier days. Yet a certain nostaligia remains for the old watering holes of West Point, where the story is still told of Hudson River ships saluting Benny Havens as they passed his dock. And even today it's not rare to hear young voices raised in that rousing invitation to

Come, fill your glasses, fellows . . . .

46. They Rallied 'Round the Flag

DESPITE THE ABUNDANCE OF CIVIL WAR MONUMENTS THROUGHOUT the region, not many people nowadays are aware of just how vital a role the Hudson Valley played in preserving the Union. In fact, New York provided the greatest amount of men, money and materiel, with much of that contribution coming from the Hudson Valley—a contribution so enormous that it can only be touched upon in this chapter.

The overt issue precipitating the war was states' rights, but "slavery was on everyone's mind, if not on his tongue." That quote comes from John Jay Chapman, a Dutchess County writer who, though little known today, was active in the abolitionist movement. Nor did Chapman's concern for the plight of blacks end with passage of the Thirteenth Amendment prohibiting slavery. After the Civil War, when he learned of lynchings going on in the South, Chapman went down there and almost got lynched himself—a terrifying experience that may have tipped his already delicate emotional balance. For it is said that Chapman spent two years locked away in the tower room at Rokeby, the Barrytown mansion off River Road (Route 103) that was the childhood home of his wife, the former Elizabeth Astor Chanler. Whether

Sited at what has been called the most scenic spot on the Hudson, the U.S. Military Academy's Trophy Point is dominated by the Battle Monument to the Union's Regular Army soldiers who died during the Civil War.

or not it was a nervous breakdown that caused his reclusion, Chapman eventually recovered and built Sylvania, a Georgian mansion near Rokeby whose serene beauty surely helped his peace of mind.

Considering Chapman's dedication to the abolitionist movement, it is possible that he was also involved in the Underground Railroad, which had several routes through the Hudson Valley. But because of the strict secrecy necessary in operating this system for helping slaves escape to freedom, there is scarce information as to the Underground Railroad's "conductors" (those who guided the fugitives), the "stationmasters" and "stations" (places of refuge), or even the exact routes.

It is known that Harriet Tubman was one of the conductors who led slaves through Westchester County, with the help of a Quaker named Moses Pierce. Pierce's Pleasantville home was the station just south of the Jay homestead in Bedford, which reputedly also served as a house of refuge. (See the chapter on "The Day Harriet Tubman Raided Troy.") Peekskill also has ties to the Underground Railroad: a stone-lined tunnel leads to the former summer home of abolitionist preacher Henry Ward Beecher off Main Street, and the old AME Zion Church on Park Street hosts a hidden chamber.

On the other side of the Hudson, the main line of the Underground Railroad went from Edward Hesdra's home in Nyack to Newburgh, and from there it branched into two routes: one heading up to Albany, and the other going west to Utica. Numerous old houses in this area have traditions linking them with the Underground Railroad, including the Ten Eyck house on Hurley's Main Street, the John Field home on Lighthouse Drive in Saugerties, and the James Andrews farm, later the site of the Lake Avenue Elementary School in the city of Saratoga Springs.

That so many Hudson Valley residents risked their own safety in aiding fugitive blacks is coupled with the fact that multitudes of the region's men— some women too—rushed to sign up when it became apparent the Civil War was going to last much longer than the brief period predicted by both sides after the opening battle of Fort Sumter in April 1861. A great many others were already in the army, including Newburgh-born General John Ellis Wool, who at the outbreak of the war had the foresight to send reinforcements to Fortress Monroe in time to save it for the Union. As regards Fort Sumter, it was General Abner Doubleday, a native of Ballston Spa in Saratoga County, who reportedly fired the first Union shot. Doubleday, by the way, was attending the U.S. Military Academy at West Point during 1839 when legend erroneously has him inventing the game of baseball at Cooperstown. Actually he didn't even like sports. His true fame lies in his military heroism, most memorably displayed at Gettysburg, where a statue now marks his contribution to the Union victory.

Mention of West Point brings to mind one of the ironical twists of the Civil War. Most of the generals—both North and South—had been trained at that military bastion in the Highlands, and frequently wound up fighting former friends, classmates and even teachers. Robert E. Lee, for instance, had been superintendent of West Point when Albany-born Philip Sheridan was a cadet, and it was Sheridan's devastation of the Shenandoah Valley in 1863 that helped in eventually bringing Lee's Army of Northern Virginia to its knees. As for Ulysses S. Grant, who graduated with William Buell Franklin in 1843, he had battlefield encounters with several other Confederate generals he had known in the class of 1842, including Richard H. Anderson, Ambrose P. Hill, and James Longstreet.

In 1861, however, there was little hope of turning the Confederate tide. Union troops suffered one defeat after another, among them the disastrous Battle of First Manassas (Bull Run). Young Philo Lewis from the Putnam County town of Kent lost his life on that hot July day—one of the first of hundreds of Hudson Valley men who made the supreme sacrifice. Not all of them died from battle wounds either; disease killed two men for every one who died in combat. In fact, some never even made it to the battlefield, as happened to John S. Mead of Amenia, who succumbed to disease at Camp Dutchess in Poughkeepsie before his regiment was sent south.

The second year of the Civil War was even bloodier than the first, for it was in the April 1862 Battle of Shiloh that more men were killed in one day than in all previous American wars. This pyrrhic victory of the North was followed by the defeat at the June Battle of Gaines' Mills, where General Daniel Adams Butterfield fought so valiantly that he was later awarded the Congressional Medal of Honor. Butterfield, who is credited with composing "Taps," settled in the Ulster County town of Esopus after the war. Then in 1893, he moved to Cold Spring, where he lived in a hillside mansion on Craigside Drive until his death in 1901.

During 1862, defeat continued to plague the North at Second Manassas (Bull Run), and then in September 12,000 Union soldiers were captured at Harpers Ferry. In the latter battle, Cold Spring's General William Hopkins Morris commanded the 6th Regiment of New York Artillery, made up of men from Putnam, Westchester, and Rockland counties, at nearby Maryland Heights. He escaped capture, only to be severely wounded in the 1864 Battle of the Wilderness, but that did not stop the gallant Morris. Upon his recovery, he went on to serve throughout the war, after which he returned to his

Undercliff home on Craigside Drive in Cold Spring. (The General, by the way, was the son of George Pope Morris, newspaper publisher and poet, who penned the once-popular patriotic song "The Flag of Our Union," but perhaps is best remembered for his "Woodman, Spare That Tree.")

The North fared somewhat better in its naval engagements during 1862. Two Putnam County brothers, Lewis and Joseph Ludington, helped to build the Union's first ironclad warship, *Monitor*, parts of which were fabricated in Troy, and which was launched from New York City in March. (Leftover hull plates for the *Monitor* can be seen at the Burden Iron Works Museum at the foot of Troy's Polk Street. The company also manufactured most of the horseshoes used by the Union Army.) Commanded by John Lorimer Worden, a native of Westchester County, the *Monitor* soon engaged the Confederate *Merrimac* at Hampton Roads, Virginia—an indecisive battle from which both ironclads withdrew, but which won the wounded Worden national renown. Worden's fame, however, was soon eclipsed by another naval hero, David G. Farragut, who had been stationed at Norfolk when the war broke out, and immediately moved to Hastings-on-Hudson in Westchester County, offering his services to the Union. His capture of New Orleans on April 25, 1862 was an outstanding achievement, but he is equally famous for the 1864 Battle of Mobile Bay, when suffering from vertigo he strapped himself to the mainmast of his ship and issued the order: "Damn the torpedoes, full speed ahead!"

If 1862 was a bloodbath, then 1863 was pure carnage—and not just on the battlefield. For the conscription law Congress passed in March caused resentments that soon flared into riots. All men between the ages of 20 and 45 were subject to the draft, but anyone could be exempted by paying $300, or by hiring a substitute. Thus, the wealthy didn't have to fight—and many of them took advantage of the exemption, including the fathers of Theodore and Franklin D. Roosevelt.

The bloodiest of the draft riots occurred in New York City from July 13 to 16, when mobs of predominantly Irish and German immigrants roamed Manhattan, killing and being killed. The violence even reached as far as Chappaqua in Westchester County, where a drunken mob advanced upon the farm of Horace Greeley, a staunch abolitionist who championed the war in the columns of his newspaper, the New York *Tribune*. Greeley wasn't home at the time, but his wife was warned of the mob's approach by a neighbor, A.J. Quinby, who advised her to flee. The courageous Mary Greeley declined; after seeing to the safety of her children, she is said to have laid a trail of gunpowder from her front yard to the house, and asked Quinby to inform the mob that she would light the fuse if they came any farther than the gate. They didn't.

Others were not so fortunate. Among the more than 100 deaths during the Manhattan draft riots, that of Orange County's Edward Dippel is one of the most tragic. On July 14, 1863, the 26-year-old policeman and some fellow officers were trying to stop a gang from attacking an abolitionist's home on 29th Street when a contingent of soldiers shot into the crowd, accidentally hitting Dippel and three other cops. When Dippel died of his wounds five days later, his body was brought back to Orange County for burial in the Monroe Cemetery on Route 17M, but his sacrifice received no official recognition for 140 years. It was not until 2003 that researchers realized Dippel's name did not appear on any of various memorials to fallen police officers. A campaign was then mounted to remedy the remission, with the result that a plaque bearing a replica of Dippel's badge, along with a medal for valor, was presented to the New York City Police Museum on East 20th Street.

Two weeks before the draft riots broke out, there had been incredible carnage at the small Pennsylvania community of Gettysburg—a name few of the region's men had ever heard before they fought and died there. But when the battle was over, and a grieving President Abraham Lincoln gave a brief speech dedicating the Union cemetery there, the name of Gettysburg would never be forgotten—certainly not in the annals of Hudson Valley heroes.

Among the regional regiments that took part in the Battle of Gettysburg, the 120th New York—made up mostly of volunteers from Greene and Ulster counties—is remarkable not only for the bravery of its members, but also because of the unique homage accorded it. The regiment's commander, Kingston-born General George H. Sharpe, was so impressed by his men that in 1896 he dedicated a statue to them. (Variously called the Patriotism Statue, or the Daughter of the 120th Regiment, the 7-foot-high, 800-pound bronze figure stands on a stone base in the northwest corner of the Old Dutch Church grounds at Fair and Main streets in Kingston.)

The 124th New York State Volunteers (nicknamed the Orange Blossoms) also served at Gettysburg, and hold a particular place of honor for their fierce defense of the Union Army's left flank near the prominence known as Little Round Top. That strategic hill was taken on July 2, 1863 by the forces of General Gouvernor Kemble Warren, a native of Cold Spring, who is credited with saving the day for the Union, and a bronze statue of him now graces the site.

Another nearby statue commemorates the heroism of Colonel Augustus Van Horne Ellis, the New Windsor-born commander of the Orange Blossoms, who supposedly had told Lieutenant Henry Ramsdell of Newburgh that he did not expect to survive the battle, and was shot through the forehead while leading a charge. Ellis' pessimism was not unfounded, considering the fact that out of the 1,000 men originally in his regiment, only 250 remained to fight at Gettysburg. Many had been lost at Chancellorsville earlier that year—as mentioned elsewhere, that battle reportedly was the basis of Stephen Crane's classic novel, *The Red Badge of Courage*, which he was inspired to write after hearing the reminiscences of Orange Blossom veterans in Port Jervis.

Unlike the Orange Blossoms, Gettysburg was the very first battle fought by Dutchess County's 150th Regiment, but these untried troops performed with great valor at Cemetery Ridge, and managed to capture 200 Confederate soldiers. The 150th then went on to pursue the retreating Rebels, until their ranks were so depleted by disease that the regiment was excused from duty until early autumn. Thereafter, the 150th was sent to guard a railroad at Tullahoma, Tennessee, and in the spring of 1864 they joined General Sherman's army to march through Georgia.

Sherman would not have been able to enter Georgia had it not been for the battles of Missionary Ridge and Lookout Mountain in November 1863. Among the Union forces gathered there was the 143rd Regiment, consisting mostly of Sullivan County men who had trained at Camp Holley on the shore of what is now called Kiamesha Lake. One of the youngest members of the 143rd was a sergeant named Thomas D. Collins, a native of Neversink Flats, who had just turned 16 when his regiment fought at Lookout Mountain. It was there, and at subsequent battles, that Collins' fearlessness under fire was demonstrated in such deeds as the single-handed capture of a Confederate regimental flag, and the rescue of his own company when it was trapped at Peachtree Ridge. His heroism earned Collins the Congressional Medal of Honor, and even the respect of the enemy. For one day when Collins went to resuce a wounded comrade during a fusillade, the officer on the opposing side was so impressed by the young Yankee's bravery that he ordered his troops to hold their fire until Collins brought the injured man to safety. Collins survived the war and spent his later years in the Orange County city of Middletown, where he was buried in the Hillside Cemetery at the end of Mulberry Street, along with 102 other Civil War veterans, including two other Congressional Medal of Honor winners: Corporal Nathan M. Hallock and Captain Lewis S. Wisner, both of the Orange Blossoms.

As the war raged on into 1864, the people at home in the Hudson Valley were playing a vital, if non-combative, role. The iron mines in the Ramapos and the Taconics were churning out tons of ore, while the West Point Foundry at Cold Spring was producing 7,000 artillery projectiles per week. Greene County tanneries turned out much-needed leather; mills like those at Rifton in Ulster County produced gunpowder and army blankets, and Troy's industrial complex operated at high gear—to give only some examples.

Yet the summer of 1864 was the Union's darkest hour, as well as for an Ulster County man named Asa A. Clyne—the same Clyne who later operated the D&H Canal store and drydock at Port Ben (present-day Accord). After enlisting in the Irish Brigade (63rd Regiment) on February 1, Clyne participated in 15 battles in less than six months. Then on June 16, he was wounded at Petersburg and sent to the infamous Confederate prison camp at Andersonville, Georgia, where thousands of Union soldiers died from neglect. Somehow Clyne survived, as did the Union's determination to win the war, which finally ended on May 26, 1865, when General Kirby Smith surrendered all Confederate troops west of the Mississippi.

Abraham Lincoln did not live to see the end of the Civil War. On April 14, he was shot by John Wilkes Booth and died the following day—a tragedy that was mysteriously anticipated in the Orange County village of Pine Bush. According to newspaper accounts, Pine Bush residents heard that Lincoln had been assassinated a full eight hours before he was shot. Was it merely rumor, or had someone prior knowledge of the plot? It was said that John Wilkes Booth had been seen in Newburgh the previous October when he was on his way to Buffalo, and the route he would have taken was along the turnpike going through Pine Bush. There is no proof that he did, though, and the Pine Bush mystery remains just that.

Secretary of State William H. Seward, who was born in the Orange County village of Florida, was also targeted for assassination on the night of April 14. However, Booth's accomplice, Lewis Paine, only succeeded in wounding Seward, who recovered and remained at his cabinet post throughout the administration of Lincoln's successor, Andrew Johnson.

The route of the train carrying Lincoln's body to its last resting place in Illinois passed along the east shore of the Hudson, and in its wake came one of the most mournful of the region's folk tales. For it is said that every April for many years thereafter, a ghostly black-draped train would be seen silently chugging north; clocks would stop as it went by, and all trains on the Hudson line that day would be late.

As intriguing as that bit of folklore may be, it is a factual account that best concludes this abbreviated look at the Hudson Valley's Civil War years. On June 14, 1865, the steamer *Mary Powell* docked at Newburgh, bringing home all that remained of the Orange Blossoms regiment. Amid cheers of the thousands who thronged the shore, the soldiers debarked, still carrying their rifles. As they marched toward the mustering-out ceremony at Washington's Headquarters on Liberty Street, women stepped forward to thrust a bouquet of spring flowers into the muzzle of each gun. Peace had come at last.

47. General Grant's Last Great Battle

THE ARRIVING STEAM LOCOMOTIVE SWIRLED CINDER-LADEN SMOKE over the thousands of people gathered at the Saratoga Springs station on the afternoon of June 16, 1885, but no one seemed to notice. Instead, all eyes were fixed on the private railway car that millionaire William H. Vanderbilt had supplied for this special Delaware & Hudson train taking a dying hero away from the stifling heat of New York City.

Doctors had felt the coolness and clear air high atop Saratoga County's Mount McGregor might help their patient, who surprised everone by walking erectly—if weakly—from the Vanderbilt coach to a narrow-gauge train waiting on a parallel track to bring him the rest of the way. The ailing man's effort elicited a subdued cheer from the crowd, who then joined the uniformed Civil War veterans lining the track in silently waving goodbye to General and ex-President Ulysses S. Grant.

There had been similar gatherings all along the route from Manhattan's Grand Central Station—a Hudson-shore route that stirred many a memory in the sad-eyed soldier-statesman. To Grant, the most significant site was the U.S. Military Academy at West Point, where he had arrived in 1839 as a 17-year-old Ohio farmboy, and quickly decided it was "the most beautiful place I have ever seen." Yet Cadet Grant had no intention of making a career of the Army. A less than assiduous scholar, he preferred to sit in a saddle than in a classroom. He wasn't much of a church-goer either, which earned him no end of demerits. So did something biographer Geoffrey Perret calls "as much military bearing as a sack of potatoes." Grant was as quiet as one too, which early in his Academy days had fooled a fellow cadet into believing he could bully the small-statured Ohioan. When a polite remonstrance failed to deter the taller tormentor, Grant promptly flattened him with one punch.

That kind of get-the-job-done courage was emblematic of Grant's life, whether as the unsuccessful businessman he became after resigning from the Army in 1854, or later as the officer Abraham Lincoln chose to lead the Union to triumph in the Civil War. And during the two-day parade at

Washington in May 1865, the marching soldiers' non-stop cheers for their general presaged Grant's election as president three
years hence.

Unfortunately Grant was no politician.
Despite his personal honesty, scandal scarred
his administration, both in his first term of
office and when he was re-elected in 1872.
Even his own brother Orville forged Grant's
signature for a widow-fleecing scam he ran
with Albany attorney J.H. Smith. No wonder then that the President sometimes sought
serener scenes in the Hudson Valley. One
such peaceful place was his friend William
Dinsmore's Dutchess County estate called
The Locusts, with its main house set on a
bluff overlooking the Hudson at Staatsburg.
Reportedly Grant was enjoying the estate's
western view one July day in 1871 when he
spied a sparkling white spot near the summit
of a blue-green mountain in the distance.
Told it was the recently opened Overlook
Mountain House in the Ulster County town
of Woodstock, the President immediately

*Ulysses S. Grant was a lieutenant general
in command of all the Union armies at
the time he sat for this portrait around
1864. (Photo courtesy of the National
Park Service, Manhattan Sites, General
Grant National Memorial)*

said he'd like to go there. But it was to be another two years bfore Grant
made that rumor-tainted trip.

Before finally heading off to Woodstock in the summer of 1873, Grant
indulged his fondness for horses by attending the June races in the Orange
County village of Goshen. It was one of several visits, for he could count on
a cabinet member's niece to provide him with a private viewing of the races.
The thoughtful lady, it is said, placed a chair for Grant in the open doors of
her barn's hayloft, overlooking the homestretch of what is now Historic Track.

The following month, a much more public Grant steamed up the
Hudson on the Day Line's *Chauncey Vibbard*, acknowledging the crowds
greeting him at every landing. Debarking at Rhinecliff on the Dutchess
County shore, Grant was met by General George H. Sharpe, a Kingston
lawyer and government official, who accompanied the President across the
river to Rondout, then by train to West Hurley, and from there a horse-
drawn carriage took them to the Overlook Mountain House. (The remains

of the resort can be reached via the red-blazed Overlook Spur Trail at the end of Meads Mountain Road north of Woodstock village.)

According to Alf Evers' wonderful history of *Woodstock*, on the evening Grant arrived—July 30, 1873—a gala ball was given at the hotel in his honor, and the following morning the President walked up to the summit of the mountain, escorted by a contingent of hotel guests. There he savored the view from various overlooks, including a boulder afterwards known as Grant's Rock. Tradition says he also took time to carve his initials into one of the rocks, but it was not this Kilroyism that caused Grant to suffer a cruel lambasting. It seems some of his political opponents viewed his Hudson Valley tour as Grant's way of "testing the waters" for a possible third-term candidacy, and they apparently decided to damage his popularity by accusing him of drunkenness during the trip. Grant's early bouts with the bottle were well known, but there had been no hint of alcohol abuse since the Civil War, and he must have been deeply hurt by the accusations printed in a Rhinebeck newspaper.

The public attack on his sobriety may have contributed to Grant's decision not to run for a third term in 1876, and he later confided to a friend that he "was never as happy in my life as the day I left the White House." Grant thereupon embarked on a two-year world tour with his beloved wife Julia, after which they moved into a Manhattan brownstone at 3 East 66 Street. The mansion was their winter home, with the warmer months spent at a New Jersey cottage or in the Hudson River region. The presence of the ex-president was, of course, a drawing card at any of the area's grand resorts, and in 1883, he was a guest at both the Catskill Mountain House in Greene County and the nearby Hotel Kaaterskill. (Both sites can be seen from trails leading from the North-South Lake Campground and Day Use area off Route 18, northeast of Haines Falls.) Mainly, however, the Grants visited their son Ulysses Jr.—called Buck—who lived with his wife and family at Merryweather Farm in the Westchester County town of North Salem. (Much altered and privately owned, the Italianate stone house stands at Grant Corners, near the intersection of June, Grant and Hawley Mountain roads.)

Through Buck, the ex-president was introduced to Wall Street wizard Ferdinand Ward, who convinced the two Grants to become partners with him in a new investment firm. Father and son, along with other members of the family, invested heavily in what turned out to be nothing more than a Ponzi scheme. On May 6, 1884, the firm of Grant & Ward folded, leaving the ex-president "literally without means." Indeed, had it not been for a RensselaerCounty man from Lansingburgh named Charles Wood—a total stranger who heard of the General's troubles and sent him $500 saying, "I owe you this for Appomattox"—there would have been no cash to run the Grant household.

A few weeks later, Grant was approached by *Century Magazine* to do a series of articles on the Civil War. He had never tried his hand at writing, but since it was the only way he might earn some money, he accepted the assignment. To his surprise, authorship came easy, and for a brief time the future seemed secure. Then in the early summer of 1884, Grant was eating a peach when he felt a searing pain in his esophagus. Though the problem persisted, he put off seeing a specialist until late October, when Manhattan's leading throat expert, Dr. John H. Douglas, diagnosed "a complaint with a cancerous tendency."

By this time, Grant had difficulty swallowing and was experiencing choking fits, so he was persuaded to give up the cigars he loved. Supposedly he enjoyed his last stogie that November when invited to an elegant horse farm on the banks of the Wallkill River in Orange County—an event recorded in a *Scribner's* illustration called "Evening in the Stony Ford Smoking Room."

Although not smoking seemed to bring about some improvement in Grant's condition, a biopsy in February 1885 showed a malignancy "sure to end fatally," and his doctors concurred that any surgical intervention would only cause him further pain. Grant reacted to the news with less concern for himself than for his family. He could not—*would not*—die before he had provided for them financially!

That was something easier said than done, for Grant's sole hope was to complete within the next few months the memoirs he had recently begun to write—a monumental task for a healthy man, let alone one in constant pain and no longer able to swallow solid food.

Mark Twain, who had long admired and liked Grant, even though they had served on opposite sides in the Civil War, was willing to gamble that the General would accomplish his goal. Twain's publishing company therefore offered a $10,000 advance, and a book contract was signed in late February 1885.

Consistent with such terminal cases, Grant's condition variously peaked and plummeted. In early spring a hemorrhage had doctors despairing of his life, but Grant rallied and went on with his memoirs, at times trying to speed things up by dictating his thoughts instead of his usual method of writing with a pencil.

As summer approached, Twain's publishing house had copy enough for a two-volume work. Grant, however, was far from finished, insisting on the careful text revisions that only he could accomplish. There was no dissuading him, so Grant's doctors did the next best thing: transfer their patient to a cooler, clearer climate where he could work in greater comfort—a relative comfort, that is, dependent on periodic applications of cocaine solution to the ravaged throat, morphine to nurture sleep at night, and as a stimulant to the ever-weakening body there were *injectio*ns of brandy (a fairly common practice in those days).

New York banker and summer Saratogian Joseph Drexel offered the use of his cottage near the summit of Mount McGregor, just north of Saratoga Springs. A roomy if rustic structure, the cottage was easily accessible from a narrow-gauge railroad and just a short walk from the lavish Hotel Balmoral, which could be counted on to supply meals. Drexel's invitation was therefore readily accepted, especially since Grant recalled earlier enjoyable sojourns in the area, including a visit to a Round Lake resort in the town of Malta during the summer of 1874, when he also was the guest of honor at a grand ball given by General George Sherman Batcheller in the latter's brand-new Saratoga Springs mansion.

When Grant and his family arrived at the Drexel cottage on the afternoon of June 16, they found an Albany man named Sam Willett standing at attention. A former Civil War soldier and a member of the Grand Army of the Republic (a veterans' organization), Willett had pitched a tent in the back yard, determined to guard his general for as long as Grant remained there. A similar devotion was seen in the crowds that began coming to Mount McGregor—from individual children with bouquets of flowers for the country's first four-star general, to cadres of soldiers and contingents of civilian organizations silently marching past the cottage, saluting Grant if he happened to be sitting on the verandah. In addition, there were countless letters, gifts, and telegrams, along with the callers whose numbers had to be restricted in order to conserve Grant's strength.

Nobody knew better than he did how near he was to the end. Shortly after his arrival at Mount McGregor, Grant had attempted a short stroll out to the escarpment offering a spectacular view to the east. Exhausted by the effort, he returned to the cottage and wrote notes to his family and doctors, unemotionally estimating his remaining time and detailing some of his last wishes. One of his greatest desires was for the reconciliation of North and South, and Grant was cheered by a visit on July 10 from Confederate General Simon Bolivar Buckner, a fellow West Pointer who had surrendered to him at Fort Donelson in 1862. But Grant's most fervent hope remained that of providing financially for his family. And to this end he continued to devote many a waking hour, aided by his sons and sometimes Mark Twain.

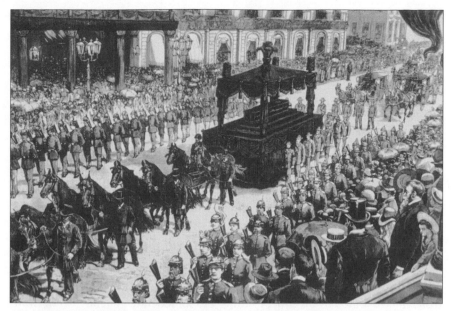

The August 8, 1885 funeral of Ulysses S. Grant was one of the largest ever seen in New York City, with a 3-mile-long line of marchers and an estimated million mourners lining the route.

PHOTO COURTESY OF THE NATIONAL PARK SERVICE, MANHATTAN SITES, GENERAL GRANT NATIONAL MEMORIAL

Actually Grant never really went to bed, because the choking he experienced kept him from lying down, and for many months he had slept semi-reclined on two large armchairs placed face to face. It was there, leaning on a lapboard, that he finished work on his book "about July the nineteenth," according to his wife Julia. A few days later, on the morning of July 23, 1885, Ulysses S. Grant peacefully passed away, content in the knowledge that his battle to complete the memoirs had been successful, and that Mark Twain's salesmen already had secured 100,000 pre-publication orders for the two-volume set. (Grant's *Personal Memoirs*, it might be added, are still popular more than a century after first appearing.)

Although the dying Grant had matter-of-factly made many of the arrangements for his funeral, the place of burial remained undecided. He had ruled out the most likely place—West Point—since wives were not allowed interment there, and he wanted Julia's last resting place to be by his side. Therefore, when New York Mayor W.R. Grace offered a site in one of the city's parks, the family responded favorably, and the high bluff of Riverside Park in northern Manhattan was chosen.

A funeral service was held at Mount McGregor on August 4, when at dawn a 13-gun salute began firing every half-hour for the 63-year-old general whose graveclothes consisted of a simple black broadcloth suit. None of his military habiliments had been available, not even his sword, for much of his wartime memorabilia had been used to repay a loan made during the Grant & Ward fiasco. After the services at the Drexel cottage, Grant's coffin was brought down the mountain in a special funeral train and taken to Albany, where he lay in state at the Capitol until the following day. The cortege then made its way to New York's City Hall, and a quarter-million people paid their last respects during the next two days.

August 8, 1885 found the streets of Manhattan filled with an estimated million mourners as a 3-mile-long line of marchers escorted Grant's catafalque—drawn by 24 black horses—the 7 miles from City Hall to Riverside Park. There a temporary brick tomb would hold the remains until the temple-like Grant Monument was completed in 1897.

All this would surely have impresssed Grant, but the thing that might have moved him most concerned his long-harbored hope of healing Civil War wounds. For the Union generals serving as honorary pallbearers at the funeral were joined by an equal number of Confederate generals. So in more ways than one, Ulysses S. Grant had won his last great battle.

[Note: Grant Cottage, off Corinth Mountain Road in the town of Wilton, is open to the public during the summer season. Grant's tomb, formally called General Grant National Memorial, is located near the intersection of Riverside Drive and 122nd Street in Manhattan, and can be visited year-round.]

VIII. PLACES NONPAREIL

48. Mill House: Monument to the American Experience

O NE OF THE BEST-KEPT SECRETS OF HUDSON VALLEY HISTORY LIES only a few hundred yards off busy Route 9W in the northeastern Orange County town of Newburgh. Just before the road crosses over into Ulster, a narrow lane leads off to the east and swoops down into a picturesque ravine. For a short distance, the lane parallels the course of a rushing stream, passing en route a rustic mill precariously perched on a small island. Then it continues east over a stone bridge as the stream makes a sharp bend to the north.

At this scenic point, an old stone-and-brick house stands tucked up against the dogwood-studded hillside. There are no large signs proclaiming its importance, and not many people are aware of its existence, but even in a region replete with historic structures, this building—called the Gomez Mill House—is outstanding. For it not only is the oldest surviving Jewish residence in North America, it is remarkable in other ways as well.

To fully appreciate the rich history of Mill House, it is necessary to travel back in time to 17th century Spain, where the Inquisition

Its blend of ancient stones and local handmade brick hint of the long history of Gomez Mill House, thought to be the oldest surviving Jewish residence in North America.

was still taking its bloody toll. Although Jews were considered heretics, and therefore prime targets for the torture rack, they were told they could avoid persecution by professing to accept Christianity—something many of them did, while secretly retaining their own religion. Such conversions were not above suspicion, though, and the Jews who made them were contemptuously referred to as *marranos* (Spanish for "swine"), while they remained under the watchful eye of the Inquisition. Despite this, several *marranos* were welcome at the court of King Philip IV, who believed Spain would benefit more by utilizing their business acumen than by burning them at the stake. Yet even Philip did not dare oppose the all-powerful Inquisition.

Isaac Gomez was one of the *marrano* courtiers the king prized most highly—so much so that Philip promised Gomez that if ever the Inquisition was about to arrest him, he would warn him by saying, "The onions are beginning to smell." The king kept his promise, and when Gomez heard the cryptic words, he managed to send his wife and infant son Moses to safety in France. But he was unable to secure his own passage, and spent the next 14 years in prison.

Somehow Isaac Gomez survived the horrors of the Inquisitiors' dungeon and, upon his release, he joined his family in France. There he gave his son the added name of Louis, out of gratitude to the French monarch who had granted them asylum. As it turned out, Louis XIV was not all that tolerant of non-Catholics, and when in 1685 he revoked the Edict of Nantes (which had allowed Huguenots limited religious freedom), the Gomezes fled to England.

Louis Gomez was by now a grown man. Following in the footsteps of other family members engaged in international trade, he recognized the opportunities offered by England's colonies across the ocean, and by 1703 he was settled in New York City, having been granted Letters of Denization (similar to citizenship papers) by Queen Anne. The queen could have made no better choice, for in addtion to being an astute businessman whose many enterprises added to her own wealth as well as his, Louis was a civic-minded individual, as quick to contribute to the construction of a Christian church steeple (that of Trinity in 1711) as he was in helping to build the city's first synagogue (the Spanish and Portuguese Congregation Shearith Israel, begun around 1728). He was also the father of five sons, and very likely it was an interest in their future that caused Louis to look ever farther afield—this time upriver, where vast tracts of land were available through patents granted by the queen.

Along with his sons Daniel and David, Louis concentrated on the Harrison and Kennedy patents around Newbugh and Marlborough, eventually buying up thousands of acres. There was more to his plan than mere land acquisition, however. For Louis had studied the area carefully and learned that several major Indian paths converged into a single trail leading to a rocky prominence called the Danskammer—an ancient ceremonial site jutting out into the Hudson, where native Americans regularly congregated. Dark tales were told of the Danskammer, so named in the early 1600s by Dutch sailors who had witnessed the native rituals there and had decided it was without doubt the "Devil's Dance Chamber." What's more, the land around it was a wilderness, with the nearest settlement six miles south at Newburgh. All this Louis knew, but it paled in importance to the fact that anyone courageous enough to establish a post along that main trail to the Danskammer could conduct an exclusive fur trade with the Indians.

It is not known whether Louis or his son Daniel undertook the arduous task of clearing the land and hauling huge fieldstones, but by 1717 (perhaps as early as 1714), a single-story trading post had been erected near a spring the Indians always stopped at when traveling along the trail to the Danskammer. With stone walls nearly 3 feet thick, and its north side set into the hill like a cellar, the fortress-like building had ceilings high enough to hang animal pelts from the beams, and two huge fireplaces where friendly Indians might gather on cold winter days as they bartered their furs for the trade goods the Gomezes brought upriver from New York City.

The trading post was a success from the very first season, and for many decades thereafter the Gomezes spent part of every year at their stone house, abandoning the operation only when the Indians began leaving the area and the fur trade fell off. Meanwhile, the family continued to be a vital force in the development of the colony, and when the Revolutionary War broke out in 1776, they sided with the new nation. In fact, Daniel Gomez volunteered for the militia, even though he was then in his eighties. Turned down because of his age, the octogenarian reportedly huffed, "I can stop a bullet as well as anyone else!"

The same fervid patriotism was displayed by Wolfert Acker, who had purchased the old Gomez trading post in 1772, and built a gristmill on the nearby stream. Instead of Indians gathering around the huge fieldstone fireplace, the main room as now filled every Sunday with Acker's fellow revolutionaries, who came there to hear the latest war news, and plan their activities. Acker would always open those meetings by reading passages from an enormous Dutch Bible, then switch to items in the *New-York Packet*, a pro-patriot newspaper printed across the river in Fishkill.

As chairman of the local Committee of Safety, Acker abhorred anyone siding with the British, and pursued those Tories with "untiring zeal." Yet he never allowed his patriotism to outdistance practicality, as was apparent in 1777 when he protested a law calling for the confiscation and sale of all a Tory's property. Pointing out that Tories thus made destitute would became public charges, he convincingly argued that some of the confiscated property be used to maintain the former owners. He also objected to a severe tax imposed on people whose sons fought for the British, saying that most of them were "not worth half the sum . . . taxed."

Had it not been for his unflagging efforts in support of the patriot cause, such protests might well have resulted in Acker's own loyalty being questioned. As it was, he was not immune to the ravages of war, and suffered the wrath of the military when he refused to condone unnecessary requisitions of farm horses and forage. But Acker survived, and when the Revolution ended in 1783, he concentrated on expanding his business interests, adding brickmaking to his milling enterprise, in addtion to establishing a ferry that operated between Wappingers Falls and the landing he built at Hampton (now Cedar Cliff).

By this time, the old Indian trail had become a well-traveled lane, and the stream Wolfert Acker had dammed to provide power for his mills was known as Acker's Creek, having originally be called Jew's Creek—a name that still appears on some maps. Speaking of names, there is a still-repeated story that Acker's home was the "Wolfert's Roost" that Washington Irving wrote about, but this is not true. Although Irving may have visited Mill House at some time during the 1800s, "Wolfert's Roost" was the author's own Sunnyside home in Tarrytown—a remodeled 17th century Dutch farmhouse originally owned by the grandfather for whom Wolfert Acker was named.

Wolfert Acker had been born in that Westchester County farmhouse in 1732, and perhaps memories of the place had some influence on the design of the brick second storey he added to the old Gomez trading post. Clay for the brick was dug from the banks of the nearby stream, then packed in wooden frames by slaves who lived in a small house adjoining the main building. Under Acker's direction, they constructed an addition as sturdy as the stone storey beneath it, using darker-colored bricks to delineate a traditional Dutch design of a heart within a diamond on the east end of the house.

Acker, it seems, was building for future generations of his family. But that was not to be. For his son and heir, William Acker, reputedly was more devoted to the "sporting life" than to his duties as a state legislator, and 31 years after Wolfert's death in 1799, Mill House was subject to a foreclosure sale. The property was purchased by the Armstrongs of Danskammer Point, a prominent Hudson Valley family that included several authors, artists and statesmen well known in their day. The exception is William Henry Armstrong, a writer who lived longer at Mill House than any other resident—60 years, it is said—but whose life and work remain something of a mystery.

According to some accounts William Henry Armstrong penned a Civil War novel called *Rutledge* while residing at Mill House, and set some of the scenes therein. His wife Sarah also was of a literary bent, and edited a collection of the writings of her father, William John Grayson. On a sadder note, the Armstrongs are said to have constructed the fieldstone wall that protectively curves around the property following the death of their daughter Emily, who had wandered down to the stream one day and drowned. However, stories that the child's tombstone was embedded at one end of the wall are erroneous; there is a small tombstone there, but it is that of a pet lamb.

Aside from that wall and a kitchen extension the Armstrongs built on the west side of Mill House, few changes were made until Dard Hunter bought it around 1912. Indeed, during the decade preceding his purchase, little had been done by way of maintenance, and the property was sorely run down. Fortunately, Hunter and his wife appreciated the proud history of Mill House and set about restoring it to pristine condition. There couldn't have been a better choice either, for Dard Hunter was an associate of Elbert Hubbard, the writer and publisher who in 1895 founded the Roycroft Shop at East Aurora, New York, to revive such ailing arts as fine printing and handmade paper. After studying papermaking in England, Hunter set up his own shop at Mill House, where he produced special editions of books virtually from scratch. The large second-floor room on the southwestern side of the house became his type foundry, where he cut and cast type, then handset every letter. But to make paper he needed a mill.

The site Hunter chose for his water-powered paper mill was the small island in Jew's Creek, just across from the house. There has been speculation that he built this structure on the ruins of Wolfert Acker's gristmill, but in his 1958 autobiography, *My Life With Paper*, Hunter stated that "of this building [Acker's mill] nothing remained." And anyone who has ever seen how springtime runoff from the hills sometimes turns the stream into a raging torrent can well understand why Acker's mill did not suvive the centuries.

Utilizing oak beams and the handmade brick left over from the time Acker had added the second storey to Mill House, Hunter designed his paper mill to look like a Devonshire cottage in England, complete with a thatched roof—the latter made from straw grown on the property. It was there that Hunter turned out some of the finest handmade paper ever produced in America, examples of which can be seen in the Mill House library.

Eventually Dard Hunter and his family moved away, and from the

1920s through the '40s Mill House experienced a variety of owners and uses. For a brief time it served as a libertarian school for children of all races run by two advocates of anarchist Emma Goldman, and later it became a tea-room and guest house, but mostly it was used as a private residence. Then in 1947 it was purchased by the Starin family, and its future became much brighter.

Mildred Starin had grown up in the neighborhood and since childhood had loved the old house, so it was a great delight to be able to raise her own four children there, while carefully maintaining what she felt was an important piece of history placed in her trust. Accompanying this feeling was a growing concern over the future of Mill House, and Mrs. Starin began researching its past, convinced it belonged on the National Register of Historic Places, and that such designation would help preserve it. Her efforts were rewarded in 1979, when Mill House was placed on the National Register, and with the listing another dream surfaced: that someday the site would become a house-museum, where the public would be welcome to learn about and enjoy what has been one of the Hudson Valley's least-known historic landmarks.

In 1984, Mrs. Starin's dream came closer to realization when the Gomez Foundation for Mill House purchased the 14-room dwelling and 28 acres surrounding it. Estblished in 1979, the foundation's membership mainly consisted of descendants of former Mill House owners, with Washington, D.C. lawyer Michael H. Cardozo at one time serving as president. Cardozo was directly descended from Louis Moses Gomez, whose penchant for patriotism was passed on to such notable family members as Captain Isaac Franks, aide to George Washington during the closing days of the Revolution, and U.S. Supreme Court Justice Benjamin Cardozo. As for Louis Gomez's chief reasons for coming to America—religious freedom and economic opportunity—it is interesting to note that another of his descendants was Emma Lazarus, who wrote the poem about the "huddled masses yearning to breathe free" that is inscribed on the base of the Statue of Liberty.

As money became available, the Gomez Foundation restored Dard Hunter's paper mill and made many other improvements to the property, as well as fostering public awareness of Mill House through programs and guided tours of the building. The large living room stretching across the front of the house is the most evocative of the Gomez era, with its enormous field-stone fireplaces at either end and exposed ceiling beams, but it is another first-floor room at the eastern end of the house that is the most fascinating for many visitors. This room is reached by a long central hall, where an ancient plank door opens to reveal a book-filled room, with a section of shelves hiding the entrance to a secret tunnel.

It is still possible to swing back the hinged bookcase, but the tunnel is no longer accessible, having been closed off in the distant past. Tradition holds that this tunnel goes underneath the road outside to exit on the stream bank, but who built it and why is anybody's guess. Some people think it was dug by the Gomezes, whose past experiences with persecution might well have prompted them to install a secret escape passage. Others point out that such tunnels were not uncommon in colonial homes—especially those lacking an in-house water source, where a sheltered passage to a nearby stream was expedient in times of attack, and could double as a getaway route. So the tunnel might have originated with Wolfert Acker during the perilous days of the Revolution.

As for the building being filled with mementoes spanning three centuries—from an antique menorah to a colonial Bible box and a 20th century fireplace lintel—some people have argued that historic structures should reflect a single era rather than many, and in the past there was some talk of returning Mill House to a Gomez-only ambiance. Even if that were physically and financially possible, few people would want to see that occur. For while the founding family represents the dream of religious and economic freedom that brought most immigrants to our shores, and without the Gomezes and their indomitable spirit there obviously would have been no Mill House, it is also the structure's subsequent history that helps make it a monument to the American experience—a heritage of which we all can be very proud.

49. Saving Grace

PREDOMINANT AMONG THE HUDSON VALLEY'S MANY DELIGHTS IS ITS amazing variety of awesome public places, some of which are surprisingly little known outside their immediate neighborhoods. A case in point is Untermyer Park and Gardens in the Westchester County city of Yonkers—a walled enclave off North Broadway that people are apt to pass by, unaware that the narrow driveway leads to the former Greystone estate and what was once one of the country's grandest horticultural designs.

It isn't until newcomers round the corner of the Charles A. Cola Community Center—site of the estate's carriage house—that they have some hint of this magnificence. A gravel path leads to a high wall pierced by a marble-framed portal over which a bas relief of the Greek goddess Artemis seems to beckon one inside. The invitation is irresistible. Beyond the portal, arrow-straight paths impel strollers past canals, fountains, flowerbeds and sculpted shrubbery to a pair of winged sphinxes at the north end of this Greek garden. Each poised atop a double Ionic column, these mythical white marble creatures oversee a colonnaded amphitheater whose purpose is proclaimed by tragedy/comedy masks set in tiny mosaic floor tiles.

If you were to visit Untermyer Park solely to see the mosaics, that would be sufficient reason, since the Grecian garden boasts over 9,000 square feet of these inlaid decorations—one of the largest collections in the country. (On the western side of the garden, don't miss the many different fish depicted in the tiled pool at the base of the open-air temple; the floor of the latter features a mosaic head of Medusa, snakes and all.) But mosaics constitute only one aspect of this outdoor wonderland, whose borders extend well beyond the formal Greek garden. At the western end of the colonnade, for instance, a 600-foot-long stepped allée called the vista leads downhill to a columned overlook offering grand views of the Hudson below and the Palisades beyond.

Although the land on the north side of the allée is now sadly overgrown, visitors can still discern the terraced gardens that in the past had turned the whole hillside into an unbelievable floral display. In one bed alone 50,000

Right: "One of the few Grand Beaux Arts landscape designs ever executed in America," the
*Grecian Gardens at Untermyer Park in Yonkers is
graced by this open-air temple.*
PHOTO CREDIT: STEPHEN PAUL DEVILLO

*Below: as befits her power to turn people into stone,
the mythological Greek Gorgon, Medusa, is depicted in one of Untermyer Park's many mosaics.*
PHOTO CREDIT: STEPHEN PAUL DEVILLO

tulips once bloomed above 50,000 pansies. There were also color-specific plots—a pink garden, a blue garden, a yellow garden, and so on—as well as a rose garden, another devoted solely to dahlias, and along the far side a five-level Italian vegetable garden complete with formal fountain on the topmost terrace. Water from this fountain cascaded down to limestone pools on succeeding levels that were bisected by beautiful blue-tiled channels.

The grounds south of the Vista were equally impressive if more parklike, with a carriage road curving uphill from the Hudson past some 30,000 rhododendrons and boxwood shrubs set amidst all sorts of statuary, specimen trees, rock gardens and even an enormous working sundial made up of living plants. And as if this weren't enough, dozens of greenhouses boasted the "finest private collection of tropical plants in America," including more than 3,000 varieties of orchids.

What manner of man—what measure of money—did it take to create such a place? Considerable is the answer in either case, with the man, Samuel Untermyer, certainly a study in contrasts. He could, for example, shell out thousands of dollars of his own money as an unpaid counsel in a lawsuit, yet bicker with Yonkers liverymen over their rates.

The son of a Bavarian immigrant who settled in the antebellum South and became a slave-holding tobacco farmer, Untermyer was born in Lynchburg, Virginia, in 1858. Tradition tells that as a youngster during the Civil War he dressed in a miniature Confederate uniform and ran around his front yard shouting, "Huzzah for Jeff Davis"—cheers that were silenced by the Union victory in 1865, when the family income was lost and his father died shortly afterward. Samuel's mother then packed up her five children and headed for New York City, where she supported the family by running a boarding house. She had hopes of Samuel becoming a rabbi, but after-school work as a lawyer's messenger boy convinced him otherwise, and before he passed the bar in 1879, Untermyer already was winning cases.

Despite being sickly and small of stature, Untermyer was a giant in the courtroom, always as perfectly attired as he was prepared, and able to call upon a photographic memory, plus a certain histrionic talent. Perhaps his greatest gift, however, was what journalist Alva Johnston called the "singular power to open the skull of a witness and exhibit the contents to a jury." Not even Henry Ford dared undergo Untermyer's cross-examination in a libel suit regarding the auto magnate's anti-Semitism. Instead, Ford opted to settle, mayhap recalling rumors that Untermyer's two-day cross-examination of J.P. Morgan during a 1912 congressional committee hearing had brought about the banker's death. It wasn't true, of course, but the wily trial lawyer in his trademark horn-rimmed glasses wasn't about to issue a disclaimer.

The only mogul that Untermyer could not melt in a courtroom was his neighbor a dozen miles to the north, icy-eyed John D. Rockefeller. The two crossed verbal swords over a small petroleum firm that Rockefeller's Standard Oil Company was trying to dominate, despite a 1911 Supreme Court ruling dissolving the huge trust. Untermyer managed to win the case for the little guy, but later admitted that the then septuagenarian Rockefeller had the "ablest and most agile mind" he'd "ever encountered on the witness stand," anticipating "five or six questions ahead all of the time." Then in his fifties, Untermyer was evolving into a crusading, oftentimes pro-bono trust-buster, after having started out as a corporation counsel with a knack for organizing industrial combinations. This early work brought him hefty fees and, along with some insider investments, he had made his first million by the time he turned 30 in 1888.

Eleven years later and several millions richer, Untermyer was easily able to afford the $171,500 auction price for a 99-room mansion on more than 100 acres in Yonkers. Called Greystone for its granite building material quarried nearby, the house had been designed in the 1860s by John Davis Hatch for hat manufacturer John T. Waring. Financial problems eventually forced Waring to sell Greystone to ex-governor of New York State, Samuel J. Tilden, who not only Americanized the spelling to Graystone, but expended $244,000 for improvements, among them additional land and 13 large greenhouses to serve his horticultural interests.

Untermyer was a botany buff too, but was far from satisfied with the estate as Tilden left it. He soon hired architect J.H. Freedlander to remodel the mansion, reportedly to the tune of $100,000, part of which paid for a Turkish bath and a second-floor swimming pool. As for the grounds, they became an ongoing enrichment project featuring fountains and statues designed by leading artists like Isidore Konti and Paul Manship, the latter perhaps best known for his gilded statue of *Prometheus* in Manhattan's Rockefeller Center. And in 1912 Untermyer contracted with William Welles Bosworth—a Beaux-Arts landscape architect who had earlier planned John D. Rockefeller's Kykuit property in North Tarrytown—to design the "finest garden in the world."

Among the sculpture that eventually graced the garden was a splendid pair of winged sphinxes created by Paul Manship in 1917—sculptures that pleased Untermyer so much that he later ordered bronze castings of the artist's statues depicting *Diana* and *Acteon*. According to Greek myth, Acteon was a hunter who accidentally viewed the goddess Artemis naked in her bath. The angered Artemis—whose Roman equivalent is Diana—thereupon turned Acteon into a stag, and his own hounds tore him to pieces. The bronze version was to suffer a somewhat similar fate when on the afternoon of October 7, 1939, someone stole *Acteon* from its place at the amphitheater entrance. How this could be accomplished without detection raised more than one eyebrow, since the four-and-a-half-foot statue weighs around 250 pounds. But Untermyer was much more interested in getting *Acteon* returned, and promptly posted a reward.

Little more than a week later, police were tipped off to a certain New Rochelle junkyard dealer named John Real, who had tried selling the statue as "old metal" for 7¢ a pound. Hearing of *Acteon* being offered for a mere $17.50, when its estimated worth was around $8,500, Untermyer publicly stated his "mortification"—a condition no doubt exacerbated by news that the statue had been cut into four pieces and buried underground. Fortunately, the severing had occurred along the seams of the bronze casting, and before long *Acteon* had been bolted back together.

That was not the estate's first case of buried treasure. Back in 1927, laborers doing some excavation work unearthed a Greek statue that turned out to be a piece long ago pilfered and buried by the butler of Greystone's former owner, Samuel Tilden. But whether this incident had any influence on the 1939 statue-napping remains a mystery, for the junkman John Real refused to reveal any details of the theft, and silently served his sentence at Elmira Reformatory.

The much-abused *Acteon* was almost lost again in 1948 when an auction was held and a California cemetery tried to purchase it as a sepulchral ornament. This time the Hudson River Museum, located just south of the Untermyer estate, came to the rescue, along with the Yonkers City Council. Permanent custodianship of *Diana* and *Acteon* was granted to the museum, where both statues were safely ensconced.

Getting back to the genesis of the "finest garden in the world," it was Untermyer's gift to his wife, the former Minnie Carl, a governess he had met at a friend's house and married in 1880. Mrs. Untermyer, it seems, desired an outdoor setting for the entertainments she enjoyed giving—a mission gloriously met by William Welles Bosworth's Greek garden, which offered various venues for gatherings. Poetry readings, for instance, were perfect in the amphitheater, with its four rows of stone benches set in a semicircle, while the garden's grassy lower terrace was ideal for legendary danseuse Isadora Duncan, who performed there in 1923. Politics came into play too, since Untermyer was an influential Democrat. Grover Cleveland and

Woodrow Wilson were overnight guests at Greystone (the spelling having been changed back to the British), and in 1924 Untermyer invited all 1,200 delegates of the Democratic Convention then meeting in Manhattan to an outdoor dinner at his estate. Alas, the affair was ruined by torrential rains that some wags insisted had been sent by the Republicans!

On a more somber note, Untermyer was devastated by the death of his wife that summer of 1924. His own fragile health compromised, the 66-year-old lawyer decided to take a trip around the world as a prelude to retirement. He only got as far as Tokyo, however, when he read some articles which he thought demeaned his role in setting up the Federal Reserve system. Suddenly energized, Untermyer shot back a rebuttal, and with clients clamoring for his services, he returned to New York, ready to resume a full-time schedule. That schedule included close attention to his Greystone gardens, for Untermyer felt that "in gardening one can work on so much larger a scale than in any other art except possibly architecture." Flowers were by far his favorite plants, with orchids topping the list—so much so that his large desk at Greystone was kept covered with blooms, except for the blotter, and for a boutonniere he always chose an orchid grown in one of his greenhouses. In fact, a few hours after Untermyer left for his Manhattan office—either taking the train or his steam launch, *Scud*, docked in the Hudson—an employee would be dispatched with a fresh supply of orchids so that Untermyer could change his boutonniere several times during the day.

When it came to vegetables and fruits, Untermyer was the fondest of those he could grow in his greenhouses and enjoy when they were out of season and unavailable on the market. At other times, it was the sheer joy of experimentation, as when he tried spiking honeydew melon vines with a combination of Benedictine, cognac and port wine—a test he didn't talk much about after the not too successfully soused melons were harvested. And although he audited every penny paid out for household expenses, once refusing to pay the Greystone electric bill for nearly *eight years* by claiming a faulty meter, he couldn't care less about garden costs, cabbages included. In that instance, his estate manager, George Chisholm, attempted to convince Untermyer the Greystone vegetable garden was an extravagance by pointing to cabbages costing nearly $1 a head to grow. Untermyer's only answer: "I never eat cabbages!"

A strong bond existed between Untermyer and Chisholm, forged in part by the Welsh landscapist being unintimidated by the famous lawyer's mien or money. Indeed, at their first meeting in the 1920s, Chisholm had called an Untermyer-designed rock garden a "geological monstrosity," and proceeded to build him a better one. Both men were horticultural experts, but the estate manager was beyond any doubt the better botanical artist.

Journalists of the day delighted in describing Chisholm's floral sculpture, sometimes made as a surprise for Untermyer when he returned home from a trip: a full-size replica of an Indian paddling a canoe, all done in yellow chrysanthemums, and a prize-winning 12-foot-high chrysanthemum Notre Dame Cathedral are just two of those creations. The public didn't have to depend on written accounts, however, for there were autumn flower shows at Greystone, as well as Tuesdays when the gardens were open to everyone. And when he finally did retire around the age of 80, Untermyer enjoyed those Tuesdays when he could mingle with visitors and listen to their compliments.

Before he died, Untermyer tried to donate Greystone, first to New York State, then to Westchester County, and finally to the city of Yonkers. But all three declined the gift, not wishing to assume the upkeep of such an extensive estate or, for that matter, to take it off the tax rolls. And this was how matters stood in March 1940, when the flower-loving lawyer's casket—covered by 300 orchids and 10,000 lilies of the valley, all from Greystone greenhouses —was laid to rest in the lavish family plot at Woodlawn Cemetery in the Bronx. Untermyer's will restated his desire for Greystone to become a public park, but again there were no takers. Contents of the mansion and greenhouses were auctioned off and before long the in-limbo estate became the target of vandals and unchecked vegetation. Finally in 1946 Yonkers agreed to accept 70 acres of the estate, 15 of which would be used for a park and the rest of the land sold to provide maintenance moneys. Two years later the mansion, whose foundations may still be seen on the southern side of the park, was demolished. By then, much of the outdoor statuary had been dispersed: the bronze fountain of three dancing maidens that stood in front of the mansion now decorates Central Park's Conservatory gardens, but others not previously sold off or donated just disappeared.

Despite desuetude, Untermyer Park remained popular with those aware of its existence, and throughout the 1950s and '60s band concerts drew crowds to the great lawn by the Greek garden. Public awareness was further enhanced by the establishment of the Old Croton Trailway State Park, since a portion of its aqueduct path passes Greystone's western gate. There a sculpted stone lion and unicorn (the latter now decapitated) silently guard the ruins of a caretaker's cottage, meanwhile enticing aqueduct strollers to follow the Greystone carriageway uphill to where the gardens are located.

The early 1970s saw some restoration of the Greek garden and in 1974

Untermyer Park was listed on the National Register of Historic Places, but much more work was needed, along with a buy-back of some of the Greystone property that had been sold.

Happily, the city of Yonkers has persevered in preserving the site, whose considerable needs were identified in a 1995 Historic Landscape Report. Since then, thanks to various grants and dedicated proponents like Parks Commissioner Mitchell Tutoni and Project Administrator Ellen Meagher, much of the infrastructure work has been completed, along with restoration of the exterior walls, with long-range plans calling for such improvements as a pedestrian/bike trail leading up from Warburton Avenue, replanting the living sundial, and refurbishing the Eagle's Nest. The latter is a man-made mound of boulders crowned by a circle of Corinthian columns with a filigreed cast-iron dome, where Samuel Untermyer supposedly enjoyed afternoon snoozes in the summertime.

After all the difficulties he had in donating his estate to the public, the old gentleman surely would applaud what has been accomplished, as well as Commissioner Tutoni's avowal that "We consider Untermyer Park to be the jewel of the city's park system, and will continue to seek . . . funding from all available sources to reach our goals."

More power to you, Yonkers!

50. *Always Room at the Inn*

THE JOURNEY HAD BEEN LONG AND COLD AND CIRCUITOUS. STARTING out from the Orange County village of Warwick on the morning of December 15, 1898, the trio of travelers had taken the train north to Newburgh, where they crossed the Hudson by ferry to Dutchess County. Then in Beacon they boarded another train for the trip south to the depot at Garrison on the Putnam County shore. From there a horse and sleigh had struggled through the heavy snow to the Albany Post Road, depositing them late that evening at a dilapidated farm cottage called the Dimond House.

Thoroughly chilled and weary, the three travelers were nevertheless jubilant, especially the one dressed in the habit of an Episcopal nun. For although she knew the long winter was to be spent in this drafty rented house, with Christmas celebrated in an unfamiliar chapel down the road, Sister Lurana Mary White was confident in her decision to co-found a new religious society —and the unique community that came to be known as Graymoor.

Her involvement had begun back in 1897, when as a 27-year-old novice at the Sisterhood of the Holy Child in Albany, Lurana White had written to an Episcopal priest named Lewis Wattson, asking if he knew of a woman's order in their church dedicated to corporate poverty, for despite her affluent background, she wanted to join such a group. Wattson was not aware of any, but as he and Sister Lurana exchanged letters concerning their mutual regard for Christian unity and the principles of St. Francis of Assisi, it became apparent they should work together for the Society of the Atonement that Watson wished to establish.

A graduate of St. Stephen's (now Bard) College at Annandale in Dutchess County, the 33-year-old Wattson was then heading a mission of semi-monastic clergymen in Omaha, Nebraska, having recently left St. John's Episcopal Church in the Ulster County city of Kingston, where he had successfully served as rector for nearly a decade. Hence, the two correspondents did not meet in person until Wattson returned to Kingston in October 1898, and Sister Lurana invited him to visit The Terrace, her wealthy family's mansion on Warwick's Main Street.

It was there that Sister Lurana told him about St.-John's-in-the-Wilderness, a small wayside chapel on the Albany Post Road across the river in Garrison.

Above, left: Lurana Mary White left behind an affluent life in her family's Warwick mansion to co-found a new religious society. Right: better known simply as Father Paul, Lewis T. Watson's dream of befriending his fellowman took him from a drafty paint shed on a mountain high above Garrison to the 400-acre complex that is there today.

PHOTOS REPRODUCED COURTESY OF THE FRANCISCAN FRIARS AND SISTERS OF ATONEMENT—GRAYMOOR

Originating in the 1870s as a small wayside chapel on the Albany Post Road, St. John's-in-the-Wilderness and its companion St. Francis Convent are two of the earliest buildings associated with Graymoor.

Built during the 1870s when a local farmer gave a piece of land to the rector of St. Philip's Church for a "union" chapel embracing different denominations, the building eventually had been abandoned and was in parlous condition when a Garrison resident named Julia Halsted Chadwick came across it in 1893. Distressed by the deterioration, Miss Chadwick and two lady friends had taken it upon themselves to clean out a decade of detritus. They then obtained permission to reopen the chapel, and personally hired a clergyman to conduct occasional services there. Subsequently the property was turned over to the three restorers, who named it Graymoor—not for any Hudson Highlands scene, but because the Reverend A.Z. Gray had built the chapel, aided by funds from a Professor Moore of Columbia University.

The three women felt it would be best to find permanent caretakers for the tiny church. So they offered it to Sister Lurana when they were told of the aborning Society of the Atonement by a mutual friend, Sister Mary Angela of the Episcopal Sisters of St. Mary in Peekskill. Consulting with Father Wattson, who enthusiastically endorsed the idea after visiting the site on October 10, 1898, Sister Lurana accepted the responsibility. But in keeping with her Franciscan beliefs, she refused outright ownership—a refusal that was to ricochet a dozen years later.

Such an unpleasant possibility doubtless was farthest from the thoughts of the few folk who gathered at St. John's-in-the-Wilderness on Christmas Day, 1898, for there was much to celebrate besides the religious observance. In addition to Graymoor becoming home to the Society of the Atonement —whose purpose was to aid the needy and promote Christian "at-one-ment"—Father Wattson also envisioned a monastery high atop the mountain at whose base the chapel was located.

Father Wattson was not among the celebrants that Christmas Day, having entered an Episcopal order in Maryland for training in monastic discipline. But he was on hand the following fall when Sister Lurana and her fellow nuns left their rented farmhouse for a new convent that had been constructed for them alongside St. John's.

On the day before St. Francis Convent was dedicated, October 3, 1899, Father Wattson arrived from Maryland, and accepted a ride from the railroad station with Joseph Davis, the contractor for the new building. Having no funds for either housing or property, yet faithful that the mountain rising above them would someday house his monastery, Father Wattson asked Davis if there was a nearby cave he might live in for the winter. The contractor immediately offered the use of an old paint shed he owned—a place Father Wattson later referred to as his "Palace of Our Lady Poverty," while he stuffed rags between the cracks to keep out the winter wind.

That crude shelter (now preserved as part of St. Elizabeth's Chapel on the Graymoor property) is a mute reminder of the sacrifice it took to achieve today's multi-building complex, as well as one of the Society's oldest and perhaps best-known missions: that of helping homeless, alcoholic, or otherwise needful human beings to reclaim their lives.

In 1900, when a benefactor provided $300 for Father Wattson to purchase 24 rocky acres on the mountain, wanderers were a common sight along the Albany Post Road below. Those hungry hoboes who stopped at St. Francis Convent, or who continued up the steep slope to the small wooden friary that had replaced the "Palace of Our Lady Poverty" shack, were never refused, even when the residents had little enough for themselves. Nor were all recipients "knights of the road," a memorable case occurring in the early 1900s when work was halted on the nearby Catskill Aqueduct shafts and the convent soup kitchen kept many laborers and their families from starving. Not long after that, Father Wattson refurbished a log-sided chicken coop for any wayfarer seeking lodging—Graymoor's first St. Christopher's Inn, named for the patron saint of travelers.

By that time, Graymoor had become affiliated with the Franciscan order of the Roman Catholic Church, following its founders' conversion in 1909, when Father Paul—as Wattson was now known—entered St. Joseph's (Dunwoodie) Seminary in Yonkers to study for the priesthood. This came as no surprise to some Valley residents who had witnessed the small-statured but charismatic Father Paul, clad in his brown monk's robe, carry his message of Christian unity into the city streets, preaching anywhere he could gather a crowd, from Beacon to Kingston, and from Newburgh to Poughkeepsie. Yet not everyone condoned the conversion, including two of the three women who had made St. John's-in-the-Wilderness available to Sister Lurana. And since she earlier had refused title to the site, the new Mother Superior of the Franciscan Sisters of the Atonement soon faced a lawsuit aimed at wresting the property away from the group.

True to the Franciscan tenet of non-resistance, Mother Lurana did not formally contest the suit, writing only a letter of explanation to the plaintiffs' lawyer. And although the case ground on for seven years, the decision finally rendered by New York Supreme Court Judge Tompkins was a foregone conclusion. His finding for the plaintiffs in 1917, along with an order for the sisters to vacate the property, didn't conclude the case, however—thanks to a chance meeting that November.

On Election Day, Father Paul had gone to Fishkill to cast his ballot when he encountered the powerful politician, Hamilton Fish, coming down the street. A three-time state assemblyman, as well as son of the same-named prior governor of New York, Fish listened with interest when Father Paul mentioned the plight of the sisters, and he wound up offering his services, despite the fact that he was senior warden of St. Philip's Episcopal Church in Garrison. Those services were exceptional too, including a petition favoring the sisters that Fish circulated among his fellow parishioners and other towns-folk, plus the introduction of a bill into the state legislature that would trans-fer the property to the sisters. The bill passed quickly and was signed by the governor a week later, on March 21, 1918.

All this had come on the heels of another serious threat to Graymoor made by a disgruntled priest whose lies caused a mass exodus from the sem-inary Father Paul established there in 1913. But Graymoor had weathered that storm too. In fact, the only problem which seemed insoluble concerned sufficient finances, for Father Paul was totally committed to aiding others, be they starving children in China, or a Peekskill priest struggling to pay off a parish debt. Besides that, there were schools and churches to build, period-icals to publish, missions to support, novices to train, and the funding of an ever-expanding Graymoor facility. (Today Graymoor covers approximately 400 acres.)

Interestingly enough, for all the donations he took in and dispersed, Father Paul refused to touch money physically—something that could cause problems, particularly when he traveled alone. He was not one to pamper himself either, sleeping on a straw-filled mattress in a narrow second-storey room of the friary, where a sliding-board window allowed him to look down on the original Episcopal chapel. He also had definite ideas about what a monastery should be: not some medieval enclave walled off from the world, but a place where seekers of help would never find themselves locked out. And that is why he did not allow gates at Graymoor.

Despite a schedule extending from dawn to dusk and oftentimes much later, Father Paul almost always managed a daily walk down to the sisters' compound, where he maintained an office. Leisure moments might find him looking west over the Hudson Valley from a seat by the tall cedarwood cross he had hewn by hand, then hauled up the mountain on his shoulder that June day back in 1900 when he took possession of the property. Or he might stroll down to the large farm acquired in 1916, which helped fill many an empty stomach during the years of the Great Depression. (Those fields are now fallow, but the farmhouse serves as a residence for Graymoor novices.)

In 1929 alone, Graymoor provided more than 69,000 meals and over

23,000 lodgings, in keeping with its policy of "no man ever turned away." That rule was considered too lenient by some, especially when an occasional escapee from Sing Sing Prison showed up at Graymoor. But Father Paul stood by the biblical admonition about entertaining strangers lest they be angels unawares, and during the dark days following the stock market crash, St. Christopher's Inn was enlarged to accommodate 100 transients. There was even a basement room left open at night so that a late arrival could find a bed.

Then, as now, religion was not thrust upon any arrival, nor did it matter what creed, color or nationality a man might be. He was respectfully referred to as a "Brother Christopher," provided with nourishing meals, a clean bed and fresh clothing, and welcomed for as long as he needed to stay. In the early years, that might mean overnight or for a couple of weeks at most, but there were such exceptions as a fellow named Kelly who started tending the sisters' garden and remained for nearly a quarter-century.

There was never any charge for staying at Graymoor, though the able-bodied usually reciprocated by helping out around the grounds or with various building projects. In fact, the lovely St. Francis Chapel, dedicated in 1912, was largely constructed by "Brothers Christopher." This tradition of mutual aid has been carried down through the years too. In 1996, for example, members of the New York-New Jersey Trail Conference and various hiking clubs pitched in to restore Graymoor's old friary, where through-hikers along the nearby Appalachian Trail have long been welcome to spend the night.

Graymoor has experienced profound changes since the death of its founders: Mother Lurana in 1935, followed by Father Paul in 1940. (Both are buried at Graymoor.) But in many ways it remains the same: the awesome mountain scenery, the serenity, the sincerity of the Franciscans, and an air of spirituality which seems to soften speech but never stifles, as well as the eclectic architecture that includes an Eastern Orthodox chapel tucked into the base of an old water tower.

Such structures give some idea of how Graymoor has kept a respectful grasp on the past while meeting modern needs. A large Pilgrim Hall, for instance, now serves the warm-weather crowds that Graymoor's small chapels and churches cannot accommodate, while picnics are encouraged on the spacious lawns or in one of the pavilions. As for St. Christopher's Inn, it has been expanded several times over the years, and its mostly drug- and alcohol-addicted residents now receive professional counseling during an average stay of 21 days. For those requiring longer rehabilitation, since 1971, the friars have operated a facility at Saranac Lake in the Adirondacks.

Still another development has been Graymoor's Christian Unity Center, which is housed in the same large building as its Ecumenical and Interreligious Institute at Garrison. Throughout the year, the center hosts a wide-ranging selection of educational programs, support groups, and overnight retreats for "people of all creeds—or none." Among them are members of Ironworkers Local 40 union, who aided in the recovery work following the destruction of the World Trade Center's twin towers on September 11, 2001. And it is through the efforts of these men that Graymoor now hosts an evocative relic of that tragic day—a 20-foot, half-ton cross made of steel beams and rods reclaimed from the site, set on a cement base containing ashes from Ground Zero. Located in Graymoor's Meditation Garden, it understandably has become one of the most frequently visited sites on the property.

Understandable, too, is the popularity of Graymoor's annual Christmas at the Friary. For while celebrating the birth at Bethlehem two millennia ago, it also recalls another Christmas back in 1898, when Graymoor was but a hope in the hearts of those congregated in a small chapel at the base of the mountain. Surely theirs is a lesson that will survive for many millennia to come.

51. The Bedford Mystique

TO FIRST-TIME TRAVELERS HEADING NORTH ALONG ROUTE 22 IN Westchester County, the village of Bedford can come as a total and tantalizing surprise. For it is not until a curve in the tree-bordered byway is rounded that there suddenly appears the epitome of a picturesque New England community, complete with ancient burying ground and sparkling white buildings abutting a comely village green. New England in New York? Incongruous but true, and only one facet of a compelling story that helped create the unique quality that sets this village apart from all others—a specialness perhaps best described as the Bedford mystique.

Tracers of that mystique, however, might prefer to forego Route 22 and approach the village via the Stamford Road (Route 104), since that was the original Indian path taken by the 22 Connecticut men who in December 1680 came here seeking land from the Indians. For 12 coats, 6 blankets, 2 yards of red broadcloth, 6 yards of cotton, and 300 guilders in wampum, Katonah and 6 other local chiefs signed away nearly 8,000 acres of the "Hopp Ground"—a name derived from the area's abundance of wild hop vines used in making both beer and medicine.

The following spring, the new landowners moved their families from Stamford, with the first dwelling being built along what is now the Poundridge Road. Like as not these "propriators" neglected to tell their womenfolk of a massacre that had occurred there in 1644, when a company of Dutch soldiers led by Captain John Underhill annihilated the native village of Nani-chiestawack in retaliation for the murder of the religious liberal Anne Hutchinson near what is now Pelham Bay. But even if told, the women need not have worried. The Indians still residing in the area did not hold the Englishmen accountable for what the Dutch had done, and relations between the two groups reportedly were amicable. (Historians differ as to the site of Nanichiestawack, but local lore places it on the southern side of Indian Hill, where a ghostly native supposedly can sometimes be seen descending the slope.)

In keeping with their New England traditions, the settlers from Stamford immediately established a "common" for grazing their livestock (now the Bedford Green), as well as setting aside land for a cemetery and a meeting house (where Historical Hall stands). The grinding of grain was also a priority, and before the first year was over, Joshua Webb had agreed to build a mill on the Mianus River in joint ownership with the town. Possibly the earliest gristmill in the county, it became part of the complex seen by the dam near where the Mianus River Road meets Millers Mill Road, the latter named for a subsequent operator.

Military and magisterial matters were addressed too, with a militia-like "Train Band" soon drilling in a field by Whipping Post Brook—a name denoting one of the punishments meted out to miscreants. And lacking a steeple bell to sound alarms or summon the citizenry to church services and such, a man was appointed to "keep the town drum . . . and to beat it when necessary."

The thriving community even got a new name—Bedford—but not because any of its settlers had been born in that British borough. Rather, the redubbing stems from the fact that the Hopp Ground was then part of the Connecticut Colony, whose General Court probably selected the name in its stated desire "to leave to posterity the memorial of several places in our dear native country of England." Nor were the settlers offended; indeed, their ties to Connecticut were so strong that when New York later claimed Bedford and Rye to be within its borders, the former Hopp Grounders nearly joined their southern neighbors in an open revolt called the Rye Rebellion.

Resolution of the conflict came in 1700, when King William III ruled against Connecticut. His loyal Bedford subjects then calmly accepted their change of colony, though the ambience of their village would ever be more New England than New York. Less lasting was their fealty to the Crown, and when the Revolutionary War broke out, most Bedford families espoused the Patriot cause. It was a decision that cost them dearly, for the town's location within the "Neutral Ground"—that no-man's-land between the American and British lines—made Bedford the repeated target of enemy raids. (The village of Bedford, it should be pointed out, is situated within the town of Bedford.)

The worst came on July 11, 1779, when British and Loyalist troops torched the entire village. Except for one house belonging to a Tory, every building was burned to the ground, including the church. The destruction of the village was no spur-of-the-moment military maneuver either, for Bedford was then the most populous part of the county, and had been serving as the wartime capital of Westchester since the Battle of White Plains three years earlier. But if the British thought they could incinerate morale as easily as material, they were dead wrong. The burned-out Bedfordites did not abandon their village, though it took them long months to rebuild—months during which some of them, it is said, lived in shanties set up against rock ledges near the Mianus River.

After the Revolution, Bedford retained its place as a seat of county government, sharing half-shire status with White Plains, and by 1788 judges were enjoying their own courthouse—the belfried, gambrel-roofed building that still anchors the north end of the village. Now headquarters of the Bedford Historical Society, and housing an excellent museum of local memorabilia, it is the oldest extant government building in Westchester, with its ground-floor courtroom just the same as when Aaron Burr argued a case there during the opening session.

Adding to Bedford's judicial prestige was the presence of the country's first Chief Justice of the Supreme Court, John Jay, who in 1801 retired to his family's farmhouse, now a State Historic Site on Route 22, a few miles north of the village. Jay, it might be added, was instrumental in securing the land for St. Matthew's, the beautiful brick church that adds a touch of Georgian grace to Cantitoe Street. (Cantitoe is a corruption of Katonah, meaning "great mountain." The Indian chief reportedly was buried near Katonah Wood Road, but no such legend is attached to the nearby lane named for his wife Mustato.)

John Jay died in 1829, but his descendants continued to make a vital contribution to the community, including his younger son William, who inherited the family farm. Although more famous for his abolitionist writings, William Jay is remembered locally as a county judge, "conducting his trials so expeditiously," Bedford historian Donald W. Marshall reported, "that it was said they never lasted more than a day."

William's son, John II, became a prominent abolitionist as well, after receiving his early education at the Bedford Academy, which his grandfather had helped to found in 1807. Now the home of the Bedford Free Library, the private academy operated for nearly a century, listing among its alumni such men as William K. Vanderbilt, Civil War General Philip Kearny, and John McCloskey, the country's first cardinal of the Roman Catholic Church. But since Bedford was basically a community of small farmers, the majority of its youngsters received their elementary education at the one-room schoolhouses that came into being when the town set up its public school system in 1813.

The village had to wait until 1829 for the building of its "Stone Jug" (the one-room school at the south end of the Green, which in more recent years served as a museum of local education). In the interim, classes were held either in private homes or at the courthouse. As for the latter site, teaching could only have been accomplished during times when the court was not in session, for judicial proceedings during the early 19th century often crowded the village to such an extent that tents had to be set up to accommodate the overflow of out-of-towners.

That booming period was all too soon doomed by the New York and Harlem Railroad, which began pushing through Westchester in the 1840s. While cognizant of the progress the iron horse promised, Bedfordites were not about to sacrifice the past for the future—as exemplified by a Mr. Smith, who then owned the land where the town's most historic tree still stands at the corner of Hook Road and Cantitoe Street. When engineers arrived to lay out the train route, Smith reputedly told them, "It's all right to survey, but if the railroad touches that oak, it can't come through here!"

As it was, the New York and Harlem line bypassed the village by some 6 miles, and so did the unbridled development that followed in the wake of the railroad. This may well have been a blessing in disguise; although the village was to lose its half-shire status in 1870, when burgeoning White Plains became Westchester's only county seat, Bedford retained its unique if rural flavor. And it was this very thing that helped bring about its second "boom."

Looking at Bedford's well-wooded landscape today, it is difficult to imagine a time when it was more fields than forest. Yet within two centuries of the first settlers' arrival, practically every tillable acre had been cleared of its primeval canopy, with few large tracts of trees left standing except in terrain too rugged for even pasture.

So important was its agrarian economy that in 1851 the Bedford Farmers Club was formed "for the improvement of agriculture and the sciences." But times were changing, and while the club remained active down through the years—making it the oldest such organization in the county, if not in the country—it evolved into a more social than scientific group, following the decline of farming in the 1880s.

Around that time, rich pegmatite deposits were discovered on the southeastern side of the village, so Bedford's economy virtually went underground, with eight different mines and quarries eventually operating in the area. Of these, the Kinkel and Bayliss quarries became the best known primarily because of the pure-white feldspar found in their pegmatite. Ground into powder, the mineral was used in manufacturing fine china, including the first official set of White House dinnerware made in

America. (That set of china was produced by the Lenox Company during Woodrow Wilson's administration in 1918. Bedford, however, had been supplying the company since 1882, and its pulverized feldspar was popularly known as "Lenox spar.")

Feldspar was also in demand for making glass, enamel and scouring powder, but it was by no means the only commercially valuable mineral to come out of the Bedford pegmatite. Massive chunks of milky quartz were shipped off to be used for porcelain and wood filler, while asterated rose quartz from the Kinkel Quarry was prized by Japanese jewelry-makers. The Kinkel boasted abundant black tourmaline and greenish-yellow beryl as well, with foot-long crystals of the latter silicate luring collectors. The quarry was a mecca for geology students too, since it contained an alphabet of other minerals, ranging from almandine to zircon.

Meanwhile, a different kind of gem began sparkling on the summits of the surrounding hills. Millionaires in the market for country estates had discovered the quiet beauty of Bedford, whose hilltops provided an ideal setting for opulent mansions with panoramic views. And in those days before reforestation took place, the views were indeed extensive, as is evident in the memoirs of Bedford sportsman Gustavus T. Kirby, who wrote that as a boy in the early 1880s, he watched the building of the Brooklyn Bridge from atop Guard Hill, using only a simple spyglass.

Closer at hand, Kirby could monitor the construction going on at James F. Sutton's estate, which covered several hundred acres on Guard Hill. Sutton was a New York City art dealer married to the daughter of merchandising magnate R.H. Macy, and their combined fortunes made possible the lavish mansion that not only helped launch Bedford's golden era of grand estates, but is one of its most legendary.

It seems a well-known French architect was hired by Sutton to design the house and supervise its construction—a project that was delayed time after time until the Suttons despaired of a completion date. Finally the Frenchman called upon the couple to report the house was ready, and said he would meet them there the next day. He did, but not in the way the Suttons expected. For when they opened the front door the next morning, they found the lifeless body of the architect hanging in the stairwell.

Despite this depressing start, the Suttons spent many years in their Guard Hill home, with its long, maple-lined driveway and rolling lawn so carefully nurtured that horses harnessed to the mower reportedly were fitted with soft leather boots so their hoofs would not mar the sod. As for the city-bred Mrs. Sutton's adjustment to country living, her husband was quick to

Local lore tells of a 19th century Bedford bride so lonely for the sound of Manhattan's Grace Church bells that her wealthy husband arranged for this clock's chimes to match the ones she missed.

act upon her complaint that she sorely missed hearing the hourly chimes from a clock tower in her old New York neighborhood. He ordered a fine E. Howard time-and-strike model to be installed in the cupola of their barn, where the clock's 550-pound bell could easily be heard from the house. That clock became such an integral part of the Bedford scene that after the Sutton barn burned down in 1929, a group of concerned citizens banded together to fund a new home for the rescued timepiece. By selling bricks for $1 apiece, they were able to erect the handsome tower that now stands at the corner of Succabone and Guard Hill roads.

Perhaps no period in Bedford's history contributed more to its mystique than the half-century from 1880 to 1930 when most of its grand estates were built. For in those days of untaxed income and seemingly endless supply of cheap labor, there developed a leisurely lifestyle likely never to occur again on such a luxurious scale, and one that resulted in the nabobs being nick-named "hilltoppers" as opposed to the "townies' living in less lofty locations.

Horticulture was then the rage, with magnificent gardens complementing mansions that came in a variety of architectural styles—from medieval Gothic and Romanesque to the colonial farmhouse Stanford White redesigned for Augustus Van Cortlandt. There was even a replica of the English Exchequer, which supposedly was built utilizing original plans the owner borrowed from a British buddy. Some of the landed gentry extended their horticultural activities to include farming, though such ventures generally were not commercially viable. One exception was Rock Gate Farm on Guard Hill, which was famous for its milk, as well as the elegant summer home the Darlington family built there in 1904, but nowadays may be more familiar as the setting for the movie *Fatal Attraction.*

According to Alex Shoumatoff, whose 1979 *Westchester* is a fascinating insider's view of the county, "the greatest estate of all in the Bedford area" was Penwood—a 500-acre enclave of Gothic buildings and gardens that Frederick Law Olmsted designed for publishing heir Carll Tucker and his wife Marcia. Their museum-like main house, started in 1912 by a cadre of Sicilian stonemasons, was not completed until 1920, owing to delays occasioned by the First World War. During that hiatus, it might be noted, a neighboring mansion became notorious because of a cannon its Germanic owner kept aimed in the direction of New York City!

Mention of the Tuckers, whose son Carll Jr. carried on the family's publishing tradition by establishing the *Patent Trader* newspaper, brings to mind the literary lights that added luster to the Bedford scene. Art historian Henry Marquand and publisher Charles Scribner both owned hilltop homes, where famous authors like Edith Wharton were frequent visitors. DeWitt and Lila Wallace, of *Reader's Digest* renown, were later arrivals, not settling in Bedford until 1937, when the great estate era was on the wane.

The Depression had sounded the era's death knell; World War II dealt the final blow. Better-paying jobs in defense plants dried up the pool of domestic help, lifestyles changed, and the cost of maintaining outmoded mansions skyrocketed. Some families hung on, but most estates wound up on the market, often to be chopped up into smaller parcels or made into housing developments.

One thing that has not changed is Bedford's pride in its past—the plebeian as well as the patrician—and its efforts at preserving this legacy can be seen in the village which is both a museum and a vital modern community. Achieving a balance between the two has not always been easy, though. In 1916, for example, the Bedford Historical Society was born as a direct result of the century-old Methodist meeting house almost being converted into apartments. The advent of automobiles caused conflict too, and realtor Beatrice Lounsbery Monroe was one of the Bedford matrons who lay down on the path of a bulldozer to prevent the paving of their rural roads. But the most colorful event (or lack thereof) occurred in 1959, when a supermarket was allowed to lease a village building only on the condition that it blend in. Reportedly the first A&P not painted a blaring red, it received national attention via a whimsical cartoon in the *New Yorker* magazine.

In 1972, the ongoing efforts of Bedford's preservationists reached an apex with the designation of the village's historic district. National Register listing came the following year, and anyone who strolls the time-machine streets of the district will agree it was a recognition well deserved. There is no way of registering an aura, however: that intangible essence which makes Bedford so special. And while this chapter has highlighted some of its facets, Bedford's mystique remains just that—an aura perhaps best summed up by historian James Wood when he said, "Those who are native here never feel quite at home elsewhere. Those who come here to reside for a time become conscious of an indescribable something which holds them here."

52. Shawangunk Shangri-La

WHEN *LOST HORIZON* AUTHOR JAMES HILTON ADDED "SHANGRI-LA" to our language in 1933, some Ulster County residents of Cragsmoor may well have wondered if their remote clifftop community had served as a model for the imaginary Himalayan haven whose name has become synonymous with idyllic beauty. Certainly it's possible that the British novelist was familiar with the local landscape paintings of the famous Cragsmoor art colony that flourished around the turn of the century. But there is no way Hilton could have known all of what makes this American Shangri-La so special—a place perhaps even more remarkable than its Himalayan counterpart because it is real.

Legends came early to this section of the Shawangunk (pronounced Shon-gum) Mountains. Set on a forested plateau girded by cliffs of sparkling white, quartz-studded conglomerate interspersed with caves and deep gullies down which mountain streams dash, the locale that would one day be called Cragsmoor hosted mainly transient hunters and trappers until the 1750s when a few families braved the rough Indian trail leading up from the valley floor.

Among those settlers was Samuel Gonsalus. His daring escape from pursuing Indians during September 1758—a feat he accomplished by leaping off a cliff and landing in the branches of a hemlock tree far below—reputedly resulted in the naming of Sam's Point, at 2,255 feet one of the highest elevations in the Shawangunks. Sam's story pales in comparison, however, to some other local lore, including that of a monstrous snake whose fiery hisses defoliated the land for several yards on either side of its slithering body. Then there is the legend of Old Ninety-Nine, an Indian who not only worked his own secret silver mine, but also led a friend to a cave containing fabulous riches. Unfortunately that friend never could find the cave afterward, and the search for Old Ninety-Nine's treasure was to become a popular pastime among summer boarders at Cragsmoor.

Those boarders began coming to Cragsmoor soon after its first real road was completed in the early 1800s. By then, timbering had helped open up the plateau for agriculture as well as scenic vistas, and farmers could harvest a handy "cash crop" by renting spare bedrooms to vacationing city folk seeking a cooler, healthier climate. Potatoes also proved profitable, for Shawangunk spuds were deemed tastier than the valley variety, thereby fetching a higher price.

For awhile there was some manufacturing too, with the mountain plateau boasting such divers businesses as shingle-cutting, hat-making, carpet-weaving, wagon-building, and even a coffin shop. But its unparalleled natural beauty turned out to be Cragsmoor's greatest resource—something anticipated by Thomas Botsford, who purchased Sam's Point in the 1850s and at the very top erected a tower offering "eatibles [sic] and drinkables" to tourists. Alas, wind flattened the tower and subsequent structures Botsford built there, so in 1871 he literally bolted a new hotel to the cliff face on a shelf just below the summit. Called the Mountain House, and noted for its 50¢ meals of fried chicken and green corn, as well as a spring running through the main room, it resisted all gales, only to burn down within a few years. Sad to say, the same fate befell a hotel Botsford's son LeGrand later built along the shore of nearby Lake Maratanza.

A similarly named Mountain Hotel had been operating under various owners since 1835 at the junction of present-day Cragsmoor and Dellenbaugh roads. This location was made even more advantageous in 1851 by the construction of a Newburgh-to-Ellenville toll road (roughly today's Route 52), and after 1862 when the Bleakley family bought it, the boarding house attracted a clientele from near and far.

One man who stayed with the Bleakleys during the summer of 1879 was to have a profound influence on Cragsmoor. He was Edward Lamson Henry, a Manhattan-based artist small of stature (no more than 5 feet 2 or 3), but tall on talent, whose success had been ensured by his election to the National Academy of Design in 1867 when he was only 26. Henry was no stranger to the region, having visited fellow artist Robert Weir at West Point in 1858, and also sketching at one of the Terwilliger homes in the Ulster County town of Wawarsing during October 1867. Boarding with the Bleakleys, however, seemed to bond him to "The Mountain"—as Cragsmoor was then called—and a few years later he and his wife Frances bought land for the home they enjoyed from Spring through Autumn for the rest of Henry's life.

A legend exists that the artist bartered some of his paintings for a "hummock of rotten shale," but records show the proper sale of several parcels that comprised Henry Park, with panoramic views and plenty of room for the three houses eventually built there. Henry served as his own architect too,

setting shingle walls on stone foundations for his studio-home, Na-pee-
nia, and two cottages called Shingle-
nook and I-e-nia.

Similar construction and colorful
toponyms marked many of the houses
that eventually made up the summer
colony at Cragsmoor—houses often
incorporating items salvaged from
demolished Manhattan mansions. The
aptly named Endridge off Schuyler
Avenue is one example. It was planned
by explorer-author-artist Frederick S.
Dellenbaugh, who in 1882 moved to
the mountain with his actress wife,
Ellenville's Harriet Rogers Otis.
Although not formally trained as an
architect, Dellenbaugh designed some
of the community's loveliest landmarks,
including the Cragsmoor Free Library
(with massive stone fireplace bordered
by chestnut tree trunks upholding interior balconies), and the Gothic Chapel
of the Holy Name on Henry Road.
Nowadays known simple as the Stone
Church, it is usually open to visitors,

*Looking northwest through the memorial arch on
the grounds of Cragsmoor's Old Stone
Church—more formally known as the Chapel of the
Holy Name—provides a panoramic view of
Ellenville and the distant Catskills.*

who shouldn't miss the adjacent memorial archway offering a spectacular
view of Ellenville and the distant Catskills.

Funding for the church was provided by Eliza Hartshorn, a wealthy
relative of E.L. Henry's wife, who visited Cragsmoor in 1886 and promptly
purchased property. Mrs. Hartshorn subsequently became a prime developer of the community, despite the fact that she very nearly bought the
farm on one of her trips up the mountain. According to the *Cragsmoor
Journal,* the driver of her carriage took too wide a turn on a rail-less bridge
along the steep road. "A plank broke . . . a horse was thrown . . . the carriage plunged into the air," but Mrs. Hartshorn miraculously escaped with
only bruises. The spunky lady spent a few days recuperating, then continued with a plan whereby she would build or buy a house for remodeling,
live there until it was finished, then move on to another. (The Barnacle, a

former barn visible from Schuyler Avenue, was one of those projects.)

To get some inkling of the kind of curving, precipitous path on which the Hartshorn carriage overturned, current visitors to Cragsmoor need only drive down South Gully Road toward Ellenville—that is, after making sure their brakes are working, and remembering that such scenic byways weren't paved in those days. In fact, an E.L. Henry painting of 1891, showing a horse-drawn cart *On the Gully Road* was purchased by Andrew Carnegie "to show some of the awful roads in the Eastern States"!

Transportation had been made a tad more convenient in 1871 when the railroad was extended to Ellenville. Travelers still faced a two-hour uphill haul by horse-drawn wagon after they got off the train, but that didn't deter artists from coming to the mountaintop community officially designated Cragsmoor in 1892. Frederick Dellenbaugh had devised that descriptive name when his first choice of Winahdin was rejected by postal authorities because it sounded too much like Windham in Greene County. Winahdin would be preserved, however, in the name of Charles Courtney Curran's home near the junction of Spring Road and Schuyler Avenue.

A leading painter possessing a mastery of light and clouds, Curran was often seen pulling a child's red wagon full of his artist's supplies along the path to Bear Hill cliff, on the southwestern rim of Cragsmoor. The fissured prominence, with its dramatic Pulpit Rock and rare dwarf pines, was a favorite subject of Curran, whose evanescent *Blue and Gold* hangs in the Cragsmoor Library for all to enjoy. It's enjoyable, as well, to stroll out to the summit of Bear Hill and see the places Curran so realistically depicted, along with the spot where the 1919 movie *The Moonshiners* was filmed.

Although the summer colony was by no means restricted to painters—writers, musicians, actors, craftsmen, and people of other professions came too—it is the artists that are most closely associated with Cragsmoor. Edward Gay, Albert Insley and Arthur I. Keller are three notable men, with the distaff side represented by such talents as Helen Turner and the Paris-trained Austa Densmore Sturdevant, whose Cragsmoor Inn proved so popular she was forced to set aside her paints for the role of full-time hotelier.

Mention must also be made of Eliza Pratt Greatorex and her two daughters, Kathleen and Eleanora. This talented trio settled on the southeastern side of the plateau in 1884, calling their home Chetolah, which supposedly is a native American word for "love." Another artist, George Inness Jr., loved it too. At the turn of the century, he and his wife purchased the estate, subsequently enlarging it to 350 acres and building the grandest of all

Visitors to Cragsmoor's Bear Hill Preserve can see some of the places Charles Curran depicted in paintings such as his Blue and Gold *(Painting reproduced courtesy of John Carmichael)*

Cragsmoor's private dwellings—a stretched-out, shingle and stucco structure of mainly Queen Anne Style, with 40 or so rooms and a large studio in one wing, all of which was set amid elegant terraced gardens off present-day Vista Maria Road.

Costing a cool million in 1902 dollars, Chetolah became the community's centerpiece for cultural gatherings of a private nature, whereas The Casino and The Pavilion on the grounds of the Cragsmoor Inn offered more public entertainments. By and large, summer residents opted for simple amusements, with nature a top priority. Hot-weather hikes to nearby ice caves, huckleberry picking in July, bird-watching and identifying some of Cragsmoor's 100 known wildflowers were popular outdoor pastimes. As for in-home gatherings, they ranged from musicales and Saturday morning literary readings to light-hearted bridge parties without cards and Barmecide feasts.

Invitations to the E.L. Henry house were welcomed, for the fun-loving, flute-playing artist might perform one of his parlor tricks or take guests on a tour of his private museum containing old carriages and costumes—items he employed to faithfully reproduce a bygone era in genre paintings that have sold for as much as $175,000. Since many of these studies in Americana show the local folk he used as models, including one of his favorites, an Ellenville toper named Peter Brown, Henry gave that village a selection which can be seen at the Pubic Library on Center Street. It was a most generous gift indeed, considering that in 1996 art historian Kaycee Benton appraised the half-dozen pictures at $35,000 to $40,000 apiece.

After Henry's death in 1919, there was some concern that the art colony he helped to establish might wither once the other founders passed away. Changing times decreed that it could not continue in quite the same manner, but then—as now—the mountain seems to exert a magnetism that attracts creative and caring people. Newcomers thus joined established residents in keeping Cragsmoor viable during Depression years that saw the decline of the resort industry and large estates.

In 1936 the elegant Chetolah was purchased by a religious order, followed three years later by the sale of the Cragsmoor Inn, which eventually was turned into a boys boarding school. Both buildings later fell into disrepair, with the Inn's condition finally deemed so dangerous that it was burned down by the local fire department. On a more positive note, the Cragsmoor Free Library opened in 1925 along Cragsmoor Road, and overall access to the area was improved when Route 52—dubbed the Shawangunk Trail—replaced the old Newburgh-to-Ellenville plank road in 1936. This was a boon to the Kinaloha Co-op, an art school started in 1935; also to the newly established (1936) Cragsmoor Playhouse, one of the region's first professional summer stock companies. And when those two enterprises faltered in the 1950s, others appeared: a golf course and a ski slope, a school for jewelry-making and pottery, plus the Roycraft Studios that exhibited the work of local craftsmen in the old Kinaloha off Sam's Point Road.

So it was that Cragsmoor changed yet remained the same, its residents ever conscious of their responsibility for stewarding the stunning landscape. That doesn't mean there never was controversy: proposals for a communications tower, a motorcycle track, and even an industrial windmill farm certainly caused that. But for the most part the community has lined up solidly behind the preservation-minded Cragsmoor Association founded in 1978. It's been a productive partnership too, starting with the rescue of Bear Hill cliff from the threat of developers. Featuring foot trails leading through thick stands of pink and white mountain laurel to the breathtaking crags that inspired so many painters, the 50-acre hilltop is now a wildlife preserve owned by the Cragsmoor Library and maintained by the Association. The Association also took part in protecting the cliffs on the other side of Cragsmoor, where the Nature Conservancy began managing a magnificent 4,600-acre tract called Sam's Point Dwarf Pine Barrens Preserve. And following a thorough renovation of an old tourist trail through the giant fissures of the Preserve's ice caves, that geological wonderland was reopened to visitors in 2002.

Understandably the hamlet's historic houses have always been a priority, so it was considered a coup when Chetolah and some of its ancillary structures were listed on the National Register of Historic Places in October 1980. (Though sorely vandalized after the 1970s departure of the religious order that owned it, Chetolah later came under private ownership and restoration began.) Then in August 1996, the bulk of Cragsmoor was designated a National Historic District.

The month of August was meaningful because that is when the community-wide Cragsmoor Festival is held to benefit the landmark library. This one-day celebration offers all the usual events—from a book sale to flea markets and children's games—but with that special Cragsmoor touch. Lunch, for instance, is available on the lawn of Orchard Cottage, where early-day artists gathered. And in years past, tours of the hamlet have been offered, with a narrator pointing out significant sites. However, it's better if tourgoers first attend the slide show usually given inside the library on Festival day. Tony award-winning actor Barnard Hughes—whose father was a coachman for the Inness family at Chetolah—occasionally narrated the show. But no matter who gives it, the slide show conveys the essence of this Shawangunk Shangri-La, concluding as it does with the capsule comment of an early resident:

> *It is Cragsmoor makes the people,*
> *not the people Cragsmoor.*

53. Pacem in Terris

I T'S NOT AS DIFFICULT TO FIND PEACE ON EARTH AS SOME PEOPLE MAY think. Just head for the southern Orange County town of Warwick, where world-renowned author-artist Frederick Franck has created a compelling sanctuary called, appropriately enough, Pacem in Terris—a place particularly pertinent at New Year's because of an unusual celebration that occurs there. For decades people of all persuasions have put aside traditional New Year's Even partying to gather along the bank of the creek that courses through Franck's sanctuary. There on the winter-chill waters bobs the centerpiece of the celebration: a hut-like structure of twigs built upon a rough wooden raft. The raft remains tethered to the shore during a short program of music and reflections on the preceding year. Then everyone is invited to crumple up newspapers—the problems of the past 12 months in print—and put them in a large basket.

An expectant hush falls over the onlookers as the basket is set inside the hut, and it is almost possible to hear the scratch of the match that ignites the twigs. Cast adrift, the now blazing raft lights up the night sky as it careens downstream to destruction, carrying with it what Franck calls "the transgressions, failings and sufferings of human beings," amid cheers from the crowd.

As impressive as this conflagration may be, it doesn't hold a candle to the gentle if unconventional genius who conceived the idea after viewing a similar way of starting off the new year with a clean slate when he was traveling in the Tibetan Himalayas. For Frederick Franck's 90-plus years have been ones of amazing accomplishment, deriving from a desire perhaps best described in the title of his 1991 book, *To Be Human Against All Odds*.

That desire dates back to the days of World War I, when as a boy in the Dutch border village of Maastricht, Franck witnessed the tragic human tide of wounded soldiers and refugees washing into neutral Holland. "There were only two ways of reacting to such suffering," he recalls. "Say to hell with it, or react against the inhumanity by being human." He chose the latter, aligning his sights on the world of art, since he considered painters to be most human in their ability to create life on canvas. Franck's mother, however, wanted him to be a physician, and silenced his protests by proposing that as a doctor he could aid humanity like the great Dr. Albert Schweitzer in Africa.

That his mother's words were prophetic did not become apparent for many years—years during which Franck earned his medical degree in Amsterdam, then went on to study dentistry in Antwerp, thinking that profession would allow him more time for painting and writing. But war clouds were again gathering over Europe. Franck served with the Dutch-East Indies government in Australia during World War II, then headed west; first to England, and then to America, where he was granted a dental diploma by the University of Pittsburgh. Art remained his raison d'etre, however, and eventually he was rewarded with a show in Pittsburgh, followed

Renowned author and artist Frederick Franck is above all a humanitarian, whose Warwick retreat called Pacem in Terris reflects his philosophy through stunning icons, serene landscapes and an old stone mill serving as a concert venue.

by one in New York. This prompted a move to Manhattan, where he divided his time between an East 65th Street dental practice and a Bleecker Street art studio. Galleries were soon exhibiting his paintings—mainly landscapes like those now at the Museum of Modern Art and the Whitney Museum—for which Franck found inspiration through frequent trips to Europe.

It was on one of these overseas jaunts that Franck began working on his first book: what might be termed a tongue-in-tooth treatise titled *Open Wide Please* (1956). The only trouble was that he needed someone to take dictation in his native tongue and then transcribe it into English—a problem permanently solved when he met a cultured Dutch lady named Claske, who became his wife, and without whom Franck says "life would be unthinkable."

Life was about to take some remarkable twists as well. Returning to New York, Franck began treating a friend of Albert Schweitzer's, who mentioned that the doctor was desperately in need of a dental clinic at his African hospital. Franck was soon on his way to Lambarene, where he donated his skills during parts of the next three years, meanwhile producing what has been called the best book ever written about the famed humanitarian, *Days With Albert Schweitzer* (1959).

It was also around this time that a chance walk in the Orange County woods one winter day brought Franck to Covered Bridge Road where it crosses Wawayanda Creek, and the sight of an old house whose "dilapidated, shabby dignity" remained in his mind long after he went back to his New York studio. A few years later, he and Claske were again hiking in the area and spotted a "for-sale" sign on the empty house. Both were struck by its Holland-like setting, and without even inspecting the property, they paid the $5,400 asking price. Only afterwards did they learn the 1840s building — which had seen service as McCann's Hotel and Saloon—was in such parlous condition that one contractor could only suggest demolition.

Fortunately a local carpenter and fellow Hollander, Bert Willemse, was certain the structure could be restored, and went about proving his point at a bare-bones hourly rate that he himself had set. There could have been no better boon for the Francks, who by now had decided they preferred a peaceful if necessarily more frugal life in Warwick to the pressures of a profitable city practice. In addition, having grown tired of the materialistic gallery scene, Franck had temporarily given up paintings.

As Willemse went about working his restorative miracles, Franck began eying a roofless stone ruin on the other side of Wawayanda Creek—the remains of an 18th century gristmill that for generations had been used as a garbage dump. An inspection proved that tons of trash would have to be hauled away, but Franck decided to buy the ruin anyway, even though he had no specific purpose for the place.

The seeds of a plan were finally sown in October 1962, when Franck picked up a newspaper reporting Pope John XXIII's opening-day speech at the 21st Ecumenical Council. Deeply moved despite his lack of any church ties, Franck hurried home to tell Claske they were going Rome, for he was determined to depict in drawings what he felt would be a "watershed in the history of the human spirit." Amazingly, he managed to do just that, thanks to influential friends who opened Vatican doors to the uninvited artist from America, and the subsequent publication of these drawings earned Franck a medal of appreciation from the Pope. News of the award arrived in Warwick on the same day John XXIII died, and after flying to Rome for the funeral, Franck knew what he wanted to do with the old mill.

To Franck's way of thinking, Pope John XXIII had superseded the strictures of any single religion to become a "prophet of human solidarity." And with this in mind, Franck started building Pacem in Terris, naming it after the Pope's last encyclical, but also honoring two other modern-day champions of peace and humanity: Daisetz Teitaro Suzuki, who introduced Buddhism to the western world, and Dr. Albert Schweitzer. Thus, Pacem in Terris is a spiritual, rather than a religious statement; "a work of art," Franck writes, "intended to be an oasis of quiet, where self and nature may reconnect."

If all this sounds a tad intimidating, a visit to Pacem in Terris proves the contrary to be true, especially on summer evenings when the reconstructed mill—with its exceptional acoustics, intriguing artwork and tiered stone seats—resounds with concerts that attract people from all walks of life. Franck began inviting musicians to perform there two years after opening Pacem in Terris to the public in 1966, and the schedule of events has since grown to include performances of his plays, as well as workshops focusing on the principles he set forth in such best-selling books as *The Zen of Seeing* (1973) and *The Awakened Eye* (1979).

By far the majority of visitors, however, simply come to stroll the serene sculpture-studded grounds, which are reminiscent of a triptych in that there are three separate areas to savor. The central panel of this triptych contains the mill, with its ancient stone foundation surmounted by the soaring triangles of its modern wooden roof. On warm-weather weekends when Pacem in Terris is open to the public, a large tubular banner is flown, its five stripes of different colors representing mankind's subdivisions of black, white, red, brown and yellow, with each stripe double to indicate male and female. And as Franck points out in his autobiographical *Pacem In Terris A Love Story* (2000), "the banner is tubular, so there is no first, or last," and though the five equal-length stripes are "united at the top, each one is free to blow in the wind according to its own nature"—a visual summary of his philosophy.

Intricately carved stepping stones lead from the gated entrance to a narrow stairway descending to the arched portal of the stream-side mill. And what a portal it is! The door is a massive wooden sculpture in the form of the sun, turning on a central axis that symbolically allows only one person to enter at a time. As for the mill's interior, no verbal description can do justice to this "non-chapel" of intricate carvings, stained glass and mosaics. It must be experienced firsthand, along with the stone and metal sculptures displayed on the path paralleling the stream. Of these, few people are apt to forget the giant hand rising out of the ground at one corner of the mill, its stigmatiferous palm surrounded by the names of sites around the world where countless humans have been inhumanely treated—and there are some very recent inscriptions too.

The second panel of the Pacem in Terris triptych is situated on the other side of Covered Bridge Road along the railroad tracks, where an inconspicuous panel directs visitors down a wooded path to Franck's "Meadow of Signs." Chief among the sculptures mounted here is the celebrated *Hiroshima*, which depicts the human image Franck saw burned onto a concrete wall when he visited the atomic-bombed city—a sculpture he and his co-worker, the talented Arthur Meyer, replicated for such places as Japan's Narzan University, the Cathedral of St. John the Divine in Manhattan, and the University of Pennsylvania. While a stark reminder of darker days, *Hiroshima* does not reflect Franck's feelings about the future of mankind. Rather, he is convinced humaneness can prevail over inhumanity, and his more serious side is complemented by a delightful sense of humor that sparks his hazel eyes, and immediately endears this kindly gray-bearded man to most to meet him. It occurs in his speech too, as when he tells people all his outdoor art works are simply icons, not sculptures, adding with eyes atwinkle that "I wouldn't want to make Michelangelo jealous."

The final panel of the Pacem in Terris triptych encompasses Franck's tavern-turned-home, along with the Daito Gallery exhibiting his recent books and drawings. The residence is not open to the public, but the gallery is, and also a slab-sided, one-room cabin called "The Other Shore." Located on a knoll in back of the Franck residence, this mini-gallery displays the artist's venture into stained glass—something he did at the behest of a friend who suggested he replicate his ink-on-paper panels of The Stations of the Cross now in the collection of the Cathedral of St. John the Divine. The impressive result is 15 rectangular stained-glass windows Franck collectively calls the *Tao of the Cross* in that they are transreligious in nature. Along the remaining wall of the cabin are ten small stained-glass circles depicting the Parable of the Oxherd as told by a 15th century Zen master. And even though the two sets are totally different in style and content, there is an overall sense of symbiosis.

Beyond the cabin is a path winding past icons inspired by both eastern and western cultures, including an 8-foot-wide wooden snake biting its tail, which Franck says is "the oldest symbol of eternal life, of life sustaining itself." There is even a sculpture derived from the Iroquois Confederacy, a massive work stretching for 32 feet called *Seven Generations*. Recalling the Iroquois admonition that any decision made should take into consideration the impact it might have on the succeeding seven generations, this cut-out steel icon has proven so evocative that copies have been fabricated for patrons as far away as Argentina. Closer to home are replicas at Dutchess County's Omega Institute in Rhinebeck—where Franck had given workshops—and the Wainwright House in the Westchester County community of Rye.

Discreet signs guide strollers to other sites like the organic "Resurgence Garden" at the end of the path, a centuries-old cherry tree, and a simple shrine built into the side of the hill. But the unmarked side-paths leading down to Wawayanda Creek should not be overlooked. For these vantage points offer lovely views of the reconstructed mill across the stream, as well as the dam where the symbol of Pacem in Terris —a carved fish with a central eye-like mirror—hangs suspended over the cascading water.

Frederick Franck's metal icons are in collections the world over. Among the most evocative of these is his 32-foot-long Seven Generations, based on an Iroquois Confederacy adage.

It is there that on New Year's Eve the sin-burning hut disintegrates beneath the reflective eye, and Franck reads aloud a poem ending with his wish that "we survive like a tree and bring forth new shoots."

What better way to say Happy New Year? What better wish than Pacem in Terris?

Acknowledgments

I N A WORK OF THIS TYPE, SO MANY PEOPLE DESERVE THANKS THAT THE list seems limitless—and there is always the accompanying fear that someone may have been inadvertently left out. If any such omission has occurred, let me apologize here and now, for I am deeply grateful to all the folks—especially my family—who helped make this book a reality:

Anne W. Ackerson, Alan C. Aimone, Timothy Albright, J. Winthrop Aldrich, Mary and Keld Alstrup, Raymond Armater, Roberta Arminio, Charles L. Ballard, Jane Campbell Bannerman, Raymond Beecher, C. Belknap, Carolyn Bennett, Kaycee Benton, Ruth Bolin, Michael Boriskin, Dennis K. Brown, A'Lelia Perry Bundles, Ken Burns, James W. Campbell, Neil Caplan, Mary R. Cardenas, John Carmichael, Madolyn V. Carpenter, Mary Jo Carpenter, Barbara Chumard, Mary Flannery Climes, Barbara Coker, Eulie J. Costello, Dorothy Crosbie, Connie M. Cullen, Diane H. Dayson, H. Ray Decker, Tom and Rae DeLeo, Janet Dempsey, Stephen Paul DeVillo, Bob Devine, Kathy Do, Harold E. Doley, Jr., Ruth and Tink Donnelly, Bob Dowd, Barbara and George Dudley, Lola Dudley, Donna M. Egan, Oliver Eldridge, Patricia Fenoff, Audrey Fitzgerald, Lynne K. Fonteneau, Lanny G. Foster, Elizabeth and Rodolphe Fouché, Claske and Frederick Franck, Elizabeth Fuller, Eva H. Gemmill, Jerry Grant, Sister Mary Anunciata Griffiths, Gayle Grunwald, Eileen M. Hayden, Don Herron, Kenneth L. Hoadley, Elizabeth Upham Howell, Geralyn T. Huba, Barnard Hughes, Virginia Kaminsky Hughes, and Norma Humphrey.

Also: Anna Janosi, Erik Johns, Melvin Johnson, Anne Jordan, Carol J. Koenig, Eileen Kolaitis, William Krattinger, Todd Kreamer, Doris Lamont, Allynne Lange, Cindy and Al Lanzetta, Billie Laroe, Richard M. Lederer, Jr., Stuart W. Lehman, Tom Lewis, Philip Lord, Jr., Dorothy G. McChesney, Scott McCloud, Gay McCreery, Robert McCully, Margaret and Tom McDonald, Linda M. McIlven, Nancy S. Mackechnie, Helen McLallen, Edward J. McLaughlin, III, Linda McLean-Connelly, Mary Lou Mahan, James Mandracchia, Scott Marshall, Gloria Mayernik, Ellen Meagher, Paul Mercer, Collis Miller, Elizabeth H. Moger, Myra Morales, James Mouw, William G. Muller, Winifred Morrison Mulvey, Susan Ness, Freda and Frank Nicklin, Janet E. Nugent, Laird Ogden, Christine M. Palmatier, Beth

Pfaffenbach, Phil Pines, and Peggy Post.

In addition: Debra Randorf, Michael P. Rebic, Kathleen M. Reilly, John P. Renwick, Mary E. G. Rhoads, Judith Rockefeller, Andrew Rolle, Heidi Rosenau, Maureen B. Russell, Jay Safran, Elizabeth D. Shaver, Marjorie Shipp, Deana Signor, Jim Sirmans, Frances Skelton, Theodore Sly, Adelaide R. Smith, Christian Sonne, Angela Strangarone, Florence Stevens, Harry R. Stoneback, Marlene Straus, April Sutherland, Florence Tate, Daniel J. Valeri, Denise Van Buren, Debbie Vargulick, Alicia Vivona, The Reverend Bob Warren, Dwight Warren, Dietrich Werner, Marylou Whitney, Peter Wing, Loretta Winkler, Mary Ann Winstanley, and Patricia Reynolds Wood.

And of course I cannot forget the expert staff at The Overlook Press, who took the manuscript and turned it into a finished product.

Selected Bibliography

Adams, Arthur G. *The Hudson. A Guidebook to the River* (Albany, NY: State University of New York Press, 1981).

Adams, Charles J., III. *New York City Ghost Stories* (Reading, PA: Exeter House Books, 1996).

Anderson, A.W. *The Story of a Pioneer Family* (Jamestown, NY: Jamestown Historical Society 1936).

Anderson, Fred. *Crucible of War* (New York: Alfred A. Knoph, 2000).

Anderson, Scott Edward. *Walks in Nature's Empire* (Woodstock, VT: Countryman Press, 1995).

Angell, Charles and Charles LaFontaine. *Prophet of Reunion. The Life of Paul of Graymoor* (New York: The Seabury Press, 1975

Balch, William Ralston. *The Life of James Abram Garfield* . . . (Philadelphia, PA: Hubbard Bros., 1881*).*

Baldwin, Neil. *Edison. Inventing the Century* (New York: Hyperion, 1995).

Bannerman, Charles S. *The Story of Bannerman Island* (Blue Point, NY: Francis Bannerman Sons, n.d.).

Barnett, James H. *The American Christmas* (New York: The Macmillan Company, 1954).

Barnum, H.L. *The Spy Unmasked* (Harrison, NY: Harbor Hill Books, 1975).

Becker, Mary Lamberton, ed. *The Home Book of Christmas* (New York: Dodd, Mead & Co., 1941).

Benstock, Shari. *No Gifts From Chance—A Biography of Edith Wharton* (New York: Charles Scribner's Sons, 1994).

Brink, Benjamin Myer. *The Early History of Saugerties* (Kingston, NY: 1902).

Bronfield, Jerry. *Rockne. The Coach, The Man, The Legend* (New York: Random House, 1976).

Brown, Harry James and Frederick D. Williams, eds. *The Diary of James A. Garfield,* vol. I (East Lansing, MI: Michigan State University Press, 1967).

Brown, Slater. *The Heyday of Spiritualism* (New York: Hawthorn Books, 1970).

Bundles, A'Lelia. *On Her Own Ground. The Life and Times of Madam C.J. Walker* (New York: Washington Square Press, 2001).

Cady, Edwin H. and Lester G. Wells, eds. *Stephen Crane's Love Letters to Nellie Crouse* (Syracuse, NY: Syracuse University Press, 1954).

Carmer, Carl. *The Hudson* (New York: Holt, Rinehart and Winston, 1939).

Cavalier, Julian. *American Castles* (Cranberry, NJ: A.S. Barnes, 1973).

Christman, Henry. *Tin Horns and Calico* (New York: Henry Holt, 1945).

Clark, Ronald W. *Edison. The Man Who Made the Future* (New York: G.P. Putnam's Sons, 1977).

Clarke, N.T. *Sixty Years Ago. Early History of Canandaigua* (Canandaigua, NY: Ontario County Times, n.d.).

Clarke, O. P. *General Grant at Mount MacGregor* (Saratoga Springs, NY: Saratogian, 1906).

Conrad, Earl. *General Harriet Tubman* (Washington,D.C.: The Associated Publishers, 1990).

Cooper, James Fenimore. *The Spy. A Tale of the Neutral Ground* (New Haven, CT: College & University Press, 1971).

Copland, Aaron and Vivian Perlis. *Copland 1900 Through 1942* (New York: St. Martin's/Marek, 1984).

———— *Copland Since 1943* (New York: St. Martin's Press, 1989).

Davis, Andrew Jackson. *The Magic Staff*, 5th ed. (New York: J.S. Brown & Co, 1859).

Davis, Linda H. *Badge of Courage. The Life of Stephen Crane* (Boston, MA: Houghton Mifflin, 1998).

Dobrin, Arnold. *Aaron Copland. His Life and Times* (New York: Thomas Y. Crowell, 1967).

Downing, A.J. *The Architecture of Country Houses* (New York: Dover Publications, 1969).

———— *Victorian Cottage Residences* (New York: Dover Publications, 1981).

Dunwell, Frances F. *The Hudson River Highlands* (New York: Columbia University Press, 1991).

Dupuy, R. Ernest. *Men of West Point. The First 150 Years of the United States Military Academy* (New York: William Sloan Assoc., 1951).

Dwight, Eleanor. *Edith Wharton. An Extraordinary Life* (New York: Harry N. Abrams, 1994).

Eager, Samuel W. *An Outline History of Orange County* (Newburgh, NY: S.T. Callahan, 1846-7).

Eddy, A.D. *The Life of Jacob Hodges . . . .* (Philadelphia, PA: American Sunday-School Union, 1842).

Ellis, Franklin. *History of Columbia County, New York* (1878; reprint Old Chatham, NY: Sachem Press, 1974).

Emery, Noemie. *Alexander Hamilton. An Intimate Portrait* (New York: G.P. Putnam's Sons, 1982).

Evers, Alf. *The Catskills From Wilderness to Woodstock* (New York: Doubleday, 1972).

Feron, Myrna V., ed. *Town of Pawling 200 Years* (Pawling, NY: Town of Pawling 200th Anniversary Committee, 1987).

Fleming, Thomas J. *West Point. The Men and Times of the United States Military Academy* (New York: William Morrow, 1969)

Follett, Wilson, ed. *The Work of Stephen Crane* (New York: Russell & Russell, 1963).

Forman, Sidney. *West Point: A History of the United States Military Academy* (New York: Columbia University Press, 1950).

Foster, Don. *Author Unknown* (New York: Henry Holt, 2000).

Franck, Frederick. *Pacem in Terris A Love Story* (New Paltz, NY: Codhill Press, 2000).

Fried, Marc B. *Tales From the Shawangunk Mountains* (Glens Falls, NY: Adirondack Mountain Club, 1981).

Friedel, Robert and Paul Israel with Bernard S. Finn. *Edison's Electric Light. Biography of an Invention* (New Brunswick, NJ: Rutgers University Press, 1986).

Funk, Robert and D.W. Steadman. *Archaeological and Paleoenvironmental Investigations in the Dutchess Quarry Caves, Orange County, New York* (Albany, NY: Persimmon Press, 1994).

Gannon, David. *Father Paul of Graymoor* (New York: The Macmillan Co., 1959).

Gekle, William F. *The Lower Reaches of the Hudson River* (Poughkeepsie, NY: Wyvern House, 1982).

Gibbons, Euell. *Stalking the Wild Asparagus* (Chambersburg, PA: Alan C. Hood & Co., 1987)

Gilchrist, Ann. *Footsteps Across Cement* (privately published, 1976)

Grant, Julia Dent. *The Personal Memoirs of Julia Dent Grant (Mrs. Ulysses S. Grant)*, ed. by John Y. Simon (New York: G.P. Putnam's Sons, 1975).

Grey, Rudolph. *Nightmare of Ecstasy. The Life and Art of Edward D. Wood, Jr.* (Portland, OR: Feral House, 1992).

Griffin, Ernest Freeland, ed. *Westchester County and Its People* (New York: Lewis Historical Publishing, 1946).

Grossman, James. *James Fenimore Cooper* (New York: William Sloane Associates, 1949).

Haagensen, Alice Monro. *Palisades & Snedens Landing* (Tarrytown, NY: Pilgrimage Publishing, 1986).

Hancock, H. Irving. *Life at West Point* (New York: G.P. Putnam's Sons, 1911).

Hansen, Harry. *Scarsdale From Colonial Manor to Modern Community* (New York: Harper & Brothers, 1954).

Hecht, Marie B. *Odd Destiny. The Life of Alexander Hamilton* (New York: Macmillan, 1982).

Headley, Russel, ed. *History of Orange County* (Middletown, NY: Van Deusen and Elms, 1908).

Hedrick, U.P. *The Grapes of New York* (Albany, NY: J.B. Lyon Co., 1908).

Hendrickson, Robert A. *The Rise & Fall of Alexander Hamilton* (New York: Van Nostrand Reinhard, 1981).

Herr, Pamela. *Jessie Benton Fremont. American Woman of the 19th Century* (New York: Franklin Watts, 1987).

Hine, C.G. *The Old Mine Road* (New Brunswick, NJ: Rutgers University Press, 1963).

Historical Sketches of Hudson, Embracing the Settlement of the City, reprint (Hudson, NY: Hendrick Hudson Chapter of the Daughters of the American Revolution, 1985).

Holdridge, Barbara C. and Lawrence B. *Ammi Phillips: Portrait Painter 1788-1865* (New York: Clarkson N. Potter, 1969).

Holton, Milne. *Cylinder of Vision. The Fiction and Journalistic Writings of Stephen Crane* (Baton Rouge, LA: Louisiana State University Press, 1972).

Hommell, Pauline. *Teacup Tales. Folklore of the Hudson Valley* (facsimile reprint of the 1958 edition, Saugerties, NY: Hope Farm Press, 1992).

Howe, Irving, ed. *Edith Wharton. A Collection of Critical Essays* (Englewood Cliffs, NJ: Prentice-Hall, 1962).

Hull, Richard W. *History of Warwick, New York. Three Centuries of a Community 1696-1996* (Unionville, NY: Royal Fireworks Press, 1996).

———— *People of the Valleys. A History of the Valleys of the Town of Warwick, NY, 1700-1976* (Warwick, NY: Historical Society of the Town of Warwick, 1975).

———— *Sugar Loaf. Its History, Mystery and Magic, 1703-1980* (Sugar Loaf, NY: privately printed, 1980).

———— *Sugar Loaf, New York, 1700-1997. The Enduring Vision* (Unionville, NY: Royal Fireworks Printing, 1997).

Irving, Washington. *A History of New York*, (Library of America ed., New York: Literary Classics, 1983).

Jackson, Herbert G. *The Spirit Rappers* (Garden City, NY: Doubleday & Co., 1972)

Johnson, Herbert Alan and Robert K. Andrist. *Historic Courthouses of New York State* (New York: Columbia University Press, 1977).

Johnson, Paul E. and San Wilentz. *The Kingdom of Matthias* (New York: Oxford University Press, 1994).

Jones, Leigh Rehner and Shirley A. Mearns. *Ammi Phillips and Company. Popular Taste in Face Painting* (Kingston, NY: Senate House Historic Site, 1982).

Kleiger, Estelle Fox. *The Trial of Levi Weeks or The Manhattan Well Mystery* (New York: Dell Publishing, 1989).

Krythe, Maymie R. *All About Christmas* (New York: Harper & Bros., 1954).

Levy, Leonard W. *Freedom of Speech and Press in Early American History. Legacy of Suppression* (New York: Harper & Row, 1963).

Linson, Corwin K. *My Stephen Crane* (Syracuse, NY: Syracuse University Press, 1958).

Lewis, R.W.B. *Edith Wharton. A Biography* (New York: Harper & Row, 1975).

Lewis, R.W.B. and Nancy. *The Letters of Edith Wharton* (New York: Chas. Scribner's Sons, 1988).

Lewis, Tom. *Empire of the Air. The Men Who Made Radio* (New York: HarperCollins, 1991).

Lossing, Benson J. *The Biography of James A. Garfield* (Henry S. Goodspeed & Co., 1882).

———— *The Hudson, From the Wilderness to the Sea* (Troy, NY: H.B. Nims, 1866; facsimile reprint Heritage Books, 1992).

Mabee, Carleton, with Susan Mabee Newhouse. *Sojourner Truth: Slave, Prophet, Legend* (New York: New York University Press, 1993).

McClausland, Elizabeth. *The Life and Work of Edward Lamson Henry N.A. 1841-1919,* New York State Museum Bulletin 339 (Albany, NY: University of the State of New York, 1945).

McCracken, Henry Noble. *Old Dutchess Forever* (New York: Hastings House, 1956).

McKissack, Patric and Fredrick. *Madam C.J. Walker. Self-Made Millionaire* (Hillside, NJ: Enslow Publishers, 1992).

McLaughlin, Edward J. III. *Around the Watering Trough* (Washingtonville, NY: Spear Printing, 1994).

Marshall, Donald W. *Bedford Tricentennial 1680-1980* (Bedford Hills, NY: Town of Bedford, 1980).

Marszalek, John F., Jr. *Court-Martial* (New York: Charles Scribner's Sons, 1972).

Martell, Alan and Alton Long. *The Wines and Wineries of the Hudson River Valley* (Woodstock, VT: Countryman Press, 1993).

Martin, I.T. *The Recollections of Elizabeth Benton Fremont* (New York: Frederick H. Hitchcock, 1912).

Miles, Clement A. *Christmas Customs and Traditions* (New York: Dover Publications, 1976).

Millen, Patricia E. *Bare Trees: Zadock Pratt, Master Tanner & The Story of What Happened to the Catskill Mountain Forests* (Hensonville, NY: Black Dome Press, 1995)

Morton, Lucie T. *Winegrowing in Eastern America* (Ithaca, NY: Cornell University Press, 1985).

Myles, William J. *Harriman Trails* (New York: New York-New Jersey Trail Conference, 1992).

Nevins, Allan. *Fremont. Pathmarker of the West* (New York: Longmans, Green & Co., 1955).

O'Donnell, Patricia M., et. al. *Historic Landscape Report—Untermyer Park* (Yonkers, NY: City of Yonkers Dept. of Parks, Recreation & Conservation, 1995).

Pearson, Hesketh. *The Man Whistler* (New York: Harper & Brothers, 1952).

Pelletreau, William S. *History of Putnam County, New York* (1886; reprint Brewster, NY: Landmarks Preservation Committee of Southeast Museum, 1975).

Perret, Geoffrey. *Ulysses S. Grant. Soldier and President* (New York: Random House, 1997).

Phillips, Sandra S. and Linda Weintraub. *Charmed Places* (New York: Harry N. Abrams, 1988).

Pines, Phil. *Tales of Whoa* (Goshen, NY: Hall of Fame of the Trotter, 1979).

Pitkin, Thomas M. *The Captain Departs. Ulysses S. Grant's Last Campaign* (Carbondale, IL: Southern Illinois University Press, 1973).

Piwonka, Ruth and Roderic H. Blackburn. *Ammi Phillips in Columbia County* (Kinderhook, NY: Columbia County Historical Society, 1975).

Platt, Edmund. *The Eagle's History of Poughkeepsie From the Earliest Settlements 1683 to 1905* (reprinted Poughkeepsie, NY: Dutchess County Historical Society, 1987).

Post, Edwin. *Truly Emily Post* (New York: Funk & Wagnalls, 1961).

Rapp, Kenneth W. *West Point. Whistler in Cadet Gray and Other Stories About the United States Military Academy* (n.l.: North River Press, 1978).

Rebic, Michael P. *Landmarks Lost & Found: An Introduction to the Architecture and History of Yonkers* (Yonkers, NY: Yonkers Planning Board, 1986).

Reische, Diana. *Of Colonists and Commuters. A History of Scarsdale* (Scarsdale, NY: The Junior League of Scarsdale, 1976).

Reynolds, Donald M., Jane Nobes Brennan and Sister Mary David Barry. *Fonthill Castle: Paradigm of Hudson-River Gothic* (Riverdale, NY: College of Mount Saint Vincent-on-Hudson, 1976).

Rhoads, Mary E.G. *The Fan Directory. A Guide to Decorative Fans For Museums and Collectors* (Kennett Square, PA: The Fan Collectors' Press, 1993).

Rifkind, Carole and Carol Levine. *Mansions, Mills and Main Streets* (New York: Schocken Books, 1975).

Ringwald, Donald C. *Hudson River Day Line* (New York: Fordham University Press, 1990).

Robinson, Ray. *Rockne of Notre Dame. The Making of a Football Legend* (New York: Oxford University Press, 1999).

Rolle, Andrew. *John Charles Frémont. Character as Destiny* (Norman, OK: University of Oklahoma Press, 1991).

Rollins, Richard M. *The Long Journey of Noah Webster* (Philadelphia, PA: University of Pennsylvania Press, 1980).

Rowson, Susanna. *Charlotte Temple* (New Haven, CT: College & University Press, 1964).

Rowson, Susanna H. *Charlotte Temple; A Tale of Truth* (New York: Funk & Wagnalls Co., 1905).

Rushmore, George M. *The World With a Fence Around It* (New York: Pageant Press, 1957).

Sanderson, Dorothy Hurlbut. *Ice Caves Mountain and Sam's Point Stories* (Ellenville, NY: Rondout Valley Publishing, 1968).

Scharf, J. Thomas. *The History of Westchester County*, 2 vols. (Philadelphia, PA: L.E. Preston, 1886).

Schmitt, Claire K. *Natural Areas of Rensselaer County, New York* (Troy, NY: Rensselaer-Taconic Land Conservancy, 1994).

Schmitt, Claire K. and Mary S. Brennan. *Natural Areas of Albany County* (Rexford, NY: Environmental Clearing House of Schenectady, n.d.).

Schoberlin, Melvin, ed. *The Sullivan County Sketches of Stephen Crane* (Syracuse, NY: Syracuse University Press, 1949).

Schuyler, David. *Apostle of Taste: Andrew Jackson Downing 1815-1852* (Baltimore, MD: Johns Hopkins University Press, 1996).

Scott, John, ed. *John Charles Frémont. The Pathfinder* (New City, NY: The Historical Society of Rockland County, 1989).

Sharts, Elizabeth. *Cradle of the Trotter. A Goshen Turf History* (Goshen, NY: Book Mill, 1946).

————— *Land O' Goshen Then and Now* (Goshen, NY: The Bookmill, 1960).

Shonnard, Frederic and W.W. Spooner. *The History of Westchester County, New York, From its Earliest Settlement to the Year 1900* (Harrison, NY: Harbor Hill Books, 1974).

Shoumatoff, Alex. *Westchester: Portrait of a County* (New York: Coward McCann & Geoghegan, 1979).

Simpson, Jeffrey. *Officers and Gentlemen. Historic West Point in Photographs* (Tarrytown, NY: Sleepy Hollow Press, 1982).

Smith, Jessie Carney, ed. *Notable Black American Women* (Detroit, MI: Gale Research, 1992).

Smith, Philip H. *Legends of the Shawangunk* (Syracuse, NY: Syracuse University Press, 1965).

Stallman, R.W. and E.R. Hagemann, eds. *The New York City Sketches of Stephen Crane and Related Pieces* (New York: New York University Press, 1966).

Stallman, R.W. and Lillian Gilkes, eds. *Stephen Crane: Letters* (New York: New York University Press, 1960).

Swanson, Susan Cochran. *Between the Lines. Stories of Westchester County, New York During the American Revolution* (Pelham, NY: Junior League of Pelham, 1975).

Sylvester, Nathaniel Bartlett. *History of Ulster County, New York* (Philadelphia, PA: Everts & Peck, 1880).

Terwilliger, Katherine. *Wawarsing Where the Streams Wind* (Ellenville, NY: Rondout Valley Publishing, 1988).

Terwilliger, Katherine T. and Marion M. Dumond. *An Old House Sampler* (Ellenville, NY: Ellenville Public Library and Museum, 1986).

Wakefield, Manville B. *Coal Boats to Tidewater* (Grahamsville, NY: Wakefair Press, 1965).

Walters, George R. *Early Man in Orange County* (Middletown, NY: Historical Society of Middletown and the Wallkill Precinct, 1973).

Warfel, Harry R. *Noah Webster. Schoolmaster to America* (New York: Macmillan Co., 1936).

Waugh, John. *The Class of 1846: Stonewall Jackson, George McClellan and Their Brothers* (New York: Warner Books, 1994).

Weigold, Marilyn, ed. *Westchester County: The Past Hundred Years 1883-1983* (Valhalla, NY: Westchester County Historical Society, 1983).

Wertheim, Stanley and Paul Sorrentino, eds. *The Correspondence of Stephen Crane,* vols. I & II (New York: Columbia University Press, 1989).

Wharton, Edith. *A Backward Glance* (New York: Charles Scribner's Sons, 1934).

White, Bouck. *The Book of Daniel Drew. A Glimpse of the Fish-Gould-Tweed Regime From the Inside* (Larchmont, NY: American Research Council, 1965).

——— *Bouckware. The New Type Pottery That is Being Made in the Helderbergs* (Voorheesville, NY: The Bouckware Studio, 1936).

Zukowsky, John and Robbe Pierce Stimson. *Hudson River Villas* (New York: Rizzoli, 1985).

Index

Where towns are indexed, county names are in parentheses. Only historic houses open to the public are listed individually.